PATERNOSTER BIBLICAL MONOGRAPHS

The Significance of Salvation

A Study of Salvation Language in the Pastoral Epistles

PATERNOSTER BIBLICAL MONOGRAPHS

A full listing of titles in this and Paternoster Theological Monographs will be found at the close of this book.

PATERNOSTER BIBLICAL MONOGRAPHS

The Significance of Salvation

A Study of Salvation Language in the Pastoral Epistles

George M. Wieland

Foreword by Philip H. Towner

Eugene, Oregon

Wipf and Stock Publishers
199 W 8th Ave, Suite 3
Eugene, OR 97401

The Significance of Salvation
A Study of Salvation Language in the Pastoral Epistles
By Wieland, George M.
Copyright©2006 Paternoster
ISBN: 978-1-49824-828-0
Publication date 6/1/2006
Previously published by Paternoster, 2006

This Edition reprinted by Wipf and Stock Publishers
by arrangement with Paternoster

PATERNOSTER BIBLICAL MONOGRAPHS

Series Preface

One of the major objectives of Paternoster is to serve biblical scholarship by providing a channel for the publication of theses and other monographs of high quality at affordable prices. Paternoster stands within the broad evangelical tradition of Christianity. Our authors would describe themselves as Christians who recognise the authority of the Bible, maintain the centrality of the gospel message and assent to the classical credal statements of Christian belief. There is diversity within this constituency; advances in scholarship are possible only if there is freedom for frank debate on controversial issues and for the publication of new and sometimes provocative proposals. What is offered in this series is the best of writing by committed Christians who are concerned to develop well-founded biblical scholarship in a spirit of loyalty to the historic faith.

Series Editors

I. Howard Marshall, Honorary Research Professor of New Testament, University of Aberdeen, Scotland, UK

Richard J. Bauckham, Professor of New Testament Studies and Bishop Wardlaw Professor, University of St Andrews, Scotland, UK

Craig Blomberg, Distinguished Professor of New Testament, Denver Seminary, Colorado, USA

Robert P. Gordon, Regius Professor of Hebrew, University of Cambridge, UK

Tremper Longman III, Robert H. Gundry Professor and Chair of the Department of Biblical Studies, Westmont College, Santa Barbara, California, USA

E te whānau
tō koutou ahau
tō koutou tōku aroha
tā tātou katoa tenei mahi

CONTENTS

Foreword by Philip H. Towner		xv
Preface		xvii
Abbreviations		xix

PART 1: INTRODUCTION — 1

1.	**Salvation in PE Scholarship**	3
1.1	A Lack of Consensus	3
1.2	A Growing Recognition of Coherence	12
1.3	The Present Study	14

PART 2: SALVATION IN 1 TIMOTHY: "God our Saviour" — 17

2.	**Introduction to Salvation in 1 Timothy**	19
3.	**1 Timothy 1:1**	21
3.1	Context	21
3.2	God Our Saviour	21
3.3	Christ Jesus Our Hope	28
3.4	Summary	33
4.	**1 Timothy 1:12-17**	34
4.1	Context	34
4.2	What Does it Mean to Be Saved?	35
4.2.1	*σῶσαι*	35
4.2.2	*ζωὴ αἰώνιος*	36
4.3	Who are Saved?	39
4.3.1	*"Sinners"*	39
4.3.2	*"Those Who . . . Believe in Him"*	42
4.4	How is this Saving Effected?	43
4.4.1	*The Historical Appearing of Christ*	43
4.4.2	*Christ's Continuing Activity*	44
4.4.3	*Paul as a Paradigm*	48
4.5	Summary	50
5.	**1 Timothy 2:1-7**	51
5.1	Context	52
5.2	What Sort of "Saving" is in View?	53
5.2.1	*A Peaceful Life*	53
5.2.2	*Coming to Knowledge of the Truth*	55
5.3	How is Salvation Provided and Received?	57
5.3.1	*God's Will to Save*	57
5.3.2	*The Christ-event*	58
5.3.3	*The Witness*	64
5.4	Summary	68

6.	**1 Timothy 2:15**	69
6.1	Context	69
6.1.1	*The Argument: Conduct in the Christian Assembly (2:8-15)*	69
6.1.2	*The Letter as a Whole: Women and Deception*	70
6.1.3	*The Immediate Context: Argument from Adam and Eve (2:13-15)*	71
6.2	Issues and Approaches	72
6.2.1	*Issues of Interpretation*	72
6.2.2	*Proposed Solutions*	73
6.2.3	*Back to the Background: Hearing the Other Voices*	74
6.2.4	*The Author's Strategy*	76
6.3	The Statement in its Context	79
6.3.1	*σωθήσεται*	79
6.3.2	*διὰ τῆς τεκνογονίας*	79
6.3.3	*ἐὰν μείνωσιν ἐν πίστει καὶ ἁγιασμῷ μετὰ σωφροσύνη*	81
6.4	Summary	84
7.	**1 Timothy 4:10**	85
7.1	Context	85
7.2	Grammatical Possibilities	87
7.3	Range of Interpretations	88
7.4	Issues	89
7.4.1	*Who are οἱ πιστοί?*	89
7.4.2	*What is the Significance of θεὸς ζῶν?*	90
7.4.3	*ἠλπίκαμεν*	95
7.4.4	*εὐσέβεια*	96
7.4.5	*The Rhetorical Function of the Salvation Statement*	96
7.5	Summary	97
8.	**1 Timothy 4:16**	98
8.1	Context	98
8.2	What Sort of "Saving" is in View?	98
8.3	In What Sense does the Human Agent "Save"?	99
8.3.1	*Who is the Agent?*	99
8.3.2	*What is Timothy Exhorted to Do?*	99
8.3.3	*How does this Activity "Save"?*	100
8.4	Summary	101
9.	**Summary of Salvation in 1 Timothy**	102
9.1	General Observations	102
9.2	Specific Aspects of the Presentation of Salvation	103
9.2.1	*The Benefits of Salvation*	103
9.2.2	*God and Christ in Relation to Salvation*	103
9.2.3	*Paul and Salvation*	104

Contents   xi

9.2.4	Those Who are Saved	105

PART 3: SALVATION IN 2 TIMOTHY: "The promise of life"   107

10.	**Introduction to Salvation in 2 Timothy**	109
10.1	Distinctive Features	109
10.2	Paraenetic Character	110
10.3	Significant Themes: Shame, Power and Witness	110
10.3.1	*Shame*	110
10.3.2	*Power*	113
10.3.3	*Unashamed Witness*	113
11.	**2 Timothy 1:9-14**	115
11.1	Context	116
11.2	The Statement about God (v. 9a)	117
11.2.1	*God has Saved*	117
11.2.2	*God has Called with a Holy Calling*	117
11.3	The Statement about Grace (vv. 9b-10a)	119
11.3.1	*Grace Explains God's Intention to Save*	119
11.3.2	*Grace was Given to Us in Christ Jesus Before Time*	119
11.3.3	*Grace has Now been Revealed through Christ's Appearing*	120
11.4	The statement about Christ Jesus (v. 10b)	122
11.4.1	*Christ Jesus is σωτήρ*	123
11.4.2	*Christ Jesus has Abolished Death*	123
11.4.3	*Christ has Brought Life and Immortality to Light*	125
11.4.4	*"Through the Gospel"*	129
11.5	The Statements about Paul and Timothy (vv. 11-14)	131
11.5.1	*The Paraenetic Effect of the Salvation Statement*	131
11.5.2	*Paul in the Soteriological Schema*	133
11.6	Summary	133
12.	**2 Timothy 2:8-13**	135
12.1	Context	135
12.2	Paul's Gospel (v. 8)	136
12.2.1	*"My Gospel"*	136
12.2.2	*"Remember"*	138
12.2.3	*"Jesus Christ"*	138
12.2.4	*"Raised from the Dead"*	139
12.2.5	*"Of the Seed of David"*	140
12.3	Paul's Suffering (vv. 9-10)	142
12.3.1	*The Character of the Suffering*	142
12.3.2	*The Motive for the Suffering*	145
12.4	Salvation (v. 10b)	148
12.4.1	*"In Christ Jesus"*	148

12.4.2	"With Eternal Glory"	149
12.4.3	ἵνα . . . τύχωσιν	150
12.5	Overview of vv. 8-10	150
12.6	The Hymn (vv. 11-13)	151
12.6.1	Dying and Living (v. 11b)	152
12.6.2	Enduring and Reigning (v. 12a)	154
12.6.3	Denying and being Denied	155
12.6.4	Our Faithlessness, His Faithfulness (v. 13)	157
12.7	Summary	158
13.	**2 Timothy 3:14-17**	160
13.1	Context	160
13.2	The Sacred Writings and Salvation (v. 15a, b)	161
13.2.1	"The Sacred Writings"	161
13.2.2	"Are Able"	162
13.2.3	"To Make Wise for Salvation"	162
13.3	Faith and Salvation (v. 15c)	164
13.4	Summary	165
14.	**2 Timothy 4:16-18**	166
14.1	Context	166
14.2	The Past Rescue (v. 17)	167
14.2.1	The Reference	167
14.2.2	The Character and Content of this Rescue	167
14.2.3	The Purpose of this Strengthening	168
14.2.4	The Metaphor	169
14.3	The Future Rescue (v. 18)	171
14.3.1	The Shift in Focus	171
14.3.2	πᾶν ἔργον πονηρόν	171
14.3.3	εἰς τὴν βασιλείαν αὐτοῦ τὴν ἐπουράνιον	172
14.3.4	The Doxology	173
14.4	Summary	174
15.	**Summary of Salvation in 2 Timothy**	175
15.1	General Observations	175
15.2	Specific Aspects of the Presentation of Salvation	176
15.2.1	The Benefits of Salvation	176
15.2.2	God and Christ in Relation to Salvation	176
15.2.3	Paul and Salvation	177
15.2.4	Those Who are Saved	178

PART 4: SALVATION IN TITUS: "The grace of God . . . bringing salvation" — 181

16.	**Introduction to Salvation in Titus**	183
16.1	Situation and Tone	183
16.2	The Presentation of Salvation	185

17.	**Titus 1:1-4**	187
17.1	Context	187
17.2	What God has Done	188
17.2.1	*God Promised Eternal Life Before Time*	188
17.2.2	*God has Manifested His Word*	191
17.3	Paul and Titus in Relation to Salvation	192
17.3.1	*Paul, δοῦλος θεου*	192
17.3.2	*Paul, ἀπόστολος Ἰησοῦ Χριστου*	193
17.3.3	*Titus, γνήσιον τέκνον κατὰ κοινὴν πίστιν*	196
17.4	Summary	196
18.	**Titus 2:11-14**	197
18.1	Context	197
18.2	Grace Appeared so that We Might Live	198
18.2.1	*Overview*	198
18.2.2	*ἐπεφάνη ἡ χάρις τοῦ θεου*	199
18.2.3	*σωτήριος πᾶσιν ἀνθρώποις*	201
18.2.4	*παιδεύουσα ἡμᾶς*	202
18.2.5	*ἵνα . . . ζήσωμεν*	203
18.3	Jesus Christ Gave Himself in Order to Redeem Us	208
18.3.1	*ὅς ἔδωκεν ἑαυτὸν ὑπὲρ ἡμῶν*	208
18.3.2	*ἵνα λυτρώσηται ἡμᾶς ἀπὸ πάσης ἀνομίας καὶ καθαρίσῃ ἑαυτῷ λαὸν περιούσιον, ζηλωτὴν καλῶν ἔργων*	209
18.4	The Language of the Unit	211
18.5	Summary	212
19.	**Titus 3:1-8**	214
19.1	Context	215
19.2	Then and Now (vv. 3, 7)	217
19.3	What Appeared? (v. 4)	219
19.4	The Saviour (vv. 4, 6)	220
19.5	"He Saved Us" (v. 5)	220
19.6	The Grounds of Salvation (v. 5a)	222
19.7	The Means of Saving (vv. 5b-6)	224
19.8	The Outcome of the Saving (v. 7)	231
19.9	Summary	233
20.	**Summary of Salvation in Titus**	234
20.1	General Observations	234
20.2	Specific Aspects of the Presentation of Salvation	235
20.2.1	*The Benefits of Salvation*	235
20.2.2	*God and Christ in Relation to Salvation*	235
20.2.3	*Paul and Salvation*	236
20.2.4	*Those Who are Saved*	236

PART 5: CONCLUSIONS — 239

21. Salvation in the Three Letters — 241
21.1 Specific Aspects Compared — 241
21.1.1 *The Benefits of Salvation* — 241
21.1.2 *God and Christ in Relation to Salvation* — 241
21.1.3 *Paul and Salvation* — 242
21.1.4 *Those Who are Saved* — 243
21.1 Similarities and Differences — 243
21.2.1 *Shared Characteristics* — 243
21.2.2 *Distinctive Features* — 244
21.2.3 *The Three Presentations of Salvation and Their Purposes* — 245

22. Implications for Understanding the PE — 248
22.1 The Individual Coherence and Distinctiveness of the PE — 248
22.2 Re-evaluation of Some Current Interpretations of the PEs' Soteriological Perspective — 249
22.2.1 *Salvation as Good Citizenship in the Present Age?* — 249
22.2.2 *Soteriology as an Ideological Stratagem?* — 250
22.2.3 *"Paulology" as a Soteriological Category?* — 251
22.2.4 *A Decline from Paul?* — 252
22.3 Principal Exegetical Results and Some Implications — 254
22.3.1 *1 Tim 1:1* — 255
22.3.2 *1 Tim 1:12-17* — 255
22.3.3 *1 Tim 2:1-7* — 256
22.3.4 *1 Tim 2:15* — 257
22.3.5 *1 Tim 4:10* — 258
22.3.6 *1 Tim 4:16* — 258
22.3.7 *2 Tim 1:9-14* — 258
22.3.8 *2 Tim 2:8-13* — 259
22.3.9 *2 Tim 3:14-17* — 260
22.3.10 *2 Tim 4:16-18* — 260
22.3.11 *Titus 1:1-4* — 261
22.3.12 *Titus 2:11-14* — 262
22.3.13 *Titus 3:1-8* — 262
22.4 Suggestions for Further Investigation — 263
22.5 Concluding Summary — 265

Bibliography — 267
Indexes — 301
    Biblical and Other Ancient Literature — 301
    Modern Authors — 322
    Hebrew Terms — 326
    Greek Terms — 327
    General Index — 334

Foreword

For most of the twentieth-century, and especially since WWII, the interpretation of the three letters commonly called "The Pastoral Epistles" has been determined in scholarly discussion by a fairly rigidly defined paradigm. This scholarly consensus has definitely evolved in the last two decades, receiving greater measures of nuance in the process. Yet there are still certain features which (with some variation) broadly characterize it. (1) Paul certainly did not write these letters; they are rather the pseudepigraphical product of a Paulinist belonging to a later generation, who wrote to address some set of issues in the church(es) of his time and thought resurrecting the image of Paul might help his program. (2) With this view of authorship in the ascendancy, the three letters have acquired the status of a pseudo-Pauline mini-corpus within the canon, which has impacted distinctly the way they are treated. (3) The theology of the letters is certainly not Paul's. Their theology, ethics and way of viewing Christian existence belong to some later time and circumstances. Where contact with the authentic Paul might be thought to exist, the theology is derivative, and it generally lacks the original eschatological impulse of Paul. However, there is within the consensus the growing agreement that the author was in fact a creative theologian, whose theology is best described with a term like Pauline tradition.

As positive a development as this last may seem to be, readings of these letters to Timothy and Titus continue to be subject to an unyielding (if largely unproven) framework of assumptions and rules. From about the 1980s on, however, a growing number of scholars, mostly postgraduate students whose works were subsequently published, have been "coloring outside the lines." And one of the broad areas of the dominant interpretation examined in various ways has been that of the theology of the letters. Of course disassembling and re-examining the components of a long-standing monolithic structure such as this takes time. Up until now one of the gaps in this exercise has been a thorough study of salvation.

Fortunately, Dr. George Wieland's, *The Significance of Salvation: A Study of Salvation Language in the Pastoral Epistles*, promises to fill this gap.

This book interrogates the consensus thoroughly on this matter. "Salvation"—that is, a corpus-reading of it in very specific non-Pauline terms, as under the custodianship of church officers, or exclusively linked to the image of a "canonized" Paul—has been a central feature of the treatment of these letters. Dr. Wieland challenges this understanding by exploring the language and concepts by which salvation in each letter is expressed. In doing so, he uncouples the letters and allows them to speak as unique, individual discourses, instead of requiring them to speak only as parts of a trilogy. There is a serious concern to read the letters within their historical and cultural contexts, and to link the salvation framework which emerges to the paraenetic and ministerial goals of the individual messages.

Scholars engaged in work on the letters to Timothy and Titus can be enormously grateful for Dr. Wieland's careful and thorough interaction with the literature on this topic. His treatment of the evidence is judicious and his engagement with scholarship is fair, constructive and irenic. In the end, he has mounted a convincing case for locating the theology of salvation in the Pastoral Epistles, and their separate expressions of salvation, within a framework that can be called Pauline.

PHILIP H. TOWNER, PHD
Director of Translation Services
United Bible Societies
Reading, England

Preface

This project began in North West Brazil, where in the course of pastoral and missionary work questions arose about the nature of salvation, "healthy teaching" and authentic Christian existence. The letters to Timothy and Titus acquired fresh relevance in that context, and the questions simmered during further years of pastoral work in the North of England.

Opportunity to explore them more fully came with doctoral studies at the University of Aberdeen, assisted by a British Academy Research in the Humanities Award. After three fulfilling years of researching, learning, thinking – but not nearly enough writing! – we returned to pastoral ministry, and the tortuous process of writing up a thesis part-time that continued through a change of continent and role until a sabbatical leave enabled it to be brought to completion.

Innumerable debts have been incurred along the way. To undertake New Testament research under the supervision of Professor I. Howard Marshall has been a singular privilege. Exemplary in his scholarship, authentic in his Christian discipleship and generous in his friendship, he is for me a *typos kalōn ergōn* (Titus 2:7). Dr Philip Towner also gave significant encouragement and stimulus. We were blessed with many new friends in Aberdeen and Dr Chiao Ek Ho and his wife Samantha were valued companions through the arduous PhD process.

The friendship of Dr Ray and Sue Baker over many years has been a great joy and amongst many acts of generosity was the gift of the computer on which much of the research was done.

I am grateful also to the following for providing hospitality and study accommodation: in Edinburgh, Dr Patricia Tweeddale and also Rutherford House; In Aberdeen, Dr Paul and Meg Wraight, whose home has been a haven for so many; Tyndale House, Cambridge; and St John's College, Auckland.

It is a privilege to share in life, learning and serving in Carey Baptist College with the principal, Rev Paul Windsor, staff and students. Dr Martin Sutherland's enthusiastic encouragement of research and writing helped move this project to completion, and colleagues in the University of Auckland School of Theology were also generous in their interest. Students at Carey and the University explored the Pastoral Epistles with me, enriching my understanding.

At one particularly stressful point in the process my Carey colleague Dr Laurie Guy came alongside offering support and friendship that helped keep both me and the project on track.

I owe a continuing debt to Spurgeon's College, London, where I undertook my initial theological studies. Through their teaching, example and encouragement over subsequent years Dr Raymond Brown and Dr Bruce Milne have had an influence greater than they can know. Dr Martin Selman supervised my first Biblical Studies dissertation and encouraged me both in pursuing further study and in taking up a teaching role. It was a great delight to be able to share with him the joy of the completion of the thesis and the prospect of this book not long before his premature death last year.

Several "households of God" have shaped and enabled our lives, faith and service: the Baptist Churches of Hunslet, Leeds; Presidente Medici, Rondônia, Brazil; Rothwell, W. Yorks.; Middleton Park, Leeds; Gerrard St., Aberdeen; Abbeyhill, Edinburgh; Eastview, Auckland; and Mangere, Auckland.

I am blessed with wonderful parents, Rev Joseph McLaren Wieland and Mary Jane Wieland, whose support, spiritual, emotional and material, is unstinting. From them I first learned to love and try to live by the Bible, and my father's faithful Biblical exposition provided my first and most formative model of careful exegesis. I am deeply grateful for the supportive interest shown throughout by my brother John McLaren Masson Wieland and the encouragement of my sister Christine Mary Macpherson, with her husband Bruce and family.

To my wife Jo I want to say thank you for all that we've done together, including this book. From selling our home to fund further study, to moving across the world (three times), ours has been a partnership demanding total buy-in from both parties. Jo, the security of your love has made many risky ventures possible. Lindsey, Jonathan and Joanne, our children and "children in the faith we share" (Titus 1:4): thank you for all you are and everything you add to who I am and anything I do.

Finally, I thank Jeremy Mudditt and Dr Anthony R. Cross for their editorial expertise and encouragement, and Louisa Bayer for invaluable assistance in formatting the text for publication.

GEORGE M. WIELAND

Abbreviations

Journals, Reference Works and General Abbreviations
AB	Anchor Bible
AnBib	Analecta Biblica
ANRW	*Aufstieg und Niedergang der römischer Welt*
ANTC	Abingdon New Testament Commentaries
ASP	American Studies in Papyrology
AzTh	Arbeiten zur Theologie
BAGD	Bauer, Arndt, Gingrich, and Danker, *Greek-English Lexicon of the New Testament and Other Early Christian Literature*
BBET	Beiträge zur biblischen Exegese und Theologie
BBR	*Bulletin*
BNTC	Black's New Testament Commentaries
BT	*Bible Translator*
BTB	*Biblical Theology Bulletin*
CBQ	*Catholic Biblical Quarterly*
CGTC	Cambridge Greek Testament Commentary
diss.	dissertation
DLNTD	*Dictionary of the Later New Testament and Its Developments*
DPL	*Dictionary of Paul and His Letters*
EKKNT	Evangelisch-Katholischer Kommentar zum Neuen Testament
ETr	English Translation
EuroJTh	*European Journal of Theology*
EvQ	*Evangelical Quarterly*
ExAud	*Ex Auditu*
ExpTim	*Expository Times*
FRLANT	Forschungen zur Religion und Literatur des Alten und Neuen Testaments
HNT	Handbuch zum Neuen Testament
HTKNT	Herders theologischer Kommentar zum Neuen Testament
HTS	Hamburger Theologische Studien

HUT	Hermeneutische Untersuchungen zur Theologie
ICC	International Critical Commentary
Int	*Interpretation*
IVPNTC	IVP New Testament Commentaries
JBL	*Journal of Biblical Literature*
JETS	*Journal of the Evangelical Theology Society*
JSNT	*Journal for the Study of the New Testament*
JSNTSup	Journal for the Study of the New Testament Supplement Series
JTS	*Journal of Theological Studies*
LCL	Loeb Classical Library
LXX	Septuagint
MBPAR	Münchener Beiträge zur Papyrusforschung und antiken Rechtsgeschichte
MNTC	Moffat's New Testament Commentary
MT	Masoretic Text
NAC	New American Commentary
NCB	New Century Bible Commentary
n, nn	note, notes
n.d.	no date
ns	new series
NIBC	New International Bible Commentary
NIDNTT	*New International Dictionary of New Testament Theology*
NIGTC	New International Greek Testament Commentary
NIV	New International Version
NIVAC	New International Version Application Commentary
NLC	New London Commentary
NovT	*Novum Testamentum*
NRSV	New Revised Standard Version
NTD	Das Neue Testament Deutsch
NTS	*New Testament Studies*
ÖBS	Österreichische biblische Studien
OTP	J. H. Charlesworth (ed.), *The Old Testament Pseudepigrapha*
p, pp	page, pages
PE	Pastoral Epistles
PNTC	Penguin New Testament Commentary
RB	*Revue biblique*
RNT	Regensburger Neues Testament
RHPR	*Revue d'histoire et de philosophie religieuses*
RRT	*Reviews in Religion and Theology*
RSV	Revised Standard Version

SBLDS	Society of Biblical Literature Dissertation Series
SJT	Scottish Journal of Theology
SNTSMS	Society for New Testament Studies Monograph Series
SNTSU	Studien zum Neuen Testament und seiner Umwelt
TDNT	Theological Dictionary of the New Testament
TJ	Trinity Journal
TNTC	Tyndale New Testament Commentary
TynBul	Tyndale Bulletin
WBC	Word Biblical Commentary
WTJ	Westminster Theological Journal
WUNT	Wissenschaftliche Untersuchungen zum Alten und Neuen Testament
ZBKNT	Zürcher Bibelkommentare zum Neuen Testament
ZWT	Zeitschrift für wissenschaftliche Theologie

Ancient Texts

Standard abbreviations are used for books of the Bible and Apocrypha. The following abbreviations are employed for other ancient texts:

1 Clem.	First Letter of Clement
1QS	Community Rule (Qumran Cave 1)
Abr.	Philo, On the Life of Abraham
Ant.	Josephus, Jewish Antiquities
Ap.	Josephus, Against Apion
Ap. John	The Apocryphon of John (Nag Hammadi)
Apol.	Justin Martyr, Apology
B.J.	Josephus, The Jewish War
Conf.	Philo, On the Confusion of Tongues
Diatr.	Epictetus, Diatribai (Discourses)
Fin.	Cicero, De finibus (On the Ends of Good and Evil)
Flacc.	Philo, Against Flaccus
Fr. Ps.	Origen, Fragments on Psalms 1-150
Haer.	Hippolytus, The Refutation of All Heresies
Haer.	Irenaeus, Against Heresies
Her.	Philo, Who is the Heir?
Hyp. Arch.	The Hypostasis of the Archons (Nag Hammadi)
Ign. Eph.	Ignatius, Letter to the Ephesians
Ign. Pol.	Ignatius, Letter to Polycarp
Ign. Smyrn.	Ignatius, Letter to the Smyrnaeans
Ios.	Philo, On the Life of Joseph

Leg.	Philo, *Allegorical Interpretation*
Legat.	Philo, *On the Embassy to Gaius*
Mor.	Plutarch, *Moralia*
Mos.	Philo, *On the Life of Moses*
Mut.	Philo, *On the Changing of Names*
Opif.	Philo, *On the Creation of the World*
Orig. World	*The Origin of the World* (Nag Hammadi)
PHerc.	*Herculaneum Papyri*
Plant.	Philo, *On Planting*
Sacr.	Philo, *On the Sacrifices of Cain and Abel*
Spec.	Philo, *On the Special Laws*
TBenj	*Testament of Benjamin* (in *Testaments of the Twelve Patriarchs*)
TDan	*Testament of Dan* (in *Testaments of the Twelve Patriarchs*)
Vita	Josephus, *Life*

Commentaries on the Pastoral Epistles

Modern commentators on the PE are generally cited simply by surname. Where the same writer has produced more than one commentary on the PE, the work referred to is identified by its title or series.

Quotations from the Bible and Apocrypha in English are taken from the NRSV except where otherwise indicated.

Part 1

INTRODUCTION

CHAPTER 1

Salvation in PE Scholarship

1.1 A Lack of Consensus

One cannot read far in the Pastoral Epistles without encountering the language or ideas of salvation. The unusually high incidence of salvation terms (σῴζω, σωτήρ, σωτηρία, σωτήριος), references to both God and Jesus Christ as σωτήρ, and the citing of much apparently traditional material with soteriological content,[1] prompts the claim that "salvation is all-important for these epistles."[2] For all that, and despite considerable interest in the PE in recent decades,[3] there have been surprisingly few studies specifically of salvation in these letters. Apart from A. Klöpper's 1904 article, "Zur Soteriologie der Pastoralbriefe (Tit. 3:4-7; 2 Tim. 1:9-11; Tit. 2:11-14),"[4] and I. H. Marshall's essay, "Salvation in the Pastoral Epistles," published almost a century later,[5] scholarly literature related to the topic outside the commentaries consists largely of either studies of

---

1   See I. H. Marshall's survey of the data in "'Sometimes Only Orthodox' - Is there more to the Pastoral Epistles?" *Epworth Review* 20.3 (1993): 12-24; also J. D. Quinn, *The Letter to Titus: A New Translation with Notes and Commentary, and an Introduction to Titus, I and II Timothy, the Pastoral Epistles* (AB 35; New York: Doubleday, 1990), Excursus V: "Salvation in the PE," 304-15. On the "faithful words" as salvation statements see R. A. Campbell, "Identifying the faithful sayings in the PE," *JSNT* 54 (1994): 73-86.
2   F. Young, *The Theology of the Pastoral Letters* (New Testament Theology; Cambridge, Cambridge University Press), 55; cf. C. Spicq, *Les Épitres Pastorales* (2 vols; 4th ed.; Paris: Gabalda, 1966), 257.
3   For surveys of recent scholarship on the PE generally and evaluations of current trends see especially I. H. Marshall, "Recent Study of the Pastoral Epistles," *Themelios* 23.1 (1997): 3-29, and M. Harding, *What Are They Saying about the Pastoral Epistles?* (New York: Paulist, 2001). On scholarship pre-1985 see W. Schenk, "Die Briefe an Timotheus I und II und an Titus (Pastoralbriefe) in der neueren Forschung (1945-1985)." *ANRW* 25.4: 3404-38.
4   A. Klöpper, "Zur Soteriologie der Pastoralbriefe (Tit. 3:4-7; 2 Tim. 1:9-11; Tit. 2:11-14)." *ZWT* 47 (1904): 57-88.
5   I. H. Marshall, "Salvation in the Pastoral Epistles," in *Frühes Christentum* (ed. H. Lichtenberger; vol. 3 of *Geschichte-Tradition-Reflexion*, ed. H. Cancik, H. Lichtenberger, and P. Schäfer; Tübingen: J. C. B. Mohr, 1996), 449-69.

particular texts that are of soteriological interest,[6] or treatments of the theme of salvation in the PE as part of broader surveys.[7]

In explanations of the general outlook of the PE, however, salvation often features prominently. Defenders of Pauline authorship find in the letters' theological passages indications of a fully Pauline soteriology. G. Fee, for example, argues that a "concern for the gospel is the driving force behind the PE,"[8] and that where aspects of the gospel are treated in these letters, "in each case the theology, as well as much of the language, is thoroughly Pauline."[9] He concludes an impressive list of Pauline soteriological elements with the assertion that,

If all of this is not as systematically set forth as some would like,

---

[6] E.g. S. M. Baugh, "'Savior of all people': 1 Tim. 4:10 in Context," *WTJ* 54 (1992): 331-40; S. Coupland, "Salvation Through Childbearing? The Riddle of 1 Timothy 2:15," *ExpTim* 119 (2001): 302-03; K. A. van der Jagt, "Women are Saved through Bearing Children: A Sociological Approach to the Interpretation of 1 Tim 2:15," in *Issues in Bible Translation* (ed. P. C. Stime; United Bible Societies Monograph Series 3; London: United Bible Societies, 1988), 288-95; repr. from *BT* 39 (1988): 201-08; S. C. Mott, "Greek Ethics and Christian Conversion: The Philonic Background of Titus 2:10-14 and 3:3-7," *NovT* 20 (1978): 22-48; S. E. Porter, "What Does It Mean To Be 'Saved by Childbirth' (1 Tim 2:15)?" *JSNT* 49 (1993): 87-102; J. D. Quinn, "Jesus as Savior and Only Mediator (1 Tim 2:3-6): Linguistic Paradigms of Acculturation," in *Fede e Cultura/Foi et culture* (Turin: Elle di Ci, 1981), 249-60; G. Wainwright, "Praying for Kings: The Place of Human Rulers in the Divine Plan of Salvation," *ExAud* 2 (1986): 117-27.

[7] E.g. F. F. Bruce, "'Our God and Saviour': a Recurring Biblical Pattern," in *The Saviour God: Comparative Studies in the Concept of Salvation Presented to Edwin Oliver James* (ed. S. G. F. Brandon; Manchester: Manchester University Press, 1963), 51-66; M. Davies, section on "Salvation and Eschatology" in *The Pastoral Epistles* (New Testament Guides; Sheffield: Sheffield Academic Press, 1996), 41-66; D. Gerber, "L'indice d'une sotériologie pensée prioritairement en lien avec la venue de Jésus?" *RHPR* 80 (2000): 463-77; I. H. Marshall, "The Nature of Christian Salvation." *EuroJTh* 4 (1995): 29-43; "Salvation, Grace and Works in the Later Writings in the Pauline Corpus." *NTS* 42 (1996): 339-58; "Sometimes Only Orthodox"; "Universal Grace and Atonement in the Pastoral Epistles," in *The Grace of God, the Will of Man* (ed. C. Pinnock; Grand Rapids: Zondervan, 1989), 51-69; J. Sumney, "'God Our Savior': The Theology of 1 Timothy," *Lexington Theological Quarterly* 33 (1998): 151-61; F. Young, discussion of "God as saviour" and "Salvation" in *Theology*, 50-59.

[8] G. D. Fee, *1 and 2 Timothy, Titus* (NIBC 13; Peasbody, Mass.: Hendrickson, 1988), 15.

[9] Fee, 16.

and if some of it appears in slightly different language, there can be no question that the substance is what Paul elsewhere calls "my gospel."[10]

Without sharing Fee's position on authorship, I. H. Marshall reaches similar conclusions with regard to the "centrality of the concept of salvation" in the PE and its essentially Pauline content:

> The thought is not different in any significant way from that of Paul, and I do not think that any slight differences in emphasis are at all important. What is significant is the much greater prominence of the vocabulary and especially the concept of God as Saviour.[11]

The majority of scholars, however, place the presentation of salvation in the PE at varying degrees of distance from what they read in the *Hauptbriefe*, whether they explain that distance in terms of a development of or a departure from the Pauline intention. Dibelius-Conzelman, in their still influential commentary,[12] find in salvation an organising principle, so that, "unity results from the constant emphasis upon the meaning of salvation for the present."[13] There is a consistent soteriological perspective which is determinative for the attitude adopted to the world and the existence of the church in it:

> The presupposition is that salvation has become a reality in the epiphany of the past; salvation in the future appears to be nothing but the shadow of this past epiphany. This consciousness of salvation forms the ultimate essential presupposition of the attitude toward the world which is expressed in the concept of good citizenship [*christliche Bürgerlichkeit*].[14]

In this view the eschatological horizon has receded far into the distance. What matters is the present and the need for the church to settle down for a long term existence in the world. With the diminution of the Pauline tension a more positive view of the

---

10 Fee, 17.
11 Marshall, "Salvation in the Pastoral Epistles", 467.
12 M. Dibelius and H. Conzelmann, *A Commentary on the Pastoral Epistles* (trans. P. Buttolph and A. Yarbo; Hermeneia; Philadelphia: Fortress, 1972); trans. of M. Dibelius, Die Pastoralbriefe (4th rev. ed. by H. Conzelmann, HNT 13; Tübingen: J. C. B. Mohr, 1966).
13 Dibelius-Conzelmann, 9.
14 Dibelius-Conzelmann, 10.

present world becomes possible. Salvation, understood as already realized in the past Christ event, is experienced in the present as the salvation event is proclaimed in the *kerygma* and life is conformed to an ethical ideal which is largely borrowed from the surrounding culture.

P. H. Towner takes issue with this interpretation.[15] His study uncovers a consistent eschatological perspective according to which the present age has significance as the age of salvation which has been inaugurated by the first epiphany of Christ, and which will culminate in his second epiphany.[16] Seven pieces on the theme of salvation are scrutinized (1 Tim.1:15; 2:5-6; 3:16; 2 Tim. 1:9-10; 2:8-13; Tit. 2:11-14; 3:4-7),[17] leading to the conclusion that though drawn from a variety of traditions they cohere into a consistent theme, and each is woven into the argument of its immediate context. The Christ event is central to each, and the author has linked various aspects of salvation to it:

> Thus he characterizes salvation as a present participation in eternal life and in Christ's resurrection life. It is the removal from the sphere of sin, and it finds visible expression in a new manner of life. Salvation is God's gracious gift, having been executed through the historical appearance of Christ. But it also emerges that salvation is a process initiated but not yet finished in the believer, a view that coincides with the understanding of the earlier Paul.[18]

The ethics of the PE are grounded in this understanding of salvation,[19] and the particular forms of life and ethically attractive behaviour proposed in the letters are motivated by a concern, in this age of salvation, for the on-going mission of the Church.[20]

For C. Spicq, the key to the letters' understanding of salvation, and a significant part of their purpose, is found in the linking of

---

15　P. H. Towner, *The Goal of our Instruction: The Structure of Theology and Ethics in the Pastoral Epistles* (Journal for the Study of the New Testament Supplement Series 34. Sheffield: Sheffield Academic Press, 1989.
16　Towner, *Goal*, 61-74.
17　Towner, *Goal*, 75-119.
18　Towner, *Goal*, 249.
19　P. Trummer, *Die Paulustradition der Pastoralbriefe* (BBET 8; Frankfurt: Peter Lang), also finds in the PE essentially Pauline doctrine, which provides "die Grundlage einer stark theologisch motivierten Ethik." (198); cf. H. Merkel, *Die Pastoralbriefe* (NTD 9.1; Göttingen: Vandenhoeck & Ruprecht, 1991), 14-15.
20　Towner, *Goal*, 21-45.

salvation to the church.²¹ So closely connected are they that in his analysis of the theology of the PE he finds it necessary to discuss soteriology and ecclesiology together.²² While he recognizes an eschatological dimension in the thought of the PE, this too is absorbed into the concept of the church, in that it is in and through the church that the salvation of the world is realized.²³ The distinctive contribution of the PE (which he regards as authentically Pauline) consists in this presentation of the church as a saving institution ("institution salutaire"),²⁴ whose hierarchical structure and sacramental activity are established by God through the apostles as the means whereby it might confer justification upon its members and lead them to eternal life.

J. Roloff also understands the PE to present the church as *Heilsanstalt*, though under the authority of the gospel.²⁵ The primary concern of the author, whom Roloff takes to be a third-generation Paulinist with access to much of the Pauline corpus, is to maintain his community in continuity with Paul and the tradition of Pauline teaching.²⁶ Within this framework, Roloff's approach consists in identifying the Pauline sources for particular sections and explaining the transformation of original Pauline ideas and statements into what is found in the PE. In general, he observes a lessening of tension and a flattening of theological concepts. With regard to salvation, the world is no longer so radically opposed to God, and sin is not the same enslaving force which brings people under the condemnation of the Law and leads to death. The Christ event accordingly loses its drama as a breaking into enemy territory, and becomes rather a manifestation of God's pre-temporal saving will.²⁷ In place of Paul's direct relationship of the believer with the crucified and risen Christ is a relating of the believer to abstract qualities which constitute the nature of the life made possible through Christ and learned through the Gospel which Christ brought.²⁸ Paul's determinative eschatological horizon has faded;²⁹

---

21 "La sotériologie des Pastorales est ecclésiologique, et sa nouveauté est de bloquer le propos divin et éternel du salut avec son accomplissement dans l'Église." (Spicq, 261.)
22 Spicq, 257-64.
23 Spicq, 264.
24 Spicq, 264.
25 J. Roloff, *Der erste Brief an Timotheus* (EKKNT 15; Zurich: Benziger, 1988), 215.
26 Roloff, 42.
27 Roloff, 361.
28 Roloff, 362.
29 Roloff, 213: "Die für die paulinische Ekklesiologie zentrale *eschatologische*

the dynamic pneumatology of Paul has been replaced by an emphasis on encounter with Christ in the Church's worship;[30] and it is in and through the Church, built upon God's sure foundation, that sinners are called to change, baptism is given and members are trained up into salvation.

For some other scholars it is not so much the church as the person of Paul himself that assumes soteriological significance in the PE. According to M. Wolter,[31] the solution of the PE to the threat to the community was to safeguard its continuity with its apostolic origins, because to them Paul represented not merely an authority figure, but an essential component of their Christian identity.[32] The faith of the Christian community had been articulated normatively by Paul, and it was only through remaining true to this Pauline heritage that the salvation of believers could be guaranteed.[33]

K. Läger goes so far as to speak of a "Paulology" in the PE, more prominent even than Christology, according to which Paul has become not only the authorized bearer of the saving message, but an integral part of that message.[34]

The views reported thus far all relate the salvation concepts of the PE in some way to Paul's teaching. Some, however, propose that the soteriological ideas derive from elsewhere. J. D. Quinn, for example, favours a Lukan source,[35] and stresses the affinity of the language and thought of the PE to that of Hellenistic Judaism. In relation to salvation, he discovers in the PE "the internal, ethical deliverance, the moral change that has been identified in the Jewish tradition represented by Philo,"[36] which in promoting ethical values admired in the Hellenistic world would represent an intentional missionary approach to that culture.[37]

V. Hasler considers the soteriology of the PE to provide one of the weightiest arguments for placing the PE outside any Pauline tradition.[38] Though he concedes that the PE do cite traditional materials which might seem to witness to a Pauline understanding

---

    Dimension fällt in den Past so gut wie völlig aus."
30 Roloff, 216-17.
31 M. Wolter, *Die Pastoralbriefe als Paulustradition* (FRLANT 146; Göttingen: Vandenhoeck & Ruprecht, 1988).
32 Wolter, *Paulustradition*, 270.
33 Wolter, *Paulustradition*, 269.
34 K. Läger, *Die Christologie der Pastoralbriefe* (HTS 12; Münster: Lit, 1996), 177.
35 Quinn, *Titus*, 19.
36 Quinn, *Titus*, 315; cf. Mott, "Greek Ethics," 22-48.
37 Quinn, *Titus*, 315.
38 V. Hasler, *Die Briefe an Timotheus und Titus (Pastoralbriefe)* (ZBKNT 12; Zürich: Theologischer, 1978), 8.

of salvation, Hasler insists that, when the theological reflection of the author and his community shows through, it bears the hallmark of a Greek Christianity whose conception of salvation is shaped by the revelation schema of Hellenistic religion.[39]

This presentation of salvation draws on ideas of the universal will to save of a benevolent deity and of the revelation of that will through the appearing of the redeeming deity in human form. Its most significant contribution to Christian theology, according to Hasler, lies in the insight that this revelation, effected in history, continues through the preaching of the Gospel.[40] The PE do offer a unified theological theory,[41] but it is so far removed from that of Paul that Hasler has some difficulty in explaining why the PE should go to such lengths to claim a direct line to Paul. He proposes that a 2nd century church leader in Greece or Western Asia Minor had aspirations to influence churches over a wider area, and reasoned that since the Paul of Christian history had exercised leadership in the whole region, he could, by writing under the apostle's name, speak with similarly extensive authority.[42]

Like Hasler, L. R. Donelson sees in the PE a unified conception of salvation which draws on the Hellenistic religious environment and finds the motive for the attempt to pass off the letters as Pauline in the desire to claim wider authority for the role and outlook of a particular leader or leadership group.[43] In his view, however, neither Hasler nor any other student of the PE had really taken account of the literary implications of the pseudepigraphical character of these letters. In consequence, studies have been concerned with constructing the author's theological system from statements plucked out of their contexts, and, "the elaborate interplays among ethical statements, Christological statements, and other dicta are ignored."[44] On Donelson's reading, there is no tension between the traditional materials and the theology of the rest of the letters,[45] rather there are intricate connections between the various units of material which lend themselves to exploration in the light of the

---

39 See, e.g., Hasler on 1 Tim. 1:15-17 (pages 16-17), and on the two texts which Trummer took as particularly powerful evidence for genuine Pauline tradition and understanding, 2 Tim. 1:9 (58-59) and Tit. 3:5-7 (96-97).
40 Hasler, 8.
41 Hasler, 9.
42 Hasler, 9.
43 L. R. Donelson, *Pseudepigraphy and Ethical Argument in the Pastoral Epistles* (HUT 22; Tübingen: J. C. B. Mohr, 1986).
44 Donelson, *Pseudepigraphy*, 135.
45 Donelson, *Pseudepigraphy*, 134.

strategies of persuasion, in particular enthymeme and paradigm, employed by Graeco-Roman ethicists. Such a study reveals that the author of the PE, "grounds his ethic in the workings of God's plan for salvation, linking his ethical claims to cosmological and Christological assertions."[46]

The author has constructed his own unique theory of salvation and has set out to invest it with apostolic authority by means of the technique of deception available to him in the device of the pseudepigrahical letter. Though such an approach uncovers many examples of "the intimate and unbreakable connection the author creates between his ethics and salvation statements,"[47] it would be a mistake to imagine that this author has begun with an understanding of salvation and gone on to deduce ethical directions from it. The reality is quite the reverse. The author knows what sort of attitudes and behaviour he wishes to inculcate, and has developed a cosmological and ethical system whereby these attitudes and behaviour lead to salvation, and those whom the author is opposing, who espouse alternative attitudes, are excluded from salvation.[48] The author of the PE has intentionally and singlehandedly created a Pauline tradition:

> The παραθήκη comes into existence out of the author's own creativity. He picks and chooses from his theological environment; he weaves various ideas into a coherent system; then he thrusts the whole collection back into a fictional past.[49]

The key to the entire system is that "quiet virtues constitute the sole means of salvation."[50] Such a life is possible because God has a plan of salvation which is in operation in this world; Jesus in his first epiphany revealed the existence of this plan, taught the ethical standards required and made available, as the means of attaining them, the Spirit given in baptism. At Jesus' second epiphany those who have lived virtuously according to the orthodox teaching within the official cultus will be rewarded. It is clear how such a scheme serves the author's purpose. It is only in the cult and by education through the teaching of particular authorized figures that the virtuous life which God requires can be cultivated and salvation guaranteed.

---

46 Donelson, *Pseudepigraphy*, 115.
47 Donelson, *Pseudepigraphy*, 85.
48 See on "The Author's Response," Donelson, *Pseudepigraphy*, 127-8.
49 Donelson, *Pseudepigraphy*, 164.
50 Donelson, *Pseudepigraphy*, 153.

There is, then, a remarkably wide range of explanations of the content and purpose of the presentation of salvation in the PE, from authentically Pauline to decidedly un-Pauline in character, from salvation by faith to salvation through good works, from universal to restrictive in scope, and from predominantly this-worldly to thoroughly eschatological in orientation. Why this lack of consensus? Mounce provides part of the answer in his judgment that, "More than perhaps for any book in the NT, exegesis of the PE is affected by one's critical assumptions."[51] It is the weight given to prior assumptions that explains a tendency that may be observed to a high degree of selectivity in the evidence cited in support of a particular position, while contrary indicators are summarily explained away or simply ignored.

Thus we see Merkel, who wants to find a Pauline doctrine of justification by faith at the heart of the PE,[52] dismissing two soteriological texts (1 Tim 2:15; 4:16) as un-Pauline aberrations,[53] while Donelson, expounding his theory of salvation through the cult from his key text, Titus 3:4-7, simply ignores the rather Pauline-sounding οὐκ ἐξ ἔργων τῶν ἐν δικαιοσύνῃ ἃ ἐποιήσαμεν ἡμεῖς (v. 5) and the reference to δικαιωθέντες τῇ ἐκείνου χάριτι (v. 7).[54] In a similar way Dibelius-Conzelmann pass over the indications of eschatological hope in Titus 2:13 and 3:7 that cause difficulties for their *christliche Bürgerlichkeit* ("Christian citizenship") interpretation with no comment on the possibility of a future dimension in 2:13 and relegating the "hope for eternal life" in 3:7 to the status of a "formulaic entity."

In each case prior assumptions about the historical context and purpose of the PE have guided the reading of the letters, leading to the privileging of certain strands of evidence over others. If the determining influence of such prior assumptions could be reduced there would be a greater possibility of an evaluation of the soteriological perspectives of these letters on their own terms, taking due account of all the internal evidence. In fact encouragement for an attempt at such an evaluation may be found in recent scholarship on the PE that utilizes literary and rhetorical approaches. A significant trend has emerged towards appreciating the internal coherence of these letters.

---

51 W. D. Mounce, *Pastoral Epistles* (WBC 46; Nashville: Thomas Nelson, 2000), xlvi.
52 Merkel, 14.
53 Merkel, 15, 40.
54 Donelson, *Pseudepigraphy*, 138-39, 143.

1.2 A Growing Recognition of Coherence

A major problem dogging earlier work on theological topics in the PE, in an environment strongly influenced by tradition-historical questions, related to the status of the evidence available. Since much of the overtly theological content was to be found in what were apparently traditional materials incorporated into the three letters, the charge could be made that it did not represent the author's own thinking and, useful as it was for studies of early Christian liturgy,[55] it should therefore be set aside in discussions of his theological outlook. Thus Dibelius-Conzelmann speak of the "disparate nature, both in form and content," of the traditional material employed, concluding that "the soteriological concepts can be used indiscriminately,"[56] and it is difficult to know how the author would have interpreted "what for him was already a traditional expression."[57] No coherent theological system could be expected in a writer who seemed to be a gatherer rather than an originator of religious thought, endowed with "an administrative, not a creative mind,"[58] and indeed, the assumption that no such order existed was the basis for some interpretations of the PE. In the judgment of A. T. Hanson,

> It is this impression of relative incoherence which, as much as anything else, makes it impossible to believe that the great bulk of the Pastorals is Pauline. This strange feature is, I believe, best accounted for by the supposition that the author of the Pastorals had no theology of his own. He is a purveyor of other men's theology. What he supplies is a fairly conventional piety and strong moral earnestness.[59]

Easton states bluntly, "We can hardly speak of the 'theology' of the Pastoral Epistles."[60]

---

55 E.g. W. Metzger, *Der Christushymnus 1.Timotheus 3,16: Fragment einer Homologie der paulinischen Gemeinden* (AzTh 62; Stuttgart: Calwer, 1979).
56 Dibelius-Conzelmann, 9.
57 Dibelius-Conzelmann, 150 (on Titus 3:7).
58 F. D. Gealy and M. P. Noyes, "The First and Second Epistles to Timothy and the Epistle to Titus, Introduction and Exegesis," in vol. 11 of *The Interpreter's Bible* (Nashville: Abingdon, 1955), 342-551, 364.
59 A. T. Hanson, *Studies in the Pastoral Epistles* (London: SPCK, 1968), 110-11.
60 B. S. Easton, *The Pastoral Epistles* (London: SCM, 1948), 22. As he reads the PE, "there is no sustained thought . . . even within paragraphs . . . the topic changes without preparation and apparently without motive. For emotional appeal the Pastor relies chiefly on citations; and these are often in glaring contrast to his own work, not only in vocabulary and style but in religious

This "impression of relative incoherence" has been strongly challenged, however, in more recent scholarship. D. Cook attempted to explode the notion that Pauline "fragments" had been embedded in otherwise pseudepigraphical letters by demonstrating that there is no difference between the language of the so-called fragments and that of the remainder of the letters.[61] This strengthens the impression that the author has purposefully integrated any source materials into his own argument. More fundamentally, the case for conceptual coherence has been greatly advanced by the work of B. Fiore,[62] L. R. Donelson,[63] and P. H. Towner.[64] Fiore and Donelson found in the PE recognizable structures of argumentation suggesting deliberate and careful literary strategies. Towner investigated the ethics of the PE, which had been considered largely autonomous and only loosely related to any theological material in their literary contexts, and was able to demonstrate that the theological pieces were integrated into a coherent structure of theology and ethics. These studies, starting from different assumptions and proceeding by different methods, all found evidence of coherence in the structure of the PE and consistency in their theological outlook,[65] even if they offered opposing profiles of that theology. Persuaded by them, F. Young accepts that, "there is a more consistent theology than has generally been suggested."[66] Against this trend, J. D. Miller has attempted to describe the PE as "composite documents" more akin to anthologies of diverse traditions than logically ordered compositions,[67] but his thesis fails to convince.[68] The anthropologist K. D. Tollefson takes

---

thought as well" (14).

61 D. Cook, "2 Tim. 4:6-8 and the Epistle to the Philippians," *JTS* ns 33 (1982): 168-71; and "The Pastoral Fragments reconsidered," *JTS* ns 35 (1984): 120-31.

62 B. Fiore, *The Function of Personal Example in the Socratic and Pastoral Epistles* (AnBib 105; Rome: Biblical Institute, 1986).

63 Donelson, *Pseudepigraphy*.

64 Towner, *Goal*.

65 See also S. E. Fowl, *The Story of Christ in the Ethics of Paul: An Analysis of the Function of the Hymnic Material in the Pauline Corpus* (JSNTSup 36; Sheffield: Sheffield Academic Press, 1990); M. Harding, *Tradition and Rhetoric in the Pastoral Epistles* (New York: Peter Lang, 1998); also the earlier work of N. Brox, *Die Pastoralbriefe* (RNT 7; Regensburger: Friedrich Pustet, 1969), who discerned "eine bestimmte theologische Grundhaltung," even in the supposedly non-theological sections of the letters (49).

66 F. Young, *Theology*, 48.

67 J. D. Miller, *The Pastoral Letters as Composite Documents* (SNTSMS 93; Cambridge: Cambridge University Press, 1997).

68 See e.g. I. H. Marshall's strong response in *The Pastoral Epistles* (ICC;

issue with Miller partly on the grounds of the general probability that "writers have some overarching purpose in mind in order to decide what should be included or excluded in a manuscript to achieve the intended objective."[69] Specifically in relation to the PE, there is in the current climate a greater readiness to allow to the author theological purpose in the choice and utilization of traditional materials, to see conceptual coherence in these letters and in particular to recognize that the ethical instructions are "grounded in a particular theological view of the way the world is."[70] If the claims to literary and conceptual coherence are to be taken seriously, then all the relevant evidence, including that contained in the "traditional material," can and should be taken into account in an investigation of an aspect of the theological outlook of these letters.

1.3 The Present Study

The present study attempts to investigate the understanding(s) of salvation in the PE, asking what is the content of the idea(s) of salvation expressed and what is the function of soteriological elements in the argument of these letters. Building on the recognition of coherence of argumentation in the letters and accepting that letters are essentially documents designed to persuade, we shall identify the material in each letter that pertains specifically to salvation and seek to understand its significance in relation to that letter's paraenetic purpose.

We shall attempt to reduce the prejudicial effect of prior assumptions particularly in two respects. First, rather than begin with a highly specific theory of authorship or supposed life-setting which then becomes the interpretive framework within which the letter is read, we shall approach "the text as text,"[71] making the internal coherence of each letter the primary reference point in interpreting its content. No one background will be assumed from the start to inform the use of salvation terms or supply soteriological concepts. Instead we shall explore a range of backgrounds, attempting to determine which gives the best sense within the argument of the letter and enables the salvation material to function in line with the letter's paraenetic purpose. Having said that, it is necessary to set some limits if the task is to be manageable. For this

---

Edinburgh: T&T Clark, 1999), 16-18.
69 K. D. Tollefson, "Titus: Epistle of Religious Revitalization," *BTB* 30 (2000): 145-57, 145.
70 Young, *Theology*, 74-75.
71 Tollefson, "Titus," 145.

investigation, the working hypothesis will be that the writer has potentially available to him early Christian traditions such as those reflected in other NT writings; the LXX; various ideas and traditions of Hellenistic Judaism as represented, e.g., by the books of Maccabees, Sirach, the Wisdom of Solomon and the writings of Philo; and notions of popular religion and philosophy current in the Graeco-Roman milieu. This hypothesis does steer the investigation in the direction of exploring possible links with or derivation from earlier ideas of salvation rather than seeking to locate the soteriology of the PE among later expressions of Christian belief such as may be found in the writings of the Apostolic Fathers. Apart from the cogent arguments for an earlier date in recent commentaries,[72] such an approach may be defended on the grounds that the comparison with other NT writings will allow any conceptual distance between the PE and those writings to become apparent. Should such a distance emerge, that would be the appropriate point at which to explore connections between the PE and other early Christian documents that may be placed at a similar remove from the NT.

The second assumption that we shall set aside is that the three letters were produced as one three-part corpus, to be read and understood in relation to each other.[73] If this assumption is in fact justified, the coherence of the three-fold presentation may be expected to emerge from a comparison of the results of the study of each separately. If, on the other hand, it is unfounded, to proceed on the basis of the essential unity of the three documents would seriously distort the findings of the investigation. It is therefore methodologically preferable to attempt to hear the voice of each distinctly before judging to what extent they are singing the same tune. This approach gains encouragement from the recent study by

---

72 See e.g. Marshall, 40-92; Mounce, xlviii-cxxix; L. T. Johnson, *The First and Second Letters to Timothy: A New Translation with Introduction and Commentary* (AB 35A; New York: Doubleday, 2001), 55-97.
73 Though the majority of scholars treat the three PE as a whole, grounds have been proposed for regarding 2 Timothy as distinctive (e.g. M. Prior, C.M., *Paul the Letter-Writer and the Second Letter to Timothy*. JSNTSup 23; Sheffield: Sheffield Academic Press, 1989; cf. J. Murphy-O'Connor, "2 Timothy Contrasted with 1 Timothy and Titus," *RB* 98 (1991): 403-10). A. Kenny's stylometric analysis (*A Stylometric Study of the New Testament*, Oxford: Clarendon, 1986) sets Titus apart from the two letters to Timothy. Further reason for caution is found in the diversity of explanations for precisely how the three work as a group, even from scholars who insist that it is only as a conceptual whole that they can be adequately understood (see e.g. Roloff, 44-45; Young, *Theology*, 142; Quinn, *Titus*, 19-20).

W. A. Richards,[74] in which he notes differences of vocabulary, form, traditions cited, structure and genre between the three letters.[75] From his epistolary analysis he finds a basis for "treating the Pastorals as three separate texts, from three different hands, set at three different points along the road after Paul."[76] This lends weight to L. T. Johnson's earlier remark that, "To reconsider one of the letters in isolation would be to open up the whole issue once more. But perhaps it is time to do so."[77]

For a soteriological investigation the explicit salvation terms in the letters and the material within which they are set furnish a convenient starting point. The body of the work will consist of a careful exegetical study of each occurrence of σῴζω and its cognates in these letters, drawing into the discussion other material as appropriate, and exploring how concepts of salvation contribute to the arguments of each letter. The results of this investigation will be gathered for each letter separately before the three are compared and conclusions drawn in relation to the content of salvation for these letters and the use made of those ideas in furthering the letters' purposes.

---

74 W. A. Richards, *Difference and Distance in Post-Pauline Christianity: An Epistolary Analysis of the Pastorals* (New York: Peter Lang, 2002).
75 Richards, *Difference and Distance*, especially the section, "Are the Pastorals all of a Piece?" (20-24).
76 Richards, *Difference and Distance*, 240.
77 Johnson, *1 & 2 Timothy*, 82.

PART 2

SALVATION IN 1 TIMOTHY

"God our Saviour"

CHAPTER 2

Introduction to Salvation in 1 Timothy

Explicit salvation language abounds in 1 Timothy. God is 3x referred to as θεὸς σωτήρ (1:1; 2:3; 4:10) and is declared to desire πάντας ἀνθρώπους . . . σωθῆναι (2:4). The "faithful word" is recorded, ὅτι Χριστὸς Ἰησοῦς ἦλθεν εἰς τὸν κόσμον ἁμαρτωλοὺς σῶσαι (1:15); Timothy is urged, καὶ σεαυτὸν σώσεις καὶ τοὺς ἀκούοντάς σου (4:16); and there is the puzzling statement that [ἡ γυνὴ] σωθήσεται. . . διὰ τῆς τεκνογονίας (2:15). Paul's own experience of salvation is depicted in some autobiographical detail as an example for others who would come to believe in Jesus Christ εἰς ζωὴν αἰώνιον (1:16). This life is later set in the future perspective of the ἐπιφάνεια of Christ (6:14-15), and Timothy is exhorted to make it his goal (6:12). Those who are rich ἐν τῷ νῦν αἰῶνι are also urged to value the life of that coming age and invest for it (6:17-19). Soteriological elements such as the mediation and ransom provided in Christ appear (2:5-6).

For all that, it would be difficult to argue that salvation *per se* formed the main interest of this letter, taken on its own. The letter can be very largely understood as a response to a perceived threat.[1] The implied addressee is an apostolic delegate who is exercising a ministry in a troubled context. Some - apparently within the church - are teaching something which the author regards as dangerous. The exponents of false teaching and elements of its content and character are vilified, attention is given to the sort of people who, in future, can be entrusted with office in the church, Timothy is himself recalled to the ministry to which he had been commissioned and urged to exercise his authority in dealing with the situation and, by contrast with the false, the faithful teaching is commended and glimpses of its content given. The author seems to entertain the hope that at least some of those whose teaching is currently threatening the health of the church may yet turn from their useless preoccupations.

We shall be better attuned to the precise significance of the

---

1   See e.g. Fee, 7-10, who argues that, "everything in the letter has to do with 1:3" (7).

statements and inferences about salvation in this letter if we hear them mindful of the implied context of conflict within which they are made. The particular purposes of the salvation statements may well be discerned within that governing purpose of dealing with a situation in which people with some influence in the congregation were perpetrating novel and damaging teaching. There are various ways in which this could affect the way that salvation would be presented. We might expect particular stress on any elements of salvation that the author considered to be distorted or missed by the false teaching, but it is also possible to wrong-foot opponents by stealing their thunder, affirming certain elements that the opponents have perhaps claimed as uniquely theirs. We must ask whether access to salvation is being used as a weapon in the conflict, presented in such a way as to exclude the author's opponents or to indicate that salvation is only available by means of the teaching or teaching agents that he has approved. In order to arrive at an adequate understanding of salvation in this letter, as in others, it is therefore necessary to ask, not only what concept(s) of salvation it contains, but also how these function within the purpose of the letter as a whole. For an exploration of these questions, the occurrences of σῴζω and cognate terms throughout the letter provide a convenient starting point.

Chapter 3

1 Timothy 1:1

Παῦλος ἀπόστολος Χριστοῦ Ἰησοῦ κατ' ἐπιταγὴν θεοῦ σωτῆρος ἡμῶν καὶ Χριστοῦ Ἰησοῦ τῆς ἐλπίδος ἡμῶν

In the opening sentence of 1 Timothy we meet what may be "the most striking theological idiosyncrasy of the Pastorals," namely, "the frequent application of the epithet σωτήρ to God."[1] Apart from this letter (3x) and Titus (3x), it occurs in the NT only in Luke 1:47 and Jude 25. The author's use of this expression therefore merits investigation.

3.1 Context

In the context of the opening salutation, in which Paul's apostolic credentials are being established, the expression θεὸς σωτὴρ ἡμῶν offers the first hint of this letter's interest in salvation. It is specifically "God our saviour" from whom Paul derives his apostleship. This characterization therefore colours not only the concept of God but also the apostolic ministry which is performed at the command of such a God and, in turn, the instructions given by the apostle of this σωτήρ. There is in fact a chain of command terms: God gives the command (ἐπιταγή, v. 1) by which Paul becomes his apostle; Paul exhorts Timothy (παρακαλέω, v. 3), who instructs others (παραγγέλλω, vv. 3-4). Thus the instructions given with regard to the situation envisaged in the letter are traced back to an ultimate source not only in God, but in God as σωτήρ, thus relating the practical and ecclesiastical concerns in some way to the saviour's purpose.

3.2 God our Saviour

In discussing the use of the term σωτήρ in an early Christian text, a range of possible backgrounds must be taken into account. It was widely used in the Graeco-Roman world,[2] not only of deities but of

---

1 Donelson, *Pseudepigraphy*, 135.
2 See W. Foerster, G. Fohrer, "σῴζω, κτλ.," *TDNT* 7:965-1024, on σωτήρ, 1003-21; J. Schneider, C. Brown, "σωτήρ," *NIDNTT* 3:216-23; Dibelius-

anyone, or even any thing,³ that rescued or preserved. In the political realm, claims to saviour status became part of imperial propaganda, illustrated by the well-known inscription at Halicarnassus honouring the emperor Augustus as σωτῆρα τοῦ κοινοῦ τῶν ἀνθρώπων γένους.⁴ Philosophers could also be called σωτῆρες,⁵ therapists of the soul,⁶ uncovering the roots of inner disturbance and guiding into a life of progress in philosophy. Epicurus in particular was regarded by his followers as σωτήρ,⁷ in that he freed people from their captivity to fear of death, τύχη and the gods.⁸

When the term was applied to a deity various saving benefits could be in view. When Isis, for example, was invoked as σώτειρα or *sospitatrix*, it could be as benefactrix of the human race in general,⁹ the giver of wealth, the discoverer of all life, the one who taught humankind just patterns of life and the skills necessary for comfort and ensured good harvests, or the fulfiller of more individual and personal hopes. Citing Isis as an example, Dibelius-Conzelmann suggest that the term σwthvr was applied in the Mystery religions to deities who had the ability to impart eternal life.¹⁰ This, however,

---

Conzelmann, "'Savior' in the Pastoral Epistles", 100-03; and see comments on the Graeco-Roman background in Marshall, "Nature of Christian Salvation."

3   Fohrer, *TDNT* 7:1011 and n. 50.
4   Quoted by Foerster, *TDNT* 7:1012, from *The Collection of Ancient Greek Inscriptions in the British Museum* vol. 4 (ed. G. Hirschfeld), 6, 37.
5   Foerster, *TDNT* 7:1007.
6   See M. C. Nussbaum, *The Therapy of Desire: Theory and Practice in Hellenistic Ethics* (Martin Classical Lectures ns 2; Princeton: Princeton University Press, 1994).
7   Schneider, Brown, *NIDNTT* 3:217; cf. BAGD, 800, citing Philodemus, PHerc. 346:4, 19: ὑμνεῖν τὸν σωτῆρα τὸν ἡμέτερον.
8   Cicero considers that Epicurus "has delivered men from the gravest errors and imparted to them all there is to know about well-being and happiness" (*Fin.* 1.14).
9   See V. F. Vanderlip, *The Four Greek Hymns of Isodorus and the Cult of Isis* (ASP 12; Toronto: A. M. Hakkert, 1972).
10 Dibelius-Conzelmann, 101-02: ". . . in the mystery religions ["Savior"] designates the god who gives new life to the mystic by effecting his rebirth." They consider that it is in this sense that Isis and Sarapis are to be regarded as "bringers of salvation", and find in the title "Savior" the suggestion of "the power to endow with divine life". The only evidence they are able to cite, however, consists of passages from Philo which show that he could use the language of mystery and revelation (*Leg.* 3.27) and speak of a soul being redeemed into freedom (*Conf.* 96), but do not mention rebirth and certainly do not lend any support to these assertions of Dibelius-Conzelmann about Isis, Serapis and the mysteries.

underestimates the extent to which even in the Mysteries the present life could be the focus of saving benefits. In Apuleius's *Metamorphoses*, Lucius is admittedly said to be "reborn in a certain way" (*renatus quodam modo*, xi.16), but this does not mean that he has entered into eternal life. Rather, he now has the opportunity to live in obedience to Isis in the hope that, when his mortal life has reached its allotted span, she will combat the decision of the fates and prolong his life in Hell. Meanwhile, devotion to the goddess brings material and temporal rewards. On Graeco-Roman religion generally Ben Witherington III comments:

> Strange though it may seem to anyone not familiar with pagan antiquity, much of ancient pagan religion had little or nothing to do with attempts to obtain eternal life or be 'saved' in the Christian sense of the term. The "salvation" most ancients looked for was from disease, disaster, or death in this life. . . .[11]

In contrast to this wide range of applications in the general Graeco-Roman milieu, a much narrower field of use emerges in the Judaism represented by the LXX. Σωτήρ appears 36x, rendering, where there is a Hebrew original, substantival forms of the root ישע (to deliver save). Fohrer, however, insists that, "σωτήρ is not a [technical term] in the LXX,"[12] on the grounds that the same Hebrew forms are also represented in the LXX by a variety of other cognate terms (σῴζω, διασῴζω, σωτηρία and σωτήριον) and in addition by βοηθέω and ῥύομαι (we could add ἐξαιρέω, Josh 10:6). Fohrer's main concern, however, seems to be to refute the suggestion that σωτήρ had become a messianic title in Judaism.[13] In his eagerness to exclude this development, however, he fails to give sufficient weight to other distinctive features of the use of the term in the LXX. Chief among them is the fact that in the vast majority of its 36 occurrences the σωτήρ is God himself. Dibelius-Conzelmann cite the four exceptions as evidence that, in the LXX, "'savior' is used of men." [14] Even there, however, the real author of the saving in view is without

---

11 "Salvation and health in Christian antiquity: the soteriology of Luke-Acts in its first century setting", in I. H. Marshall and D. G. Peterson (eds.), *Witness to the Gospel: The Theology of Acts*, Grand Rapids: Eerdmand, 1998. Even Plutarch, writing to a bereaved friend, can offer no clarification of the post-mortem state (*Mor.* 2.102-21).

12 *TDNT* 7:1013.

13 *TDNT* 7:1012-13, including notes 56, 57. This also colours Dibelius-Conzelmann's discussion of 'savior' in the LXX (100-01).

14 Dibelius-Conzelmann, 100, citing the application of the term σωτήρ to judges in Judg 3:9, 15 and Neh 9:27 (given erroneously as 19:27) and to a "helper in battle" in Judg 12:3.

exception God himself, and the human "saviours" are deliverers whom God has gifted to his people. Even when Gideon is commanded to "save Israel" (Judg 6:14) it is in fact God who will save by the hand of Gideon (vv. 36-37), and the means of the saving is designed to demonstrate that it is due to (7:2). The only other instance of σωτήρ predicated of a human being is in Judg 12:3, where the point is to deny that the human subject was in fact a saviour.

The LXX translators of Judges and Nehemiah seem to have taken greater pains than the MT to insist that even where there are human agents, the effective saving must be ascribed to God. In MT Neh 9:27, for example, God gives the messiahs, who perform the saving: תִּתֵּן לָהֶם מוֹשִׁיעִים וְיוֹשִׁיעוּם מִיַּד צָרֵיהֶם ("you gave them saviours who saved them"). In the LXX, however, God both provides saviours and himself saves: ἔδωκας αὐτοῖς σωτῆρας καὶ ἔσωσας αὐτούς ("you gave them saviours and you saved them").[15] In the light of this we may concur with Fohrer's negative finding that, "LXX seems to avoid σωτήρ for the kings,"[16] but move beyond it to the positive conclusion that the LXX largely reserves σωτήρ for God. Quinn's statement that "Thirty-six times the LXX adopted *sōtēr* to describe the persons through whom Yahweh had rescued Israel as a corporate entity from physical peril and death"[17] is uncharacteristically inaccurate. Judg 3:9 and 15, cited by Quinn as exemplifying Septuagintal usage, are rather among the small handful of exceptions. Fourteen of the sixteen LXX books where the term appears (Deuteronomy, 1 Samuel, Judith, 1 Maccabees, 3 Maccabees, Psalms, Odes of Solomon, Wisdom, Sirach, Psalms of Solomon, Micah, Isaiah, Baruch) reserve it exclusively for God, and when human beings are described as σωτῆρες in Judges and Nehemiah they are clearly agents through whom God accomplishes his saving.

In the Greek LXX σωτήρ is reserved exclusively for God (Wis 17:7; Sir 51:1; Bar 4:22; 1 Macc 4:30; 3 Macc 6:29, 32; 7:16) and, with one exception (Bar 4:22), occurs in the context of address to God. This could suggest that the predication developed particularly in the language of worship. True, the title was not a technical term for the messiah, but it was an almost exclusively divine predicate. As σωτήρ God is the giver of benefactions to pure worshippers (Ps 23:5 [24:5]), the one who directs and teaches so that the true way can be followed

---

15 The same contrast applies to the deliverance through the judges (שֹׁפְטִים, κριταί) in Judg 2:16.
16 *TDNT* 7:1013.
17 Quinn, *Titus*, 308.

(Ps 24:5 [25:5]), and a protector from enemies (ὑπερασπιστὴς τῆς ζωῆς μου parallels σωτήρ μου in Ps 26:1 [27:1]), whether the attack takes the form of physical assault or slander and scheming (Ps 61:3 [62:2]). In a congregational setting there is the general exhortation to "rejoice in God our Saviour" on the grounds of his greatness as creator and special relationship with and care for his people, and in the context of national disaster a Psalm of Asaph turns to ὁ θεὸς ὁ σωτὴρ ἡμῶν with the plea, ῥῦσαι ἡμᾶς καὶ ἱλάσθητι ταῖς ἁμαρτίαις ἡμῶν (Ps 78:9 [79:9]).

Some stereotyping of the phrase, "God my/our saviour" may perhaps be detected.[18] In Psalms σωτήρ appears nine times, always of God, and, with only two exceptions (Pss 27:1 [LXX 26:1]; 62:3 [61:3]), with a possessive pronoun, so that God is not simply σωτήρ in the absolute way that he is κύριος, but "my/our/their saviour". The LXX translators seem to have adopted θεὸς σωτήρ μου/ἡμῶν as the equivalent of the Hebrew phrase, אֱלֹהֵי יִשְׁעִי (Pss 24:5 [LXX 23:5]; 25:5 [24:5]; 27:9 [26:9]; 62:6 [61:7]; 65:5 [64:6]; 79:9 [78:9]; 95:1 [94:1]), which is rarely represented by other expressions.[19] Outside the Psalms, the phrase occurs 4x in the MT, rendered θεὸς σωτήρ μου/σου in Isa 17:10, Mic 7:7 and Hab 3:18, and ὁ θεὸς τῆς σωτηρίας ἡμῶν in 1 Chr 16:35. God's identity and function as σωτήρ belong primarily within his relationship with his people. He is κύριος of all the earth (LXX Ps 96:5 [97:5]; cf. 23:1 [24:1]), but σωτήρ specifically of Israel. There is, however, just the hint of a wider scope. God is worshipped in LXX Ps 64:6 [65:5] as, ὁ θεὸς ὁ σωτὴρ ἡμῶν, ἡ ἐλπὶς πάντων τῶν περάτων τῆς γῆς καὶ ἐν θαλάσσῃ μακράν. This stops short of describing God as σωτήρ of all: he is still σωτὴρ ἡμῶν, and the psalm enumerates the particular blessings enjoyed by the community centred on the temple in Zion as well as the general benefits of a fruitful earth which all may enjoy. Nonetheless, there is a suggestion here of some continuity between what God is and does for Israel and what he can be for all.[20]

Outside the LXX, Josephus seems to avoids using σωτήρ of God, but applies it extensively to human deliverers such as his hero

---

18 See also Bruce, "Our God and Saviour."
19 Only in LXX Pss 84:5 [85:5] (θεὸς τῶν σωτηρίων ἡμῶν)and 61:8 [62:7] (θεὸς τὸ σωτήριόν μου), which could be a stylistic variation on the standard formulation in v. 7 [v. 6].
20 In Wis 16:7 God is ὁ πάντων σωτήρ (cf. v. 12 and 11:23) but in the context the interest is not in the actual saving of all people but in the saving of Israel, demonstrating God's reality in contrast to the futile idols of Israel's oppressors (see v. 8).

Vespasian (*B.J.* 3.459) or even himself (*Vita* 244).²¹ By contrast, in Philo, while it may be used of Roman emperors (*Flacc.* 74.126; *Legat.* 22), σωτήρ is most frequently God. The context may be of individual deliverance (e.g *Abr.* 176; *Ios.* 195), but principally God is εὐεργέτης καὶ σωτὴρ θεός of the whole human race (*Opif.* 169; cf. σωτὴρ καὶ φιλάνθρωπος, *Abr.* 137). It is however the privilege of the φιλόθεος ψυχή (*Leg.* 2.55-56; cf. ἡ ποθοῦσα τὰ καλὰ ψυχή, *Leg.* 3.27) to draw near and come to a fuller knowledge of him.

Against this background of both Jewish and Graeco-Roman usage, the considerable restraint in the use of σωτήρ in early Christianity is notable.²² As a predicate of God it is conspicuously absent from the greater part of the NT, appearing outside the PE (1 Tim 1:1; 2:3; 4:10, Titus 1:3; 2:10; 3:4) only in Luke 1:47, in the Song of Mary which draws on the language of the LXX,²³ and in the formulaic setting of the doxology in Jude 25. It is used more frequently with reference to Christ, but again in a limited range of writings, namely, Luke-Acts (3x), The Johannine corpus (2x), 2 Peter (5x), Phil (1x), Eph (1x) and the PE (2 Tim 1x; Titus 3x). Where the term is used of Jesus in Luke-Acts it is always in addresses to Jews, designating him as the agent of God's deliverance sent in fulfilment of his promise to Israel (Luke 2:11; Acts 5:31; 13:23). The Graeco-Roman background probably lies behind the choice of the term in Phil 3:20 to present Jesus, in contrast to the Roman emperor, as the protector and deliverer awaited by the citizens of Heaven.²⁴ In Eph 5:23, however, σωτήρ carries specific theological content in relation to Christ's self-giving with its sanctifying effect.

---

21   Foerster, *TDNT* 7:1014.
22   Foerster, *TDNT* 7:1020-21, suggests: "Except in the Past. and 2 Pt. one can only say that there is a restraint in the use of σωτήρ which is to be explained by the fact that in the Jewish sphere σωτήρ could easily be linked with the expectation of a liberator from national bondage, while in the pagan world it suggested the idea of an earthly benefactor, especially in the figure of the emperor. Hence the word might kindle hopes and ideas which the Gospel could not promise to fulfil."
23   I. H. Marshall, *The Gospel of Luke: A Commentary on the Greek Text* (NIGTC; Grand Rapids: Eerdmans, 1978), 82, offers Hab 1:18; Ps 34:9 [35:9]; and 1 Sam 2:1 as the nearest parallels to Luke 1:47.
24   See R. P. Martin, *Philippians* (TNTC; London: Tyndale, 1959), 161-62: "The use of the term [σωτήρ] here may be justified on the ground that Paul has employed an imagery in which the contrast with the Roman emperor was inevitable. Therefore, he opposes the true Emperor, *the Lord Jesus Christ*, against the head of imperial Rome. . . . Paul uses the word here in a descriptive sense."

In the Johannine corpus Jesus is twice declared ὁ σωτὴρ τοῦ κόσμου (John 4:42; 1 John 4:14). Again, this may be explicable in Hellenistic terms as a counter claim to those of other saviour figures,[25] but in the context of the discussion with the Samaritan woman in John ch. 4 it is also a statement about the scope of the salvation offered by this Jewish (vv. 9, 22) messiah (vv. 25, 29) that would stand in overt opposition to exclusivism. Apart from 2 Timothy and Titus, it is only in 2 Peter that σωτήρ seems to have the character of "a common title for Christ,"[26] usually paired with κύριος (1:11; 2:20; 3:2, 18) and once with θεός (1:1). Kelly's assessment is unnecessarily pessimistic:

> In the 2 Peter passages [the title Saviour] is formalized, appearing always in solemn-sounding, stereotyped phrases, so that it is useless to attempt to pinpoint its exact theological content.[27]

The context is often specifically soteriological, and the thought of final salvation is not far away. It is in this connection that Christ is σωτήρ.

Surveying the uses of σωτήρ in the Apostolic Fathers, Foerster observes that, as with the NT usage, the most striking feature is its rarity. He can find only eight examples of σωτήρ applied to Christ, four of them in Ignatius, and concludes that, "while σωτήρ is a title for Jesus it usually has a specific content, and is not particularly common. At any rate, ὁ σωτήρ is never used as a current unequivocal designation in the way that ὁ κύριος is."[28] Kelly's depiction of a "growing, and increasingly confident, readiness to hail Christ as Saviour" that "rapidly established itself and became

---

25 As suggested with regard to the Gospel usage by R. E. Brown, *The Gospel According to John* (2 vols.; Brit. ed.; AB 29-29A; London: Geoffrey Chapman, 1971), 1:175. His finding that, "The term 'Saviour' was a common post-resurrectional title for Jesus, particularly in the Lucan and Pauline works" is, however, challenged by our survey of NT usage.
26 Foerster, *TDNT* 7:1018.
27 J. N. D. Kelly, *The Epistles of Peter and Jude* (BNTC; London: A&C Black, 1969), 298. Nor is Foerster completely fair in his comment that, "The three titles of Jesus, θεός, κύριος, and σωτήρ alternate for no obvious reason" (*TDNT* 7:1018). Jesus is never "God and Lord" in the way that he is "Lord and Saviour" (4x) and "God and Saviour" (1x); Foerster cites 1:2, ἐν ἐπιγνώσει τοῦ θεοῦ καὶ Ἰησοῦ τοῦ κυρίου ἡμῶν as an example of the first combination, but here God and Jesus-our-Lord are distinguished; θεός is not predicated of Jesus.
28 *TDNT* 7:1018-19.

normal" must therefore be questioned.²⁹ It cannot be said that early Christianity freely and generally adopted σωτήρ as a standard designation for either God or Christ; its use is specific to certain texts and the attempt to chart a gradual increase over time from the later NT writings onwards founders on the paucity of use in the Apostolic Fathers. It is therefore methodologically sound to admit the possibility that those texts which did utilize the term might have had particular reasons for doing so, and that its content may be specific to each context rather than supplied by some universal Christian usage.³⁰ 1 Timothy is one such text, and its ascription of the predicate σωτήρ to God (1:1; 2:3; 4:10) is an unusual feature that merits investigation.

3.3 Christ Jesus our Hope

Θεὸς σωτὴρ ἡμῶν is paired in 1:1 with Χριστὸς Ἰησοῦς ἡ ἐλπὶς ἡμῶν. This linking may help to elucidate the θεὸς σωτήρ concept here. What is the content of this "hope," and what is meant by its identification with Christ? Again, there are a number of possible backgrounds. In LXX Psalms, ἐλπίς and ἐλπίζω (much more than πιστεύω or πείθω) represent the attitude of those who receive salvation from God; indeed God is characteristically ὁ σῴζων τοὺς ἐλπίζοντας ἐπὶ σέ (LXX Ps 16:7 [17:7]; cf. 61:8 [62:7]; 7:2 [7:1]; 12:6 [13:5]; 17:3 [18:2]; 21:9 [22:8]). As the one in whom hope is placed, the Lord can be referred to as "my/his etc. hope," usually in a context in which salvation is being sought (e.g. Pss 13:6-7 [14:6-7]; 70:4-5 [71:4-5]). In LXX Psalms ἐλπίς as a divine predicate usually represents the Hebrew מַחְסֶה, "refuge" (13:6 [14:6]; 90:9 [91:9]; 141:6 [142:6]), translated elsewhere in LXX Psalms by such terms as βοηθός (61:9 [62:9]) or καταφυγή (103:18 [104:18]). This serves to indicate the extent to which, for the LXX translators, "hope" directed towards the Lord meant trust in him for saving help and protection.³¹

The saving in view here is mainly from troubles in the present life. In certain of the later Septuagintal writings, however, the horizons of ἐλπίς stretch beyond the present life to God's eschatological

---

29 J. N. D. Kelly, *The Pastoral Epistles: I & II Timothy and Titus* (BNTC; London: A&C Black, 1963), 163. Perhaps his perception is disproportionately shaped by his studies of the PE and 2 Peter, which in this respect are most untypical of the NT and early Christian literature.
30 Dibelius-Conzelmann, 100-03, rightly judge that it "seems impossible to find only one derivation for the Christian title 'savior'" (103).
31 Cf. the same overlap of concepts in *Pss. Sol.* 15:1.

future.³² In 2 Maccabees, for example, is found both the hope that God will intervene to restore the nation (2:18) and the personal hope of resurrection for the martyrs. It is this hope that the brothers declare in the face of torture and death:

> αἱρετὸν μεταλλάσσοντας ὑπ' ἀνθρώπων τὰς ὑπὸ τοῦ θεοῦ προσδοκᾶν ἐλπίδας πάλιν ἀναστήσεσθαι ὑπ' αὐτοῦ, σοὶ μὲν γὰρ ἀνάστασις εἰς ζωὴν οὐκ ἔσται.
>
> One cannot but choose to die at the hands of mortals and to cherish the hope God gives of being raised again by him. But for you there will be no resurrection to life!
>
> (2 Macc 7:14; cf. 7:11)

The martyr chooses death, παντελῶς ἐπὶ τῷ κυρίῳ πεποιθώς ("putting his whole trust in the Lord," 7:40), and the godly mother is able to endure her sons' death in hope of a post-mortem restoration of life (7:20, 23). By contrast, the tyrant has only ἄδηλοι ἐλπίδες ("vain hopes") and the prospect of punishment after death (7:34-37).

This illustrates the "synthesis of the eschatologies of the nation and the individual"³³ in intertestamental Judaism, whereby the hope of a glorious future for the righteous nation in God's eschatological kingdom was fused with the conviction that righteous and worthy individuals would participate in this blessedness, whether by resurrection of the body (as in 2 Macc 7:11, 14; cf. Dan 12:2, 13), or by receiving immortal souls from God (4 Macc 18:23) and entering into eternal blessedness (4 Macc 17:18). In Wisdom, the righteous possess the "hope of immortality" (ἡ ἐλπὶς αὐτῶν ἀθανασίας πλήρης, 3:4), whereas the hope of the ungodly is empty (κενὴ ἡ ἐλπὶς αὐτῶν, 3:18; cf. 5:14), and they must dread the reckoning of their sins (4:20). The content of ἐλπίς, therefore, is the hope of being reckoned worthy at the time of judgment and receiving eternal life.

These elements reappear in the NT. What is distinctive there is the claim that this hope, founded on God's promise to Israel, is fulfilled for believers in Christ, whether Jew or Gentile. To achieve this, the realization of the hope had to be related to Christ and its scope had to be extended beyond the Jewish nation. The Lukan Paul makes these moves in his four defence speeches in Acts 23-28. In each he insists that the belief system of the Christian movement may be

---

32 Temporal references continue, however, as in the Theodotionic version of Susanna 60, where ὁ θεός ὁ σῴζων τοὺς ἐλπίζοντας ἐπ' αὐτόν rescues from unjust accusation and death).
33 D. S. Russell, *Between the Testaments*, London: SCM, 1960, 146.

identified with a particular ἐλπίς of Judaism,[34] to the extent that he can claim to be on trial for "my hope in the promise made by God to our ancestors" (Acts 26:6). This hope has a specific content, namely, the future resurrection of both righteous and unrighteous (23:6; 24:15, 21; 26:8), implying a coming judgment (cf. 24:25); it is "the hope of Israel" (28:20), promised to the fathers (26:6), testifed to by the Law and the Prophets (24:14-15) and cherished by the Jewish nation (26:7). At the same time, his message can be summarized as περὶ τῆς εἰς Χριστὸν Ἰησοῦν πίστεως (24:24), and περὶ τοῦ κυρίου Ἰησοῦ Χριστοῦ (28:31; cf. v. 23). The hope of resurrection is therefore linked to the message about Christ, who as the first to rise from the dead brings light to others both Jew and Gentile (26:23; cf. vv. 17-18, 20).[35]

Paul the letter-writer also "understands Christian hope as a fulfilment of God's promises to Israel."[36] The content of Christian hope is defined as ἐλπὶς τῆς δόξης τοῦ θεοῦ (Rom 5:2), which includes the expectation of a future inheritance as the children of God, involving the "redemption of our bodies" (8:16-25). In Gal 5:5 it is the ἐλπὶς δικαιοσύνης, the hope of attaining righteousness as the means of entry into that future (5:2-6). In Colossians, "the hope laid up for you in heaven" (1:5) is the promise of the gospel (1:5-6, 23), summed up as Χριστὸς ἐν ὑμῖν, ἡ ἐλπὶς τῆς δόξης (1:27). Apart from 1 Tim 1:1, this is the nearest the NT comes to predicating ἐλπίς directly of Christ.[37]

In varying degrees and in different ways the NT presents Christian hope against the background of the hope of those sections of Judaism that envisaged a future Kingdom of God implying a restored nation and resurrection to eternal life for the righteous who will share in it. The point at issue in these writings is not so much the content of the hope but how it is realized and received. As

---

34 Five of the eight occurrences of ἐλπίς in Acts are in these speeches, always with this specific content. The remaining occurrence is in Peter's Pentecost sermon in a citation of LXX Ps 15:9 [16:9] which is interpreted as a reference to the resurrection of the messiah (2:31-32).

35 Cf. Paul's synagogue address in Acts 13:16-41, presenting the resurrection of Jesus as the fulfilment of God's promise to Israel's ancestors, and belief in Jesus as the means to forgiveness of sins, leading to eternal life (v. 46). With Isa 49:6 as warrant, this salvation is offered to the Gentiles (cf. Acts 28:28).

36 J. M. Everts, "Hope," *DPL*, 415-17.

37 Even here, however, it seems to be less Christ himself than the fact of his being ἐν ὑμῖν that constitutes ἡ ἐλπὶς τῆς δόξης. R. P. Martin takes it to mean that the Messiah's presence among the Gentiles confirms their salvation (*Colossians and Philemon* (rev. ed.; NCB; London: Marshall, Morgan & Scott, 1978), 72).

1 Thessalonians illustrates, however, the same essential content is maintained even where there is little or no overt engagement with Judaism. The readers are commended for their ὑπομονὴ τῆς ἐλπίδος τοῦ κυρίου ἡμῶν Ἰησοῦ Χριστοῦ (1:3), looking for rescue from coming wrath (1:10) and participation in God's kingdom and glory (2:12). Again Christ's resurrection is the ground of confidence both that Christ will return (1:10) and that there is a future beyond physical death for believing individuals (1:14). Because of this, those Gentile readers (1:9; 2:14) are no longer among οἱ μὴ ἔχοντες ἐλπίδα (4:13; cf. Eph 2:12).

Beyond the NT, Ignatius makes use of the formula Χριστὸς Ἰησοῦς ἡ ἐλπὶς ἡμῶν (*Trall.* inscr.; 2; *Magn.* 11) or Χριστὸς Ἰησοῦς ἡ κοινὴ ἐλπὶς ἡμῶν (*Eph.* 21; cf. ὑπὲρ τοῦ κοινοῦ ὀνόματος καὶ ἐλπίδος, 1; *Phld.* 11; and cf. τὸ εὐαγγέλιον τῆς κοινῆς ἐλπίδος, 5).[38] In *To the Magnesians* Ignatius contrasts Judaism with a "new hope" (8-9) and prays that none may turn aside to the κενοδοξίαι of Judaism from Jesus Christ our hope (10-11). In *To the Philadelphians* the reference to the "Gospel of the common hope" (5) is immediately followed by the command not to listen to anyone who expounds Judaism (6); and it is after arguing that the old (patriarchs and prophets) and the new (apostles and church) are to be held together within the unity of God, while recognizing the primacy of Christ the High Priest over other priests and of the Gospel of the coming of the saviour over the message of the prophets that pointed to him (9), that Ignatius salutes his readers "in Christ Jesus, our common hope" (11). The cause of concern in *To the Trallians* is a form of Docetism, in response to which the Christian hope of future life is grounded firmly in the death and resurrection of Jesus; he is their hope ἐν τῇ εἰς αὐτὸν ἀναστάσει (inscr.) and in the sense that it is by believing in his death that Christians escape death (2). *To the Ephesians* is an appeal for unity, particularly for its expression in meeting in common assembly, to which the final greeting in "God the Father and Christ our common hope" (21) is a fitting conclusion; not only is the unity of the Father with Christ a model for the community (as argued in 5), but the eternal life that they aspire to is provided through the "one bread, which is the medicine of immortality", by which they have eternal life in Jesus Christ (20). In the letters of Ignatius, then, the "hope" is of eternal life and to describe Christ as "our hope" is to insist that it is through him that Christians receive it. The motif of "Christ our hope" can be employed variously to

---

[38] For these and other references see W. Lock, *A Critical and Exegetical Commentary on the Pastoral Epistles* (ICC; Edinburgh: T&T Clark, 1924), 6; Dibelius-Conzelmann, 13 n. 2.

counter teaching that Judaistic observance is the means of attaining that future life, to draw attention to the actual death and resurrection of Jesus as the basis for the believers' post-mortem hope, or to exhort to unity in one goal and the one means to attaining it.

In the Christian texts included in this survey the essential benefit hoped for, namely deliverance from death into eternal life with God, remains constant. This was also the hope expressed in the examples of intertestamental Jewish writing that we looked at, though not, on the whole, of the Psalms, whose hope was directed more to deliverance in the present life.

There is one instance in 1 Tim where the verb ἐλπίζω could be read as indicating trust in God for the needs of the present, where the widow, without other support, has put her trust in God (5:5).[39] Elsewhere in the letter, however, there is ample evidence that the author looked towards a future, eternal life which was to be valued above the present life (1:16; 4:8; 6:12,17-19). It is therefore reasonable to refer the Χριστὸς Ἰησοῦς ἡ ἐλπὶς ἡμῶν in 1:1 to that general Christian hope, with Christ identified as the basis for it and means of attaining it. The bringing together of "Christ our hope" with "God our Saviour" accordingly links the idea of God's saving with that hope. This suggests both that salvation for this author includes eternal life, and also that he conceived of God's saving activity as involving Christ. Paul's apostolic ministry and message (1:11) is in turn associated with this complex of ideas, so that it too takes its place within the emerging soteriological schema. Paul is the authorized bearer of the saving God's message of salvation.[40]

Beyond the general background of Jewish and early Christian hope, it may be possible to detect a specific septuagintal allusion in the pairing of ἐλπίς and σωτήρ in 1 Tim 1:1. Ideas of hope and saving are often linked, but although Spicq refers to "Le parallélisme σωτήρ - ἐλπίς, fréquent dans l'Ancien Testament,"[41] the coincidence of the substantives σωτήρ and ἐλπίς is in fact very rare.[42] They

---

39 See e.g. A. T. Hanson, *The Pastoral Epistles* (NCB; Grand Rapids: Eerdmans, 1982), 96; Kelly, 114; though it is possible to take even this as having future salvation in view: e.g. Roloff, 290: "Diese Hoffnung ist mehr als bloßes Gottvertrauen. Sie ist das Sich-Einlassen auf das Handeln des »lebendigen Gottes« (vgl. 4,10), das geschichtsmächtig ist und heilvolle Zukunft eröffnet."

40 See e.g. Hasler, 11.

41 Spicq, 316.

42 The nearest equivalents are Jer 14:8, where the Lord is both ὑπομονὴ Ισραηλ and σῴζεις ἐν καιρῷ κακῶν, and Sir 34, where the Lord is ὁ σῴζων (v. 13) and ἡ ἐλπίς (v. 14); cf. also *Pss. Sol.* 5:11; 15:1.

appear in combination as divine predicates only in Ps 64:6 [65:6], where God is addressed: ἐπάκουσον ἡμῶν ὁ θεὸς ὁ σωτὴρ ἡμῶν ἡ ἐλπὶς πάντων τῶν περάτων τῆς γῆς καὶ ἐν θαλάσσῃ μακράν. Hanson may well be correct in detecting an echo of this line in our author's expression.[43] If so, it may be significant that this combination of ideas in Ps 64:6 is the nearest that LXX Psalms comes to an explicit extension of God's role as σωτήρ beyond Israel.[44] God's function as σωτήρ and the attitude of ἐλπίς/ἐλπίζω both belong in Psalms primarily within the particular relationship of God with his people, but insofar as this Psalm at least conceives of the whole earth adopting that attitude, it could have been congenial both to outward looking Hellenistic Judaism and to missionary minded early Christianity, and of service to each in countering narrower soteriological outlooks. In any event, 1 Tim 1:1 both lays claim to God's saving and attaches the "hope" with which that saving is associated to Christ.

3.4 Summary

In this opening sentence of 1 Timothy, an interest in salvation is signalled by the ascription of the title σωτήρ to God. The pairing of the expressions θεὸς σωτὴρ ἡμῶν and Χριστὸς Ἰησοῦς ἡ ἐλπὶς ἡμῶν, possibly echoing the combination of the elements σωτήρ and ἐλπίς in LXX Ps 64:6, serves to associate the idea of God's saving with the concept of hope. It is quite plausible in an early Christian text that, as in other NT writings, this includes the specific hope of eternal life articulated in the later LXX and interpreted christologically. This suggests a willingness to appropriate for the Christian community Jewish concepts of God and salvation. Paul's apostleship, and by extension the roles of Timothy and the local teachers, are of soteriological significance in that they derive their validity and character from the intention of the saviour God.

---

43 Hanson, *Epistles*, 55.
44 See above, p. 25.

Chapter 4

1 Timothy 1:12-17

Χάριν ἔχω τῷ ἐνδυναμώσαντί με Χριστῷ Ἰησοῦ τῷ κυρίῳ ἡμῶν, ὅτι πιστόν με ἡγήσατο θέμενος εἰς διακονίαν τὸ πρότερον ὄντα βλάσφημον καὶ διώκτην καὶ ὑβριστήν, ἀλλὰ ἠλεήθην, ὅτι ἀγνοῶν ἐποίησα ἐν ἀπιστίᾳ· ὑπερεπλεόνασεν δὲ ἡ χάρις τοῦ κυρίου ἡμῶν μετὰ πίστεως καὶ ἀγάπης τῆς ἐν Χριστῷ Ἰησοῦ. πιστὸς ὁ λόγος καὶ πάσης ἀποδοχῆς ἄξιος, ὅτι Χριστὸς Ἰησοῦς ἦλθεν εἰς τὸν κόσμον ἁμαρτωλοὺς σῶσαι, ὧν πρῶτός εἰμι ἐγώ. ἀλλὰ διὰ τοῦτο ἠλεήθην, ἵνα ἐν ἐμοὶ πρώτῳ ἐνδείξηται Χριστὸς Ἰησοῦς τὴν ἅπασαν μακροθυμίαν πρὸς ὑποτύπωσιν τῶν μελλόντων πιστεύειν ἐπ' αὐτῷ εἰς ζωὴν αἰώνιον. Τῷ δὲ βασιλεῖ τῶν αἰώνων, ἀφθάρτῳ ἀοράτῳ μόνῳ θεῷ, τιμὴ καὶ δόξα εἰς τοὺς αἰῶνας τῶν αἰώνων, ἀμήν.

The statement Χριστὸς Ἰησοῦς ἦλθεν εἰς τὸν κόσμον ἁμαρτωλοὺς σῶσαι (v. 15) is introduced with the phrase πιστὸς ὁ λόγος καὶ πάσης ἀποδοχῆς ἄξιος. There are five such formulae in the PE (see 3:1; 4:9; 2 Tim 2:11; Titus 3:8; cf. Titus 1:9), generally thought to indicate traditional liturgical or didactic material.[1] While the extent and *Traditionsgeschichte* of each saying so identified is not always clear, the value for the present study lies in that the formula "has a definite purpose in commending teaching that the author wishes to emphasize."[2] In at least the majority of cases that teaching has to do with salvation.[3]

4.1 Context

The section 1:12-17 continues the theme of Paul's appointment to Christian service signalled in the opening address (1:1) and reappearing with the entrusting of the gospel to Paul in vv. 10-11. After a thanksgiving to Christ Jesus for Paul's appointment to service despite his sinfulness (vv. 12-14), the salvation saying (v. 15)

---

1 Cf. Mounce, 48-49; Quinn, *Titus*, 273; Dibelius-Conzelman, 28-29; Campbell, "Faithful Sayings," 73-86.
2 Marshall, 329; see his Excursus 9: "The trustworthy sayings," 326-30.
3 See Young, *Theology*, 56-59 (but note Marshall's caution, 328).

universalizes the thought of saving sinners, proposing Paul as an example (vv. 15b-16), before a doxology concludes the unit (v. 17). The story of Paul, therefore, provides both the occasion for the salvation statement and the material for its development.

4.2 What Does It Mean To Be Saved?

4.2.1 σῶσαι

This is the first occurrence of the verb σῴζω in 1 Timothy. Here it refers to the purpose of Christ's coming into the world (1:15); elsewhere it designates that which God desires for all people (2:4); what will happen to [the] woman through childbearing (2:15); and what Timothy should aspire to do for himself and his hearers (4:16). The range of use of σῴζω in both Hellenistic Greek and in the NT has been well surveyed elsewhere.[4] Hellenistic Greek uses it of saving from, e.g., dangers of war, sea travel, judicial condemnation or illness.[5] In the Synoptic Gospels it can also represent this-worldly deliverance such as physical healing (Matt 9:21, 22 pars. Mark 5:28, 34 and Luke 8:48; Mark 6:56), deliverance from shipwreck or drowning (Matt 8:25; 14:30) and escape from death (Matt 27:40, 42 pars. Mark 15:30, 31 and Luke 23:35). In other instances, however, end-time salvation is in view, as in the dominical saying, ὁ δὲ ὑπομείνας εἰς τέλος οὗτος σωθήσεται (Matt 10:22; 24:13 par. Mark 13:13), and when used in relation to the Kingdom of God and eternal life (Matt 19:25 pars. Mark 10:26 and Luke 18:26).[6] Discipleship may involve choosing eschatological over temporal saving (Matt 16:25 pars. Mark 8:35 and Luke 9:24). Being saved is linked with having sins forgiven (Luke 7:48-50; cf. Matt 1:21), and is associated with faith (e.g. Matt 9:22 pars. Mark 5:34 and Luke 8:48; Luke 7:50; 8:11-12; 8:50; 18:42). In John's Gospel, Jesus came to save the κόσμος (3:17; 12:47), and individuals are "saved" by believing Jesus (5:34). Acts knows the general meaning of σῴζω (Acts 4:9; 27:20, 31), but more often it refers to final salvation (2:21, 40, 47; 11:14; 15:1, 11; 16:30, 31), promised to those who call on the name of the Lord (2:21) and believe in Jesus (16:31).

In the NT epistles, however, σῴζω is reserved almost entirely for ultimate salvation,[7] and in the *Hauptbriefe*, "limited quite

---

4 E.g., Foerster, Fohrer, *TDNT* 7:965-1003; C. Brown, J. Schneider, "σῴζω," *NIDNTT* 3:205-16; Quinn, *Titus*, 304-07.
5 Foerster, *TDNT* 7:966-67.
6 See also the equating of being saved with participation in the messianic banquet (Luke 13:23, 29).
7 Leaving aside 1 Timothy for the moment, the only possible exceptions are

intentionally to the relation between man and God."[8] Foerster claims to find a wider range of usage in the Apostolic Fathers,[9] but some of his supposedly non-theological examples could equally carry fuller soteriological significance. In place of LCL's "May you gain salvation" for the final greeting, σώζεσθε, in *Barn.* 21.9,[10] he has simply, "Fare you well." The "saving" of *1 Clem.* 2.4 (εἰς τὸ σώζεσθαι μετ᾽ ἐλέους καὶ συνειδήσεως τὸν ἀριθμὸν τῶν ἐκλεκτῶν αὐτοῦ) he reads as merely "keeping up the number," [11] apparently overlooking the reference in 58.2 to one enrolled and chosen εἰς τὸν ἀριθμὸν τῶν σωζομένων διὰ Ἰησοῦ Χριστοῦ, where ultimate salvation is surely intended. Perhaps, then, the Apostolic Fathers provide more support than Foerster allows for the prevalence of soteriological uses of σώζω in early Christian writings.

Here in 1 Tim 1:15 the context is clearly theological. This saving is directed towards sinners and it is the purpose for which Christ came into the world. Through the example of Paul, who as πρῶτος is the first in a series of τῶν μελλόντων πιστεύειν ἐπ᾽ αὐτῷ (v. 16),[12] it is associated with divine mercy, grace, and patience and received through believing in Christ (vv. 13, 16). Its outcome, ζωὴ αἰώνιος, must now be explored.

4.2.2 ζωὴ αἰώνιος

Only once in the LXX does ζωὴ αἰώνιος represent a Hebrew original, rendering חַיֵּי עוֹלָם, to which the righteous will rise at the end time in Dan 12:2. In the Greek Maccabean literature, however, 2 Macc 7:9 anticipates rising to "an everlasting renewal of life" (αἰώνιον ἀναβίωσιν ζωῆς), and in 4 Macc 15:2-3 the pious mother refuses to seek temporal preservation for her sons (σωτηρία πρόσκαιρος), preferring εὐσέβεια that "saves for eternal life" (σώζουσαν εἰς αἰωνίαν). In the Synoptic Gospels, to inherit ζωὴ αἰώνιος (Matt 19:16 pars. Mark 10:17 and Luke 18:18; cf. Luke 10:25) is equivalent to entering into life (Matt 19:17; cf. Luke 10:28) or the kingdom of heaven/God (Matt 19:23, 24 pars. Mark 10:23, 24, 25 and Luke 18:24, 25; cf. Matt 25:34, 46) and to being "saved" (Matt 19:25 pars. Mark 10:26 and Luke 18:26). This life is future, ἐν τῷ αἰῶνι τῷ ἐρχομένῳ (Mark 10:30 par. Luke 18:30) with connotations of reward,

---

Jude v. 5 and James 5:15, but even these have soteriological overtones.
8   *TDNT* 7:992.
9   *TDNT* 7:998-99.
10 *The Apostolic Fathers* 1.409 (translated by Kirsopp Lake).
11 *TDNT* 7:998 and n. 153.
12 Spicq, 345.

being bestowed at the παλινγενεσία and the final judgment (Matt 19:28-29).¹³ It is promised to those who follow Jesus, suffering temporal loss for his sake (Matt 19:29 pars. Mark 10:30 and Luke 18:30).

John's Gospel and 1 John, where the expression is ubiquitous, diverge from this usage in two significant respects. First, ζωὴ αἰώνιος "does not . . . just begin in the future, it is already the possession of those who have entered upon fellowship with Christ."¹⁴ The believer has (ἔχει, present tense) ζωὴν αἰώνιον (John 3:36; 5:24; 6:47; cf. 1 John 3:15; 5:13). In John people already encounter the eschatological realities of judgment and life in Jesus. To know God in Christ is eternal life (John 17:3). There is still, however, a future dimension: ζωὴ αἰώνιος contrasts with existence ἐν τῷ κόσμῳ τούτῳ (12:25; cf. 6:27), physical death will not extinguish it (11:25-26; cf. 14:2-3), and a resurrection is awaited on the last day (6:40, 54). The difference is not so much that John and the Synoptics locate ζωὴ αἰώνιος at different points on the same time-line as that they set the concept within different frameworks: that of the Synoptics is chronological, John's, ontological. A further distinctive of the Johannine literature is that where the Synoptics associate ζωὴ αἰώνιος with following Christ (Matt 19:21, 27 pars. Mark 10:21, 28 and Luke 18:22, 28), in John it is the outcome of believing in Christ (3:15, 16, 36; 5:24; 6:40, 47; 1 John 5:13).¹⁵

In Romans Paul recites as generally accepted the view that God will give ζωὴ αἰώνιος to those who seek immortality and do good (2:6-7). Since none qualify, however, it must be a gift of God's grace (6:23), bestowed through and in Christ (5:21; 6:23). In Gal 6:8, the only other reference in the *Hauptbriefe*, it is the outcome of life in the Spirit, the antithesis of φθορά, the end of life in the flesh.

The link in 1 Tim 1:16 between ζωὴ αἰώνιος and believing in Christ fits the Johannine picture, as does Christ's coming εἰς τὸν κόσμον (v. 15). Despite the shared language, however, it cannot be assumed that 1 Timothy's concept of eternal life is the same as John's.¹⁶ Indications of its content must be sought in the context and the letter as a whole. The idea of ζωὴ αἰώνιος seems to be picked up in the ensuing doxology: τῷ δὲ βασιλεῖ τῶν αἰώνιων, ἀφθάρτῳ ἀοράτῳ μόνῳ θεῷ, τιμὴ καὶ δόξα εἰς τοὺς αἰῶνας τῶν αἰώνων,

---

13 Cf. Jude v. 21.
14 J. Guhrt, "αἰών," *NIDNTT* 3:826-33, 832.
15 The link with believing is also explicit in Acts (13:46, 48).
16 As is the case in G. W. Knight III, *The Pastoral Epistles: A Commentary on the Greek Text* (NIGTC; Grand Rapids: Eerdmans, 1992), 101.

ἀμήν (v. 17).[17] The phrase εἰς τοὺς αἰῶνας τῶν αἰώνων suggests an infinite future,[18] as does the description of God as ἀφθάρτος. In 4 Maccabees ἀφθαρσία awaits the martyrs (9:22; 17:12) and in Paul, together with ἀθανασία, it represents the post-resurrection condition of believers (1 Cor 15:42, 50, 53, 54). The doxology, then, with its notion of God as imperishable and everlasting, ruling into the infinite future, serves to connect the believers' ζωὴ αἰώνιος with God's eternal nature.

Later in the letter Timothy is urged, ἀγωνίζου τὸν καλὸν ἀγῶνα τῆς πίστεως, ἐπιλαβοῦ τῆς αἰωνίου ζωῆς (6:12). Possibly the aorist imperative ἐπιλαβοῦ contrasts with the present imperative ἀγωνίζου representing a continuing struggle now to take hold of life in a single future action at Christ's ἐπιφάνεια (vv. 14-15).[19] In a parallel injunction (vv. 17-19), the rich are to live now in such a way as to lay a good foundation for the coming age, ἵνα ἐπιλάβωνται (aorist subjunctive) τῆς ὄντως ζωῆς (v. 19). Against this future life, present wealth is impermanent and uncertain (v. 17; cf. v. 7). Again, the mention of eternal life is followed by a doxology highlighting God's immortality (ὁ μόνος ἔχων ἀθανασίαν, vv. 15-16). The link between eternal life and faith also reappears in ὁ καλὸς ἀγών τῆς πίστεως, and ἡ κάλη ὁμολογία (v. 12).[20]

In 4:6-10 the expression ζωὴ αἰώνιος is lacking, but again the focus is ζωὴ ... ἡ μέλλουσα as the appropriate orientation for one nourished on οἱ λόγοι τῆς πίστεως (4:6), whose trust is in θεὸς ζῶν (4:10). Once more, concepts of a future life, faith, and the nature of God's own life combine to shape present priorities and behaviour by directing Christians towards a future guaranteed by the life of God. The concept of eternal life therefore serves an important paraenetic function in 1 Timothy. While the ground of hope is in God's nature and his salvation-historical programme rather than explicitly in the resurrection of Christ (though this is possibly alluded to in 3:16), eternal life is received by those who believe in Christ and live in the present so as to gain that future.

---

17 Cf. Fee: "The *King eternal* ... picks up the theme of *eternal life*" (54).
18 See H. Sasse, "αἰών, αἰώνιος," *TDNT* 1:197-209, esp. 198-201.
19 See Spicq, 568; Knight, 263. Barrett, however, sees eternal life inherited in the future but grasped now (C. K. Barrett, *The Pastoral Epistles* (NCB; Oxford: Clarendon, 1963), 24); cf. J. L. Houlden, *The Pastoral Epistles* (PNTC; Handsworth: Penguin, 1976), 100.
20 The occasion of the ὁμολογία may be baptism (e.g. Houlden, 100; Kelly, 141-42; Lock, 71) or ordination (Knight, 264-65). Hasler's assumption that infant baptism would have been the norm in a third Christian generation requires him to interpret the confession more generally (49).

4.3 Who Are Saved?

4.3.1 "Sinners"

The objects of Christ's saving activity are ἁμαρτωλοί (v. 15). The term has already appeared in v. 9, paired with ἀσεβεῖς,[21] as part of the characterization of those who stand in antithesis to the δίκαιοι. If a correspondence to the two tables of the Decalogue may be found here,[22] ἁμαρτωλός would designate one who fails to give God his rightful place. In any event, the attitudes and behaviours listed in vv. 9-10a are depicted as contrary not only to ὁ νόμος (vv. 8, 9) but to apostolic teaching (vv. 10b-11). In this context, then, "sinners" are those who do not live by the ethical imperatives of Paul's gospel.

The term ἁμαρτωλός, however, also carried connotations from its general and religious background. In the Hellenistic environment it was "always used with a strongly derogatory meaning, if not as an actual term of abuse."[23] As such it was avoided by both Greek philosophers and Philo and Josephus, but it offered the LXX translators a suitable equivalent for רָשָׁע, one who, in antithesis to the צַדִּיק (e.g. Gen 18:23), sets himself by attitude and action in opposition to God.[24] Since the Torah expressed the will of God, a Gentile could be a ἁμαρτωλός almost by definition, "in virtue of his not being a Jew and his failure to regulate his conduct according to the Torah."[25]

NT usage of ἁμαρτωλός continues from that of Judaism, representing someone "who forfeits a correct relationship to God by his culpable attitude to the Jewish Law."[26] It tends to characterize a state of being rather than the committing of a particular offence, as in the τελῶναι καὶ ἁμαρτωλοί of the Synoptics (Matt 5:9 par. Mark 2:15; Matt 9:11 pars. Mark 2:16 and Luke 5:30; Matt 11:19 par. Luke 7:34; Luke 15:1). In the dominical saying, however, it is ἁμαρτωλοί, rather than δίκαιοι, who are the express objects of Jesus' mission (Matt 9:13 par. Mark 2:17; cf. Luke 5:32). Luke especially stresses the possibility of acceptance and transformation for sinners in Jesus' ministry. There is rejoicing in heaven over the ἁμαρτωλός who repents (Luke 15:7, 10) and it is a ἁμαρτωλός who seeks God's mercy who is justified (δεδικαιωμένος), not one who considers

---

21 Cf. ὁ ἀσεβὴς καὶ ἁμαρτωλός opposed to ὁ δίκαιος in 1 Pet 4:18, and ἁμαρτωλοὶ ἀσεβεῖς in Jude v. 15.
22 E.g. Kelly, 49-50; Knight, 84-88; Roloff, 75-76.
23 K. H. Rengstorf, "ἁμαρτωλός," TDNT 1:317-33 (320).
24 TDNT 1:320-24.
25 TDNT 1:326.
26 TDNT 1:327.

himself δίκαιος (Luke 18:13-14; cf. v. 9).²⁷ In John the term appears only as a term used to slander Jesus in the dispute provoked by his healing of the blind man (John 9:16, 24, 25, 31). Paul argues in Romans that Jew and Gentile alike are in the condition of ἁμαρτωλοί, having failed to attain righteousness (Rom 3:7; 5:8-10, 19). In Gal 2:15 the close association of the ideas of "sinner" and "Gentile" is glimpsed when Paul includes himself among ἡμεῖς φύσει Ἰουδαῖοι καὶ οὐκ ἐξ ἐθνῶν ἁμαρτωλοί, but he then acknowledges that "we ourselves have been found to be sinners" (v. 17) in need of God's grace.²⁸

In the NT, then, ἁμαρτωλός retains its connotations of unrighteousness, opposition to God and unworthiness of God's acceptance. These references illustrate, however, not only that sinners can be saved but that all who are saved were sinners. The usage in 1 Tim 1:9, 15 fits this pattern. These ἁμαρτωλοί had failed to meet God's conditions, whether expressed in the OT Law or in the apostolic teaching (vv. 8-11), thus forfeiting the possibility of eternal life (v. 16). Christ, however, came to offer salvation into eternal life precisely to sinners such as these. The "Gentile-sinners" association would be particularly appropriate if there is any polemical thrust against a Judaizing exclusivism.

Paul is himself πρῶτος among the sinners whom Christ came to save (v. 15; cf. v. 16). Whether this represents foremost-in-degree or first-in-a-series in the two references, or one in v. 15 and the other in v. 16, is much discussed.²⁹ In v. 16 the thought of Paul as ὑποτύπωσις for subsequent believers suggests the sense of first-in-a-series. This need not mean that the author understood Paul to be the first Christian believer, but simply that his salvation would serve as exemplar for those who would receive salvation through his ministry, particularly as apostle to the Gentiles. In v. 15, however, unless the author actually believed that Paul was the first person whom Christ saved, it gives better sense to read the expression as qualitative (cf. 1 Cor 15:9), with Paul's persecution of the church constituting the especially heinous act that explains what might otherwise seem a rather hyperbolic characterization.³⁰ In this context the concept of "sinner" acquires a Christological reference in that the specific sinful behaviour consisted in persecuting the church and thereby opposing Christ. The statement ἀγνοῶν ἐποίησα ἐν

---

27 Interestingly ἁμαρτωλός is not used in Acts, though ἁμαρτία are forgiven.
28 See F. F. Bruce, *Galatians* (NIGTC; Grand Rapids: Eerdmans, 1982), 136-41.
29 See summary and assessment in Marshall, 399-401.
30 E.g. Mounce, 56-57.

ἀπιστίᾳ (v. 13) must also be interpreted in relation to Christ: Paul's ignorance was specifically of the truth about Christ and it was Christian belief that he lacked.

The question arises of the significance of this ignorance with respect to salvation: is sin committed in ignorance not culpable? Hasler sees evidence of a Hellenized Christianity adopting the idea of salvation as an awakening from ignorance.[31] Paul's activity, however, was still morally reprehensible, enough to make him "the first of sinners." Does the author then envisage degrees of guilt comparable to the OT distinction between wilful and unwitting sins (e.g. Num 15:22-31), implying that "sins of ignorance are more capable of pardon than sins against knowledge"?[32] This is an uncomfortable distinction for some who look for a thoroughly Pauline theology in the PE,[33] as Houlden's appraisal illustrates:

> The impression is that God overlooked Paul's apparent unsuitability . . . because there was the extenuating circumstance that in opposing Christ he had acted in ignorance. How fair-minded of God! And how remote from the Pauline dynamic of total unworthiness and unmerited grace.[34]

For Paul, however, the combination of ethical failure with ignorance of God characterizes the Gentiles, τὰ ἔθνη τὰ μὴ εἰδότα τὸν θεόν (1 Thess 4:5, echoing Jer 10:25). It is against this background that in Romans ignorance (10:3) and unbelief (10:14) explain Israel's resistance to the gospel. Notwithstanding the apparent mitigation (see 10:2), their culpability is undisputed. The argument is that having become like the Gentiles in disobedience (through their ignorance and unbelief), now, like them, Israel needs and may receive God's mercy (11:30-32).[35] The portrait of the pre-

---

31 Hasler, 16.
32 E. K. Simpson, *The Pastoral Epistles: The Greek Text with Introduction and Commentary* (London: Tyndale, 1954), 34; cf. Kelly, 53.
33 E.g. Knight, 96; Fee, 51. Guthrie, however, believes Paul could regard his ignorance as "a reason for the mercy" (D. Guthrie, *The Pastoral Epistles: An Introduction and Commentary* (TNTC; Leicester: Tyndale, 1957), 64; cf. Simpson, 34).
34 Houlden, 52. Cf. Hanson: "Paul's view would be that Christ had called him *despite* his ignorance" (*Epistles*, 60-61); and Gealy: "Paul is gently shielded from the full impact of his pre-Christian wickedness by the attributing of it to unbelief as a result of ignorance. . . . Would Paul have recognized human ignorance as a ground of divine mercy?" (389).
35 See also A. Nygren's exposition of Rom 11:25-36 in terms of the σκεύη ὀργῆς/σκεύη ἐλέους theme in *Romans* (Philadelphia: Fortress, 1949), 403-

Christian Paul in 1 Tim 1:13 is consonant with that presentation of Israel, on account of whom τὸ ὄνομα τοῦ θεοῦ . . . βλασφημεῖται (Rom 2:24), who have become ἐχθροί (11:28), but to whom God intends to show mercy (11:31). In Acts, not only had pagans been living in χρόνοι τῆς ἀγνοίας, which God would overlook, but now commanded repentance (Acts 17:30), but Jews also had acted in ignorance towards Christ, but now had opportunity for repentance and forgiveness (Acts 3:17-19; 13:27, 38). In both Paul and Acts, then, ignorance and sinfulness characterize both the Gentile world and Jews who resist Christ. In a similar way, salvation in 1 Tim 1:15 is for "sinners", understood as people who, in unbelief (in Christ), oppose Christ (1:13) and live in ways contrary to the apostolic gospel (1:9-11).

4.3.2 "Those Who . . . Believe in Him"

The saving is effective for those who move from ἀπιστία to πιστεύειν ἐπ᾿ αὐτῷ (1:16). With regard to the human appropriation of salvation, then, this contrast between ἀπιστία (v. 12) and πιστεύειν (v. 16) is crucial. This is also the critical distinction in Romans: the Jews were cut off because of ἀπιστία, but if they do not persist in it, they will be restored (11:20, 23; cf. 10:8-17). The promise to Abraham is ἐκ πίστεως, ἵνα κατὰ χάριν (4:16). In 1 Tim 1:13, the syntax emphasizes the "unbelief" rather than the "unknowing," with a primary statement, "I acted in unbelief," supplemented by the adverbial participle ἀγνοῶν.[36] The thought is that, ignorant of the truth about Christ, Paul had not believed in him and had persecuted his followers, making himself an enemy of God, a sinner on a par with the Gentiles; but God's grace had brought faith, and he became the first in a series of sinners to believe in Christ and, by God's mercy, receive eternal life.

The form πιστεύω + ἐπί + dat. is rare in the NT,[37] found apart from the present text only in Rom 9:33; 10:11; and 1 Pet 2:6, always in citations of its sole occurrence in the LXX, Isa 28:16.[38] Does this text

---

08.
36 See N. Turner, *Syntax* (vol. 3 of J. H. Moulton, W. F. Howard and N. Turner, *A Grammar of New Testament Greek*, 3 vols.; Edinburgh: T&T Clark, 1963), 150, 153-54.
37 See R. Bultmann, "πιστεύω κτλ.," *TDNT* 6:174-228; Dibelius-Conzelmann, 30; Knight, 103-04; Roloff, 98.
38 Luke 24:25 and variant readings of Matt 27:42 and John 3:15 have similar forms (see M. J. Harris, "Prepositions and Theology in the Greek New Testament," *NIDNTT* 3:1171-1215).

supply the background for 1 Tim 1:16?[39] The expression may have become stereotyped in ecclesiastical usage, but the observation that "ignorance" and "mercy", significant in 1 Tim 1:12-16, also feature in both 1 Peter and Romans chs. 9-11, increases the possibility that a common interpretive tradition related to Isa 28:16 lies behind each occurrence of the form. Existence prior to faith in Christ for both Jews (Rom 10:2-3, 21) and Gentiles (1 Pet 1:14; 18, 22) is marked by ignorance and disobedience. The alteration in their condition depends upon divine mercy (Rom 9:15-18, 23; 11:30-32; 1 Pet 2:10b). In these contexts the citation of Isa 28:16 indicates that to believe in Christ is to recognize him to be the corner-stone of God's new structure into which believers will be incorporated. Even without alluding directly to Isa 28:16, the expression πιστεύειν ἐπ' αὐτῷ in 1 Tim 1:16 could reflect that tradition. In any event, the preposition ἐπί, indicating "position on something which forms a support or foundation,"[40] associates this "believing" with basing confidence upon Christ, who is both "le fondement et l'objet de la foi." [41] Possibly in implied contrast to alternative grounds such as nomistic achievement (1:7) or esoteric knowledge (1:4), Christ is the basis for the confidence of attaining eternal life.

4.4 How is this Saving Effected?

4.4.1 The Historical Appearing of Christ

That Christ came εἰς τὸν κόσμον is an almost uniquely Johannine emphasis in the NT (John 3:17; 9:39; 10:36; 16:28; 17:18; 18:37; cf. as φῶς, 12:46; 1:9; 3:19; and as the prophet, 6:14; 1 John 4:9; elsewhere only here and in Heb 10:5). Nonetheless, a Johannine understanding cannot be read into the present text without further evidence.[42] What is clear is that "the Christ-event as a matter of historical record"[43] is, for this author, significant for the provision of salvation (cf. 2:5-6; 3:16). Quinn understands the κόσμος as "the human community," which "needs rescue."[44] It is not, however, the object of rescue, but the arena within or out of which the rescue takes place.[45] Furthermore, the emphasis that Quinn recognizes on "the rescue of

---

39 See J. Jeremias, "λίθος, λίθινος", TDNT 4:268-80, 272 (cited, more or less approvingly, by, e.g., Dibelius-Conzelmann, 30; Knight, 104; Roloff, 98).
40 Harris, "Prepositions", 1193.
41 Spicq, 346.
42 Cf. Dibelius-Conzelmann, 29; but see Knight, 101.
43 Towner, Goal, 79.
44 Quinn, Titus, 306.
45 Cf. H. Sasse, "κοσμέω, κτλ.," TDNT 3:867-98, 893.

sinners,"⁴⁶ the example of an individual, Paul, and the anticipated coming to faith of discrete human beings (v. 16),⁴⁷ all suggest that the saving of individuals rather than of humankind as an entity is in view.

Christ's coming into the world is therefore vital to this salvation. D. Gerber takes the absence here of any overt reference to Christ's death as an indication of a tendency in the PE to stress the coming of Christ over against a supposed excessive emphasis on the cross at the end of the first Christian century.⁴⁸ The evident importance of Christ's coming into the world for this author need not, however, imply any purposeful de-emphasizing of Christ's death. Had that been the author's intention it is difficult to see why he would include a reference to Christ's self-giving (2:6).⁴⁹

4.4.2 Christ's Continuing Activity

The story of Paul illustrates that Christ's activity continues beyond his historical coming into the world. Paul was empowered by Christ (v. 12); the love that is in Christ was poured out upon him (v. 14); and through showing mercy to Paul Christ demonstrated his patience, which he will continue to exercise for those who will believe in him (v. 16). Remembering, however, that the account of Paul concerns his commissioning as well as his saving, we must consider to what extent these aspects of Christ's role pertain specifically to salvation.

a. ἠλεήθην

Paul's being shown mercy (ἠλεήθην, vv. 13, 16) is certainly associated with his being saved (v. 15), but although the two concepts overlap they are not necessarily identical, as is often assumed.⁵⁰ This may be demonstrated by substituting ἐσώθην for

---

46 Quinn, *Titus*, 307.
47 Chiao Ek Ho underlines the point that "the author envisages that people will be converted" ("Do the Work of an Evangelist: The Missionary Outlook of the Pastoral Epistles," Ph.D. diss., University of Aberdeen, 2000, 144).
48 Gerber, "1 Tm 1,15b", 474-75.
49 To make his case Gerber has to disallow any allusion to Christ's death in the *Hingabemotiv*, claiming that the tradition about Christ's self-giving had by then been absorbed into the concept of epiphany ("1 Tm 1,15b", 474).
50 E.g. Barrett, 43-44; Brox, 109-110; M. Davies, *The Pastoral Epistles* (Epworth Commentaries; London: Epworth, 1996), 67; Dibelius-Conzelmann, 27; Easton, 114-15; Fee, 51; Guthrie, 64; Hasler, 15-16; W. Hendriksen, *Commentary on 1 and 2 Timothy and Titus* (London: Banner of Truth, 1959),

ἠλεήθην in v. 13. "I was saved because I acted ignorantly in unbelief" is not quite the same thought. If the appointing of a self-evidently unworthy man to ministry is to the fore, ἠλεήθην would give the sense that it was a merciful judgment that considered Paul πιστός (v. 12). Similar ideas are found in 2 Cor 4:1 (ἔχοντες τὴν διακονίαν ταύτην καθὼς ἠλεήθημεν) and 1 Cor 7:25 (ὡς ἠλεημένος ὑπὸ κυρίου πιστὸς εἶναι). This could be in view here even when the idea of Paul as ὑποτύπωσις is introduced. The interjection, ὧν πρῶτός εἰμι ἐγώ (v. 15) refers to Paul as a saved sinner, but rather than continue with this thought, the reiteration of ἠλεήθην (v. 16) would then resume the earlier theme of his merciful appointing to ministry. Dibelius-Conzelman's somewhat disingenuous comment that, "[Paul's] conversion seems to have no other purpose than to serve as a prototype,"[51] misrepresents the flow of thought. V. 16 explains not why Paul was saved, but why a sinner like Paul was appointed to ministry: he could not only declare the gospel but also serve as an illustration of it's efficacy.

b. ἐνδυναμώσαντι

Paul's commissioning clearly dominates the thought in v. 12 where Christ empowers him (ἐνδυναμόω),[52] judges him (ἡγέομαι) to be

---

74-75; Kelly, 53; Knight, 96; Merkel, 21; Young, *Theology*, 124.
51 Dibelius-Conzelmann, 30.
52 Knight observes, "ἐνδυναμόω is usually used of religious and moral strengthening, as in all the NT occurrences" (93). The only occurrence of this compound in the LXX is in the Codex Vaticanus text of Judg 6:34, καὶ πνεῦμα κυρίου ἐνεδυνάμωσεν τὸν Γεδεων καὶ ἐσάλπισεν ἐν κερατίνῃ. There are suggestive correspondences between the commissioning of Gideon in Judges 6 and the story of Paul in 1 Timothy: each was a surprising choice, the Lord's evaluation differing from that of the men themselves, and each was empowered (ἐνδυναμόω) for a task; in both cases the Lord's patience was displayed. Could there be echoes in our text of this Gideon story, which "illustrates the theme of total dependance on God" (T. M. Willis, "Gideon," in *The Oxford Companion to the Bible* (ed. B. M. Metzger and M. D. Coogan; Oxford: Oxford University Press, 1993), 253)? Marcus Bockmuehl has shown that sounding the trumpet was used in early Christianity as a metaphor for preaching the gospel (M. Bockmuehl, "'The Trumpet shall sound.' Shofar symbolism and its reception in early Christianity," in *TEMPLUM AMICITAE: Essays on the Second Temple Presented to Ernst Bummel* (ed. W. Horbury, JSNTSup 48; Sheffield: Sheffield Academic Press, 1991), 199-225. One of his clearest examples comes from Origen, *Fr. Ps.* 80.4, a reference to "the trumpet of the gospel" sounding out to all the earth. This suggests another correspondence: Gideon was

faithful and appoints him (τίθημι) to service.

c. ὑπερεπλεόνασεν δὲ ἡ χάρις τοῦ κυρίου ἡμῶν

The reference of the overflowing of grace in v. 14 is, however, not so clear. It is usually related to the saving in v. 15, either as a particular example of that general truth,[53] or in explication of ἠλεήθην (v. 13).[54] Comparisons are often drawn with Rom 5:20, οὗ δὲ ἐπλεόνασεν ἡ ἁμαρτία, ὑπερεπερίσσευσεν ἡ χάρις.[55] There grace is expressly salvific, overcoming sin and producing righteousness which leads to eternal life (v. 21; cf. v. 17); as such it is contrasted with the law as a means of salvation (6:15). Similar content is possible in 1 Tim 1:14, but alternatively the reference to the Lord could connect the thought with v. 12 (τῷ ἐνδυναμώσαντί με Χριστῷ Ἰησοῦ τῷ κυρίῳ ἡμῶν). This χάρις would then be the gift to Paul of a particular role and enabling for it. There are precedents in the *Hauptbriefe* for such an idea, where Paul characterizes his ministry as a "grace" (e.g. Rom 1:5; 15:15-16; 1 Cor 3:10; cf. Gal 2:9, where the specific content of the χάρις is ὅτι πεπίστευμαι τὸ εὐαγγέλιον τῆς ἀκροβυστίας, v. 7). The context in 1 Tim 1:12-16 allows us to see both the saving and the commissioning of Paul attributed to "the grace of our Lord".

d. μετὰ πίστεως καὶ ἀγάπης τῆς ἐν Χριστῷ Ἰησοῦ

With this overflowing grace have come "faith and love in Christ Jesus" (v. 14b). Are the faith and love qualities of Christ or characteristics produced in Paul by grace?[56] Whether they take the preposition μετά to indicate "the closest possible connection between the grace of God and the two co-ordinate Christian virtues,"[57] or allow it little force in such formulaic language,[58] most commentators take the latter approach, seeing a contrast with the ἀπιστία and aggression manifested prior to the outpouring of grace (v. 13).[59] There is less agreement on what the qualification ἐν Χριστῷ Ἰησοῦ signifies. J. A. Allan has argued that what he takes to be the

---

empowered and sounded the trumpet; now Paul is empowered and proclaims the gospel.
53 So Kelly, 54; Donelson reads vv. 12-14 as an inductive paradigm leading to the conclusion in v. 15 (*Pseudepigraphy*, 101-03).
54 So Guthrie, 65; cf. Brox, 109-10.
55 E.g. Barrett, 45; Easton, 115; Kelly, 53.
56 See E. G. Hinson, "1 & 2 Timothy and Titus," in vol. 11 of *The Broadman Bible Commentary* (London: Marshall, Morgan & Scott, 1972), 299-376, 309.
57 Guthrie, 64.
58 Dibelius-Conzelmann, 28.
59 E.g. Brox, 111; Lock, 15; Mounce, 54.

characteristic Pauline mystical sense of the expression "in Christ" (as in, e.g. Rom 6:11; 8:1; Phil 3:9) is absent from the PE.⁶⁰ The formula "which is in Christ," qualifying an abstract noun to which it is predicated by a definite article, is however somewhat different. This usage is found not only in 1 Timothy (1:14; 3:13) and 2 Timothy (1:1,13; 2:1,10; 3:15; cf. 1:9; 3:12), but also, as Allan observes (citing Rom 3:24; 8:39; 1 Cor 4:17; Gal 1:22), in the *Hauptbriefe*.⁶¹ It is strange, then, that Allan insists that the form in the PE represents the former Pauline expression with diminished force, rather than the latter, to which it corresponds more precisely.⁶² In 1 Tim 1:12-16, the empowering of Paul (v. 12), coming into the world to save sinners (v. 15), and displaying divine patience (v. 16), are all explicitly attributed to Χριστὸς Ἰησοῦς. In this context the phrase ἐν Χριστῷ Ἰησου (v. 14) continues the thought of Christ's saving agency. Kelly goes beyond the internal evidence of the letter to discover here Paul's mystical faith-union with Christ, but he is justified in seeing "much more than a periphrasis for 'Christian'." ⁶³

e. ἐνδείξηται Χριστὸς Ἰησοῦς τὴν ἅπασαν μακροθυμίαν

Houlden understands patience and mercy in Hellenistic terms as "a quality of God's quiet, static, long-term existence rather than his vigorous, dynamic saving work."⁶⁴ Showing mercy is, however, an action, expressed by an aorist verb (vv. 13, 16) and the salvation saying (v. 15) describes an event. What is described in v. 16 is not merely a benevolent disposition but an aspect of the divine saving function, specifically attributed to Christ.⁶⁵ This echoes the μακροθυμία of Yahweh in the LXX, which "does not imply renunciation of the grounds for wrath. What it does mean is that alongside this wrath there is a divine restraint which justifies the postponement."⁶⁶ Similarly in the NT God's μακροθυμία explains

---

60 J. A. Allan, "The 'In Christ' Formula in the Pastoral Epistles," *NTS* 10 (1963): 115-21. His reading of the Pauline evidence is, however, open to criticism (e.g. Marshall, 395-96).
61 Allan, "In Christ," 117.
62 J. D. Quinn and W. C. Wacker comment that the phrase in v. 14 draws "various aspects of meaning from different forms of the *in Christ* phrase in the Pauline tradition"(*The First and Second Letters to Timothy: A New Translation with Notes and Commentary*, Grand Rapids: Eerdmans, 2000, 132).
63 Kelly, 53-54. E. F. Scott understands it as "imparted through a living relation to Christ" (*The Pastoral Epistles*, MNTC, London: Hodder & Stoughton, 1936, 13).
64 Houlden, 52.
65 See Merkel, 22.
66 J. Horst, "μακροθυμία, κτλ.," *TDNT* 4:374-87, 377. Cf Roloff, *1.Timotheus*,

the delay of judgment to give opportunity for repentance (2 Pet 3:9, 15; cf. 1 Pet 3:20; Rom 2:24;[67] 9:22[68]). Rhetorically, this suggestion would conclude the unit by holding out to "sinners," including opponents, the possibility of change.

4.4.3 Paul as a Paradigm

Precisely what does Paul exemplify? Since the relative clause, ὧν πρῶτός εἰμι ἐγώ (v. 15) places Paul among the ἁμαρτωλοί whom Christ came to save, and he is a ὑποτύπωσις for others (v. 16), he could serve as "the supreme model of the saved sinner," perhaps reflecting the situation of typical Gentile converts.[69] If so, the description of Paul here might be expected to indicate the author's notion of a typical sinner and the process and outcome of salvation. On that basis Knight reads vv. 14-16 as an explication of the concept of being shown mercy (v. 13), which therefore includes, "salvation from sin," "union with Christ in the sphere of faith and love," "eternal life through faith in him," and "being counted trustworthy and being put in service."[70]

Michael Wolter, however, has suggested that the description of Paul as βλάσφημος καὶ διώκτης καὶ ὑβριστής (v. 13) is better understood in terms of another paradigm.[71] Whereas the pre-Christian Paul is elsewhere depicted as a persecutor of the church, to describe him as βλάσφημος and ὑβριστής is almost unparalleled in the NT and early Christian literature.[72] Dibelius-Conzelmann regard these as standard components of vice-lists,[73] but from his survey of secular Greek, Jewish and early Christian literature, Wolter argues that the terms ὕβρις and βλασφημία identify a specific stereotype, the θεομάχος or enemy of God. Paul is thus associated with other recognized figures who opposed God.[74] In fact, even without such a

---

97; Spicq, 345.
67 Mounce, also citing the ἀνοχή of God in Rom 3:25 (58).
68 Spicq, 345.
69 Young, *Theology*, 124; Roloff describes Paul as a "Typus des gottlosen Menschen schlechthin" (93); cf. Brox, 110-11; Merkel, 21.
70 Knight, 95-96.
71 M. Wolter, "Paulus, der bekehrte Gottesfeind. Zum Verständnis von 1.Tim. 1:13," *NovT* 31 (1989): 48-66.
72 Wolter finds only one example, *Acts Pet.* 2.1.47, which he regards as dependent upon 1 Timothy ("Gottesfiend", 49-50, n. 9; also 57-58, n. 39).
73 Dibelius-Conzelmann, 28. G. Bertram, however, disputes that ὑβριστής belongs in such lists ("ὕβρις, κτλ.," *TDNT* 8: 295-307).
74 Wolter, "Gottesfeind", 52-58. He finds this incompatible with Gal 1:14 and Phil 3:6 (62), though Marshall disagrees (391-92).

stereotype, the terms βλάσφημος and ὑβριστής could serve to portray persecution of the church as enmity against God.⁷⁵ The resulting thought, that Paul was unfit for service because he had persecuted Christians and thereby opposed Christ, agrees with 1 Cor 15:9: οὐκ εἰμὶ ἱκανὸς καλεῖσθαι ἀπόστολος, διότι ἐδίωξα τὴν ἐκκλησίαν τοῦ θεοῦ.

What purpose might have been served by associating Paul not only with sinners but specifically with opponents of the church? An overview of the section reveals ministry as the principal theme, with ideas of faith and faithfulness, indicated by the recurring πιστ- terms, running through the material. The springboard for the thanksgiving is not the gospel as such, but that it was ἐπιστεύθην ἐγώ (v. 11);⁷⁶ Paul is thankful ὅτι πιστόν με ἡγήσατο (v. 12), which he attributes to mercy, because he had acted in ἀπιστίᾳ (v. 13), but the grace of the Lord endowed him with πίστις (v. 14). This illustrates the πιστός saying that Christ came to save sinners (v. 15), and in dealing thus with Paul Christ has provided an example for τῶν μελλόντων πιστεύειν ἐπ' αὐτῷ (v. 16). Timothy is in turn to hold on to πίστις, for some have gone disastrously off course with regard to ἡ πίστις (v. 19). These last may provide a clue to the paraenetic purpose. 1:12-18 is sandwiched by material concerned with false teachers (vv. 3-10, 19b-20). They are to be opposed, but the instructions do imply the possibility of change. The goal is that they cease to teach heresy (vv. 3-4) and even where discipline is applied, it's purpose is education and change (ἵνα παιδευθῶσιν μὴ βλασφημεῖν, v. 20).⁷⁷ To present Paul himself as one once in error but now considered faithful and serving Christ would exemplify for those opponents the possibility of receiving mercy and becoming trustworthy ministers, making Paul "the prototypical converted heretic."⁷⁸ This could represent an approach to those Judaizing opponents whom the letter identifies (1:3-4).⁷⁹ That Paul acted ἀγνοῶν . . . ἐν ἀπιστίᾳ implies a very negative evaluation of his life in Judaism. He has become, however, the commissioned blasphemer, sharpening the appeal to those now characterized as blasphemers (1:20).⁸⁰ Perhaps it is not so much Paul who is "gently

---

75 Cf. Bertram, *TDNT* 8:306; Fee, 51; Knight, 95; Spicq, 341-42.
76 See, e.g., Barrett, 44; Roloff, *1.Timotheus*, 84; Knight, 92.
77 Donelson comments, "Gentleness and hope for repentance will characterize all rebuke in the Pastorals" (*Pseudepigraphy*, 103).
78 Donelson, *Pseudepigraphy*, 101.
79 R. J. Karris, "The Background and Significance of the Polemic of the PE," *JBL* 92 (1973): 549-564.
80 The negative characterization of Paul's pre-Christian zeal would have an

shielded"[81] from the full force of the offence as the opponents, whom the author hopes not to repel but to reform.

4.5 Summary

In this passage Paul is presented as the erstwhile opponent who now serves Christ. While ministry is the primary thought (with a glance at opponents who may yet become faithful servants), the larger theme of salvation is also treated. The turning of Paul from the status of enemy to that of servant illustrates the assertion that it is specifically sinners who are the objects of Christ's saving work. This highlights the soteriological conviction that saving is due not to human deserving but to the divine attributes of mercy, grace and patience. This saving is inextricably bound up with Christ and his coming into the world, which has brought the possibility of salvation. The outcome of saving is eternal life, appropriated by believing in Christ, which seems to imply trusting him for that outcome on the basis of the message about him. A conversion, a coming to believe with resultant transformation of life, is in view. Within such a framework the proclamation of the message is significant, and Paul's effectiveness as a missionary is heightened by the encapsulation in his own history of the saving that he proclaims.

---

additional polemical edge if the false teaching had a Judaizing character.
81 Gealy, 389.

Chapter 5

1 Timothy 2:1-7

Παρακαλῶ οὖν πρῶτον πάντων ποιεῖσθαι δεήσεις προσευχὰς ἐντεύξεις εὐχαριστίας ὑπὲρ πάντων ἀνθρώπων, ὑπὲρ βασιλέων καὶ πάντων τῶν ἐν ὑπεροχῇ ὄντων, ἵνα ἤρεμον καὶ ἡσύχιον βίον διάγωμεν ἐν πάσῃ εὐσεβείᾳ καὶ σεμνότητι. τοῦτο καλὸν καὶ ἀπόδεκτον ἐνώπιον τοῦ σωτῆρος ἡμῶν θεοῦ, ὃς πάντας ἀνθρώπους θέλει σωθῆναι καὶ εἰς ἐπίγνωσιν ἀληθείας ἐλθεῖν. εἷς γὰρ θεός, εἷς καὶ μεσίτης θεοῦ καὶ ἀνθρώπων, ἄνθρωπος Χριστὸς Ἰησοῦς, ὁ δοὺς ἑαυτὸν ἀντίλυτρον ὑπὲρ πάντων, τὸ μαρτύριον καιροῖς ἰδίοις. εἰς ὃ ἐτέθην ἐγὼ κῆρυξ καὶ ἀπόστολος, ἀλήθειαν λέγω οὐ ψεύδομαι, διδάσκαλος ἐθνῶν ἐν πίστει καὶ ἀληθείᾳ.

The interpretation of this statement about "our Saviour God" and his desire to save (vv. 3-4) will be influenced by what the main thought and purpose of 2:1-7 is understood to be, which in turn is affected by how the letter's general outlook and purpose is perceived. This may be illustrated by two contrasting approaches. For Dibelius-Conzelmann, the overriding goal of the PE is "a structuring of life under the ideal of good Christian citizenship."[1] The fact that prayer is urged for all, including pagan authorities, ἵνα ἤρεμον καὶ ἡσύχιον βίον διάγωμεν ἐν πάσῃ εὐσεβείᾳ καὶ σεμνότητι (v. 2) is therefore highly significant.[2] It reveals a concept of salvation whose outcome is peaceful temporal existence,[3] attained through the rational acceptance of the Christian message ("recognition of the truth," v. 4).[4] Admittedly the doctrinal material in vv. 5-6 is "not easy to connect with what precedes," but if it is traditional, it need not be expected to relate closely to its context.[5]

---

1 Dibelius-Conzelmann, 40.
2 Cf. Epictetus: "For God made all mankind to be happy, to be serene" (*Diatr.* 3.24.2, cited by Dibelius-Conzelmann, 41).
3 Dibelius-Conzelmann, 38 nn. 21, 22.
4 Dibelius-Conzelmann, 41.
5 Dibelius-Conzelmann, 41; cf. Houlden: "The fact that it is a set form is confirmed by its not being integral to the thought of the passage." (67)

Fee, on the other hand, "assumes that everything in the letter has to do with 1:3,"[6] the command to curtail the activity of false teachers. From this perspective, he interprets the reiterated concern for "all people" in 2:1-7 as a corrective to the false teachers' "elitist or exclusivist mentality."[7] A coherent flow of thought may be traced from the preceding section into 2:1-7, and the theological statements, far from being incidental, serve the unit's purpose. Fee's difficulty, however, is with the prayer (v. 2), which becomes "something of a digression, albeit . . . a meaningful one."[8] Is it possible to offer an explanation that gives due weight to both the doctrinal material and the prayer?

5.1 Context

After the parenthetical allusion to specific opponents (1:19b-20), παρακαλῶ οὖν (2:1) picks up the exhortation to Timothy from 1:18-19a,[9] which is in relation to the on-going missionary task (τῶν μελλόντων πιστεύειν, 1:16) associated with Paul and his gospel (1:12-17). In this wider context the reiteration of "all" through 2:1-7 is significant. It also enables connecting lines to be drawn from the salvation statement to the surrounding material. God's desire that all should be saved (πάντες ἄνθρωποι, v. 4) echoes the prayer for all (πάντων ἀνθρώπων, v. 1, and πάντων τῶν ἐν ὑπεροχῇ ὄντων, v. 2) and prepares for the claim that Christ gave himself for all (πάντων, v. 6). The salvation statement thus functions as the basis for the instruction in vv. 1-2, with the thought: Pray for <u>all</u>, because the Saviour God wants <u>all</u> to be saved, as Christ's self-giving for <u>all</u> demonstrates. This central soteriological conviction then establishes the rationale for Paul's ministry to <u>all</u>, and specifically to Gentiles (v. 7),[10] before the thought returns to prayer in the context of the community's worship (v.8).

---

6   Fee, 7.
7   Fee, 62.
8   Fee, 62.
9   Marshall, 418.
10 On three occasions in the *Hauptbriefe* Paul protests, οὐ ψεύδομαι (Rom 9:1; 2 Cor 11:31; Gal 1:20), always reinforcing not doctrinal but personal claims. Similarly 1 Tim 2:7 affirms Paul's call and its scope.

5.2 What Sort of "Saving" is in View?

With the verb σωθῆναι, σωτήρ (v. 3) "has therefore its own force here and is not a mere title."[11] Of what does this "saving" consist?

5.2.1 A Peaceful Life

If the content of the saving (v. 4) is found in the prayer ἵνα ἤρεμον καὶ ἡσύχιον βίον διάγωμεν ἐν πάσῃ εὐσεβείᾳ καὶ σεμνότητι (v. 2b), this is a less radical salvation than in other NT writings.[12] If, however, this purpose clause supplies not the content of salvation but a means to its realisation, a quite different result is obtained: the conditions of a well ordered state and freedom from persecution make it possible for the Christian community to fulfil its soteriological task for the world and for all people (v. 4).[13]

This saving, promoted by conditions conducive to the spread of the "knowledge of the truth" (v. 4b, summarized in vv. 5-6a) and Christian mission (v. 7), accords with the concept in 1:15-16, where Christ saves sinners as they come to believe in him for eternal life. The details of the clause fill out the picture.

a. ἤρεμος καὶ ἡσύχιος

In Hellenistic popular philosophy ἡσυχία represented quiet and tranquillity,[14] and it is this "ideal of a peaceful life" that Dibelius-Conzelmann find in v. 2.[15] The term could also, however, carry religious overtones. Philo recommends ἡσυχία as the appropriate disposition for receiving instruction in the synagogue (*Spec.* 2.60-64). He tells of the LXX translators seeking seclusion to quieten and still themselves (ἐνησυχάσαι καὶ ἐνερημῆσαι) and "commune with the laws" free from distractions (*Mos.* 2.36). This sense of attaining conditions, external and attitudinal, in which hearing God becomes possible, fits the worship context of 1 Tim 2:2. It is also interesting that Philo credits the creation of such conditions to a βασιλεύς (*Mos.* 2.29-31). Making God's laws available to half the human race was of such magnitude that only kings could undertake it.[16] A prayer that rulers would so govern as to create peaceful conditions in which all could hear the gospel is intelligible from that perspective. Philo's

---

11 Dibelius-Conzelmann, 41.
12 Houlden, 66.
13 See L. Oberlinner, *Die Pastoralbriefe. Ersten Timotheusbrief* (HTKNT 11.2-1; Freiburg: Herder, 1994), 68; cf. Roloff, 125.
14 See M. J. Harris, "ἡσυχία," *NIDNTT* 3:111-12.
15 Dibelius-Conzelmann, 39.
16 *Mos.* 2.28.

translators pray (stretching out their hands to heaven; cf. 1 Tim 2:8[17]), "In order that most or even all of the human race (γένος ἀνθρώπων) should be profited (ὠφεληθῇ χρησόμενον) as they make use of wise and supremely noble directions for the rectifying of life (εἰς ἐπανόρθωσιν βίου)."[18] Similarly, 1 Tim 2:1-2 seeks benefit for all, in part at least through hearing God's message (vv. 3-4, 7).

b. εὐσέβεια

The desired life is ἐν πάσῃ εὐσεβείᾳ καὶ σεμνότητι. As is commonly remarked, εὐσέβεια and its cognates appear with unusual frequency in the PE,[19] with thirteen out of twenty-two NT occurrences.[20] Less often noticed is the variation in frequency between the letters. Nine of these references are in 1 Timothy (εὐσέβεια in 2:2; 3:16; 4:7, 8; 6:3, 5, 6, 11; εὐσεβεῖν in 5:4), with only two each in 2 Timothy and Titus (εὐσέβεια in 2 Tim 3:5; Titus 1:1; εὐσεβῶς in 2 Tim 3:12; Titus 2:12). It is therefore particularly in 1 Timothy that the concept is prominent.[21] In the Hellenistic milieu εὐσέβεια represented an ideal of reverence shown in cultic observance and respectful acquiescence within familial and societal orders.[22] The adoption of the term in the PE has been attributed to an increasingly Hellenized Christianity,[23] missionary strategy,[24] or the adoption of the opponents' vocabulary in order to counteract them.[25]

NT scholars have given little attention, however, to the political and legal implications of εὐσέβεια. The legal historian R.A. Bauman has documented the concerns of Roman jurists and politicians about unscrupulous exploitation of the vaguely defined charge of *impietas*,

---

17 The verbs are ἀνατένω in Philo and ἐπαίρω in 1 Timothy.
18 Cf. 2 Tim 3:16, where the scriptures are ὠφέλιμος . . . πρὸς ἐπανόρθωσιν.
19 See discussions in Marshall, 135-44; Quinn, *Titus*, 282-91; Roloff, 117-19; Spicq, 482-92.
20 Elsewhere only in Acts (4x) and 2 Peter (5x).
21 W. Foerster, noting that εὐσέβεια appears among Christian qualities in 1 Tim 6:11 but not in 2 Tim 2:22, concludes that "it is not a central and indispensable concept in the Pastorals" ("σέβομαι, κτλ." *TDNT* 7:168-96, 182). He overlooks the possibility that it could be central to 1 Timothy but not to 2 Timothy.
22 See W. Günther, "σέβομαι," *NIDNTT* 2:91-93.
23 E.g. Hanson, *Epistles*, 67; Houlden, 59, 63-65.
24 E.g. Quinn: "The values grounded on *pietas* in pagan Rome offered a point of departure for showing what Christians meant by *eusebeia*" (*Titus*, 289).
25 E.g. Fee, 63. R. Schwarz, *Bürgerliches Christentum im Neuen Testament? Eine Studie zu Ethik, Amt und Recht in den Pastoralbriefen* (ÖBS 4; Klosterneuburg: Österreichisches Katholisches Bibelwerk, 1983), 116-17, explains it as a positive term countering the opponents' world-denying stance.

"irreverence," in Roman law.²⁶ For considerable periods no such charges were entertained, but during certain times (such as in Nero's reign), authorities used the *impietas* legislation against groups or individuals whom they wished to attack but could not easily prosecute on other grounds. Could the unusual concern for εὐσέβεια in 1 Timothy reflect a local or national situation in which the Christian movement was vulnerable to this strategy?²⁷ The activity of praying for rulers might be hoped to demonstrate "piety and reverence" and deflect suspicion of *impietas*. A defensive stance in such a context should not be assumed incompatible with a missionary desire that "the effective leadership of the State will maintain an environment conducive to witness."²⁸ On the contrary, "peaceful existence is not an end in itself but facilitates missionary endeavour."²⁹ In its worship, then, the church should express that concern for the salvation of all that is here attributed to God himself.

5.2.2 Coming to Knowledge of the Truth

Καί connects the verb σωθῆναι to the clause εἰς ἐπίγνωσιν ἀληθείας ἐλθεῖν. If copulative, it would permit the ideas of being saved and coming to a knowledge of the truth to be distinguished. Simpson tentatively suggests two levels of saving, general preservation (first element) and spiritual salvation (second element).³⁰ There is, however, no hint of two classes of beneficiary or of the possibility of receiving one element without the other. It gives better sense to read the καί epexegetically ("to be saved, that is to come to a knowledge of the truth") or take the two infinitives as a hendiadys

---

26 R. A. Bauman, *Impietas in Principem. A Study of Treason Against the Roman Emperor with Special Reference to the First Century A.D.* (MBPAR 67; München: C. H. Beck, 1974).
27 The same question could be asked of 2 Peter. Titus, where Paul's message is κατ᾽ εὐσέβειαν (1:1), and living εὐσεβῶς is a goal (2:12), could have a similar apologetic intent. The tone in 2 Timothy, however, is markedly different. There the opponents are said to have the appearance, but not the true dynamic, of εὐσέβεια (3:5), and whereas such deceivers go unchecked, those who want to live εὐσεβῶς in Christ are persecuted (3:12-13). The contrast with 1 Timothy would be compatible with a shift in circumstances. Despite the efforts in 1 Timothy to demonstrate that they are no threat to the state, churches are suffering under charges of *impietas*, while pretenders put on a show of piety and escape persecution.
28 Marshall, 423.
29 Ho, "Missionary Outlook," 337.
30 Simpson, 41-42.

("to be saved through coming to a knowledge of the truth").³¹ Whichever of these overlapping interpretations is adopted, "to come to a knowledge of truth" explicates the idea of being saved.

The phrase ἐπίγνωσις ἀληθείας is restricted in the NT to the PE (1 Tim 2:4; Titus 1:1; 2 Tim 2:25; 3:7) and Heb 10:26.³² The noun ἀλήθεια appears 5x in 1 Timothy, characterizing the teaching of Paul (ἐν πίστει καὶ ἀληθείᾳ, 2:7³³) and the church (στῦλον καὶ ἑδραίωμα τῆς ἀληθείας, 3:15) over against false teaching (4:3; 6:5). These contexts suggest the sense of "true teaching or faith."³⁴ An idiosyncrasy of the three PE is that the noun ἐπίγνωσις occurs only in the expression ἐπίγνωσις ἀληθείας (1 Tim 2:4; 2 Tim 2:25; 3:7; Titus 1:1),³⁵ suggesting to Bultmann that, "the compound ἐπίγνωσις has become almost a technical term for the decisive knowledge of God which is implied in conversion to the Christian faith."³⁶ The construction εἰς ἐπίγνωσιν ἀληθείας ἐλθεῖν suggests a movement into a state of recognition (cf. the perfect participle ἐπεγνωκόσι in 4:3, defining "the believers" as those who "have come to recognize the truth").³⁷ With ἀλήθεια as its object, this conversion is envisaged through acceptance of the truth taught by Paul (v. 7).³⁸ Since 1 Timothy also associates salvation with coming to believe in Christ (1:15-16; cf. 4:10), it seems that believing in Christ and recognizing the truth are contiguous if not equivalent concepts. Nonetheless, while recognition of truth must include a "noetic component,"³⁹ more is implied than "the intellectual acceptance of Christianity."⁴⁰ The concept embraces a decisive "moment of recognition, i.e. of appropriation and practical realization" which shows itself in a life conformed to the truth of the gospel.⁴¹

---

31 See Marshall, 427-28 and n. 44.
32 Although knowing the truth is a Johannine theme (John 8:32; 2 John v. 1; cf. John 14:7; 1 John 3:19; 4:6),
33 "The sphere and the subjects in which he teaches" (Lock, 29; followed by Knight, 127).
34 R. Bultmann, "ἀλήθεια," *TDNT* 1:238-47, 244.
35 The same applies to Hebrews (10:26); cf. 1 Timothy's only example of ἐπιγινώσκω, in ἐπεγνωκόσι τὴν ἀλήθειαν (1 Tim 4:3).
36 R. Bultmann, "γινώσκω, κτλ.," *TDNT* 1:689-719, 707, citing 1 Tim 2:4, Titus 1:1; 2 Tim 2:25; 3:7; cf. Kelly, 62.
37 Cf. 2 John 1; also Col 1:6, where conversion took place when, ἠκούσατε καὶ ἐπέγνωτε τὴν χάριν τοῦ θεοῦ ἐν ἀληθείᾳ.
38 Mounce, 87.
39 Roloff, 120; followed by Knight, 120.
40 Lock, 27; followed by Hanson, *Epistles*, 68.
41 Oberlinner, *1.Timotheusbrief*, 73.

1 Timothy 2:1-7

Finally, against elitist restrictions, the phrase indicates "the openly accessible nature of Christian faith and life."[42]

5.3 How Is Salvation Provided and Received?

If the prayer in v. 2 envisages the conditions for salvation, v. 4 indicates the means whereby it is effected.

5.3.1 God's Will to Save

The source of salvation is in God as σωτήρ and the fact that he πάντας ἀνθρώπους θέλει σωθῆναι (v. 4). "Die Wille Gottes wird bestimmt als universaler Heilswille."[43] If this is "the divine sovereignty in disposing to salvation,"[44] however, does the Almighty will something which apparently does not eventuate?[45] Spicq takes θέλει to express a desire of God's heart or wish that is not infact accomplished,[46] but his attempt to circumvent the problem by distinguishing θέλω (expressing a desire) from βούλεσθαι (giving a command) is not convincing.[47] "The sovereignty of God" as defined in later debates is simply not the issue here. As Fee writes,

> [The statement] implies neither that all (meaning everybody) will be saved (against 3:6; 4:2; or 4:10, e.g.) nor that God's will is somehow frustrated since all, indeed, are not saved. The concern is simply with the universal scope of the gospel . . . .[48]

With the affirmation, εἷς γὰρ θεός (v. 5), the implication is that "God our Saviour" (v. 3) is the one God, and hence the one Saviour, for all of humanity.[49] This parallels Paul's argument in Rom 3:29-30 that there is one God, therefore one God for all, whose saving activity extends to all.[50]

---

42 Houlden, 67; cf. Hanson, *Epistles*, 68; Spicq, 364; Oberlinner, *1. Timotheusbrief*, 72.
43 Oberlinner, *1. Timotheusbrief*, 72.
44 G. Schrenck, "θέλω, κτλ." *TDNT* 3:44-62, 47.
45 See Barrett, 50.
46 Spicq, 365.
47 See βούλεσθαι in 2 Pet 3:9; cf. Mounce, 86.
48 Fee, 64.
49 Cf. Brox: "Die Einheit aller Menschen im universalen Heiswillen Gottes hat ihren Urgrund in dem einen Gott und in dem einen Mittler." (127)
50 Cf. Barrett, 50; Kelly, 63; Lock, 27.

5.3.2 The Christ-event

As well as carrying forward the argument that God's saving will is universal (vv. 1-4), vv. 5-6 may specify that "truth" which God wants people to come to know (v. 4). Following εἷς γὰρ θεός, affirming "the basic tenet of Judaism,"[51] Christ is introduced in a series of terse theological dicta: εἷς καὶ μεσίτης θεοῦ καὶ ἀνθρώπων, ἄνθρωπος Χριστὸς Ἰησοῦς, ὁ δοὺς ἑαυτὸν ἀντίλυτρον ὑπὲρ πάντων (vv. 5-6). While this may well reflect some liturgical source,[52] it is utilized here to elaborate the role of Christ in this saving, disclosing more of the author's soteriological outlook.[53]

a. μεσίτης

Christ Jesus is the "one mediator between God and humankind" (v. 5). While it is evidently significant here, the precise content of the term μεσίτης is difficult to establish. It is relatively rare in the NT, and the Hellenistic environment supplies a range of mediator concepts.[54] It represented a range of legal functions, from arbitrator to guarantor.[55] There were also various religious usages,[56] from pagan mediators, such as the Persian Mithra or Plato's δαίμονες,[57] to Gnostic intermediaries and human (or once-human) mediators of mystic knowledge.[58] In Judaism both human figures such as Moses and angelic beings could exercise mediatorial functions.[59]

Hanson traces the adoption of the term to its sole occurrence in the LXX, Job 9:33.[60] He translates Job's appeal, εἴθε ἦν ὁ μεσίτης

---

51 Kelly, 63. In Hellenistic Judaism, according to Bultmann, "the knowledge of God . . . means specifically, recognition of the fact that there is only one God" (*TDNT* 1:702).
52 Hasler, 22.
53 *Contra* Easton, 122.
54 See Mounce, 88.
55 See O. Becker, "μεσίτης," *NIDNTT* 1:372-76; A. Oepke, "μεσίτης, μεσιτεύω," *TDNT* 4:598-624.
56 See, e.g., Brox, 127-28; Hasler, 21-22; Lock, 27-28; Merkel, 25.
57 Oepke, *TDNT* 4:604-07.
58 Amongst the examples they offer to illustrate possible backgrounds to 1 Timothy ch. 2, R. C. and C. C. Kroeger refer to female figures who might serve as mediators of knowledge, supporting the notion of the feminine as the source of enlightenement, in *I Suffer Not a Woman: Rethinking 1 Timothy 2.11-15 in Light of Ancient Evidence* (Grand Rapids: Baker, 1992), 105-13. They have been criticized, however, for applying evidence from later Gnosticism to a New Testament setting (see e.g. Mounce, 140-41).
59 E.g., the angelic μεσίτης θεοῦ καὶ ἀνθρώπων in T*Dan* 6:2 (see Easton, 122); cf. Heb 2:2.
60 Hanson, *Epistles*, 68-69; *Studies*, 56-62. The suggestion that Job provides a

ἡμῶν καὶ ἐλέγχων καὶ διακούων ἀνὰ μέσον ἀμφοτέρων, "I wish there were our mediator and reprover and one to hear the case between us both," and reasons, "A Christian reading his Job in LXX could easily take this as a prophecy of the mediator who was to come."[61] The setting is, however, juridical: "In language suffused with legal terms, Job denounces God's disregard of his right."[62] In this forensic context the term μεσίτης represents a neutral third party whose role is to ensure a fair hearing for each disputant. As Hanson recognizes, Job's μεσίτης is "an arbitrator between God and man."[63] This is not at all the function of the mediator in 1 Tim 2:5-6, and Hanson offers no explanation of the relationship of the arbitrator concept to the material in v. 6, surmising only that vv. 5 and 6 comprise separate formulae with different histories.[64] Even if this were the case, however, it could be argued that if the author has combined two distinct sayings he probably took them to be in agreement, the second explicating the idea announced in the first. Clues to the term's significance for the author must be sought in the context, and perhaps the other NT references to Christ as μεσίτης could provide points of comparison.

In v. 5, Christ shares the human condition of those who benefit from his mediatorship: as ἄνθρωπος he can mediate between God and ἄνθρωποι (v. 5; cf. vv. 1, 4). Hasler argues that the pairing of the "one God" and "one mediator" statements demonstrates the divine status of the mediator,[65] but this does not necessarily follow. While there may be some suggestion of divine essence in the εἶς predication,[66] and 1 Timothy does place Christ alongside God as an apparently divine figure (e.g. 1:1-2; 5:21; 6:13),[67] in 2:5-6 it is specifically Jesus' human-ness that qualifies him for the role of mediator. That role is fulfilled in his self-giving as a ransom, which affects the relationship between God and humankind. All these

---

background for the use of the term in 1 Timothy is noted with cautious approval by Houlden (68) and without comment by Oberlinner (*1. Timotheusbrief*, 74). Towner (*Goal*, 53) thinks that there is insufficient content between Job 9:33 and 1 Tim 2:5 to permit conclusions to be drawn regarding literary links.

61 Hanson, *Epistles*, 68.
62 M. Greenberg, "Job," in *The Literary Guide to the Bible* (eds. Robert Alter and Frank Kermode; London: HarperCollins, 1989), 283-304, 289.
63 Hanson, *Epistles*, 69.
64 Hanson, *Studies*, 63.
65 Hasler, 22.
66 Dibelius-Conzelmann, 42; cf. Oepke, *TDNT* 4:619.
67 See I. H. Marshall, "The Christology of the Pastoral Epistles," *SNTSU* 13 (1988): 157-77.

ideas are also present in Hebrews, which is the only other NT writing to predicate μεσίτης of Christ (Heb 8:6; 9:15; 12:24).[68] Jesus is διαθήκης καινῆς μεσίτης (9:15), not primarily as its communicator, although God spoke supremely through him (1:2; 2:1-5), but rather as the high priest through whose ministry its benefits are realized (8:6; 9:11-28; 12:24). The points of contact are tabulated below:

Concept	1 Tim 2:5-6	Hebrews
Solidarity of Christ with the human beneficiaries of his ministry	ἄνθρωπος (v. 5)	ἐπεὶ οὖν τὰ παιδία κεκοινώνηκεν αἵματος καὶ σαρκός, καὶ αὐτὸς παραπλησίως μετέσχεν τῶν αὐτῶν (2:14) ὅθεν ὤφειλεν κατὰ πάντα τοῖς ἀδελφοῖς ὁμοιωθῆναι (2:17)
Christ's self-giving (to death)	ὁ δοὺς ἑαυτὸν (v. 6)	ἐφάπαξ ἑαυτὸν ἀνενέγκας (7:27) ἑαυτὸν προσήνεγκεν (9:14) cf. διὰ δὲ τοῦ ἰδίου αἵματος (9:12) διὰ δὲ τῆς θυσίας αὐτοῦ (9:26) διὰ τῆς προσφορᾶς τοῦ σώματος Ἰησοῦ Χριστοῦ (10:10)
Ransom/redemption	ἀντίλυτρον (v. 6)	εἰς τὰ ἅγια αἰωνίαν λύτρωσιν εὑράμενος (9:12) θανάτου γενομένου εἰς ἀπολύτρωσιν (9:15)
For/on behalf of all/everyone	ἀντίλυτρον ὑπὲρ πάντων (v. 6)	ὑπὲρ παντὸς γεύσηται θανάτου (2:9)

---

68 To my knowledge the presence of these elements of Mark 10:45 in Hebrews has not been noted in the literature.

The mediator's role in Hebrews includes the priestly tasks of sacrifice and intercession (7:25; 9:24; cf. 6:20). Christ is both priest and sacrifice, who, on the basis of his singular act of atonement, is able to "save" (σῴζω) by his efficacious intercession (7:25), a pattern of substitutionary suffering issuing in effective intercession found in Isaiah 53:12 and 4 Macc 6:27-29.

Without using the term μεσίτης, Paul's presentation in Romans of Christ's role in the provision of salvation exhibits the same elements. The death of Christ is an atoning sacrifice (ἱλαστήριον, 3:25) which has effected redemption (ἀπολύτρωσις, 3:24). The need, and the solution, apply to all (πάντες, 3:23). The representative aspect of Christ's ministry is highlighted in the contrast between Adam and ὁ εἷς ἄνθρωπος Ἰησοῦς Χριστός (5:12-21). Intercession is part of Christ's salvific ministry, and is associated with his death (Χριστὸς Ἰησοῦς ὁ ἀποθανών . . . ὃς καὶ ἐντυγχάνει ὑπὲρ ἡμῶν, 8:34). The sole appearance of μεσίτης in the *Hauptbriefe* (Gal 3:19-20) is in a quite different sense, in an illustration drawn from judicial practice. It is sometimes assumed that Paul is comparing Moses, as mediator of the old covenant, with Christ, mediator of the new.[69] It is not certain, however, that Paul had Moses in mind,[70] and the contrast in Gal 3:15-22 is between the promise and the Law, not Christ and Moses.

The idea of Moses as a mediator between God and the people is present, however, in the Jewish background to the NT. Philo describes Moses as μεσίτης in *Mos.* 2.166, which Fee takes to mean that he " 'mediated' the Law to God's people."[71] In fact the mediatorship works in the opposite direction, Moses approaching God on behalf of the people rather than conveying something from God to them. Finding the people worshipping the golden calf, Moses might have fled from such apostasy, but instead he remained to act as μεσίτης καὶ διαλλακτής ("mediator and reconciler") and ὁ κηδεμὼν καὶ παραιτητής ("protector and intercessor"). His mediatorial activity consisted of intercession on behalf of (ὑπέρ) the nation, "pleading that those who had sinned might be pardoned." Philo does depict Moses elsewhere as an intermediary being between God and humankind, οὔτε ἀγένητος οὔτε γενητὸς ὡς ὑμεῖς ("neither uncreated as God nor created as you"),[72] but when Moses is designated μεσίτης it is in the sense of one who intercedes on behalf of others. The intercession's specific content is significant:

---

69 E.g. Hasler, 21-22.
70 See Bruce, *Galatians*, 178-79.
71 Fee, 65; cf. Mounce, 88.
72 *Her.* 206 (quoted by Dibelius-Conzelmann, 42, n. 44).

he seeks to avert the divine punishment that the people's sin should incur. The account of this sin and Moses' selfless and efficacious intercession is given twice in the Pentateuch (Exod 32; Deut 9:11-21; 25-29) and remembered in Ps 106:23 [LXX 105:23], where Moses "stood in the breach before [God], to turn away his wrath from destroying them." Here, without the term μεσίτης, is the concept of mediatorship. Brevards S. Childs comments on Exodus ch. 32:

> God vows the severest punishment imaginable, but then suddenly he conditions it, as it were, on Moses' agreement. 'Let me alone that I may consume them.' The effect is that God himself leaves the door open for intercession. He allows himself to be persuaded. That is what a mediator is for![73]

Moses' role in this tradition is a priestly one. He approaches the Lord to "make atonement" for the people's sin (ἵνα ἐξιλάσωμαι περὶ τῆς ἁμαρτίας ὑμῶν, Exod 32:30); there is a self-offering, with a hint of substitution, in the request that he himself might be blotted out of God's book if he will not forgive the people (v. 32). It is to describe this function that Philo employs the term μεσίτης in *Mos.* 2:166.

The understanding of mediatorship in 1 Tim 2:5-6 fits readily into this priestly framework observed in Philo and in Hebrews. The mediator, qualified by his solidarity with those for whom he acts (ἄνθρωπος), gives himself (ὁ δοὺς ἑαυτὸν) on behalf of (ὑπέρ) and in the place of (ἀντι-) others, thus providing a ransom (-λυτρον) which affects the relationship between God and people (θεοῦ καὶ ἀνθρώπων). Though Christ's intercession is not specifically mentioned we recall that the material supports the exhortation to intercede for all: since Christ's atoning sacrifice was offered on behalf of all, effectual intercession for all is now possible.[74]

This unit displays twin polemical emphases: Christ alone is able to deal with God on behalf of humankind, and the salvation thereby provided is available to all.[75] The notion of a mediator is consonant

---

73 B. S. Childs, *Exodus* (Old Testament Library; London: SCM, 1974), 567.
74 Cf. Spicq: "il insinue que la prière des disciples (v. 1) s'insère dans l'intercession même du Christ prêtre et victime" (367).
75 M. Goulder goes beyond the internal evidence of the letter to propose a specific polemic: "Jewish Christians thought in terms of a multiplicity of aeons, one of whom had taken possession of Jesus. This was an error. There was only one intermediary who had brought us salvation, and he was human, ἄνθρωπος, the divine Christ-Jesus incarnate." ("The Pastor's Wolves. Jewish Christian Visionaries behind the Pastoral Epistles," *NovT* 37 (1996): 242-56, 252.)

1 Timothy 2:1-7

with the representative functions of the OT priesthood, offering sacrifice to atone for sin and through intercession making forgiveness available to the people. 1 Tim 2:5-6 depicts the soteriological significance of the Christ event in these terms, emphasising the uniqueness, the divine source and universal application of Christ's mediatory ministry.

b. ἀντίλυτρον

As mediator, Christ gave himself ἀντίλυτρον ὑπὲρ πάντων (v. 6), a Hellenized form of the dominical saying in Mark 10:45.[76] There may be more here, however, than stylistic refinement. The substitution of πάντες, whether by the author or his source, may represent an intentional universalising extension of πολλοί,[77] especially if "the many" in Mark 10:45, might have been open to a more exclusive interpretation.[78] In addition, the compound ἀντίλυτρον seems to intensify the idea of representation.[79] The term λύτρον already has substitutionary connonations,[80] and with the addition of ἀντι- Harris sees "notions of exchange and substitution."[81]

In any event the ideas of atoning sacrifice and the intercession for which it provided the basis were already closely linked. In the OT Day of Atonement ritual (Leviticus chs. 16-17) the life given in exchange was an important ground of the priest's plea for forgiveness (e.g. Lev 17:11). The LXX illustrates a converging of the ideas. Ps 105:30 [106:30] represents Phinehas's interceding (Heb. פלל, "to interpose, intercede") by ἐξιλάσκομαι, which usually translates כפר, "to expiate, atone" (83 of 105 occurrences). The climax of the Servant's ministry in Isa 53:12 is in the MT יַפְגִּיעַ וְלַפֹּשְׁעִים ("and made intercession for the transgressors") but in the LXX, καὶ διὰ τὰς ἁμαρτίας αὐτῶν παρεδόθη ("and he was given over [to death] for their sins"). Utilising elements of this idea of

---

[76] "Instead of the Semitic τὴν ψυχὴν αὐτοῦ we have the good Gk. ἑαυτόν; instead of the indefinite πολλῶν the expressly universal (cf. 2:4) πάντων; instead of the simple form the elegant compound." (O. Procksch, F. Büschel, "λύω, κτλ.," *TDNT* 4:328-56, 349) Cf. Oberlinner, *1. Timotheusbrief*, 75-76.

[77] W. Mundle, C. Brown, "λύτρον," *NIDNTT* 3:189-200, 197-98.

[78] Brown compares its use at Qumran to refer to "the elect community" (*NIDNTT* 3:196).

[79] See Oberlinner, *1. Timotheusbrief*, 76; cf. Towner, *Goal*, 85; Mounce, 89-90.

[80] Marshall, 432.

[81] Harris, "Prepositions," 1180; cf. J. R. W. Stott, *The Message of 1 Timothy & Titus* (The Bible Speaks Today; Leicester: IVP, 1996), 70.

vicarious atonement,[82] 4 Maccabees interprets the deaths of the martyrs in substitutionary terms as ransom (ἀντίψυχον, 6:29; 17:21) and atoning sacrifice (ἱλαστήριον, 17:22) on behalf of others (ὑπέρ, 6:28), securing salvation (διασῴζω, 17:22) for the nation of Israel. Eleazar pleads,

> ἴλεως γενοῦ τῷ ἔθνει σου ἀρκεσθεὶς τῇ ἡμετέρᾳ ὑπὲρ αὐτῶν δίκῃ. καθάρσιον αὐτῶν ποίησον τὸ ἐμὸν αἷμα καὶ ἀντίψυχον αὐτῶν λαβὲ τὴν ἐμὴν ψυχήν

> Be merciful to your people and let our punishment suffice for them. Make my blood their purification, and take my life in exchange for theirs.

> (4 Macc 6:28-29)

Similarly in 1 Tim 2:5-6 Christ's mediatorship involves self-giving that is both on behalf of and in the place of all.[83]

5.3.3 The Witness

a. τὸ μαρτύριον

Partly because it "seems to stand without obvious grammatical connection to what has gone before,"[84] the phrase τὸ μαρτύριον καιροῖς ἰδίοις (v. 6b) has been found "enigmatic,"[85] "very obscure,"[86] and even "tellement elliptiques qu'ils en sont presque inintelligibles."[87] If τὸ μαρτύριον is in apposition to the verb διδόναι (v. 6a), the "testimony" becomes Christ's self-giving,[88] as witness to or proof of God's will to save (e.g. NEB; NIV; Knox).[89] On the other hand τὸ μαρτύριον may stand in apposition to Χριστὸς Ἰησοῦς (v. 5), defining not Christ's death but Christ himself. In LXX

---

82 See H. Anderson, "4 Maccabees: A New Translation and Introduction" (*OTP* 2:531-64), who cites *TBenj* 3:8; 1QS 5:6; 8:3-4, 10; 9:4 to illustrate intertestamental developments.
83 Cf. Guthrie, 72.
84 Fee, 66.
85 Kelly, 64.
86 Hanson, *Epistles*, 69.
87 Spicq, 368.
88 So Dibelius-Conzelmann, 42; cf. Brox, 128.
89 According to H. Strathmann, μαρτύριον in non-biblical Greek "denotes the objective witness, the proof, which can be adduced to confirm a statement or fact" ("μάρτυς, κτλ.," *TDNT* 4:474-514, 477). Cf. Barrett, 52; Hanson, *Epistles*, 69; Houlden, 69; Kelly, 64.

Isa 55:4-5 David is μαρτύριον ἐν ἔθνεσιν, serving through God's work in him as "a factual proof of Yahweh's grace and power."[90] In material which exhibits other Isaianic allusions,[91] it is not implausible to see Christ presented in similar terms.[92] Yet another approach is suggested by Strathmann's observation that in the LXX,

> Yahweh Himself is the subject of the μαρτυρεῖν contained in the μαρτύριον. But this μαρτυρεῖν is worked out in the revelation imparted to Moses. The full appropriation of the word μαρτύριον and its plural μαρτύρια for the self-witness of God in the Mosaic legislation is a highly significant process for the development of OT nomism.[93]

Does the author of 1 Timothy conceive of the Christ-event as the new "self-witness of God," superseding the Mosaic Law (cf. 1:8-11)?[94]

Referring back to vv. 5-6, then, τὸ μαρτύριον could be the death of Christ, Christ himself or the self-witness of God in Christ. In such a tightly compacted unit none of these proposals may be excluded solely on syntactical grounds. Nonetheless, a slightly smoother reading is achieved when, rather than identifying it with some element in vv. 5-6a, τὸ μαρτύριον is understood as the testimony to that which is described in these verses (e.g. "this was attested," NRSV). The textual variant οὗ τὸ μαρτύριον καιροῖς ἰδίοις ἐδόθη provides an early illustration of this interpretation.[95] For Oberlinner, τὸ μαρτύριον stands for the totality of statements concerning the concrete historical fulfilling of God's saving purpose in the self-giving of Jesus.[96] This is consistent with other NT passages where τὸ μαρτύριον seems to represent the content of apostolic preaching

---

90 TDNT 4:485. A messianic interpretation is considered possible by J. A. Motyer, *The Prophecy of Isaiah* (Leicester: IVP, 1993), 454-55.
91 Hanson, *Epistles*, 67, suggests that vv. 4-5 originally formed "a sort of Christian midrash on Isa. 45:21-22," in an interpretive tradition which envisaged the conversion of the Gentiles.
92 A similar range of ideas is found in Sir 36:1-22, with concepts of the uniqueness of God (v. 5), the set time (v. 10, though it is here a time of judgment), the witness (v. 20), the prayers of God's people (v. 22a) and the whole earth coming to know God (v. 22b).
93 TDNT 4:486.
94 Hasler is in a shrinking minority in debarring any Judaizing tension from the PE (14). More representative is Roloff: "das atl. Gesetz für das Lehren der Gegner eine besonders hervorgehobene Rolle spielte" (*1.Timotheus*, 71).
95 See Knight, 124; Mounce, 75; Roloff, 123 n. 75. Cf. RSV.
96 Oberlinner, *1.Timotheusbrief*, 76.

(e.g. Acts 4:33, τὸ μαρτύριον . . . τῆς ἀναστάσεως τοῦ κυρίου Ἰησοῦ) or be equivalent to τὸ εὐαγγέλιον (2 Thess 1:8, 10; 2 Tim 1:8, 10-11).[97] With this significance in 1 Tim 2:6b, the thought would flow from the Christ-event (vv. 5-6a) to the testimony about it (v. 6b) to Paul's commissioning as bearer of that witness (v. 7). Picking up the concern for "knowledge of the truth" (v. 4), this gives good sense in this context.

b. καιροῖς ἰδίοις

Still puzzling, however, is the phrase καιροῖς ἰδίοις. Some salvation-historical moment is in view,[98] but what? In 6:15, the same expression refers to the future epiphany of Christ, but in 2:1-7 "the context needs a present witness."[99] If τὸ μαρτύριον were Christ's self-giving, καιροῖς ἰδίοις could characterize it as "a fulfilment of God's promises in God's good time,"[100] but if, as we judged, τὸ μαρτύριον is the message rather than the event, then it is the time of the declaring of the testimony that acquires salvation-historical significance here (cf. Titus 1:3).[101] The point being made is that God has himself set the time in which this witness will take place.[102]

Rarely discussed in this connection is the role of witness in the Synoptic apocalyptic tradition. A turbulent period is envisaged prior to the coming of the Son of Man during which Jesus' followers will stand before kings and authorities, εἰς μαρτύριον τοῖς ἔθνεσιν (Matt 10:18; 24:14; Mark 13:9-10; cf. Luke 21:12-13[103]). This μαρτύριον is a feature of this penultimate era, during which the gospel is to be preached to the nations.[104] Might the author of 1 Timothy understand Paul's preaching to be part of that eschatological witness to the nations? If he was aware of the tradition reflected in the Synoptics it would be difficult to conceive of him not attaching such

---

97 Roloff proposes that μαρτύριον functions in the Deuteropaulines as a technical term for the apostolic preaching (*1.Timotheus*, 123); cf. Marshall, 433.
98 Dibelius-Conzelmann, 43.
99 Mounce, 91; cf. Kelly, 66.
100 Hanson, *Epistles*, 69; cf. Houlden, 69; Kelly, 64.
101 Cf. Marshall, 433.
102 Oberlinner, *1.Timotheusbrief*, 76.
103 On various interpretations of Luke 21:13 see Marshall, *Luke*, 767-68.
104 In Matthew the εἰς μαρτύριον τοῖς ἔθνεσιν motif is referred both to the appearance of the disciples before rulers (10:18) and to the worldwide preaching of the gospel (24:14). On Mark 13:9-10 see C. E. B. Cranfield, *The Gospel According to St. Mark* (3rd impression with additional supplementary notes; CGTC; Cambridge: Cambridge University Press, 1966, 1955), 398.

significance to Paul's mission.¹⁰⁵ In 1 Timothy Paul's preaching is specifically to the Gentiles (2:7) and the author understands himself and his readers to be living in times of a particular salvation-historical significance (ἐν ὑστέροις καιροῖς, 4:1-2) while they await God's determined time for Christ's appearing (6:15). This is in accord with both the time frame and the Gentile emphasis in these Synoptic passages concerning the μαρτύριον.¹⁰⁶ The "kings and all who are in authority" (2:2) also resonate against this background as anticipated hearers of the witness.¹⁰⁷ The Synoptics and 1 Timothy agree that deceivers would also be active in this era of witness (Mark 13:5-6 pars. Matt 24:4-5, Luke 21:8; Mark 13:22 par. Matt 24:11, 23-24; cf. 1 Tim 4:1-3). In this context, the "surprising violence of Paul's protest,"¹⁰⁸ ἀλήθειαν λέγω οὐ ψεύδομαι (v. 7), is perhaps not so out of place.

As with the *Hingabemotiv* discussed earlier, the sharing of apocalyptic elements need not imply any literary relationship between 1 Timothy and the Synoptics. In fact the notion of testimony to the nations preceding the end was already present in Judaism. Isa 43:8-13 envisages the nations gathered for a judicial hearing; God calls his people as witnesses, so that the nations may know that there is only one God (v. 10) and Saviour (v. 11), and that the ends of the earth may turn to him and be saved (v.15, LXX).¹⁰⁹ Perhaps this,

---

105 The author of Acts, who knew both Synoptic and Pauline traditions, describes Paul as chosen to bring the Lord's name ἐνώπιον ἐθνῶν τε καὶ βασιλέων (9:15).

106 Interestingly in 1 Cor 1:6-7, the only reference in the *Hauptbriefe* to the μαρτύριον in the sense of message about Christ (2 Cor 1:12 has "the testimony of our conscience"), it is associated with Gentile fruit and the expectation of Christ's appearing. Cf. 2 Thess 1:10.

107 Cf. 2 Tim 4:16-18.

108 Kelly, 65.

109 On the intra-Jewish debate about whether Gentiles would be saved see, e.g., E. P. Sanders, "The Covenant as a Soteriological Category and the Nature of Salvation in Palestinian and Hellenistic Judaism," in *Jews, Greeks and Christians: Religious Cultures in Late Antiquity* (ed. R. Hamerton-Kelly and R. Scroggs; Leiden: E. J. Brill, 1976), 11-44. NT citations of Isaiah in support of mission to the Gentiles include Matt 12:17-21 (Isa 42:1-2); Luke 3:4-6 (Isa 40:3-5); Acts 13:47; 26:23 (Isa 49:6); Rom 10:20 (Isa 65:1); 15:12 (Isa 11:10). At certain points LXX Isaiah seems more open than the MT to the possibility of Gentiles being saved. In, e.g., 41:1, the MT commands the אִיִּים, "islands," הַחֲרִישׁוּ אֵלַי, "keep silence before me," like the guilty before a judge. The LXX, however, has, ἐγκαινίζεσθε πρός με, νῆσοι, a call to dedicate themselves to God, or possibly be renewed towards him. This appeal recurs in LXX 45:15-16, with no MT source, where the nations acknowledge Israel's God to be the only God. In place of the MT's אַתָּה אֵל מִסְתַּתֵּר, "You are a

rather than the Davidic μαρτύριον in 55:4-5, is the most illuminating Isaianic background to 1 Tim 2:6b.

5.4 Summary

The peaceful life for which prayer is offered in this passage is not the content of salvation but an environment in which salvation may be extended to people through their hearing and coming to acknowledge the message about Christ. A universalising tendency is apparent in the insistence that God's will to save and Christ's self-giving are directed towards all, strengthened, perhaps intentionally, by the phrasing of the *Hingabemotiv*. Christ's role in the provision of salvation is mediatorial, carrying OT priestly and sacrificial overtones. Again the missionary activity of bearing testimony is of vital importance in making salvation available, and within a salvation-historical framework, the present age is the time of the eschatological witness to the nations which constitutes Paul's calling.

God who hides himself," the LXX has the Gentiles confess, σὺ γὰρ εἶ θεός καὶ οὐκ ᾔδειμεν. Does this plea of ignorance mitigate their former failure to recognize him (cf. 1 Tim 1:13)?

Chapter 6

1 Timothy 2:15

σωθήσεται δὲ διὰ τῆς τεκνογονίας, ἐὰν μείνωσιν ἐν πίστει καὶ ἀγάπῃ καὶ ἁγιασμῷ μετὰ σωφροσύνης

As Houlden wryly comments, "There are obscurities here."[1] This is nonetheless one of the four occurrences of the verb σῴζω in 1 Timothy and we must ask whether it has anything to contribute to an understanding of the concept of salvation in this letter. To discover what sort of content the reference to being "saved" might bear we must first explore the way the argument develops in the unit within which the statement appears, and what function it serves.

6.1 Context

6.1.1 The Argument: Conduct in the Christian Assembly (2:8-15)

The statement about being saved concludes a series of gender-specific instructions on behaviour in the Christian assembly (2:8-12) which are supported by apparently theological considerations (2:13-14). Whatever the saving in v. 15 is, it must relate in some way to

---

1 Houlden, 77; cf. Spicq, 383. Guthrie reckons it "among the most difficult expressions in the whole of the Pastorals" (77). Many discussions of the letter's soteriology omit this passage, preferring to derive their conclusions from less obscure material (e.g. Towner, *Goal*, 75-119; A. Y.-Y. Lau, *Manifest in Flesh: the Epiphany Christology of the Pastoral Epistles* (WUNT 2.86; Tübingen: J. C. B. Mohr, 1996), 272-77). The debate over women's roles in the Church continues to generate a vast literature on this passage (see recent bibliography in Mounce, 94-102). The focus of this study, however, is on what notion of salvation might lie behind the statement in v. 15. On soteriological questions see, e.g., van der Jagt, "Saved through Bearing Children"; A. J. Köstenberger, "Ascertaining Women's God-Ordained Roles: An Interpretation of 1 Timothy 2:15," *BBR* 7 (1997): 107-44; A. J. Köstenberger, T. R. Schreiner and H. S. Baldwin (eds.), *Women in the Church: A Fresh Analysis of 1 Timothy 2:9-15* (Grand Rapids: Baker, 1995); P. B. Payne, "Libertarian Women in Ephesus: A Response to Douglas J. Moo's Article, '1 Tim 2:11-15: Meaning and Significance'," *TJ* 2 (1981): 177-8; Porter, "Saved by Childbirth".

this material, either backing up the instructions or developing the theological argument. The instructions and their rationale form part of a larger unit which begins with the injunction to pray for all, so that a peaceable and godly life would become possible (vv. 1-2). Attention then turns to conduct in the Christian assembly (vv. 8-12), and it transpires that this peaceable and godly ideal of ἡσυχία with εὐσέβεια also applies to public worship. For men, it is expressed in how they pray, exhibiting the positive quality of purity of life and deed (ὅσιοι χεῖραι) and avoiding the negative characteristics of anger and arguing (χωρὶς ὀργῆς καὶ διαλογισμοῦ, v. 8). For women there are also positive goals, lives adorned with good deeds (vv. 9-10) and learning in a quiet and submissive manner (vv. 11-12), and a negatively coloured activity to avoid (διδάσκειν δὲ γυναικὶ οὐκ ἐπιτρέπω οὐδὲ αὐθεντεῖν ἀνδρός, v. 12), which represents non-ἡσυχία in contrast to the ἡσυχία expressed in learning submissively. It is not necessary here to enter the debate over precisely what women are not to do.[2] It is sufficient to note that a restriction is imposed on women's teaching,[3] and that whatever αὐθεντεῖν represents it would certainly be contrary to this peaceable and submissive attitude. The instruction is followed by two observations from the Genesis story of Creation and the Fall: Adam was created first (v. 13) and Eve, not Adam, was deceived (v. 14). The author seems to intend the practical implications that women should show due respect for men (or their husbands) and not usurp their place, and specifically that, humbly recognising the danger of their being deceived, they should not take it upon themselves to teach.

6.1.2 The Letter as a Whole: Women and Deception

Deception is a major theme in 1 Timothy (1:3-4, 6, 19-20; 2:7, 14; 4:1-

---

[2] For contrasting views see D. J. Moo, "What Does It Mean Not to Teach or Have Authority Over Men? 1 Timothy 2.11-15" in *Recovering Biblical Manhood & Womanhood: A Response to Evangelical Feminism* (ed. J. Piper and W. Grudem, Wheaton: Crossway, 1991), 179-93, and Kroeger and Kroeger, *Suffer Not a Woman*.

[3] This assumes that the dative γυναικί is the subject and not the indirect object of the verb διδασκεῖν. If αὐθεντεῖν ἀνδρός were taken to specify the teaching content and οὐδέ read as a redundant negative (noted as a possibility by Kroeger and Kroeger, *Suffer Not a Woman*, 37), it would be a prohibition (following "let a woman learn") on teaching a woman to usurp her husband's place. This would, however, be very awkward grammatically.

3, 7; 5:11-13, 15; 6:3-5, 9-10, 17, 20-21).[4] The declared occasion of the letter is a problem of false teaching in the church (1:3-7) which derives ultimately from "deceitful spirits and demons" active in these "last days" (4:1). Furthermore, there are indications of particular difficulties with respect to women, especially some younger widows. In ch. 2 instructions regarding women receive five times as much space as the exhortation to men, and in ch. 5 although the whole area of providentia for widows requires attention,[5] the younger widows give the author particular anxiety (5:11-15). In 2 Timothy these two problem areas combine, again in the "last days" environment, when false teachers influence certain women (2 Tim 3:6-7). It is not unreasonable to read 1 Tim 2:9-15 against the general background of deceiving teachers to whom some women are especially vulnerable.

6.1.3 The Immediate Context: Argument from Adam and Eve (2:13-15)

As Hanson points out, "We have here a treatment by the author of the Pastorals of a piece of *Haggada*."[6] The author is not, then, generating new material but is engaging with an interpretive tradition with which he and, presumably, those with whom he is in dispute are familiar. Houlden notes that this is the PEs' only venture into "the world of Jewish speculative theology."[7] This might suggest that it is not the author's preferred medium in these letters, and that he enters it to answer his opponents.[8] It is the more necessary therefore to take account of other voices in the discussion; we may not be able to hear them distinctly, but at least we must be aware that the author's statements will make most sense not as free-standing declarations of his creed but as one side of an engagement with other positions.

A second observation is that the transition to the final clause in v. 15b is awkward, shifting from a singular to a plural subject. J. D.

---

4   For Fee, reading 1 Timothy against a background of deception within the church "makes sense of every detail of the letter" (7).
5   See B. W. Winter, "Providentia for the widows in 1 Tim 5:3-16," *TynBul* 39 (1988): 83-100.
6   Hanson, *Epistles*, 72. See also his enquiry into the Jewish tradition of Eve's seduction by the serpent in "Eve's Transgression: 1 Timothy 2.13-15," *Studies*, 65-77.
7   Houlden, 71.
8   C. S. Keener's comment on 1 Corinthians 11:2-16 is apposite: "In ancient rhetoric, one's arguments for a position need not be the same as the reasons for which one actually held the position." ("Man and Woman," *DPL*, 583-92, 585.)

Miller suggests that, "15a and 15b have been combined from two different sources, thus resulting in the bizarre grammatical construction."[9] Miller explains the PE as compilations of disparate materials without clear design or significant progression of thought. Given the recognition of purpose and sustained argumentation in the structure of these letters,[10] Miller's general thesis is scarcely tenable, but perhaps in this instance there are grounds for detecting the joining of once separate materials.

Bringing these two observations together, could it be that, having been drawn onto a battleground favoured by his opponents, the author has contrived to bring the discussion round to a point where he can affirm his own understanding of the way of salvation, perhaps with the citation of a formula which sits more comfortably with his own theological outlook?

6.2 Issues and Approaches

6.2.1 Issues of Interpretation

Each element of the statement about being saved raises interpretive questions. First, what content should be allowed to the verb σωθήσεται? Is it final, eschatological salvation,[11] this-worldly preserving,[12] or deliverance from the sort of behaviour that is proscribed in v. 12?[13] And what is ἡ τεκνογονία? Is it an activity of the woman who is to be saved, bearing or rearing children or by extension fulfilling domestic duties, or does it refer to a particular child-bearing, whether of Eve or of Mary, or allude to the one born of Mary, the Messiah? Then there is the key question of how this τεκνογονία is related to the saving outcome,[14] for which the force of διά (instrumental or temporal) is critical. The significance of the second subordinate clause, ἐὰν μείνωσιν ἐν πίστει καὶ ἀγάπῃ καὶ ἁγιασμῷ μετὰ σωφροσύνης, must also be estimated. Does the ἐάν indicate that the saving is conditional upon what follows or that these things accompany salvation? Do these qualities represent

---

9   Miller, *Composite Documents*, 73. Hanson posits another source document, following H.-W. Bartsch, *Die Anfänge urchristlicher Rechtsbildugen* (Hamburg: Reich, 1965), 73 (*Epistles*, 74). Barrett explains it simply as a lapse (57).
10 See above, pp. 11-14.
11 E.g. Oberlinner, *1.Timotheus*, 103-04; Fee, 75.
12 As in Moffatt's translation, "woman will get safely through childbirth"; cf. Barrett, 56-57.
13 S. Jebb, "A Suggested Interpretation of 1 Tim 2:15," *ExpTim* 81 (1969): 221-22.
14 See Oberlinner, *1.Timotheusbrief*, 100-04.

1 Timothy 2:15

Christian character in general or is this a virtuous ideal particularly appropriate to women?

Crucial to the understanding of the statement in v. 15 is deciding who the author is talking about. Who are the subjects of the verbs σωθήσεται (3rd person singular passive) and μείνωσιν (3rd person plural active)?

6.2.2 Proposed Solutions

Varying judgements on these interconnected issues produce a range of soteriological explanations.[15] Some wish to take seriously both the eschatological content of σωθῆναι and τεκνογονία as something women do. So Porter has to conclude, "for the woman who abides in faith, love and holiness, her salvation will come by the bearing of children."[16] Oberlinner (following Brox) discerns a theology of creation in which the creation order serves also as the salvation order.[17] Since within this creation order the woman fulfils the will of God by bearing children, this becomes for her the way of salvation.[18] Marshall interprets it as a commendation of motherhood more generally, in a polemical context:

> Women who bore children were fulfilling a God-ordained task that would lead to eternal life, just as much as those believers who taught and did other apparently more 'spiritual' tasks.[19]

For interpreters who wish to affirm the Pauline character of the thought of the PE, to make eschatological salvation "conditional upon a work," whether bearing or raising children, is problematic. As Waters remarks, "It is . . . highly unlikely that the author of this epistle would depart so greatly from typical Pauline thought that he would suggest that literal childbirth is somehow important for the salvation of women.[20] Solutions have been sought in different interpretations either of the saving or of τεκνογονία. Barrett, e.g., inclines to view "saving" as safekeeping through childbirth, carrying

---

15 See surveys and categorisation of possibilities in Knight, 144-46; Marshall, 467-70.
16 Porter, "Saved by Childbirth", 102.
17 Oberlinner, 1.Timotheusbrief, 103-04, citing Brox: "Die Dinge dieser Welt, die Ordnungen der Schöpfung haben unmittelbar mit dem Heil zu tun." (138).
18 Oberlinner, 1.Timotheusbrief, 104.
19 Marshall, "Salvation in the Pastoral Epistles", 462.
20 K. L. Waters Sr, "Saved through Childbearing: Virtues as Children in 1 Timothy 2:11-15." JBL 123 (2004): 703-35, 735. Guthrie also protest that, "it is inconceivable that Paul meant this" (78); cf. Knight, 145.

religious significance as a reversal of the curse of Gen 3:16.[21] Retaining eschatological salvation, Ellicott understands the childbearing as a reference to the birth of the Messiah, persuaded that, "the Apostle, in speaking of women's transgression, would not fail to specify the sustaining prophecy which even preceded her sentence."[22] Waters, finding in Plato and elsewhere the notion of the human soul giving birth to virtues, proposes that the childbearing be understood metaphorically as the production of the four virtues of faith, love, holiness and temperance.[23] With such a range of interpretations, depending upon differing assumptions about the general purpose and character of the letter, it is the more necessary to explore the literary context of the statement in search of clues to the nature of the conversation of which this passage is part. With whom might the author be in dialogue, and what sort of debate could provoke this rare venture into *haggada* on Gen 2-3?

6.2.3 Back to the Background: Hearing the Other Voices

Hanson has gathered Jewish and early Christian examples of treatments of Eve's deception by the serpent and the ensuing curse. He proposes that the author of 1 Timothy simply adopted a commonly held perception of Eve's temptation as a seduction with sexual overtones, and drew conclusions about women, men and the possibility of rehabilitation for women through fulfilling the duties of a wife and mother.[24] The purpose would be to reinforce traditional domestic roles in reaction against the opponents' devaluing of them (e.g. 4:3, and the idle widows in 5:13). This concurs with the advice to younger widows, which esteems marriage, procreation and motherhood (5:14).

This may not, however, be the whole explanation. The Kroegers offer examples of versions of the story of Eve that disagree markedly from that in 1 Timothy.[25] Specifically, they cite Gnostic claims that

---

21 Barrett, 56-7. Cf. R. W. Pierce, "Evangelicals and Gender Roles in the 1990s: 1 Timothy 2:8-15: A Test Case," *JETS* 36 (1993): 343-56, especially 351; C. S. Keener, *Paul, Women & Wives: Marriage and Women's Ministry in the Letters of Paul* (Peabody, Mass.: Hendrickson, 1992), 118-19.
22 C. J. Ellicott, *The Pastoral Epistles* (London: Parker & Son, 1866; repr., Eugene Oreg.: Wipf and Stock, 1998), 37. Cf. more recently Knight, 146; Stott, *1 Timothy & Titus*, 87.
23 Waters, "Virtues as Children", 703-35 (especially 716-22, 734-35).
24 Hanson, *Epistles*, 72-74; also "Eve's Transgression: 1 Timothy 2.13-15," in *Studies*, 65-77.
25 Kroeger and Kroeger, *Suffer Not a Woman*, Part 3: "The Prohibition's Rationale (1 Tim.2:13-15)," 117-77, and Appendix 7: "Alternate Versions of

Eve, "the mother of all living," pre-existed Adam and was the source of his spiritual life, and that Adam had been deceived into believing that he had been created first by the true God, whereas in fact he was the creation of a lower power.[26] If the false teachings troubling the author included such notions, it would make good sense to see in vv. 13-14 "a refutation of a widespread heresy."[27] The feasibility of such a background has been questioned on the grounds that the evidence cited post-dates the PE,[28] but the ideas may well have been current earlier.[29] According to Sterling, "there is a growing consensus that Gnosticism drew on Jewish exegetical traditions for the development of its anthropology."[30] His study of Paul's Corinthian opponents, who have been compared on other grounds to those in the PE,[31] discovers an understanding of creation traditions that "is not Gnostic but represents a religious position which naturally led to Gnosticism."[32] More seriously for the Kroegers' position, it is not clear that all the evidence cited actually does indicate the specific ideas that they claim to find.[33] At the least, however, they do succeed in illustrating that versions of the Adam and Eve stories had a place in certain heterodox systems.

One aspect of the opponents' teaching in relation to women about which there is no doubt is the negative view of marriage (4:1; cf. 5:11-15). To require abstinence from marriage could indicate disapproval not only of sexual intercourse but even of femaleness *per se*. This tendency is found in, e.g., Sir 25:24: "From a woman sin

---

the Creation Story," 215-22.
26 Kroeger and Kroeger, *Suffer Not a Woman*, 117-25, 215-22, citing the Nag Hammadi Tractates, *Hyp. Arch., Orig. World* and *Ap. John*; the beliefs of the Peratae in Hippolytus, *Haer.* 16.6.12-13; and Irenaeus, *Haer.* 1.30.7.
27 Kroeger and Kroeger, *Suffer Not a Woman*, 117.
28 E.g. Mounce, 140-41.
29 See e.g. Goulder, "Wolves." Stating that, "A Jewish root to Gnosticism is now widely conceded" (247 n. 19, with references), he finds in the PE a response to a "proto-gnostic myth which seems similar to the first part of the Barbeliot myth" (256).
30 G. E. Sterling, "'Wisdom among the Perfect': Creation Traditions in Alexandrian Judaism and Corinthian Christianity," *NovT* 37 (1995): 355-84, 384 (references in n. 102).
31 Cf. P. H. Towner, "Gnosis and Realized Eschatology in Ephesus (of the Pastoral Epistles) and the Corinthian Enthusiasm." *JSNT* 31 (1987): 95-124; also *Goal*, 28-45.
32 Sterling, "Wisdom," 384.
33 Irenaeus, *Haer.* 1.30.7, for example, does not require the priority of Eve in creation.

had its beginning, and because of her we all die."³⁴ The Gospel of Thomas witnesses to a strand of early Christianity that considered females ineligible for eschatological salvation:

> Simon Peter said to them: Let Mary go forth from among us, for women are not worthy of the life. Jesus said: Behold, I shall lead her, that I may make her male, in order that she also may become a living spirit like you males. For every woman who makes herself male shall enter into the kingdom of heaven.
>
> (Gos. Thom. 114)

The Kroegers provide further examples of the denigration of women in general and childbearing in particular in Gnostic texts, noting the incongruity of denigrating actual women while exalting the feminine principle.³⁵

We know, then, that among the voices in the conversation to which our text bears witness were some which disapproved of marriage and procreation. Given the general environment sketched it is not inconceivable that some were teaching that these states disqualified women from salvation. The possibility has also been raised of the presence of proto-gnostic ideas, which could include alternative versions of the Biblical account of the creation and fall. While any attempt to reconstruct the actual or even a fictive situation addressed in 1 Tim 2:12-15 must be treated with caution, the argument would make sense in relation to a hypothetical background including both misogynist attitudes and heterodox teaching concerning Eve, Adam and the Fall.

6.2.4 The Author's Strategy

We have noted that the salvation material occurs in the context of instructions concerning conduct in the Christian assembly and specifically with regard to women. He wants the assembly to be characterized by ἡσυχία, or peaceableness, with connotations of reverent receptivity to God and his word. That which militates against such ἡσυχία, namely hostility and argumentativeness on the part of the men (v. 8) and ostentation and aggressive arrogation to themselves of a teaching role (perhaps in particular of wives over their husbands) on the part of the women (vv. 9-11), is decried. It is

---

34 See J. Levison, "Is Eve to Blame? A Contextual Analysis of Sirach 25:24," CBQ 47 (1985): 617-23.
35 Kroeger and Kroeger, *Suffer Not a Woman*, 172-76 (and see footnotes on p. 238).

in support of these instructions that the statement about Eve, Adam and being saved is made (vv. 13-15). The answer to the question "Why did Paul mention Eve's Deception?"[36] must therefore be sought in this context.

It should be observed first that the author mentions Eve in order to make points about the women in the church; he intends them to understand that what he says about Eve has implications for them. There is therefore a split focus, and at any given point it must be judged how much it is Eve and how much the church women who are in the frame. This shifting focus can be illustrated by looking for the subject in each of the four parts of the statement. First it is Eve (v. 13), then ἡ γυνή (v. 14), then "she," the indeterminate singular subject of σωθήσεται (v. 15a), and finally "they," the plural subject of μείνωσιν (v. 15b). Eve dominates the first frame (v. 13); she is still prominent in the second, but the church women have also come into view (v. 14); by the third, the women in the author's audience know that it is their salvation that is being discussed, though still in terms of the Genesis story (v. 15a); and by the final frame the focus has shifted fully to the women (v. 15b).

When this sequence is superimposed upon a background that possibly includes both proto-gnostic readings of the creation account and negative attitudes towards marriage and procreation, a picture emerges of the sort of engagement within which that part of the conversation that we hear might make sense. It might have gone as follows:

Author	I am not allowing women to push themselves forward into a teaching role; I want them to exhibit a peaceable, reverent attitude.
Opponent	But it is woman who is the source of enlightenment. Do you not know that Eve is the first-created, the mother of all living?
Author	Absolutely not! Go to the Scriptures and you'll see that Adam was created first, then Eve - so, incidentally, you women should show some humility.
Opponent	Ah, but Adam was duped into believing that he had been created first! He blundered on in his ignorance, while Eve, on the other hand, was enlightened by the

---

36 Against Barnet's more general application, T. J. Harris relates the instructions to a particular historical situation in, "Why did Paul mention Eve's Deception? A Critique of P. W. Barnet's Interpretation of 1 Timothy 2," *EvQ* 62 (1990): 335-52.

	serpent and awakened to true spiritual life.
Author	You see how those deceiving spirits pervert the truth! No, it was the woman who was deceived, as is proved by the consequence - she fell into sin. And that, I fear, is what is happening among you. Women are being deceived by promulgators of these worthless myths and led into sin.
(Male!) voice from the congregation	
	Well, that's women for you. They're not fit for salvation, they're under the curse.
Opponent	There is certainly no salvation for those who indulge their feminine weakness and choose the way of animal passion and the abhorrent function of giving birth to children. To have any chance of escape from that earth-bound existence into true spiritual life they must renounce such practices.
Author	You are both mistaken. There <u>is</u> provision of salvation for the woman – it is there in our text in Genesis. Even before the curse the promise was given that the woman's seed would crush the serpent's head. So her salvation - and not only hers but that of the whole world - has come ultimately through this childbearing that you consider accursed, when God sent his Son, born of a woman, to defeat the great serpent and deceiver, Satan. Therefore, women, do not despise childbearing, for it is a divinely appointed role, and God worked through it to bring salvation. But let's not forget how salvation is to be attained. Those will be saved, as the Faithful Word says, "who continue in faith, love and holiness" - to which I might add, in the light of what we have been discussing, "with propriety"!

Fanciful though this reconstruction is, it does illustrate the serious point that the author would have been in dialogue with other positions, possibly at variance with each other. It will have been observed that the reconstruction involved a number of exegetical decisions. These may now be set out.

6.3 The Statement in its Context

6.3.1 σωθήσεται

a. Meaning

A number of considerations support the attribution of full theological weight to the verb σωθῆναι. It carries the sense of ultimate salvation in its earlier appearances in the letter (1:15; 2:4). The conditional clause ἐὰν μείνωσιν ἐν πίστει καὶ ἀγάπῃ καὶ ἁγιασμῷ μετὰ σωφροσύνης lists qualities that elsewhere accompany the receiving of final salvation (e.g. πίστις καὶ ἀγάπη, 1:14). The indicator πιστὸς ὁ λόγος (3:1) has been taken to refer either backwards or forwards.[37] If the former is correct, it would strengthen the suggestion that each of the πιστοὶ λογοί has to do with salvation.[38]

b. Subject

As detailed above, our reading allows a double focus to the verb. The author finds indication of saving for Eve within the Genesis account, but as his practical concern is the salvation of the Christian women in the church, it is both Eve and the women concerning whom the Eve story enables him to speak that are in view as subject.

6.3.2 διὰ τῆς τεκνογονίας

a. The Sense in Which διά is Used

The meaning we have taken for σωθῆναι requires an instrumental use of διά. Although διά + gen. could technically carry a temporal sense there would usually be some clear time reference (e.g. δι᾽ ἡμερῶν τεσσεράκοντα, Acts 1:3)[39]. Exceptions are possible (as perhaps in 1 Cor 3:15, σωθήσεται, οὕτως δὲ ὡς διὰ πυρός), but in the overwhelming majority of its occurrences with σῴζω in both the LXX and the NT, διά indicates instrumentality or efficient cause.[40]

---

37 The discussion continues on this issue: see, e.g., Knight, 152-53; Campbell, "Faithful Sayings".
38 See Young, *Theology*, 56-57.
39 See Porter, "Saved by Childbirth", 169-70.
40 See in the LXX: 4 Kgdms 14:27; Ps 33:16; Wis 10:4; 16:7; Isa 14:32; 63:9; in the NT: John 3:17; Acts 15:11; Rom 5:9; 1 Cor 1:21; 15:2; Eph 2:8; Titus 3:5; 1 Pet 3:21.

b. The Reference of τεκνογονία

If the author has embarked upon a debate on the significance of Genesis 2-3 for the women he is addressing, it would not be unreasonable that the next step in his argument should also refer to that OT text. There are two possible referents, the seed that shall bruise the serpent's head (Gen 3:15) and the giving birth in pain (Gen 3:16). The term τεκνογονία is rare, a NT hapax, and 1 Timothy also provides the only NT occurrence of its verbal form (τεκνογονεῖν, 5:14). The LXX has neither and there is no direct verbal association with Genesis 3 (v. 15 has σπέρμα; v. 16, τεκνεῖν τέκνα).

The concept could, however, encompass both aspects. For Eve, the arena in which the effects of the Fall are felt (v. 16) becomes at the same time the focus of hope and promise (v. 15), as she looks through the pain of childbirth to the ultimate defeat of the serpent through her offspring. For the author such a notion could have both salvation-historical and practical implications. We have already noticed elements of a salvation-historical schema,[41] and although it is not explicit, nor is it impossible that in the reference to the τεκνογονία the author was alluding to the beginning of the process by which eventually Christ ἐφανερώθη ἐν σαρκί (3:16). This is not quite the same as referring it to the bearing of Jesus by Mary, to which Guthrie objects that, "if that were the writer's intention he could hardly have chosen a more obscure or ambiguous way of saying it."[42] It is rather to Eve's childbearing, but looking on to its far-off consequence in the birth of the Messiah.

Although this salvation-historical framework would not sit easily with the "creation theology" that Brox and Oberlinner claim to find,[43] the value placed on the activity of childbearing for Eve gives illustrative (rather than deductive) support for the author's insistence, against teaching to the contrary, that motherhood has its place within the sphere of salvation. To that extent those who read the unit as an exhortation to Christian women to work out their salvation in domestic life have grasped something of the author's

---

41 On the καιροὶ ἴδιοι see above on 1 Tim 2:6 (pp. 66-68).
42 Guthrie, 78; cf. Marshall, 469. Davies, 21, would have expected the name, Christ Jesus, to appear if the reference were to his birth.
43 See p. 73 and n. 17. Oberlinner's restriction of the key issues to the verb σωθήσεται and its relation to διὰ τῆς τεκνογονίας relegates the final conditional clause ἐὰν μείνωσιν. . . σωφροσύνης to a supplementary role and compels him to find the major soteriological significance in the relationship between saving and childbearing (*1.Timotheus*, 102-04). The approach taken here reverses that weighting.

practical intention. This, however, is a practical implication of what is said about Eve, not a condition of salvation for women generally or Christian women specifically. That would indeed be, in Michel's widely quoted phrase, "in einer urchristlichen Schrift fast unerträglich."[44]

6.3.3 ἐὰν μείνωσιν ἐν πίστει καὶ ἀγάπῃ καὶ ἁγιασμῷ μετὰ σωφροσύνῃ

a. The Shift from Singular to Plural Subject

The suggested reconstruction of the author's "dialogue" construed the change from singular to plural subject as an indication that the author has moved from a discussion of Eve with implied reference to the women of the church to a final statement which has these women in clear focus.[45] It is also possible that the author is weaving into his text a piece of pre-formed material which already had the plural subject. We have suggested that the Genesis debate might have been initiated not by the author but by the opponents, and that he enters the field not to pitch camp but to deal with insurrectionists who want to use (or, to his mind, misuse) this Biblical material as ammunition. On this reading it is in v. 15b, as he leaves that battlefield, that the author is finally able to choose his ground and establish his own position. This final clause, then, is not merely a rider to the substantive statement but is itself the primary salvation statement.

b. The Force of ἐάν

The conjunction ἐάν with the subjunctive normally introduces the protasis of a conditional statement. Here, with a future passive verb in the apodosis, we have a straightforward condition for salvation (allowing for the shift in subject): those who continue in faith and love and holiness with propriety will be saved.

c. The Subjects of μείνωσιν

Although it has been proposed that it is husband and wife,[46] or even

---

44 Quoted by Roloff, 140; Oberlinner, 1.Timotheusbrief, 101; and Merkel, 28, from O. Michel, "Grundfragen der Pastoralbriefe," in *Auf dem Grunde der Apostel und Propheten* (ed. M. Loeser; Stuttgart: Quell, 1948), 83-99, 93.
45 cf. Roloff, 141; Oberlinner, 1.Timotheusbrief, 101.
46 Brox, 137.

the children,⁴⁷ who are to remain in faith, etc., the context does not require any other subject than the women who have been in view from the beginning of the discussion of women's behaviour and salvation (v. 9). The conditions for the attaining of salvation that are set out in this statement could of course apply more widely, and it may be that a general statement about salvation has been pressed into service to make the point here, but in this context the women in the church remain the primary subjects.

d. ἐν πίστει καὶ ἀγάπῃ καὶ ἁγιασμῷ

If childbearing is the condition for salvation then this string of terms must supplement or otherwise qualify that condition. Thus Fee, having stretched the reference to τεκνογονία to represent "being a model, godly woman,"⁴⁸ continues,

> But Paul could never leave the matter there, as though salvation itself were attained by this 'good deed', so he immediately qualifies, 'Provided of course that she is already a truly Christian woman,' that is, a woman who *continues in faith, love and holiness*.⁴⁹

If, however, this final clause is itself the condition for being saved, then what is affirmed is that salvation is attained by continuing in faith and in the love and holiness which characterize the saved life. This is consonant with the illustration of salvation in the portrait of Paul, the saved sinner (1:12-16). There also, faith and love are in evidence (1:14) and faith in Christ is the means of entry into the life of the saved (1:16). The three terms πίστις, ἀγάπη and ἁγιασμός are grouped by two copulatives to form one expression. This, together with the absence of either a specific objective referent or the definite article, suggests that in this instance the emphasis lies on faith as an activity.

e. The Contribution of σωφροσύνη

The term σωφροσύνη denotes self-control or restraint (quite the opposite of ὕβρις; cf. Paul as ὑβριστής in 1:13), and especially in relation to feminine virtue, decency.⁵⁰ Two of the three NT occurrences are in this passage, in vv. 9 and 15, forming an inclusio and bringing the thought back to its starting point, the demeanour of

---

47 E.g. Houlden, 72-73.
48 Fee, 75.
49 Fee, 76.
50 BAGD, 802.

Christian women. This lends support to our reconstruction of the flow of thought, reinforcing the judgment that the initial subject (the women in the church, v. 9) is again in view at the end.[51]

f. The Verb μένω

The content of the term μένω ("remain," "continue in") is appropriate to the concern in 1 Timothy about the danger of falling away from the faith.[52] Clearly, in agreement with the dominical saying in the Synoptics that, ὁ δὲ ὑπομείνας εἰς τέλος, οὗτος σωθήσεται (Matt 10:22; 24:13; Mark 13:13),[53] salvation is yet to be fully attained. The combination of the –μενω compound with the future passive σωθήσεται might suggest a verbal link with the tradition. Equally suggestive, however, are the particular associations of the simple verb μένω in the NT.

Although use of the term in its general sense is distributed fairly widely through the NT, it is almost exclusively in the Johannine writings that μένω is used of "remaining" in someone or something that relates to faith and salvation. In John, believers remain in Jesus (6:56; 15:4 (2x), 5, 6, 7), in Jesus' love (15:9, 10) and in Jesus' word (8:31). In 1 John they remain in the Son (2:6, 24 (with the Father), 27, 28; 3:6, 24; 4:13), in God (4:15, 16), in the light (2:10) and in love (4:16). 2 John speaks of remaining in the teaching of Christ (v. 19 (2x)).[54] The concept of continuing in the faith, etc. is present elsewhere (e.g 1 Cor 15:2; Col 1:23), but the only uses of μένω in this sense outside the Johannine literature are in 1 Tim 2:15 and 2 Tim 3:14, μένε ἐν οἷς ἔμαθες καὶ ἐπιστώθης. This prompts the question whether the PE have utilized materials that have some affinity with the canonical Johannine writings. If 1 Tim 2:15 is correctly identified as one of the πιστοὶ λόγοι,[55] does this group of sayings in particular exhibit Johannine characteristics? Although it unfortunately lies beyond the scope of the present study, this is an intriguing question that might merit investigation.

---

51 Cf. J. M. Bassler, *1 Timothy, 2 Timothy, Titus* (ANTC; Nashville: Abingdon, 1996), 61.
52 See e.g. 1:5-6, 19; 4:1; 6:10, 21; also comments on 1 Tim 1:12-16 above (pp. 49-50).
53 Luke has ἐν τῆς ὑπομονῆς ὑμῶν κτήσασθε τὰς ψυχὰς ὑμῶν (21:19).
54 Cf. the many Johannine examples of Jesus or Jesus' love, word, etc. remaining in people.
55 See p. 79 and n. 37.

6.4 Summary

It emerges that this puzzling statement in 2:15 is indeed a declaration by the author of the way of salvation as he understands it: salvation is received through faith that perseveres and shows itself in love and holiness. In the course of a haggadic excursion in support of paraenesis to Christian women, the salvation now claimed for the Christian community is traced back to the beginning of the human story and the promise in Gen 3:15 that the seed of the woman would bruise the serpent's head. Eve's childbearing therefore contributes to the history of salvation. This has the practical effect of affirming motherhood as a sphere within which salvation may be realized, countering tendencies to exclude women from salvation. The "faithful word," which may have a Johannine flavour, recalls listeners from the enticing notions of false teachers to the trustworthy way of salvation.

CHAPTER 7

1 Timothy 4:10

εἰς τοῦτο γὰρ κοπιῶμεν καὶ ἀγωνιζόμεθα, ὅτι ἠλπίκαμεν ἐπὶ θεῷ ζῶντι, ὅς ἐστιν σωτὴρ πάντων ἀνθρώπων μάλιστα πιστῶν.

In 4:10 the striking but enigmatic claim is made that, θεὸς ζῶν ἐστιν σωτὴρ πάντων ἀνθρώπων μάλιστα πιστῶν. In what sense is God "saviour of all people"? How is this concept qualified by the clause, "especially of believers"? Does it restrict God's role as saviour to a specific group or does it extend the function to include additional benefits for those so designated? The soteriological outlook must be explored in the light of possible backgrounds, grammatical considerations and the rhetorical function of the statement in this context.

7.1 Context

4:1 is often viewed as the start of a major division of the letter,[1] with 3:16 either concluding the preceding section or constituting a "brief digression."[2] On the other hand, the δέ of 4:1 could suggest that the thought continues from the previous verse.[3] Lau's careful study of the function of the *Christushymnus* in its context concludes that it connects significantly with both preceding and ensuing units, defining τὸ τῆς εὐσεβείας μυστήριον (3:16a) and serving as a "launching pad" for the following polemics (4:1-5) and personal instructions (4:6-16)."[4] The string of ταῦτα references that threads through the letter from this point onwards (ταῦτα σοι γράφω, 3:14; ταῦτα ὑποτιθέμενος τοῖς ἀδελφοῖς, 4:6; παράγγελλε ταῦτα καὶ δίδασκε, 4:11; ταῦτα μελέτα, 4:15; ταῦτα παράγγελλε, 5:7; ταῦτα φυλάξῃς, 5:21; ταῦτα δίδασκε καὶ παράγγελλε, 6:2; ταῦτα φεῦγε, 6:11; cf. the earlier ταύτην τὴν παραγγελίαν παρατίθεμαί σοι, 1:18)

---

1 E.g. Roloff, 218.
2 Kelly, 93.
3 See, e.g., Quinn-Wacker, 348; Fee, 97
4 Lau, *Manifest*, 113-14. Houlden also proposes a unit of 3:14-4:16, although he finds no conceptual coherence (81).

may offer support for tying 3:14-16 to the paraenesis that follows. Excluding the final ταῦτα (6:11) which refers to what Timothy is to shun (6:3-10), these references, from an introductory, "I am writing to you these things" (3:14) to a final, "Teach and urge these things" (6:2), consistently indicate and specify the teaching passed on to and by Timothy.

This suggests that 4:10 should be read as part of a larger section, taking in both the doctrinal material in 3:16 and the paraenesis of 4:1-16. There are in particular two points of contact between 3:14-16 and 4:7-10 that must not be ignored. The statement that, "we have put our hope in the living God" (4:10), recalls "the church of the living God" (3:15), and εὐσέβεια is commended to Timothy (4:7, 8) against the background of the formula, ὁμολογουμένως μέγα ἐστὶν τὸ τῆς εὐσεβείας μυστήριον, which introduces the doctrinal summary in 3:16.

The literary context of the statement in 4:10, then, goes back to 3:14-15, where, after a series of instructions expressed as third-person optatives (2:1-3:13), the singular addressee in ταῦτά σοι γράφω . . . ἵνα εἰδῇς signals the resumption of personal paraenesis to Timothy. "These things" concern life in the Christian community. The depiction of the church (οἶκος θεοῦ . . . ἐκκλησία θεοῦ ζῶντος . . . στῦλος καὶ ἑδραίωμα τῆς ἀληθείας, 3:15) suggests a community defined by its relationship with the living God and marked by faithful adherence to "the truth." A confessional summary of that truth, characterized as τὸ τῆς εὐσεβείας μυστήριον, is offered which outlines the Christ event from incarnation to exaltation, particularly highlighting its revelatory aspect (3:16).[5] Continuing the sense of advancing chronology, we find ourselves in the troubled "last times" (4:1), when some will turn from the faith to "deceitful spirits and teachings of demons," including a severe asceticism that denies the essential goodness of God's creation (4:3-5). By contrast, Timothy is to feed on the λόγοι τῆς πίστεως (4:6), cherishing the "good teaching" which he has received (4:6) In place of the ascetic disciplines he is to train for εὐσέβεια (4:7), bringing benefit for both the present life and that which is to come (4:8). Reference is then made to the "toiling and striving" of Paul and Timothy (4:10a), and it is at this point, apparently in explanation of this exertion, that the salvation statement is introduced: ὅτι ἠλπίκαμεν ἐπὶ θεῷ ζῶντι, ὅς ἐστιν σωτὴρ πάντων ἀνθρώπων μάλιστα πιστῶν (4:10b).

---

5 Note the string of passive verbs to this effect: "revealed" - "vindicated" - "seen" - "proclaimed" - "believed" - "lifted up."

The immediate context includes the formulation, πιστὸς ὁ λόγος, supplemented, as in 1:15, with καὶ πάσης ἀποδοχῆς ἄξιος (4:9). It is not clear which "word" is meant, whether v. 10,[6] or all or the second part of v. 8.[7] It is not necessary for our purpose to determine this issue. As Young points out,

> If it refers back, it is about *eusebeia* which holds promise for the present life and the life to come, which, as we shall see, is what salvation is all about; if it refers forward, it is about hope in the living God who is the Saviour of all.[8]

7.2 Grammatical Possibilities

Until the appearance in 1979 of a brief article by T. C. Skeat,[9] commentators had little choice but to understand the adverb μάλιστα along the lines of "especially," "very greatly," etc., specifying a sub-group within a larger group.[10] So in 4:10, within the set of those for whom God is saviour (πάντες ἄνθρωποι), there is a sub-set (πιστοί) for whom God is saviour in a special way. The challenge for interpreters was to define the different saving outcomes for the set and the sub-set. Skeat, however, presented evidence from non-literary Greek that μάλιστα could have the sense of "that is to say" or "in other words." This opened up new possibilities for interpetation. Applied to 4:10, the effect would be that there is just one group for whom God is saviour, πάντες ἄνθρωποι who are πιστοί: "God is saviour of all people, that is, all who believe." The suggestion has gained wide acceptance, at least among English speaking scholars.[11] Despite its popularity, however, it remains one among a number of possibilities that must be kept

---

6   Guthrie prefers it, judging its theological content more suited to "catechetical purposes" than v. 8 (95-96). Dibelius-Conzelmann suggest that in v. 10 the author may be citing, "a phrase from Col 1:29, which has already become traditional for him." (68).
7   See Fee, 104-05; Marshall, 554; and support listed in Oberlinner, *1.Timotheusbrief*, 196 n. 23.
8   Young, *Theology*, 57.
9   T. C. Skeat, "Especially the Parchments: A Note on 2 Timothy 4:13," *JTS* ns 30 (1979): 173-77.
10 See e.g. Spicq, 509-10.
11 See, e.g., Hanson, *Epistles*, 92; Towner, 108-09 (n.); Stott, *1 Timothy & Titus*, 118; Knight, 203-04; Bassler, 85; Marshall, 556-57; cf. R. A. Campbell, "ΚΑΙ ΜΑΛΙΣΤΑ ΟΙΚΕΙΩΝ - A New Look at 1 Timothy 5:8," *NTS* 41 (1995): 157-60, 159.

open.¹²

7.3 Range of Interpretations

The interpretation of 4:10 is also affected by which background is thought to colour the σωτήρ concept and what judgements are made concerning the author's theological outlook. With several factors in play a variety of readings have emerged. Some see two types of saving. Spicq, for example, takes σωτήρ to represent the Hellenistic "provident-protecteur-donateur." In this Benefactor sense, God is the saviour of the whole of humanity, and the qualifying clause does not restrict God's saving to believers, but identifies them as a privileged category within the economy of salvation, to whom God's beneficence applies superlatively.¹³ Barrett distinguishes between a general temporal preserving, in which sense, "God is indeed the Creator and Preserver of all mankind," and "the eschatological salvation of Rom. 13:11" which is given to believers.¹⁴

Others argue for a single concept of saviour and saving, and variously explain how this could apply to "all people." From the future orientation of the immediate context and the usage of σωτήρ and cognate terms elsewhere in the PE, Marshall judges that the emphasis here is on eternal salvation. Utilizing Skeat's proposal, he understands the saying to affirm that this salvation is potentially available to all, though actually received by those who believe.¹⁵ Knight also reads σωτήρ in terms of eternal salvation, but avoids the conclusion that God will actually save all by explaining πάντες ἄνθρωποι as "all sorts of people."¹⁶

---

12 Mounce lists it as one of four options (256-57). It does not seem to have come to the attention of recent German commentators Roloff and Oberlinner.
13 Spicq, 509.
14 Barrett, 70; cf. Guthrie: "the word *Saviour* is used in a double sense" (96).
15 See Marshall, "Salvation in the Pastoral Epistles", 449-69. He responds here to the critique of his earlier article, "Universal Grace and Atonement", by Baugh in "Savior of All People", who locates σωτὴρ παντῶν ἀνθρώπων within the Reformed theological category of "common grace." While not ruling out Skeat's understanding of μάλιστα, Baugh prefers the sense of "especially," indicating that for this group God is saviour in an additional (eternal) sense (338).
16 Knight, 203-04. Baugh reads 2:4 in this way, but not 4:10 ("Savior of all people", 333, 338-40); see Marshall, "Salvation in the Pastoral Epistles", 465.

To Oberlinner, it seems that the attempt to reconcile the universality of the first part of the statement with the particularity of the second may be futile. Perhaps for the author himself the universality of God's saving purpose was so important that he insisted on it notwithstanding the resulting tension between "all people" and "believers".[17] Similarly, Bassler sees the first part as a product of the author's consistent inclusive emphasis, with the final clause providing a necessary corrective to the "theological exuberance" of the preceding expression.[18]

7.4 Issues

The exploration of other features of the text may throw some light on precisely what is being affirmed. Who are the πιστοί, and is the concept linked to the other πιστ- terms in the context? Why is it specifically θεὸς ζῶν who is described as σωτὴρ πάντων ἀνθρώπων? Does the choice of the verb ἐλπίζω contribute to the soteriological presentation? What is the contribution of εὐσέβεια (4:8) to benefits present and future, and how does this fit into the scheme of salvation? A satisfactory interpretation must also account for the rhetorical function of the salvation statement, in particular how it encourages the toiling and striving of v. 10a.

7.4.1 Who are οἱ πιστοί?

The basic meaning of the adjective πιστός is "faithful," "trustworthy," etc., and this accounts for most of its occurrences in the LXX. There are also examples of absolute uses, however, apparently indicating a category of people who exhibit faithfulness and trust in God. Thus in Ps 100:6 (101:6) it is οἱ πιστοὶ τῆς γῆς who enjoy God's favour and live in fellowship with him. Wis 3:9 declares that οἱ πιστοί will abide with God in love. These are also οἱ πεποιθότες ἐπ' αὐτῷ and οἱ ἐκλεκτοί, building a picture of the πιστοί as God's chosen ones, marked out by their faith in him. Rev 17:14 also combines ἐκλεκτοί with πιστοί to describe those with the Lamb, and Eph 1:1 addresses the πιστοὶ ἐν Χριστῷ Ἰησοῦ. In such cases, including 1 Tim 4:10, a judgment has to be made concerning

---

17 Oberlinner, 1.Timotheusbrief, 197. We might compare the tension that some have detected in Romans between universalizing statements and indications that those who will in fact be saved constitute a particular group. See e.g. R. H. Bell, "Rom 5.18-19 and Universal Salvation", NTS 48 (2002): 417-32.

18 Bassler, 85.

which aspect, whether the quality of trustworthiness, activity of believing or religious identity, predominates.

Two references in the context may help to explicate the meaning of the term in 4:10. In 4:3, οἱ πιστοί are those who "have come to know the truth" (cf. 2:4), and are accordingly able to recognize the goodness of what God has created (including marriage and food) and enjoy it with thanksgiving (4:3-4). These πιστοί, "those who believe" are contrasted with those who have "wandered from the faith (ἡ πίστις)" by believing deceitful teaching (4:1). Here the cognitive dimension is significant. In 4:12 the πιστοί are those for whom Timothy is to serve as an example. There is nothing to suggest that these are a particular group within the church; "the believers" or "the faithful" denotes the Christians, and it is the community identification aspect of the term that is to the fore.[19] The idea of οἱ πιστοί in the immediate context, therefore, shades from actual description ("those who believe") to technical descriptor ("the believers"). We may conclude that the "believers" whom the author holds to be especially the objects of God's saving are those who have acknowledged "the truth" about God (as outlined, e.g., in 2:5-6; 3:16) and hence constitute the Christian community.

7.4.2 What is the Significance of θεὸς ζῶν?

a. The Idea of Life

In the immediate context the description θεὸς ζῶν recalls the promise of life, present and future, in 4:8,[20] associating this hope with a God who is himself characterized by life. The same expression has just occurred in the phrase ἐκκλησία θεοῦ ζῶντος (3:15), which associates the idea of the life that is inherent in God with the community gathered about him. Since it is expressly θεὸς ζῶν who is σωτήρ, this life colours the idea of the saving that he effects. Dibelius-Conzelmann remark on σωτήρ that,

> here the word seems to have an especially pregnant meaning, in which the divine predicate "the Living One" (ζῶν) is understood in a causative way: "it is the Living God who makes the promise of

---

19 P. Trebilco concludes that, "οἱ πιστοί . . . came to be used as an insider term for one who has faith and accepts 'the faith'" ("What Shall We Call Each Other? Part One: The Issue of Self-designation in the Pastoral Epistles," *TynBul* 53.2 (2002), 239-58, 256).
20 See e.g. Fee, 106; Knight, 203; Bassler, 84-85.

life (ἐπαγγελία ζωῆς) come true."[21]

b. The "Living God" in the Bible

Mounce comments that, "The description of God as the θεῷ ζῶντι, 'living God', is a common theme in the Bible."[22] This observation may be refined. In the LXX, the expression θεὸς ζῶν appears in the account of the meeting with God at Sinai that established Israel as God's people (Deut 4:33; 5:26). It heightens the solemnity of the occasion and underlines Israel's unique privilege. In LXX Psalms it occurs only twice, in the Korahitic Psalms 41:3 (42:2) and 83:34 (84:2) which are concerned with the worshipper's existential encounter with God at the temple. In Hos 1:10 (LXX 2:1) God's people are defined by their relationship to "the living God": καὶ ἔσται ἐν τόπῳ οἱ ἐρρέθη αὐτοῖς οὐ λαός μου ὑμεῖς ἐκεῖ κληθήσονται υἱοὶ θεοῦ ζῶντος. Elsewhere, it appears most often in contexts where God's people are under threat,[23] encouraging trust in a God who is alive and able to save, in contrast to the impotent gods and idols of the nations. In appears relatively frequently in LXX Daniel (4:21; 5:23; 6:26, 27; 12:7) and Bel and the Dragon (vv. 5-6, 24, 25), pressing the polemical identification of the God of the Jews as the only real, living God, whom even kings of Babylon ought to acknowledge. Reading 1 Tim 4:10 against this background throws its inclusivist character into sharp relief. This "living God," who spoke to a particular people at Sinai, made them "children of the living God" and saved them from their enemies, is actually σωτὴρ πάντων ἀνθρώπων. An epithet associated with exclusive claims on God is enlisted for a radically inclusive affirmation. This rhetorical move exactly parallels 2:3-4, where it is affirmed that ὁ σωτὴρ ἡμῶν θεός (traditionally exclusive) πάντας ἀνθρώπους θέλει σωθῆναι (radically inclusive). This assumes that the epithet still carries polemical connotations and has not had its force blunted by absorption into general Christian vocabulary. We must explore the NT for indications of its use in early Christianity.

The expression appears only twice in the Gospels, where it seems to heighten the solemnity of a confession (Matt 16:16) and a charge (Matt 26:63). The only reference in Revelation has the same effect (7:2). It occurs in a missionary context, however, in Acts, where in Gentile Lystra, Paul argues that rain and harvests constitute a

---

21 Dibelius-Conzelmann, 69.
22 Mounce, 256.
23 E.g., Josh 3:10; 1 Sam 17:26, 36; 4 Kgdms 19:4, 16 (= Isa 37:4, 17); 3 Macc 6:28.

witness to the existence of "the living God," creator of all, in contrast to worthless idols and pagan gods (Acts 14:15-17). The same contrast appears in 1 Thess 1:9, where, to converts from paganism, Paul writes, ἐπεστρέψατε πρὸς τὸν θεὸν ἀπὸ τῶν εἰδώλων δουλεύειν θεῷ ζῶντι καὶ ἀληθινῷ. The thought moves on to the raising of Jesus from the dead and to rescue from coming wrath (v. 10). As is frequently the case in the OT, the concept of "the living God" is associated with his power to save. The living God gave life to Jesus, and is linked with the promise of life.

The remaining Pauline uses of θεὸς ζῶν are all in contexts where features of the OT concept of Israel as the people of God are appropriated for the new Christian community, including Gentiles. Thus in Rom 9:25-26 Paul appeals to Hos 1:10 (cited above) and 2:23 to support his argument that the beneficiaries of God's mercy and call are "not from the Jews only but also from the Gentiles" (Rom 9:24).[24] The living God's revelation at Sinai is recalled in 2 Cor 3:3, when Christians are described as "a letter from Christ, written . . . with the Spirit of the living God . . . on tablets of human hearts" . Whereas in LXX Pss 41 and 83 the temple was where communion with the living God could be enjoyed, Paul writes, ἡμεῖς γὰρ ναὸς θεοῦ ἐσμεν ζῶντος (2 Cor 6:16), relocating the dwelling of God in the Christian community. Hebrews similarly utilizes θεὸς ζῶν as part of its general project to redefine the people of God by proposing a Christological reinterpretation of key Jewish concepts (Heb 3:12; 9:14; 10:31; 12:22).[25] This survey, then, has yielded three categories of use of the θεὸς ζῶν epithet in the NT: a general use, imparting solemnity; a role in missionary apologetic; and as one of several OT expressions appropriated by early Christianity in its redefinition of the people of God to include Gentiles. Any of these three categories would give reasonable sense in 1 Tim 4:10.

c. Paul's Missionary Preaching

Mark J. Goodwin, however, has recently argued for a more specific connection.[26] Citing the Acts of Paul and Thecla (3:17; 7:2; 11:4-5) as

---

24 J. Ziesler explains: "In Hosea the words have to do with the lapse and return of the northern kingdom of Israel, but as Paul uses them they concern the incoming of the Gentiles . . . . The effect . . . is to give Scriptural backing for 'also from the Gentiles' in v. 24." (*Paul's Letter to the Romans*. London: SCM, 1989, 248).

25 On the argument of Hebrews see B. Chilton and J. Neusner, *Judaism in the New Testament: Practices and Beliefs* (London: Routledge, 1995), 175-88.

26 M. J. Goodwin, "The Pauline Background of the Living God as Interpretive

well as canonical Acts and the Pauline letters, he concludes that θεὸς ζῶν belongs to a standard characterisation of Paul's missionary preaching. In 4:10 it evokes not only Paul's missionary role but also the central content of Paul's message, the resurrection of Jesus as the ground of future hope:

> Paul preached the living God to Gentiles as part of his monotheistic kerygma. The very mention of the epithet would have recalled Paul's role as missionary to the Gentiles. Further, the living God in Paul also raised Jesus from the dead, signalling the future resurrection of all believers. The living God was the source of resurrection life for all who had turned from idols and believed.[27]

The verbs κοπιάω and ἀγωνίζομαι are also taken by Goodwin to indicate Paul's missionary work, appealing to the parallels with Col 1:29, where the context is Paul's missionary commission. This enables him to explain the relationship between the two clauses in v. 10:

> Paul toiled and strove because he was an apostle of the living God, sent by the living God as the instrument of divine salvation. Paul's hope in the living God was a hope based on his personal experience of call and commission. The ὅτι clause, with its use of the epithet, thus clarifies the ultimate origin and ground of Paul's toiling and striving.[28]

It is perhaps too much to claim that, "The very mention of the epithet would have recalled Paul's role as missionary to the Gentiles,"[29] but Goodwin has shown that the Pauline Gentile mission provides a plausible interpretive context for v. 10. With this accenting, it would connect Paul's mission with Israel's one, living God, but extend his saving to all nations.

d. ἡ ἐκκλησία θεοῦ ζῶντος

Unfortunately the scope of Goodwin's article does not permit him to take into consideration the reference to the ἐκκλησία θεοῦ ζῶντος in 3:15, although he acknowledges its relevance.[30] The expression

---

Context for 1 Timothy 4.10," *JSNT* 61 (1996): 65-85.
27 Goodwin, "Living God," 76.
28 Goodwin, "Living God," 84-85.
29 Goodwin, "Living God," 76.
30 Goodwin, "Living God," 66-67 and nn. 3, 4.

ἐκκλησία θεοῦ could justifiably be described as characteristically Pauline. In the NT it is found only in Pauline letters (1 Cor 1:2; 10:32; 11:16, 22; 15:9; 2 Cor 1:1; Gal 1:13; 1 Thess 2:14; also 2 Thess 1:4; 1 Tim 3:5, 15; cf. ἐκκλησία ἐν θεῷ, 1 Thess 1:1; 2 Thess 1:1) and in Luke's record of Paul's Miletan address (Acts 20:28). The fuller expression ἐκκλησία θεοῦ ζῶντος is, however, a NT hapax. Nor is it found in the LXX, but the elements of "assembly" and "living God" appear together in the early chapters of Deuteronomy when, on "the day of the assembly" (τῇ ἡμέρᾳ τῆς ἐκκλησίας, Deut 4:10; 9:10; 18:16), Israel gathered at Sinai and heard the voice of "the living God" (Deut 4:33; 5:26). The context is Moses' final address to Israel in which he reminds them of God's laws, and commissions Joshua as his successor.

There are suggestive points of correspondence between 1 Tim 3:14-4:16 and Deuteronomy. The implied situations involve reminders, exhortations and warnings from a foundational leader and the commissioning of a younger successor. Apostasy is predicted (4:1-5; cf. Deut 4:25-31; 31:16-22, etc.); the commissioning reference emphasizes the bestowal of spiritual power through the laying on of hands (4:14; Deut 34:9);[31] teaching constitutes a large part of the responsibility; and the injunction ἔπεχε σεαυτῷ (4:16) closely echoes the reiterated πρόσεχε σεαυτῷ by which Deuteronomy urges diligence in remembering, transmitting and obeying the teaching and in guarding against being led astray (Deut 4:9; 6:12; 8:11; 11:16; 12:13, 19, 30; 15:9; 24:8). While not essential to the point, any such echoes in ἐκκλησία θεοῦ ζῶντος in 3:15 would reinforce the notion of the Christian community as a people gathered to heed the one living God. This colouring would heighten the inclusivism of the statement in 4:10, appropriating for the Christian church, including Gentiles, this OT image of the constituting of the people of God.[32] It also links the ideas of the πιστοί (4:10) and the ἐκκλησία (3:15). The emerging picture is of

---

31 Note also that Timothy's commissioning was κατὰ . . . προφειτείας (1:18), as Joshua's came through the superlative prophet Moses (Deut 34:10).

32 Cf. G. A. Couser, "God and Christian Existence in 1 and 2 Timothy and Titus" (Ph.D. diss., University of Aberdeen, 1992), 37-48, who argues *contra* D. C. Verner, *The Household of God: The Social World of the Pastoral Epistles* (SBLDS 71; Chico: Scholars Press, 1983) that OT and Pauline tradition rather than the Graeco-Roman household supply the primary background for the images of the church in 3:15.

salvation from the one true God, received by people of all nations who believe his message and are gathered into his church.

7.4.3 ἠλπίκαμεν

We have already noted the close relationship in the LXX between the idea of God as saviour and the activity of trusting in him for that saving, expressed predominantly by ἐλπίς and cognates.[33] Three times in 1 Timothy the verb ἐλπίζω appears in the perfect tense, suggesting the singularity of a beginning point together with the continuity of a sustained action or attitude. In each case God is the object of trust. In 5:3-8 the "real widow" ἤλπικεν ἐπὶ θεόν, expressing that trust in constant prayer (5:5). Though hope of eternal salvation need not be excluded, the focus is on trusting God for the necessities of this life. In 6:17, those who are rich ἐν τῷ νῦν αἰῶνι are warned not to be haughty, μηδὲ ἠλπικέναι ἐπὶ πλούτου ἀδηλότητι, ἀλλ' ἐπὶ θεῷ τῷ παρέχοντι ἡμῖν πάντα πλουσίως εἰς ἀπόλαυσιν. They are to pursue true life realized in the coming age (6:19), but again the attitude of trust in God envisages humble dependence upon God as the source of all good things (6:17-19). Neither of these references restricts the focus of hope to future salvation. Rather, we seem to have the OT disposition of hope in the saving God for this life, extended to include the greater benefits of life in the coming age.

Is there scope for this-worldly as well as next-worldly hope in 4:10? Two readings would accommodate such an understanding. First, if the σωτήρ concept here is principally that of the universal Benefactor, the statement would express trust in God for the needs of this earthly life. This reading can take some encouragement from the stress on God's good creation in 4:3-4. The other possibility is that the trust exercised by Paul and Timothy is for what is required to fulfil their ministry. There is a Pauline parallel in 2 Cor 1:8-10. Writing of dangers encountered in the course of their mission (v. 8), Paul testifies that God ("who raises the dead," v. 9) had delivered them, and they have put their hope in him to do so again: εἰς ὃν ἠλπίκαμεν καὶ ἔτι ῥύσεται (2 Cor 1:10). They persist in their ministry in spite of the dangers, because they trust God to preserve and help them to fulfil it. If 1 Tim 4:10b were read like this the thought would flow naturally from "toiling and striving" in v. 10a.

---

33 See above on 1 Tim 1:1 (pp. 28-30).

7.4.4 εὐσέβεια

The noun εὐσέβεια occurs 5x in 1 Timothy, more than in any other NT document. According to Foerster, it "denotes a particular manner of life."[34] This interpretation fits well in 2:2, 6:11 and probably 6:6. On the other hand this stress on the behavioural aspect perhaps takes insufficient account of the cognitive dimension implied in 6:3 and 4:7, where εὐσέβεια is contrasted with false doctrines and myths, and the dogmatic content of τὸ τῆς εὐσεβείας μυστήριον (3:16). An adequate understanding must embrace both behavioural and cognitive aspects. A similar ambivalence is found in Philo, in whose writings, "εὐσεβ- and ἀσεβ- are a matter of thought as well as action."[35] It is possible to have the outer form of εὐσέβεια without true understanding (e.g. *Plant.* 70), but in that case it has descended to mere superstition (*Sacr.* 18; cf. 24). It ranks among the ἐπιστῆμαι κατ' ἀρετήν, as a system of knowledge (especially of God, as in *Mut.* 76) that produces virtue. Similarly, 4 Maccabees argues that ὁ εὐσεβὴς λογισμός is supremely effective in that most severe of tests for a philosophy, its ability to overcome the passions (1:1; 6:31; 7:16; 13:1; 15:23; 16:1; 18:2).

In 4:7-8 εὐσέβεια appears in the context of education and training (γυμνάζε . . . σωματικὴ γυμνασία; see also the προκοπή urged in v. 15). In this setting, the pursuit of Christian εὐσέβεια would involve grasping a specific dogmatic content (see 3:16; cf. οἱ λόγοι τῆς πίστεως and ἡ καλὴ διδασκαλία, 4:6) and following the behavioural instruction integral to this system of belief and practice. The author commends it as fruitful both in the present life and in that which is to come (v. 8), thereby connecting it through the idea of "life" with the statement about hope in the living God, who is the saviour (v. 10). Those who practise εὐσέβεια have learned τὸ τῆς εὐσεβείας μυστήριον, which is encapsulated Christologically in 3:16. Like the πιστοί, they have come to believe the truth and order their lives in accordance with it. For this author piety and faith seem to be two sides of the same coin, aspects of his characterisation of those who will receive the full salvation provided by the saviour God.

7.4.5 The Rhetorical Function of the Salvation Statement

What is this statement about God as saviour (v. 10b) intended to motivate? Some commentators refer back to the training in godliness

---

34 Foerster, *TDNT* 7:182.
35 Foerster, *TDNT* 7:181, citing *Opif.* 172, μακαρίαν καὶ εὐδαίμονα ζωὴν βιώσεται δόγμασιν εὐσεβείας καὶ ὁσιότητος χαραχθείς."

(v. 7), assuring those who strive for godliness that the promised outcome (life) is grounded in "the living God."[36] Alternatively, if the verbs κοπιάω and ἀγωνίζομαι refer to missionary activity (as in, e.g. Col 1:27; Rom 16:12; 1 Cor 15:2), v. 10b would provide motivation for persisting in the envisaged "struggle against the opposing teachers and on behalf of the gospel."[37] This accords with the paraenetic purpose of the passage. Timothy must press on with mission to all, because God is the saviour for all; and he must teach "the faith" (v. 6; cf. v. 1) because it is through embracing it that hearers become πιστοί and are set on the way of salvation.

7.5 Summary

This statement about God the saviour (4:10) in its context illuminates several aspects of the author's concept of salvation. The source of salvation is God, the one true living God whom Israel knew but who is saviour not only for Israel but for all people. This saviour God bestows benefits here and now, in a good creation to be enjoyed, in the rewards of godly living and in provision for his servants in the fulfilment of their mission. The greatest benefit and goal of salvation remains, however, eschatological life, related to the life of God himself. It is received by faith, conceived as an attitude of trust and hope in God allied to the acceptance of a body of teaching about Christ and the living out of its behavioural implications. It is assumed that such faith and life belong within the church, the community of Christian believers, which relates to God in a manner analogous to Israel in the OT. The nature of God and the promise of salvation provide motivation for the continuing work of mission.

---

36 E.g., Dibelius-Conzelmann 68-69; Barrett, 70. For Fee, it explains why Timothy is to discipline himself in godliness (105-06).
37 Bassler, 84.

Chapter 8

1 Timothy 4:16

ἔπεχε σεαυτῷ καὶ τῇ διδασκαλίᾳ, ἐπίμενε αὐτοῖς· τοῦτο γὰρ ποιῶν καὶ σεαυτὸν σέσεις καὶ τοὺς ἀκούοντάς σου.

The impressive claim is made that Timothy could "save" both himself and his hearers. What sort of saving is in view? And does the suggestion of saving as a human achievement mark a departure from Paul's understanding of salvation?[1]

8.1 Context

The paraenesis, which has run from 3:14,[2] reaches its climax in 4:16. The instruction to Timothy to teach (4:6, 11, 13), with indications of the teaching content (e.g. 3:16; 4:4-6, 10) is accompanied by exhortation to train in godly living (4:7b-8) and demonstrate practical progress (προκοπή) in a life nurtured by this teaching (4:12, 15-16).[3] The ultimate motivation is that the outcome of this teaching and and activity is salvation.

8.2 What Sort of "Saving" is in View?

In this context of concern about false teachers (4:1-4 and the letter generally), the mention of "teaching" being salvific for "hearers" could suggest that saving from error is in view.[4] The διδασκαλία commended, however, includes in its content God's identity and activity as σωτήρ (2:3; 4:10; cf. 1:1), the salvific effects of the Christ event (2:5-6; cf. 1:15) and the prospect of life to come (4:8; cf. 6:19). Rather than being itself the goal, preservation from erroneous teaching is rather a means to the ultimate end of attaining the salvation of which the διδασκαλία speaks.[5]

---

1 See e.g. Easton, 149-50; Merkel, 40; cf. Hanson, *Epistles*, 95.
2 See discussion of context of 4:10 above (pp. 84-86).
3 The Hellenistic concept of προκοπή as moral progress through philosophy is illustrated in, e.g., Diogenes Laertius 7.91; cf. progress in παιδεία in Sir 51:16-17.
4 Knight, 211, lists supporters of this view.
5 Knight comments, "It is true that διδασκαλία does deliver from error and

8.3 In What Sense does the Human Agent "Save"?

8.3.1 Who is the Agent?

It is Timothy who is addressed. In the immediate context there are references to his personal circumstances (his youth, v. 12a) what his work consists of (teaching, v. 13) and his equipping or commissioning "through prophecy with the laying on of hands by the council of elders" (v. 14). The soteriological setting of this mention of Timothy's commissioning (cf. that of Paul in 1:1, 12-16), indicates that in the perspective of this letter, the ministries of Paul and Timothy are means by which God effects his saving purpose. By implication the encouragement given to Timothy in v. 16 could be appropriated by others engaged in the same activity, such as the teaching elders (οἱ κοπιῶντες ἐν λόγῳ καὶ διδασκαλίᾳ, 5:17), for whom Timothy provides a model of "a properly ordained ministry that is loyal to its origins (v. 14) and attentive to its responsibilities, especially that of good teaching (vv. 6, 16)."[6]

8.3.2 What is Timothy Exhorted to Do?

The means by which Timothy is to save is expressed in the commands, ἔπεχε σεαυτῷ καὶ τῇ διδασκαλίᾳ, and ἐπίμενε αὐτοῖς. The verb ἐπέχω, with the basic meaning of to hold onto someone or something, is used in the NT for giving close attention to something (e.g. Luke 14:7; Acts 3:5), holding fast to something (e.g. Phil 2:16) or remaining somewhere (e.g. Acts 19:22). The sense of giving close attention could serve in 4:16, with ἔπεχε . . . τῇ διδασκαλίᾳ closely following the exhortation, πρόσεχε τῇ ἀναγνώσει, τῇ παρακλήσει, τῇ διδασκαλίᾳ (v. 13).[7] On the other hand, since continuing in something is suggested by the companion expression, ἐπίμενε αὐτοῖς, that could influence the meaning towards something like, "Hold on in your life and your teaching." Possibly the phrase ἔπεχε σεαυτῷ, a biblical hapax, carries something of the admonitory flavour of the more common πρόσεχε σεαυτῷ, found (in singular or plural form) particularly in contexts where a senior figure is warning a junior.[8] This would be

---

bring to truth, but that seems to be included in the ultimate goal expressed in σῴζω." (211).
6 Bassler, 88.
7 E.g. Marshall, 571.
8 In Deuteronomy the phrase sounds a recurring note of warning against falling away from the book's commands (see above on 4:10, pp. 93-94). It also appears in other warning contexts in the LXX, in Gen 24:6; Exod 10:28; 19:12; 23:21; 34:12; Tobit 4:12, 14 (moral exhortation from a father to his son);

appropriate to the implied "father" to "son" setting of 1 Timothy (cf. 1:2, 18), and would produce an effect such as, "Watch yourself! - particularly the teaching."

If such is the attitude that Timothy must adopt, the specific activity that is urged is that of teaching. This is in view in the immediate context (vv. 11, 13, 16), and it includes not only declaring instructions but also providing a living example (v. 12) and demonstrating progress (v. 15). All this is summed up in the exhortation in v. 16.[9] Accordingly, the companion instruction, ἐπίμενε αὐτοῖς, is a call to persevere in those activities. By the exercise of his ministry Timothy will "save" both himself and those who to whom he ministers.

8.3.3 How does this Activity "Save"?

The author has just indicated that those for whom God is σωτήρ are the πιστοί (v. 10), i.e., those who have come to know the truth (4:2) and comprise the community to whom Timothy is ministering (4:12). The object of believing is Christ Jesus, who himself saves, and the outcome is eternal life (1:15-16). The salvific efficacy of the teaching ministry is readily understood within this framework. One who teaches the faith and guides in its outworking becomes a means by which faith in Christ is exercised and lived. He can be said to "save" others in that he is an agent of God's saving through Christ and faith in him. The description of those saved through his ministry as "your hearers" confirms that the salvific role is specifically that of the communicator of the message.

In addition to saving his hearers, Timothy is to be concerned for his own salvation (v. 16). The two savings are not different in kind. Timothy is to walk the way of salvation himself, as he exemplifies it for others (v. 12). There may also, however, be an allusion to the particular responsibility of one to whom God's saving message is entrusted. The concept of the messenger's accountability (perhaps drawn from Ezek 3:16-21 and 33:1-9) may be seen in Acts 20:26-27, where Paul declares to the Ephesian elders that he is free of their blood, because he has declared the whole of God's message to them: καθαρός εἰμι ἀπό τοῦ αἵματος πάντων· οὐ γὰρ ὑπεστειλάμην τοῦ

---

and Sir 29:20 ("take heed to yourself lest you fall"). In the NT the plural προσέχετε ἑαυτοῖς occurs 5x, all in Luke-Acts, communicating warnings from Jesus (Luke 12:1; 17:3; 21:34), Gamaliel (Acts 5:35) and Paul (Acts 20:28).

9   See Fee, 109.

μὴ ἀναγγεῖλαι πᾶσαν τὴν βουλὴν τοῦ θεοῦ ὑμῖν.[10] This allusion to the minister's accountability is immediately followed by the exhortation, "Keep watch over yourselves and over all the flock" (προσέχετε ἑαυτοῖς καὶ παντὶ τῷ ποιμνίῳ, v. 28). As in 1 Tim 4:16, those in a pastoral role are to have concern for the spiritual well-being both of the church members and of themselves.

Easton's comment on v. 16, that the "language could hardly be more un-Pauline,"[11] overlooks the apostle's declared goal, "that I might by all means save some" (ἵνα πάντως τινὰς σώσω, 1 Cor 9:22). The same Pauline passage answers Hanson's accusation that v. 16 betrays "a prudential ethic that has more in common with the old dispensation than the new," in contrast to "Paul's reckless abandonment of himself to God's will."[12] Paul himself professed anxiety, "that after proclaiming to others I myself should not be disqualified"(μή πως ἄλλοις κηρύξαν αὐτὸς ἀδόκιμος γένομαι, 1 Cor 9:27).

8.4 Summary

The exhortation in 4:16 posits a close connection between the activity of the Christian minister and the realization of God's saving purpose.[13] Since salvation is linked to faith, one who teaches the Christian faith becomes an agent of God's saving.

---

10 See e.g., I. H. Marshall, *The Acts of the Apostles* (TNTC; Leicester: IVP, 1980), 333; F. F. Bruce, *The Book of Acts* (2nd ed. NLC; London: Marshall, Morgan & Scott, 1972), 415.
11 Easton, 150.
12 Hanson, *Epistles*, 95.
13 Cf. Oberlinner, *1.Timotheusbrief*, 212.

CHAPTER 9

Summary of Salvation in 1 Timothy

9.1 General Observations

The presentation of salvation in 1 Timothy centres on "God our saviour" (1:1; 2:3), the one living God of Judaism (2:5; 4:10), who, it is asserted, is in fact God and saviour for all (2:4; 4:10). While the letter recognizes God's universal beneficence in a kindly created order, so that there is much to be enjoyed and to look to God for in this life (e.g. 4:3-5; 6:13, 17), the specifically Christian hope is of eternal life in the coming age (1:16; 4:8; 6:18-19). This saving has been made possible through the Christ event (1:15; 2:5-6; cf. 3:16), and it will be consummated at Christ's return (6:13-15). Since it is received by those who exercise faith and pursue godliness of life (1:16; 2:15; 4:6-8, 10; 6:17-19), great importance is attached to right teaching (e.g. 2:3-7; 3:14-15; 4:6, 16; cf. 1:18-20; 6:20-21). Indeed, being saved is equated with coming to a knowledge of the truth (2:4), and through faithful teaching and example the minister may be a means of salvation for himself and for others (4:10, 16). The ministries of Paul, Timothy and those who succeed them are essentially soterial in that they derive from the command of God as saviour (1:1).

The conviction that there is one living God, who in his providential ordering of creation and time shows his kindly disposition towards all people, but is known by Israel as "God our saviour," may be found in Hellenistic Judaism. The author is among those who, operating within this framework, see it as God's purpose that he should also come to be acknowledged as saviour of all peoples (cf. the missionary approach of the Lukan Paul in, e.g., Acts 14:15-17; 17:23-28). An underlying salvation-historical schema comes to the surface in the allusion to the promise of salvation that mitigated the curse upon Eve (2:15) and the concept of the proper time, both for the testimony concerning Christ's self-giving (2:6) and for the future coming of Christ (6:14-15). There are indications that this view of God's saving plan and its dissemination is being set over against an alternative reformulation of Jewish soteriological concepts within the author's constituency (e.g. 1:3-11, and discussion above on 2:8-15).

Various materials are utilized in the interests of the author's presentation of his soteriological perspective, some of which have something of a Johannine ring (e.g. Christ coming into the world, 1:15; salvation through abiding in faith, etc., 2:15). These are woven into the passages of which they are part in such a way that the thought of each sections is carried forward, indicating that the author has not merely adopted traditional language but has utilized materials to express and support his own understanding.

9.2 Specific Aspects of the Presentation of Salvation

Specific aspects of the idea of salvation in this letter may be summarized as follows:

9.2.1 The Benefits of Salvation

The salvation that Christ came into the world to accomplish is into eternal life (1:15-16). In comparison with this present transient existence (see, e.g., 6:7), it is that future life that "really is life" (6:19), and is worth aspiring to and struggling for (4:8; 6:12, 18-19). For the person on the way to that salvation, however, there is also a heightened enjoyment of the things of this life. As they "believe and know the truth" (4:3) they are able to recognize such things as the creation and gift of a generous benefactor God (4:3-4), and receive them with thanksgiving (4:4-5). Their faith enables them to look to God for the necessities of this life (5:5; 6:17) and there are benefits even now from the εὐσέβεια which those who hope in God cultivate (4:8).

9.2.2 God and Christ in Relation to Salvation

In the first sentence of 1 Timothy God is introduced as "God our saviour" (1:1). Together with references to the "one God" (2:5) and the "living God" (3:15; 4:10) this evokes the OT concept of Israel's God, the only true God who alone is able to save. Yet this letter insists that God is not only "our saviour" but also "the saviour of all" (4:10). There may even be an intentional progression in the letter's three references to God as σωτήρ, from "God our saviour" (1:1) to "God our saviour, who desires everyone to be saved" (2:3-4) to "God, who is the saviour of all" (4:10). In one sense God is already the "saviour of all" in that he "gives life to all" (6:13). God's providential care as universal benefactor is seen in his ordering of human society, instituting marriage (4:3-5) and structures of government (implied in 2:1-2), and in his pleasure in the εὐσέβεια of children fulfilling their duties of care for their parents (5:4). God provides what is necessary for the enjoyment of this life (4:3-5), and it is right to trust and pray to him for these things (5:5; 6:17). In another sense, however, God is "especially" the savour of believers (4:10), who receive eternal life (1:16). His desire is that this degree of salvation should also extend to all as they "come to the knowledge of the truth" (2:3-4), and become believers. It is specifically to this end that God, as saviour, has commissioned Paul to take the gospel to the nations (1:1, 11; 2:3-7). Consonant with the idea of God's providence is the indication that he is in control of time. The witness was borne "at the right time" (2:6), and God will bring about the coming of Christ "at the right time" (6:15). These moments are key points on the time-line of the history of salvation, and a further salvation-historical allusion may be glimpsed in the elusive reference to "the childbearing" in connection with Eve and the women (2:15). Though God is himself eternal and immortal (1:17; 6:16), it is part of his sovereign rule (6:15) to order the progression within human history of his salvation purpose.

In so far as the content of the message is seen in this letter, it relates final salvation intimately to Christ, and particularly the Christ event. His coming into the world was for the purpose of saving sinners (1:15) and eternal life is received through believing in him (1:16); in his incarnation (3:16) he was able to act as mediator between God and humankind, giving himself as a ransom for all (2:5-6); and this event also had the character of costly witness (6:13). Alongside these past elements, Christ's involvement in the provision of salvation has future and present dimensions. The consummation of eternal salvation awaits Christ's future manifestation (6:14-15), and the references to Christ's patience with Paul (1:16) and his experience of "the faith and love that are in Christ Jesus" (1:14) suggest the continuing activity of Christ in relation to the process of salvation.

9.2.3 Paul and Salvation

Paul is introduced in this letter as an apostle "by the command of God our saviour" (1:1). His ministry therefore derives its character from God's identity as saviour. His specific role in God's scheme of salvation is in relation to the gospel, which God entrusted to Paul (1:11). Not only is he a proclaimer of the gospel, but he himself exemplifies it as an erstwhile sinner and persecutor of the church who has received grace and mercy from Christ (1:12-16). The goal of his ministry is that people should come to believe in Christ and receive eternal life (1:16). The content of Paul's witness concerns the

Christ event and its saving effects (2:5-7), and it has its place "at the right time" in God's saving plan (2:6b). Its scope explicitly includes the nations (2:7b). Ministry is often "toil and struggle," but Paul persists in it because he can be sure of its effectiveness, first because God is indeed the saviour of all, so Paul's ministry to the nations has a secure basis, and also because God saves specifically those who believe, so a ministry that brings about such belief is eminently valid. Paul's is not, however, the only salvifically efficacious ministry. Timothy will "save" both himself and his hearers through the faithful exercise of his ministry and gift (4:16), and as Paul was entrusted with the gospel, so Timothy must guard what has been entrusted to him (6:20).

9.2.4 Those Who are Saved

In a number of places 1 Timothy specifies categories of people who are or may expect to be beneficiaries of the divine saving or of the eternal life that is its ultimate goal. These are "sinners" (1:15); "all," indicating especially the inclusion of the Gentiles (2:4, 7); women, specifically married women with children (2:15); the faithful minister and his hearers (4:16; cf. 6:12); and those who are rich in the present age (6:17-19). What qualifies such people for this salvation is faith with godliness. The "sinners" (1:15), despite what they have done "ignorantly in unbelief" (1:13), qualify for eternal life when they come to believe (1:16). The "all" whom God wishes to be saved enter into that salvation as they come to "the knowledge of the truth" (2:4; cf. 4:3) and believe (4:10); the women are saved if they continue in faith (2:15).

This believing, however, has a significant behavioural dimension. The letter links faith with love and holiness (1:5; 2:15; 4:12; 6:11) and propriety (2:15), keeping a good conscience (1:5, 19-20; 3:9), the pursuit of godliness (4:7-10; 6:6, 11), and being rich in good works (6:17-19), valuing the promise of the life to come over the attractions of the present age (4:8; 6:19). To "fight the good fight of the faith" (6:12) seems to involve both cultivating such a life (6:11) and remaining faithful to the confession of Christ (6:12-14). The faithful exercise of ministry will save both minister and those ministered to (4:16). On the other hand it is possible to miss the faith that issues in salvation through rejecting conscience (1:19; cf. 4:2), heeding erroneous teaching, characterized as demonic lies (4:1-2) and profane chatter "falsely called knowledge" (6:20-21), or being ensnared by temporal temptations (6:9-10).

Salvation, therefore, is open to all, but it is received by those who hear the truth, believe in Christ and pursue godliness. Since it is the faithful exercise of ministry that enables such hearing, believing and living, it may be said that from one perspective, salvation comes to those who are the beneficiaries of the sort of ministry promoted by this letter.

PART 3

SALVATION IN 2 TIMOTHY

"The promise of life"

CHAPTER 10

Introduction to Salvation in 2 Timothy

10.1 Distinctive Features

2 Timothy is distinguished from the other Pastoral Epistles by the paucity of practical instruction concerning church administration. Instead, the burden of the letter is intensely personal with Paul's death apparently imminent and urgent exhortation directed to Timothy himself,[1] charging him to preserve the integrity of Paul's gospel and transmit it to others. In common with the other PE, there is a threatening background. Proponents of what the author considers to be a damaging perversion of the gospel are active within the church (2:14-18, 23-26; 3:1-9, 13; 4:3-4, 14-15); specifically, there are those who "have swerved from the truth by claiming that the resurrection has already taken place. They are upsetting the faith of some." (2:18). To 1 Timothy's theme of turning away from the faith (1 Tim 1:6, 19; 4:1; 6:10, 25) 2 Timothy adds the motif of personal abandonment: "all who are in Asia have turned away from me" (1:15; cf. 4:10, 16). To some scholars this letter seems so much closer to the *Hauptbriefe* in content and atmosphere than 1 Timothy and Titus that they are persuaded of its authenticity even if the other PE are pseudonymous.[2] Others explain the apparent proximity to Paul as successful imitation,[3] or by the requirement of verisimilitude in a testamentary letter.[4] The question is not resolved.

---

1   2 Timothy has the greatest density of 2nd person singular imperatives with 31, compared with 30 in the longer 1 Timothy and 12 in Titus. The emphatic σὺ δέ appears 1x each in 1 Timothy (6:11) and Titus (2:1) but 3x in 2 Timothy (3:10, 14; 4:5).
2   See Prior, *Letter-Writer*, and Murphy-O'Connor, "2 Timothy Contrasted".
3   E.g. Houlden, 106. Easton speculates that in 2 Timothy, his first pseudepigraphon, the author "took pains to preserve the Pauline atmosphere", whereas later in 1 Timothy, "pseudonymity is a bare convention" (19).
4   E.g. Bassler, 22-23; Young, *Theology*, 142; L. Oberlinner, *Die Pastoralbriefe. Zweiten Timotheusbrief* (HTKNT 11.2-2; Freiburg: Herder, 1995), 1-5.

10.2 Paraenetic Character

The letter's paraenetic character must be borne in mind as we read it for indications of the author's soteriology. In such a context theology is at the service of praxis, with themes and emphases affected by hortatory goals. For a study of salvation this is not altogether a disadvantage. To motivate his readers, the author rehearses soteriological convictions. In this letter all five occurrences of σῴζω and cognate terms are in ministry contexts. Timothy's call is from God, τοῦ σώσαντος ἡμᾶς (1:9); his ministry is part of a revelatory process inaugurated διὰ τῆς ἐπιφανείας τοῦ σωτῆρος ἡμῶν (1:10); its goal is ἵνα καὶ [οἱ ἐκλεκτοί] σωτηρίας τύχωσιν (2:10); its primary resource is τὰ ἱερὰ γράμματα . . . τὰ δυνάμενά σε σοφίσαι εἰς σωτηρίαν (3:15); and the faithful minister is confident that, ῥύσεταί με ὁ κύριος ἀπὸ παντὸς ἔργου πονηροῦ καὶ σώσει εἰς τὴν βασιλείαν αὐτοῦ τὴν ἐπουράνιον (4:18). This personal paraenetic letter proves to be an appropriate medium for an "applied soteriology"!

10.3 Significant Themes: Shame, Power and Witness

Before examining these references in detail, two general features of the letter that have a bearing on the interpretation of the salvation material should be noted. These are the themes of shame (and specifically not being ashamed, μὴ/οὐκ ἐπαισχύνομαι) and power (δύναμις and cognates).

10.3.1 Shame

Timothy is urged not to be ashamed of the testimony or of Paul, the Lord's prisoner (1:8). Paul himself exemplifies not being ashamed of the gospel (1:12) and Onesiphorus, not being ashamed of Paul the prisoner (1:16). Given the potency of shame-honour systems in the first-century Mediterranean world, Bassler concludes that the author is constructing a new honour system, "to encourage bold proclamation of the gospel - in spite of the potentially 'shameful' consequences - among an honor-sensitive people." So he avoids "shameful" components in the summary of the gospel (1:10) and infuses "shame-linked items" such as Paul's imprisonment with "new categories of honor."[5] These insights from the Graeco-Roman environment are frutiful, but the "sacred writings" that he commends (3:16) and the traditions of Hellenistic Judaism also

---

5   Bassler, 131.

provided concepts of being ashamed/put to shame.

The hope of not being "put to shame" appears frequently in LXX Psalms (e.g., Pss 21:6 [22:5]; 24:2, 3, 20 [25:2, 3, 20]; 30:2, 18 [31:1, 17]; 33:6 [34:5]; 36:19 [37:19]; 68:7 [69:6]; 70:1 [71:1]; 73:21 [74:21]; 118:31, 46, 80, 116 [119:31, 46, 80, 116]; 126:5 [127:5]),[6] along with the expectation that the ungodly will be put to shame (e.g. Pss 6:11 [6:11]; 24:3 [25:3]; 30:18 [31:17]; 34:4 [35:4]; 39:15 [40:14]; 43:8 [44:7]; 52:6 [53:5]; 69:3 [70:2]). Not being put to shame often parallels positive concepts such as rescue or saving, which similarly depend on trust in God, e.g.:

πρὸς σὲ ἐκέκραξαν καὶ ἐσώθησαν ἐπὶ σοὶ ἤλπισαν καὶ οὐ κατῃσχύνθησαν

To you they cried, and were saved; in you they trusted, and were not put to shame.

(Ps 21:6 [22:5])

φύλαξον τὴν ψυχήν μου καὶ ῥῦσαί με μὴ καταισχυνθείην ὅτι ἤλπισα ἐπὶ σέ

O guard my life, and deliver me; do not let me be put to shame, for I take refuge in you.

(Ps 24:20 [25:20])

A contrast is pointed between those who look to the Lord and the ungodly:

κύριε μὴ κατασχυνθείην ὅτι ἐπεκαλεσάμην σε αἰσχυνθείησαν οἱ ἀσεβεῖς καὶ καταχθείησαν εἰς ᾅδου

Do not let me be put to shame, O LORD, for I call on you; let the wicked be put to shame; let them go dumbfounded to Sheol.

(Ps 30:18 [31:17])

There is also the example, suggestive in the context of 2 Tim 2:8, of:

καὶ ἐλάλουν ἐν τοῖς μαρτυρίοις σου ἐναντίον βασιλέων καὶ οὐκ ᾐσχυνόμην

I will also speak of your decrees before kings, and shall not be put to shame;

---

6 In the LXX αἰσχύνω and the compounds ἐπ- and καταισχύνω seem interchangeable (see R. Bultmann, "αἰσχύνω, κτλ.," *TDNT* 1:189-91, 189).

(Ps 118:46 [119:46])

Outside Psalms, Isa 28:16, ὁ πιστεύων ἐπ' αὐτῷ οὐ μὴ καταισχυνθῇ, links not being put to shame to trust in God's "cornerstone," which Rom 9:33; 10:11 and 1 Pet 3:16 interpret as faith in Christ.

Although there are examples of a more psychological aspect (e.g. Jer 6:15), OT shame is for the most part, "not so much the state of the soul of the αἰσχυνθείς as the situation into which he is brought,"[7] an objective condition, usually brought about by God, in consequence of which there is reason to feel shame. Even in the later LXX where Graeco-Roman influence may be detected, e.g. in Sirach's lists of what it is proper to be ashamed of (41:17-42:1a) and not to be ashamed of (42:1b-8), the older sense of not being "put to shame" is still found (e.g. Sir 24:22; 51:18, 29), illustrating the capacity of Hellenistic Judaism to absorb influences from its environment while retaining distinctively Jewish concepts, and employ vocabulary now with Hellenistic and now with traditional Jewish colouring.

"Shame" references in the NT are often best explained in terms of the Hellenistic socio-psychological concept. In certain contexts, however, particularly those associated with the judgment of God, OT resonances of being "put to shame" may be heard. The two fields surely overlap in the dominical saying,

ὃς γὰρ ἐὰν ἐπαισχυνθῇ με καὶ τοὺς ἐμοὺς λόγους ἐν τῇ γενεᾷ ταύτῃ τῇ μοιχαλίδι καὶ ἁμαρτωλῷ, καὶ ὁ υἱὸς τοῦ ἀνθρώπου ἐπαισχυνθήσεται αὐτὸν ὅταν ἔλθῃ ἐν τῇ δόξῃ τοῦ πατρὸς αὐτοῦ μετὰ τῶν ἀγγέλων τῶν ἁγίων.

(Mark 8:38, par. Luke 9:26)

Paul's pivotal affirmation, οὐ γὰρ ἐπαισχύνομαι τὸ εὐαγγέλιον (Rom 1:16), includes psychological ("I do not feel shame with respect to the gospel") and sociological ("I refuse to accept a categorisation of the gospel and its ministry as shameful") dimensions. The references to God's power to save and to believing/trusting, however, place it in succession to those OT declarations of faith: "I am not put to shame on account of the gospel, because God's power will save (through it) all who put their trust in him."[8] Both Hellenistic and OT backgrounds should also be taken into account in interpreting the references to shame in 2 Timothy.

---

7   Bultmann, *TDNT* 1:189.
8   Cf. Rom 5:5, ἡ δὲ ἐλπὶς οὐ καταισχύνει, "hope does not disappoint" (or, metonymically, "the one who hopes is not put to shame").

10.3.2 Power

"Power" language (δύναμις, δύνατος, ἐνδυναμόω) is ubiquitous in 2 Timothy. Timothy has received a spirit of power (πνεῦμα . . . δυνάμεως, 1:7); suffering for the gospel is possible by God's power (κατὰ δύναμιν θεοῦ, 1:8); Paul puts his trusts in the one who is powerful (δύνατος, 1:12); Timothy is to be empowered in grace (ἐνδυναμοῦ, 2:1); the opponents have relinquished the power of true godliness (τὴν δὲ δύναμιν αὐτῆς ἠρνημένοι, 3:5); and the Lord endued Paul with power to fulfil his calling (ἐνεδυνάμωσέν με, 4:17). Uses of the verb δύναμαι would not normally be remarkable but in light of this series of δυν- forms perhaps it too should be heard as contributing to the "power" theme. It indicates what Christ does not have power to do (ἀρνήσομαι γὰρ ἑαυτὸν οὐ δύναται, 2:13), what the women influenced by false teachers have no power to do (μηδέποτε εἰς ἐπίγνωσιν ἀληθείας ἐλθεῖν δυνάμενα, 3:7), and what the sacred scriptures have power for (τὰ δυνάμενά σε σοφίσαι εἰς σωτηρίαν, 3:15). All three occurrences are in soteriologically significant contexts, where the "power" allusion could well be intentional. The chain of δυν- terms threaded through the letter serves to connect the gospel and its ministry to the power of God, in contrast to the impotence of the opponents' life and teaching.

10.3.3 Unashamed Witness

The motifs of shame and power come together in the theme of enabling for unashamed witness. Explicit in the appeal with which the letter's main content begins (1:8), it is also implicit at the close in Paul's testimony (4:16-18). Bereft of human support, he received from the Lord power to declare the message. He is confident that God who has saved (1:9) will save (4:18). Like his OT forebears, he has put his hope in the Lord, and has not been put to shame. While there is no shame vocabulary in 4:16-18, the courtroom setting and the requirement to bear witness would certainly recall the warning against being ashamed in the opening appeal. Furthermore, if, as has often been suggested, the imagery of Ps 22 is in the background,[9] it need not be fanciful to hear echoes of vv. 4-5 [LXX 21:5-6]:

ἐπὶ σοὶ ἤλπισαν οἱ πατερές ἡμῶν, ἤλπισαν, καὶ ἐρρύσω αὐτούς· πρὸς σὲ ἐκέκραξαν καὶ ἐσώθησαν, ἐπὶ σοὶ ἤλπισαν καὶ οὐ κατησχύνθησαν.

---

9 E.g. Bassler, 177-78; Fee, 298; Lock, 119.

> In you our ancestors trusted; they trusted, and you delivered them.
> To you they cried, and they were saved; in you they trusted, and were not put to shame.

So the story ends not in shame but with an ascription of glory (4:18).

CHAPTER 11

2 Timothy 1:9-14

[θεοῦ] τοῦ σώσαντος ἡμᾶς καὶ καλέσαντος κλήσει ἁγίᾳ, οὐ κατὰ τὰ ἔργα ἡμῶν ἀλλὰ κατὰ ἰδίαν πρόθεσιν καὶ χάριν, τὴν δοθεῖσαν ἡμῖν ἐν Χριστῷ Ἰησοῦ πρὸ χρόνων αἰωνίων, φανερωθεῖσαν δὲ νῦν διὰ τῆς ἐπιφανείας τοῦ σωτῆρος ἡμῶν Χριστοῦ Ἰησοῦ, καταργήσαντος μὲν τὸν θάνατον φωτίσαντος δὲ ζωὴν καὶ ἀφθαρσίαν διὰ τοῦ εὐαγγελίου εἰς ὃ ἐτέθην ἐγὼ κῆρυξ καὶ ἀπόστολος καὶ διδάσκαλος, δι' ἣν αἰτίαν καὶ ταῦτα πάσχω· ἀλλ' οὐκ ἐπαισχύνομαι, οἶδα γὰρ ᾧ πεπίστευκα καὶ πέπεισμαι ὅτι δυνατός ἐστιν τὴν παραθήκην μου φυλάξαι εἰς ἐκείνην τὴν ἡμέραν. Ὑποτύπωσιν ἔχε ὑγιαινόντων λόγων ὧν παρ' ἐμοῦ ἤκουσας ἐν πίστει καὶ ἀγάπῃ τῇ ἐν Χριστῷ Ἰησοῦ· τὴν καλὴν παραθήκην φύλαξον διὰ πνεύματος ἁγίου τοῦ ἐνοικοῦντος ἐν ἡμῖν.

This unit is rich in soteriological language and concepts, but are they the author's? The "kerygmatic style," with "characteristics of formulaic participial predication,"[1] suggests traditional material,[2] and some terms and phrases in 1:3-12 are evocative of Pauline letters,[3] especially the thanksgiving in Rom 1:8-17.[4] The presence of terms distinctive of the PE (ἐπιφάνεια, σωτήρ), however, hint at the author's handiwork. Moreover, the thought flows coherently through the passage, so that any traditional material has evidently been woven into the author's composition.[5] In any event, as

---

1 Dibelius-Conzelmann, 99.
2 Bassler regards it as "a liturgical fragment that summarizes the gospel for which Paul and Timothy are to suffer" (127).
3 Lock lists Rom 1:16; 8:15; 1 Cor 15:55; Eph 2:5-9, but judges that, "none suggest conscious adaptation." (84).
4 See U. Luz, "Rechtfertigung bei den Paulusschülern," pages 365-83 in *Rechtfertigung: Festschrift für E. Käsemann* (eds. J. Friedrich, W. Pöhlmann and P. Stuhlmacher; Tübingen: Mohr-Siebeck, 1976), 378; Oberlinner, *2.Timotheusbrief*, 11-12.
5 Towner, *Goal*, 94; cf. Lau, *Manifest*, 114-15.

Marshall points out, he is likely to be persuaded by what he writes.[6] Particularly regarding the gospel, for whose integrity the author shows such concern, it is reasonable to expect that what he writes agrees with the παραθήκη as he understands it.

11.1 Context

A series of participles gives rhythm and structure to the unit. There are three pairs, σώσαντος . . . καλέσαντος (v. 9), δοθεῖσαν . . . φανερωθεῖσαν (vv. 9-10) and καταργήσαντος . . . φωτίσαντος (v. 10), each pair qualifying a main subject, respectively θεός, χάρις and Χριστός Ἰησοῦς. In each case a prepositional clause appended to the participial clauses both qualifies the statement and provides the subject for the subsequent pair of participles. The piece begins with God, who has saved and called. This is attributed to God's grace, the second main subject, first given and then revealed in and through Christ Jesus. He, the third subject, destroyed death and brought life and immortality to light through the gospel. Statements about God, grace, Christ and the gospel are thus woven into a tightly structured soteriological presentation.

That said, it cannot be assumed that every detail functions primarily to elucidate salvation. In the context of 1:3-12, vv. 9-10 support the appeal to suffer for the gospel by the power of God (v. 8), from which the thought of God and his saving revealed in the gospel develops (vv. 9-10). The flow of thought continues in vv. 11-12 affirming Paul's commissioning with respect to the gospel and his unashamed suffering for it, before the charge to Timothy is elaborated (vv. 13-14) with reference back to the faith, love and the Spirit already associated with him (vv. 5-7). Three lines of persuasion, then, are advanced in support of the exhortation. The example is offered of Paul, who, entrusted with the gospel, suffered but was not ashamed (vv. 12-13); the resources by which Paul succeeded, namely faith in God's power (v. 12), are shown to have been supplied to Timothy also (vv. 5, 7, 13-14); and the demonstration of the power and purpose of God in the gospel and in specific relation to Paul and Timothy provides further encouragement (vv. 9-10). The passage must therefore be heard in the context of the summons to costly service.

---

6   I. H. Marshall, "Faith and Works in the Pastoral Epistles," *SNTSU* 9 (1984): 203-18, 205.

11.2 The Statement about God (v. 9a)

11.2.1 God has Saved

With God as subject, the verb σώσαντος represents a divine activity. The aorist tense, together with other references to the past in vv. 9b-10, suggests something already achieved. In 4:18, on the other hand, σῴζω with God as subject depicts a future saving εἰς τὴν βασιλείαν αὐτοῦ τὴν ἐπουράνιον. The author, it seems, could conceive of salvation as both in one sense already accomplished and awaiting full realization in the coming age.[7]

11.2.2 God has Called with a Holy Calling

Does the second participial predicate, καλέσαντος, indicate a "calling" to faith,[8] or to ministry?[9] Schmidt considers that it serves as "a technical Pauline or deutero-Pauline term that conveys the sense of God's gracious calling to and promise of salvation" (Rom 11:29; 1 Cor 1:26; 7:20; Eph 1:18; 4:1, 4; Phil 3:14; 2 Thess 1:11; Heb 3:1; 2 Pet 1:10).[10] This may be an over-generalisation. While in Rom 11:26-32 and 1 Cor 1:26 the sovereign call of God independent of human criteria of worth is in view, in Phil 3:14 Paul strives for the prize of the ἄνω κλῆσις of God. Other references focus on the blessings into which people are called (Eph 1:18; 4:11; cf. Heb 3:1). In 2 Tim 1:9 Barrett finds the "Biblical doctrine of predestination,"[11] appealing to the attribution of the calling to God's purpose and grace as against human works, and the reference to the pre-temporal gift of grace in Christ (v. 9). It is difficult, however, to sustain this interpretation through the next element, φανερωθεῖσαν δὲ νῦν διὰ τῆς ἐπιφανείας τοῦ σωτῆρος ἡμῶν Χριστοῦ Ἰησοῦ (v. 10), for it is surely the gift of salvation generally, not the particular election of Paul and Timothy, that was revealed through Christ's appearing.

The content of καλέσαντος in v. 9 must be explored in relation to its companion term σώσαντος. Although the terms are not synonyms,[12] the association makes this "calling" soteriological. Concepts of saving and calling are also found together in the later chapters of Isaiah. As the (only) Saviour (e.g. 43:3, 11), the Lord "calls" his people and his servant, in contexts suggesting both saving

---

7 As in Rom 8:24, although Davies argues that the past tense distances this text from Paul (66).
8 Towner, 162.
9 Bassler, 132.
10 K. L. Schmidt, "καλέω," *TDNT* 3:491-92.
11 Barrett, 95; cf. Knight, 374.
12 *Contra* Easton, 40.

(e.g. 41:8-10; 43:1-7) and commissioning (e.g. 42:1, 5-9). Among the latter is the calling, before his birth (49:1),[13] of the servant through whom salvation will reach the nations (49:6). In Isaiah, then, God's calling is part of his activity as saviour, and includes both the gracious election of Israel and the commissioning of an agent of salvation for the benefit of Israel and the world. Perhaps in 2 Timothy, as in Isaiah, the ideas of calling to belong to God and to serve him should not be too sharply distinguished. The later notion of *vocatio* to Christian ministry is not present in the NT uses of κλῆσις,[14] nor of the verb καλέω.[15] In relation to Paul, however, the ideas of conversion and calling to service consistently overlap (e.g. Acts 9:5-6, 15; 22:14-16; 26:15-18; Gal 1:15-16; 1 Tim 1:12-16). Both are aspects of the one divine call, so that in 1 Tim 1:12-16 Paul's appointment to service can confirm the proposition that Christ came into the world to save sinners.

In 2 Tim 1:9 the "calling" is qualified by the phrase, κλήσει ἁγίᾳ, a biblical hapax described by Spicq as a semitism whose sense is impossible to determine.[16] In fact the calling to be holy,[17] and the calling from a holy God,[18] are best understood as essentially one idea, "a calling from a holy God which should lead to a holy way of life."[19]

---

13 In Isa 49:1 the MT has two parallel statements of the pre-natal call: קְרָאָ֔נִי מִמְּעֵ֥י אִמִּ֖י הִזְכִּ֥יר שְׁמִֽי יְהוָה֙ מִבֶּ֣טֶן "Yahweh from the womb called me; from my mother's body he mentioned my name" (Motyer's translation, *Isaiah*, 385). In place of the first the LXX has, διὰ χρόνου πολλοῦ στήσεται, λέγει κύριος, ("Through much time it will stand, says the Lord"), emphasising the enduring force of the Lord's decision.

14 Cf. Kelly, 162. Even in 1 Cor 7:11, this idea "cannot be legitimately attributed to Paul" (L. Coenen, "καλέω," *NIDNTT* 1:271-76, 275).

15 Of over 140 occurrences only Heb 5:4 (the call of Aaron) and possibly Matt 4:21 par. Mark 1:20 (the call to follow Jesus) could have this reference.

16 Spicq, 714; cf. Fee, 229. In the LXX κλῆσις occurs only in Jer 38:6 [MT 31:6], Jdt 12:10 and 3 Macc 5:14, always representing an invitation. The only soteriological context is in Jeremiah, where on the ἡμέρα κλήσεως the people are summoned to Zion, because God is gathering them in (embracing both God's initiative and human response).

17 As in 1 Thess 4:7. Cf. Dibelius-Conzelmann, 99.

18 Cf. Easton, 40.

19 Marshall, 705.

11.3 The Statement about Grace (vv. 9b-10a)

11.3.1 Grace Explains God's Intention to Save

When the *Hauptbriefe* speak of "grace given" to Paul the reference is almost always to his ministry, which is ἡ χάρις ἡ δοθεῖσα μοι (Gal 2:9; cf. Rom 12:3; 15:15; 1 Cor 3:10; and of all Christians in Rom 12:6).[20] While mention in 2 Tim 1:9 of the gift of ministry roles to Paul and Timothy would fit comfortably with the letter's practical concern, the setting of God's "gracious purpose"[21] in antithesis to human works as the basis for saving and calling suggests that saving grace rather than a grace-gift for ministry may be in view.

Hasler considers that the radical Pauline doctrine of sovereign grace declaring sinners justified is reduced here to the condescending, compassionate act of the divine Benefactor,[22] but while justification and sin are not specified, there is no necessary conflict between the idea of justification and the soteriological elements highlighted in vv. 9-10. The concern is to root salvation in God, and grace is that aspect of God's nature and attitude towards humankind that explains his decision to save. The strongly adversative οὐ κατά . . . ἀλλὰ κατά construction sets "our" in antithesis to "his own," and "works" to "purpose and grace," insisting that salvation owes nothing to human merit, but is willed and gifted by God.

11.3.2 Grace was Given to Us in Christ Jesus Before Time

Personal, christological, and cosmological aspects of the author's concept of grace are indicated. First, it was given "to us." In a traditional piece, the original reference might have been to beneficiaries of salvation in general. It is utilized here, however, in a markedly personal context (see the second person singular address in vv. 4, 5, 6, 8, 13, 14; first person plural in v. 7; first person singular in vv. 11, 12), suggesting that Paul and Timothy are in view as specific recipients of grace. Secondly, grace has been given "in Christ Jesus before time."[23] This gift "in Christ" is utterly objective, although the exhortation, ἐνδυναμοῦ ἐν τῇ χάριτι τῆς ἐν Χριστῷ Ἰησοῦ (2:1) reveals a more subjective dimension to grace. The point in 1:9 is that in God's saving engagement with humankind the purpose and gift of salvation have from the outset been conceived

---

20 Cf. Eph 3:2, 7, 8; 4:7.
21 Barrett, reading πρόθεσιν καὶ χάριν as a hendiadys (95).
22 Hasler, 58.
23 On "in Christ" see above on 1 Tim 1:14 (pp. 46-47 and n. 60).

and realized christologically. The location of the gift πρὸ χρόνων αἰωνίων discloses a cosmological framework. Hanson comments, "It is a characteristic of the deutero-Pauline literature to be concerned about the relation of God's salvation in Christ to the cosmos as a whole and the whole of human history."[24] While no concept of the pre-existence of Christians is required, the statement does seem to affirm that Paul and Timothy, or perhaps all who have in fact received grace, were in the saving purpose of God already its designated beneficiaries before time began (cf. Gal 1:15). The effect is to underline the priority of God's initiative and its independence of any human act.

11.3.3 Grace has Now been Revealed through Christ's Appearing

a. The Time-frame

That which was purposed and grace-gifted before time is now made manifest. This "once hidden - now revealed" schema is also found elsewhere in the NT, as illustrated in the table below. These statements assume a time frame that includes a pre-temporal decision of God and its manifestation in the present age. 2 Timothy utilizes the same chronological (or, better, "kairological") framework to depict two stages in the provision of salvation, "given before time" and "revealed in the present age."

---

24 Hanson, *Epistles*, 122-23.

Reference	"once hidden"	"now revealed"
Rom 16:25-26	God's mystery kept hidden χρόνοις αἰωνίοις σεσιγημένου	Now revealed φανερωθέντος δὲ νῦν
1 Cor 2:7-10	God's secret wisdom decreed ἀποκεκρυμμένην . . . πρὸ τῶν αἰώνων	Now revealed ἀπεκάλυψεν
Eph 3:9-10	Mystery hidden ἀποκεκρυμμένου ἀπὸ τῶν αἰώνων	Wisdom of God now made known φωτίσαι . . . ἵνα γνωρισθῇ νῦν
Col 1:26	Mystery hidden ἀποκεκρυμμένον ἀπὸ τῶν αἰώνων καὶ ἀπὸ τῶν γενεῶν	Mystery now made known νῦν δὲ ἐφανερώθη
2 Tim 1:9-10	God's (purpose and) grace given in Christ Jesus δοθεῖσαν . . . πρὸ χρόνων αἰωνίων	Grace now revealed φανερωθεῖσαν δὲ νῦν
Titus 1:1-3	Hope of eternal life promised ἐπηγγείλατο . . . πρὸ χρόνων αἰωνίων	Revealed in due time ἐφανέρωσεν δὲ καιροῖς ἰδίοις
1 Pet 1:20	Christ (the ransom) destined προεγνωσμένου . . . πρὸ καταβολῆς κόσμου	Christ revealed φανερωθέντος δὲ ἐπ' ἐσχάτου τῶν χρόνων

b. Revelation Through Epiphany

The saving purpose and grace of God were made known, διὰ τῆς ἐπιφανείας τοῦ σωτῆρος ἡμῶν Χριστοῦ Ἰησοῦ (v. 10). This "epiphany" is commonly assumed to represent Christ's incarnation,[25] an identification "unique in the NT."[26] From this

---

25 E.g., Barrett, 95; Dibelius-Conzelmann, 104 (and n. 53); Fee, 230; Guthrie, 129; Hanson, *Epistles*, 123; Houlden, 113; Kelly, 163; Merkel, 59; Young,

alleged novelty Easton infers that, "eschatological concepts (1 Cor 15.26, etc.) have been read back into the past,"[27] following Dibelius-Conzelmann, for whom it confirms that the PE are adjusting to the delay in the parousia:

> The whole sequence of concepts with its terminology . . . is intended to transfer to Christ's *first* epiphany all those effects which were originally expected from the glorious epiphany in the last days.[28]

This would be more convincing if it could be demonstrated that epiphany language had earlier been used of the parousia and only later appropriated by the PE for the incarnation, but in fact all save one of the NT occurrences of ἐπιφάνεια are in the PE themselves, and all, with the exception of 2 Tim 1:10, refer to Christ's future appearing (1 Tim 6:14; 2 Tim 4:1, 8; Titus 2:13; cf. 2 Thess 2:8). While Dibelius-Conzelmann have to concede that the PE also use ἐπιφάνεια of the future appearing, they insist that, "the formula quoted in v10 knows only of the first epiphany." [29] On this basis it could equally well be argued, if somewhat mischievously, that the author, inheriting a tradition that describes Christ's earthly existence in epiphanic terms (1:10), creatively reapplies the language to Christ's second appearing (4:1, 8)! It is arbitrary to suggest that the intention in 1:10 is to heighten the significance of Christ's first appearing at the expense of his second. Lau offers a broader explanation: "God's plan and purpose is now actualized in the historical process," so that, "what happened on earth (with the Christ-event) was only the manifestation in space and time of the things of eternity."[30] There may, however, be a more specific reference that makes better sense of both the Hellenistic background of ἐπιφάνεια and the particular theological context. We shall return to this in the discussion of φωτίσαντος below.

11.4 The Statement about Christ Jesus (v. 10b)

Christ is designated σωτήρ, and said to have "abolished death" and "brought life and immortality to light through the gospel." Here are

---

Theology, 63.
26   Easton, 43; although the verb φαίνω represents the incarnation in 1 Tim 3:16; 1 Pet 1:19-20; 1 John 1:2; 3:5, 8.
27   Easton, 43-44.
28   Dibelius-Conzelmann, 104-05.
29   Dibelius-Conzelman, 105 n. 55.
30   Lau, *Manifest,* 118, 119; cf. Scott, 93.

indications of the content of the saving (σῴζω) ascribed to God (v. 9) and the work of the saviour (σωτήρ) Christ Jesus (v. 10).

11.4.1 Christ Jesus is σωτήρ

To refer to Christ as σωτήρ highlights the salvific character of the epiphany (v. 10a). Although the high incidence of this term in the PE is commonly noted it is less often observed that 2 Timothy supplies only one of the ten examples. Since our approach is to assessing each letter on its own terms, the significance of σωτήρ here must be determined from the context rather than from generalisations about the PE as a whole. The content of the idea in vv. 9-10 is suggested by the images of epiphany, victory (destroying death) and proclamation of benefit (declaring life through the gospel). In the Hellenistic milieu this might be expected of a military benefactor, which would make the choice of σωτήρ appropriate even without Christological connotations. The main theological significance, however, is that whereas God is said to save, Christ is made saviour. Conceptually, God and Christ are brought together in the provision of salvation,[31] as Christ becomes the agent through whose epiphany God's saving will and grace are actualized.

11.4.2 Christ Jesus has Abolished Death

That Christ has "abolished death" is a dramatic assertion. Packer's survey of καταργέω in the NT finds a constant meaning of "rendering something inoperative."[32] In what sense could death be rendered inoperative? Since 2 Timothy expects physical death even for the faithful (4:6; cf. 2:11b), it must be another "death" that has been annulled. Christ's victory by his resurrection over his own death is affirmed (2:8), but in 1:10 more is in view than the reversal of one historical death. The idea is related to the proclamation of life in the gospel (cf. the "promise of life," 1:1), which requires that in some way Christ's own victory nullifies death for others also. Spicq suggests that θάνατος with the article might represent death, either personified or as the work of the devil, as the defeated enemy of Christ.[33] The statement does not, however, specify the beneficiaries of this achievement. Has death been defeated for all or some? And does the gospel declare that all are now in a new condition of immortality or announce the possibility of this new condition,

---

31 See Mounce, cxxxv.
32 J. I. Packer, "Abolish, Nullify, Reject," *NIDNTT* 1:73-74.
33 Spicq, 716. Cf. Heb 2:14.

calling people to appropriate it? While it could be argued that 1:9-10 does not provide a clear answer, 2:11-13 does indicate that the author of 2 Timothy regards enjoyment of the life provided through the Christ event as conditional.

In the accomplished act suggested by the aorist tense of καταργήσαντος, some see a shift from Paul's future hope that, ἔσχατος ἐχθρὸς καταργεῖται ὁ θάνατος (1 Cor 15:26).[34] This, however, misrepresents both Paul and 2 Timothy. Regarding 1 Cor 15:26 M. de Boer argues,

> The fact that Paul employs a present tense in v.26 (as in 2.6!) suggests that the destruction of death is certain and that, because Christ has been raised from the dead, its destruction, and those of the other powers, has in fact begun.[35]

The apparent "futurity" of the Corinthians passage is no "eschatological reservation," but a counter to an over-realized eschatology.[36] While acknowledging the "almost unbearable tension" in Paul between Christological claims and soteriological reality, de Boer insists that Paul's essential understanding is that death is already defeated, hence the declaration that death no longer rules over Christ (Rom 6:9), "a view no different from that found in 2 Tim 1.10."[37] If this is correct, 2 Timothy exhibits the standard Pauline perspective, and it is 1 Corinthians which, for situational reasons, diverges from the norm.[38]

The past tense may also owe something to the formulaic nature of the material, on the pattern of the OT's "prophetic" or "precative" perfect. Several of the LXX Psalms employ the Greek aorist to declare God's deliverance even when it is evidently not yet realized (e.g. 53:9 [54:7]; 55:14 [56:13]; 85:13 [86:13]). Faith that God will act is expressed as praise that he has done so. It is quite conceivable that an early Christian "liturgical fragment"[39] should articulate praise for God's saving and Christ's defeat of death without denying that their full realization was still awaited.

---

34 E.g. Merkel, 59.
35 M. C. de Boer, *The Defeat of Death. Apocalyptic Eschatology in 1 Corinthians 15 and Romans 5* (JSNTSup 22; Sheffield: Sheffield Academic Press, 1988), 122.
36 de Boer, *Defeat of Death*, 123.
37 de Boer, *Defeat of Death*, 123.
38 de Boer, *Defeat of Death*, 123; cf. Guthrie, 130.
39 Bassler, 127.

11.4.3 Christ has Brought Life and Immortality to Light

Paul's apostleship is intimately connected to "the promise of life that is in Christ Jesus" (1:1; cf. 1:10-11) and "life" is clearly a significant element in the "good news." What is this life, and what precisely is Christ said to have accomplished in relation to it?

a. ζωὴ καὶ ἀφθαρσία

Does this expression represent two ideas or one? A distinction has been proposed between new life in the present age (ζωή) and postmortem life (ἀφθαρσία),[40] but 2 Timothy gives no suggestion of two separable gifts of life. The "promise of life that is in Christ Jesus" (1:1) must be identified with "the salvation that is in Christ Jesus with eternal glory" (2:10),[41] reinforced by the eschatological συ[ν]ζάω concept in 2:11. Accordingly, with an epexegetical καί, 1:10 proclaims "life, even immortality."[42]

The terms ἀφθαρσία, ἀθανασία and their cognates represent a Greek concept that was adopted into Hellenistic Judaism. This is illustrated by its almost total restriction in the LXX to the Greek writings, 4 Maccabees and the Wisdom of Solomon.[43] 4 Maccabees sees immortality as the righteous martyrs' reward. Wisdom depicts humankind as created for immortality (2:23), to be attained through the righteousness achieved by loving Wisdom and heeding her instruction (6:17-20).[44] There is some continuity between such ideas and the NT. The noun ἀφθαρσία occurs 7x (Rom 2:7; 1 Cor 15:42, 50, 53, 54; Eph 6:24; 2 Tim 1:10), the adjective ἄφθαρτος 5x (Rom 1:23; 1 Cor 15:52; 1 Tim 1:17; 1 Pet 1:4, 23) and ἀθανασία 3x (1 Cor 15:53, 54; 1 Tim 6:16). Paul's discussion of resurrection in 1 Corinthians 15 accounts for almost half of these references. There, "imperishability," virtually synonymous with "immortality" (see vv. 53, 54), is a quality of the resurrected body which can "inherit the kingdom of God" (v. 50). Victory over death will be realized when the perishable and mortal is clothed with imperishability and immortality (v. 54), at the end-time event which includes

---

40 See Barrett, 95; cf. Spicq, 717; J. R. W. Stott, *The Message of 2 Timothy* (The Bible Speaks Today; Leicester: IVP, 1973), 39.
41 Quinn considers δόξα here to be almost synonymous with ζωή (*Titus*, 300); see also on "The Terminology for Life in the PE" (291-303).
42 See also Kelly, 164.
43 4 Macc 7:3; 9:22; 14:5, 6; 16:13; 17:12; 18:23; Wis 1:15; 2:23; 3:4; 4:1; 6:18, 19; 8:13, 17; 12:1; 15:3; 18:4; elsewhere only in Sir 17:30, denying that a human being is ἀθάνατος.
44 This sorites concludes with the enjoyment of immortality (v. 19) in God's kingdom (v. 20).

resurrection (v. 52). In Romans, ἀφθαρσία is an attribute of God (1:23) and a goal to which good people aspire (2:7). Polemical concerns shaped the presentations in both letters. To counter an over-realized eschatology in Corinth Paul emphasizes the futurity of God's gift of life and the impossibility of corruptible human bodies participating in the incorruptible life of God's kingdom. Concerned in Romans to demonstrate that God's justice is impartial and that he deals with Jew and Gentile on the same basis, Paul articulates "a broad principle which would gain wide acceptance among people with any degree of moral sensibility,"[45] that those who seek ἀφθαρσία by doing good will receive God's gift of ζωὴ αἰώνιος. Common to both is the idea of incorruptible life as the gift of God, unattainable by human effort alone, and not fully possessed until bestowed by God in the future. 1 Corinthians links ἀφθαρσία with the resurrection and inheritance in the Kingdom of God. Romans sees the aspiration to ἀφθαρσία answered in God's gift of ζωὴ αἰώνιος (cf. Rom 5:21).

The reference to "incorruptible life" in 2 Tim 1:10 does not make all of those ideas explicit, but nor does it conflict with them. Quinn writes, "the Pauline usage of *aphtharsia* is presumed, above all that of Rom 2:6-7."[46] God's gift is affirmed over against human achievement (v. 9) and "that day" is anticipated (v. 12; cf. v. 18; 4:8). The resurrection is yet to take place (2:18) and the believer's goal is to reach the "heavenly kingdom" (4:18) beyond physical death (4:6). 2 Timothy presents immortality as life beyond physical death enjoyed in God's coming kingdom. Though entry is via the judgment hall on the day of accounting, it is nonetheless the gracious gift of God, and the achievement of Jesus Christ the saviour.

b. A Sacramental Soteriology?

Noting that Ignatius describes the eucharist as φάρμακον ἀθανασίας, "the medicine of immortality" (Ign. *Eph.* 20), Hanson suggests that v. 10 represents an extract from a eucharistic prayer, in which context ζωή refers to new life in baptism and ἀφθαρσία to the eucharist.[47] Building on this, Oberlinner sees the act of baptism, as the means by which God's saving purpose for humankind takes

---

45 Dunn, *Romans*, 1:86.
46 Quinn, *Titus*, 301.
47 Hanson, *Epistles*, 123, and *Studies*, 97-109. Ignatius, however, does not make this distinction between ζωή and ἀφθαρσία. His φάρμακον ἀθανασίας is ἀντίδοτος τοῦ μὴ ἀποθανεῖν, ἀλλὰ ζῆν ἐν Ἰησοῦ Χριστῷ διὰ παντός. He also describes the gospel as "the consummation of immortality" (ἀπάρτισμα . . . ἀθανασίας, Phld. 9.2).

concrete form, in the foreground.⁴⁸ He explains vv. 9-10 as elements of a baptismal hymn, according to which the saving benefits of Christ's epiphany take effect in the sacramental act.⁴⁹ 2 Timothy, however, exhibits no overt sacramental interest. Rather, what emerges is a pervasive concern for the activity and content of teaching. Salvation is linked not to sacramental ministry but to the gospel and its proclamation (e.g. 1:1, 9b-11; 2:8-10). Where Ignatius appeals for unity around the sacrament (e.g. Ign., *Eph* 5.2), 2 Timothy honours the solitary but faithful proclaimer of the message (4:16-18).

c. φωτίσαντος

Some have seen a baptismal allusion in the statement that life and immortality have been "brought to light" (φωτίζω, v. 10). According to Scott, this term was used in the mystery religions for "the illumination of the initiate by means of secret rites."⁵⁰ With these connotations, a notion of baptismal illumination might be suggested.⁵¹ Conzelmann, however, judges that in the NT, "The use of the verb φωτίζω remains within modest limits . . . . No theory of illumination is developed."⁵² A further objection to an initiatory reading of 2 Tim 1:10 is that, as Scott concedes,⁵³ the object of the verb is not the person illuminated, as in the Mysteries, but the content revealed.⁵⁴

---

48 Oberlinner, *2.Timotheusbrief*, 38 (following Hasler, 58) and 41(citing Hanson, *Epistles*, 123). It is however certainly not self-evident that baptism stands "im Vordergrund" or even "im Hintergrund" of the text!
49 Oberlinner, *2.Timotheusbrief*, 43; cf. Hasler, 58-59. Oberlinner cites Towner, *Goal*, 98-99 in support (n. 70), but in fact Towner disputes both Hasler's removal of salvation to the future and Luz's "early catholic" baptismal emphasis. He does employ water imagery, but as a metaphor for spiritual experience, not baptism.
50 Scott, 94; cf. Hasler, 58-59.
51 Scott, comparing Heb 6:4; 10:32 (94); cf. Spicq, who adds Eph 5:14 (717). P. Ellingworth, *The Epistle to the Hebrews* (NIGTC; Grand Rapids: Eerdmans, 1993), 319-20, and W. L. Lane, *Hebrews 1-8* (WBC 47A; Dallas: Word, 1991), 141, consider but dismiss a baptismal reference in Hebrews.
52 H. Conzelmann, "φῶς, κτλ.," *TDNT* 9:310-58, 343. His caution extends to Justin's characterisation of τὸ λουτρόν (baptism?) as φωτισμός in *Apol.*, 61.12 (357-58). In their commentary Dibelius-Conzelmann take φωτίζω not as a technical term of mysticism but as "liturgical language of revelation," although a "purely figurative use" is also allowable (105 and n. 58).
53 Scott, 94.
54 Unlike the Johannine concept of τὸ φῶς τὸ ἀληθινόν, ὃ φωτίζει πάντα ἄνθρωπον (John 1:9).

Alternative connotations of the term must therefore be sought. Interestingly, imagery of light is prominent in the Acts accounts of Paul's conversion and mission. Noting that of ten occurrences of "light" in Acts, six refer to the blinding light of Paul's Damascus road experience (Acts 9:3; 22:6, 9, 11; 26:13, 18), S. A. Hunt continues,

> Paul, blinded by epiphanic light, would later see his ministry in terms of bringing light to the Gentiles (Acts 13:47; quoting Isa 49:6; cf. *Barn.* 14.8) and thereby 'opening blind eyes' (Is 42:27; see especially Acts 26:18; cf. *Barn.* 14.7).[55]

This provides an interpretive context for the description of the resurrected Christ as a light-bringer in Acts 26:23 (φῶς μέλλει καταγγέλλειν τῷ τε λαῷ καὶ τοῖς ἔθνεσιν). The proclamation of light in Acts 26:23 and the bringing of life and immortality to light in 2 Tim 1:10 are related if not equivalent concepts. The "light" in Acts is more than knowledge about life, it is a metaphor for that life; 2 Timothy's "life and immortality" is not something upon which light shines but the content of that light. Christ is therefore not only a communicator but the bringer of light-and-life.[56]

This suggests a different perspective on the epiphany reference. To reveal God's "purpose and grace" (v. 9), it would have to comprise "the whole manifestation of Christ on earth," [57] or at least the incarnation. If, however, what is revealed is the outcome of that purpose, life (v. 10), then the singularly appropriate focus would be Christ's resurrection. In Acts it is specifically the risen Christ whom Paul encounters in dazzling light (Acts 9:3-6; 22:6-11; 26:12-18), and his preaching is in obedience to the "heavenly vision" (οὐρανίος ὀπτασία, Acts 26:19). In the *Hauptbriefe* Alan Segal finds Paul's vision of the risen Christ central to his perception of his mission and the promise of the gospel.[58] On 1 Cor 15:5-7, where the risen Christ is said to have been "seen" (ὤφθη, used in the LXX for the seeing of visions), he comments:

> Because Jesus has been *seen* or *revealed* in this very way, we know that the general resurrection has begun and we also know that Paul and all those who saw him in this transformed state are the first apostles and prophets of this new epoch in human history. It is very important to note that Paul knows this because of his

---

55 S. A. Hunt, "Light and Darkness," *DLNTD* 657-59, 658.
56 Cf. the association of life and light in the Psalms (e.g. LXX Ps 12:4 [13:3]).
57 Ellicott, 127.
58 Alan F. Segal, "Paul's Thinking about Resurrection in its Jewish Context," *NTS* 44 (1998): 400-19.

visions, in which the embodied Christ was revealed to him.⁵⁹

Against the background of this tradition of the appearing in light of the risen Christ, the appropriateness of φωτίζω in 2 Tim 1:10 is appreciated. Having annulled death, Christ in his epiphany (post-resurrection appearing) "shines forth" life and immortality, manifesting that which in God's gracious purpose had already been gifted in Christ before time.⁶⁰ Paul's commission, given by the risen Christ, was to proclaim that light, "the promise of life that is in Christ Jesus" (1:1).

11.4.4 "Through the Gospel"

The bringing of light and life is further qualified by what may be the final clause of the traditional material, διὰ τοῦ εὐαγγελίου. This fills out the soteriological picture by clarifying the relationship between the historical Christ-event and the author's present and indicating the role of proclamation in the realization of salvation.

a. Proclamation and Actualization

This clause διὰ τοῦ εὐαγγελίου "brings the salvific effects of the Christ event into the present age."⁶¹ Without it the "now" of the historical saving manifestation would become a "then" as time passed, but with it the saving event continues in the "now" of the author and his readers, as both objective and subjective reality, "a present reception or even proleptic experiencing of eternal life."⁶² "We" (note the three first person plural pronouns in v. 9) participate in this reality through the hearing of the gospel, which is preached not as a mere passing on of doctrine but as a powerful, life-giving word.⁶³ For this author, the proclaiming of the εὐαγγέλιον is the key to immortality for people in this present age.

---

59 Segal, "Resurrection," 404.
60 Spicq, 717, offers a similar reading: "Le Christ surgissant du tombeau apparaît en triomphateur des ténèbres. Glorifié, il est lumineux, faisant resplendir en sa personne - avant de les communiquer aux siens - vie et incorruptibilité. Cette luminescence est précisément celle des épiphanies religieuses." Although dismissed by Hanson (*Epistles*, 123) and barely noticed elsewhere, this interpretation does give due weight to ἐπιφάνεια imagery.
61 Towner, *Goal*, 98; cf. "The Present Age in the Eschatology of the Pastoral Epistles," *NTS* 32 (1986): 427-48.
62 Towner, *Goal*, 99.
63 Oberlinner, *2.Timotheusbrief*, 44.

This contemporization does not nullify future and past aspects of salvation. Dibelius-Conzelmann's view that this bringing of salvation into the present represents a "realized eschatology"[64] fails to take due account of the letter's hope of immortality (v. 10b) and consciousness of "that day" to come (v. 12). Bassler's assessment that, "as long as the revelatory aspect of the Christ-event is stressed, the act of proclamation is put almost on a par with the event itself,"[65] must be balanced by the recognition that without the event from which it derives there would be no proclamation. As Oberlinner points out, where the church's preaching is interpeted as a salvation-effecting word, the concern for the guarding of the gospel acquires soteriological significance.[66]

b. ἡ παραθήκη μου

In common with the expressions τὸ εὐαγγέλιον (1:8, 10-11), ὑποτύπωσις ὑγιαινόντων λόγων (1:13), ἃ ἤκουσας παρ' ἐμοῦ (2:2; cf. 1:13), and ὁ λόγος τοῦ θεοῦ (2:9) in this letter, ἡ καλὴ παραθήκη (1:14) implies a particular didactic content. In addition the term παραθήκη, found in the NT only in 2 Tim 1:12, 14 and 1 Tim 6:20 (always with φυλάσσειν), conveys the sense of "deposit, property entrusted to another."[67] The referent in v. 12 is debated.[68] If the μου were an objective genitive the παραθήκη would be something deposited with Paul, continuing the thought of God entrusting him to proclaim the gospel (v. 11). Wolter offers linguistic evidence, however, that the usage here must be possessive,[69] making the παραθήκη something that Paul deposits, either with God (e.g. his destiny) or with Timothy (the gospel and its proclamation). It is in this latter sense that παραθήκη is used in v. 14, and it fits the the paraenetic context (cf. 2:1-2). Since, however, that which Paul deposits with Timothy is what God first entrusted to him (v. 11), much the same thought results whether the μου is read as objective or possessive: God has entrusted something to Paul, which he now hands on to Timothy, trusting that God himself will safeguard it. Similar confidence is expressed in 2:8-10 in relation to τὸ εὐαγγέλιον μου: despite the limiting of Paul's activity, God's

---

64 Dibelius-Conzelmann, 99.
65 Bassler, 133.
66 Oberlinner, 2.Timotheusbrief, 44.
67 BAGD, 616.
68 See, e.g., Bassler, 133-34; Fee, 231-32; Knight, 379-80; Quinn-Wacker, 604; Spicq, 719-20.
69 Wolter, Paulustradition, 116-18, discussed by Marshall, 710-11; Oberlinner, 2.Timotheusbrief, 47-49.

salvation-working message still operates (ἀλλὰ ὁ λόγος τοῦ θεοῦ οὐ δέδεται, v. 9), and its success is assured (v. 10). The expressions τὸ εὐαγγέλιον μου (2:8) and ἡ παραθήκη μου (1:12) are effectively equivalent in relation to the transmission of Paul's message, and "verse 12, read in this light, expresses the confidence that God has the power to watch over that important process."[70]

d. God, the Object of Trust

On the phrase, οἶδα γὰρ ἐν ᾧ πεπίστευκα (v. 12b), Guthrie comments, "The statement would have lost immeasurably if Paul had said 'what' instead of 'whom'."[71] For all the stress on the content of teaching, it is God himself who is δυνατός and he is the object of trust, echoing the OT affirmation that he who puts his trust in God will not be put to shame (ἀλλ' οὐκ ἐπαισχύνομαι, v. 12).[72] With the reference to "that day," the concept is transposed into eschatological categories (cf. 1:18; 4:8).[73]

11.5 The Statements about Paul and Timothy (vv. 11-14)

11.5.1 The Paraenetic Effect of the Salvation Statement

The salvation material (vv. 9-10) is set within a carefully constructed exhortation to suffer for the sake of the gospel. It is bracketed by the appeal to Timothy (v. 8) and the example of Paul (vv. 11-12) which, as the table illustrates, mirror each other:[74]

---

70 Bassler, 134.
71 Guthrie, 131.
72 The theme of unashamed witness is described in ch. 10: "Introduction to Salvation in 2 Timothy" above; cf. Fee, 231.
73 *Contra* Hanson, who reads it as the day of Paul's martyrdom, so that, "The reference to the parousia thus becomes little more than decorative detail" (*Epistles*, 124). Even if Paul's martyrdom is in view here, however, Hanson still has to resort to strained exegesis to eradicate any eschatological horizon from the PE. "Those who have loved his appearing" (4:8), for example, become "those who have shown their love by the Christian life they live" (156).
74 Lau suggests a chiastic pattern extending through vv. 6-14: Spirit (vv. 6-7), Paul's call and life (v. 8), Gospel (vv. 9-10), Paul's call and life (vv. 11-13), Spirit (v. 14) (*Manifest*, 128-29).

Appeal (v. 8)	Common Element	Example (vv. 11-12)
μὴ ἐπαισχυνθῇς	Not ashamed	οὐκ ἐπαισχύνομαι
τὸ μαρτύριον τοῦ κυρίου ἡμῶν	Activity of testifying/ proclaiming	ἐτέθην ἐγὼ κῆρυξ καὶ ἀπόστολος καὶ διδάσκαλος
συγκακοπάθησον	Suffer	ταῦτα πάσχω
τῷ εὐαγγελίῳ	Gospel	[τὸ εὐαγγέλιον] εἰς ὃ ἐτέθην ἐγὼ κῆρυξ
κατὰ δύναμιν θεοῦ	Power of God	δυνατός ἐστιν τὴν παραθήκην μου φυλάξαι

Combining exhortation with example, the paraenesis runs:
    (a) Do not be <u>ashamed</u> to <u>testify</u> - I am not <u>ashamed</u>, I <u>proclaim</u>
    (b) but <u>suffer</u> for the <u>gospel</u> - I am <u>suffering</u> [for the <u>gospel</u>]
    (c) by the <u>power</u> of God - I trust the one who is <u>powerful</u>.

The salvation material supports each element of this appeal. The summary of the Gospel demonstrates that there is no need for shame. Subjectively, there is no need to feel embarrassment about proclaiming such a triumph and participating in the eternal saving purposes of God; objectively, the prospect of eschatological shame is banished by the gospel assurance of immortality. The prevalence of revelation language (φανερωθεῖσαν . . . ἐπιφανείας . . . φωτίσαντος) stresses the activity of making known, while implying that the human witness is participating in the divine process of disclosure. The prospect of suffering is set in the context of an already accomplished saving and calling, the presence of a saviour and the conviction that even death has been nullified. Finally, the salvation material "explains the δύναμις θεοῦ in terms of the execution and the operative power (i.e., its effect) of God's salvation in the present age," demonstrating that "God's power, as revealed in the Christ-event, is now available to sustain Timothy in his gospel ministry."[75] This salvation material, then, motivates towards 2 Timothy's recurring motif of empowered witness.

---

75 Lau, *Manifest*, 128.

11.5.2 Paul in the Soteriological Schema

Timothy's suffering is "for the gospel" (τῷ εὐαγγελίῳ, v. 8), Christ has brought life and immortality to light "through the gospel" (διὰ τοῦ εὐαγγελίου, v. 10) and Paul's commissioning was "for the purpose of" (εἰς ὅ) the gospel (v. 11). Thus links are established between the gospel, the Christ event which it declares, and those charged with its proclamation. It is this last relationship that must now be explored. Is it fair to judge that, for this author, "Paul and the tradition are essential components of the event of salvation"?[76] Merkel makes the valid observation that when the PE speak of the gospel, they speak also of Paul.[77] In his view 2 Tim 1:13 indicates that it is Paul's message which has become the definitive expression of the church's teaching.[78] Läger goes further. She sees not only an assertion of the correctness of Paul's message but also a binding of the gospel to the person of Paul, establishing Paul and his preaching as the exclusive means of transmission of the benefits of the Christ event.[79] No such reading, however, is required by the text. As Marshall points out, while Paul was certainly appointed κῆρυξ καὶ ἀπόστολος καὶ διδάσκαλος (v. 11), "the article is conspicuously missing."[80]

11.6 Summary

This passage expresses a concept of salvation in relation to which highly developed theological, eschatological, christological and missiological aspects may be discerned. It is properly theological in that salvation is understood to be the act of God (who saves and calls) and it is grounded in the character and purpose of God. It is set within a "kairological" schema which extends from before time (v. 9) through the present age (v. 10) and on into a future of indestructible life, which is the focus of the gift of salvation. Salvation is therefore experienced as both already and not yet, living as God's holy people now while anticipating the eschatological gift of life. The concept is thoroughly Christological; although God saves, Christ is the "saviour," and even the pre-temporal saving purpose and grace of God have been given in Christ before his coming into the world. God's gift of life is revealed epiphanically in

---

76 Dibelius-Conzelmann, 105.
77 Merkel, 59: "Wo wom Evangelium die Rede ist, ist in den Pastoralbriefen auch von Paulus die Rede."
78 Merkel, 60.
79 Läger, *Christologie*, 71-72.
80 Marshall, 708.

Christ, possibly in his resurrection. Human witness participates in the divine disclosure as, through the gospel entrusted to Paul and thence to Timothy, salvation is extended to those who will yet be saved. It is however God who continues to guard it and guarantee its ultimate success.

Chapter 12

2 Timothy 2:8-13

Μνημόνευε Ἰησοῦν Χριστὸν ἐγηγερμένον ἐκ νεκρῶν, ἐκ σπέρματος Δαυίδ, κατὰ τὸ εὐαγγέλιόν μου, ἐν ᾧ κακοπαθῶ μέχρι δεσμῶν ὡς κακοῦργος, ἀλλὰ ὁ λόγος τοῦ θεοῦ οὐ δέδεται· διὰ τοῦτο πάντα ὑπομένω διὰ τοὺς ἐκλεκτούς, ἵνα καὶ αὐτοὶ σωτηρίας τύχωσιν τῆς ἐν Χριστῷ Ἰησοῦ μετὰ δόξης αἰωνίου.

πιστὸς ὁ λόγος·
εἰ γὰρ συναπεθάνομεν, καὶ συζήσομεν·
εἰ ὑπομένομεν, καὶ συμβασιλεύσομεν·
εἰ ἀρνησόμεθα, κἀκεῖνος ἀρνήσεται ἡμᾶς·
εἰ ἀπιστοῦμεν, ἐκεῖνος πιστὸς μένει,
ἀρνήσασθαι γὰρ ἑαυτὸν οὐ δύναται.

With its summary of "my gospel", the statement linking ministry to salvation, and a "faithful saying", this short section is replete with soteriological terms and ideas. Much of the detail, however, is puzzling. What is the significance of the "seed of David" reference (v. 8), and why is it mentioned after the resurrection? Who are "the elect," and how does Paul's enduring contribute to their salvation (vv. 9-10)? Does the hymn conclude with a threat or a promise? If resolved, these questions would supply glimpses of the author's idea of salvation.

12.1 Context

Again, it is a paraenetic context in which salvation vocabulary is found. In 2:1-26 Timothy is charged to pass on Paul's teaching (v. 1), accepting the suffering and hard work required by the task (vv. 2-7). In the passage under scrutiny, Paul himself exemplifies suffering and toiling for the gospel, something of whose content is indicated, confident of its salvific efficacy (vv. 8-13). By contrast, certain opponents illustrate the activity, content and outcomes of destructive teaching (vv. 14, 16-19). Timothy is urged to choose the way of usefulness to the Lord (vv. 15, 20-26), taking care over his own teaching and life while trying to win over his opponents.

The gospel summary and the hymnic fragment raise tradition-historical questions, and the referent of the πιστὸς ὁ λόγος formula is uncertain.[1] Insofar as these issues affect the interpretation they will be discussed in due course, but the focus of our investigation is the soteriological outlook suggested by the author's utilization of these materials in this context.

12.2 Paul's Gospel (v. 8)

12.2.1 "My Gospel"

The message summarized as "Jesus Christ, raised from the dead, of the seed of David," is described as "my gospel," inviting comparison with the summary of Paul's gospel in Rom 1:3-4:[2]

περὶ τοῦ υἱοῦ αὐτοῦ τοῦ γενομένου ἐκ σπέρματος Δαυὶδ κατὰ σάρκα, τοῦ ὁρισθέντος υἱοῦ θεοῦ ἐν δυνάμει κατὰ πνεῦμα ἁγιωσύνης ἐξ ἀναστάσεως νεκρῶν, Ἰησοῦ Χριστοῦ τοῦ κυρίου ἡμῶν.

If this is a direct source for 2 Tim 2:8,[3] however, the differences are problematic, notably the inverted order of Davidic descent and resurrection, different terms for the resurrection, and the absence from 2 Timothy of both the Son of God reference and the κατὰ σάρκα/κατὰ πνεῦμα antithesis. Either the author has misremembered,[4] misunderstood,[5] or adapted the Romans text to his own theological purpose.[6] Alternatively, both Rom 1:3-4 and 2 Tim 2:8 could draw upon the same pre-Pauline source,[7] to which the less elaborate 2 Timothy could well be the closer.[8] This would be congruent with the current tendency in Romans scholarship to understand 1:3-4 as a modification of an earlier Jewish Christian formula,[9] although of course Rom 1:3-4 could still be 2 Timothy's

---

1 See G. W. Knight III, *The Faithful Sayings in the Pastoral Epistles* (Kampen: Kok, 1968), 112-15, 131-37.
2 E.g. Towner, *Goal*, 101-02; Lau, *Manifest*, 130-31.
3 E.g. Easton, 53.
4 Goulder thinks it more a reminiscence rather than a redaction ("Wolves," 253).
5 Easton, 53.
6 Trummer, *Paulustradition*, 203-04; Oberlinner, *2.Timotheusbrief*, 76.
7 E.g. Dibelius-Conzelmann, 108; Fee, 251-52.
8 See Lau, *Manifest*, 131.
9 See discussion in D. J. Moo, *The Epistle to the Romans* (NICNT; Grand Rapids: Eerdmans, 1996), 45-46 and nn. 30, 31, with bibliography; also J. D. G. Dunn, *Romans* (2 vols.; WBC 38 A-B; Dallas: Word, 1988), 1:22-24.

immediate source. To seek the author's distinctive perspective in his supposed emendation of Paul's redaction of a hypothetical original would, however, be precarious![10]

Little discussed in relation to 2 Tim 2:8, but also purporting to represent Pauline tradition, is Luke's account of Paul's preaching in Acts 13:16-41.[11] The content offers intriguing points of comparison with 2 Timothy. God's election of "the fathers" (v. 17) is affirmed, and Israel's salvation history recounted to the point where God "raised up" (ἤγειρεν) David as king (v. 22). The thought shifts to Jesus, of David's seed (τούτου [of David] . . . ἀπὸ τοῦ σπέρματος),[12] given (or "raised up"[13]) as σωτήρ to Israel, according to God's promise (v. 23). John had "pre-preached" (προκηρύσσω) a baptism of repentance (v. 24), and the "message of this salvation" (ὁ λόγος τῆς σωτηρίας ταύτης, v. 26) was sent to Abraham's descendants. Failing to understand "the words of the prophets" (v. 27), the residents of Jerusalem unwittingly fulfilled them, having Jesus killed (vv. 28-29). God, however, raised him from the dead (ἤγειρεν αὐτὸν ἐκ νεκρῶν, v. 30), he was seen (ὤφθη, v. 31) by witnesses (μάρτυρες, v. 31). Paul can therefore proclaim the good news (εὐαγγελιζόμεθα, v. 32) that God has fulfilled his promise to the fathers (v. 32). This is confirmed by the scriptures (Pss 2:7; 16:10 [LXX 15:10]; Isa 55:3) (vv. 33-35). The Davidic hope is realized in Jesus, raised by God and consequently not suffering decay (v. 37). Forgiveness of sins is available through believing in him (vv. 37-38), and hearers must beware of unbelief (vv. 40-41). After this preaching of "the word of God" (ὁ λόγος τοῦ κυρίου/τοῦ θεοῦ, vv. 44, 46) some join Paul and are exhorted to "continue in the grace of God" (v. 43), while others blaspheme and oppose his message (v. 45), showing themselves "unworthy of eternal life" (v. 46). With Isa 49:6 as warrant, the missionaries turn to bring light (φῶς) and salvation (σωτηρία) to the Gentiles (v. 47), and all "appointed for eternal life" (τεταγμένοι εἰς ζωὴν αἰώνιον) believe (v. 48). Some of these correspondences between Luke's tradition of Paul's missionary preaching and 2 Timothy will be explored as the exegesis proceeds.[14]

---

10 But see Trummer's attempt (*Paulustradition*, 203-04).
11 Lau, *Manifest*, 136, n. 358, observes that Acts 13:30-36 contains Davidic descent, God's promised saviour and the resurrection.
12 C. K. Barrett notes the "unusual emphasis on David" in *The Acts of the Apostles I* (ICC; Edinburgh: T&T Clark, 1994), 636.
13 The variant ἤγειρεν for ἤγαγεν (see F. F. Bruce, *Acts*, 256 n. 64) illustrates that "raising up" could be apply to Jesus' messiahship as well as his resurrection.
14 Without endorsing the conclusions of S. G. Wilson, *Luke and the Pastoral*

12.2.2 "Remember"

To Stott, "The command to 'remember Jesus Christ' at first seems extraordinary."[15] It may be compared, however, with the repeated OT command to "remember the LORD your God" (e.g. Deut 8:18, etc.;[16] Neh 4:14; Tob 4:5). The activity recommended goes beyond intellectual recall to a continuing, conscious orientation of life. In the NT, while recall of the teaching of Jesus and the apostles is certainly urged (e.g. Matt 26:75 and par.; Mark 11:21; Luke 24:6, 8; John 2:22; 12:16; 16:4; Acts 11:16; 20:35; 2 Pet 3:2), the thought of imitation is also present (e.g. 1 Cor 11:2; cf. Heb 13:7, where μνημονεύετε τῶν ἡγουμένων ὑμῶν includes μιμεῖσθε τὴν πίστιν).[17] Both dimensions are evident in 2 Timothy ch. 2. The cognitive content is specified in terms of key doctrinal points, ἐγηγερμένον ἐκ νεκρῶν, ἐκ σπέρματος Δαυίδ, and by extension the whole of τὸ εὐαγγέλιον μου, reappearing in the instruction, ταῦτα ὑπομίμνῃσκε (v. 14), which utilizes a "specific vocabulary" pertaining to the transmission of apostolic tradition.[18] In addition, this received teaching is to be maintained (cf. v. 2) and the example of the one who died and was raised is to be followed (cf. vv. 1b-12a). The call, μνημόνευε Ἰησοῦν Χριστόν, then, requires both adherence to certain truths as taught in Paul's gospel and practical obedience, echoing the solemn summons to Israel to "remember the LORD your God."

12.2.3 "Jesus Christ"

The order of the two terms is unique for this letter, which prefers "Christ Jesus" (11x). It has been suggested that it could represent the movement of thought, with a "stress on the historic life as the first thought, and Χριστόν perhaps consciously a predicate. 'Jesus - as

---

Epistles (London: SPCK, 1979) (who gives little attention to either 2 Tim 2:8-13 or Acts 13), this raises the question whether Luke and the author of 2 Timothy drew on similar traditions.

15 Stott, *2 Timothy*, 61.
16 O. Michel, "μιμνήσκομαι, κτλ.," *TDNT* 4:675-83, speaks of Deuteronomy's "theology of remembering," which stimulates obedience and trust. "All recollection serves to maintain the purity of faith." (675) Fee finds a recurring "memory" motif in 2 Timothy (245), but perhaps this is a by-product of the testamentary setting.
17 S. Bénétreau comments on Heb 13:7, "Le souvenir doit alors déboucher sur l'imitation: *et imitez leur foi.*" (*L'Épître aux Hébreux II* (Vaux-sur-Seine: Édifac, 1990), 214).
18 Michel, *TDNT* 4:677-78.

the Messiah',"[19] and to bring the human Jesus to the fore would be appropriate to the idea of personal imitation included in μνημονεύω. It would be unwise, however, to exact much theological significance from an order that seems virtually interchangeable in much of the NT.[20] It is perhaps better explained with reference to the correspondence of the order here to that in Rom 1:4, as a reflection of traditional wording that may lie behind both texts.

12.2.4 "Raised from the Dead"

The formulation Ἰησοῦς Χριστὸς ἐγηγερμένος ἐκ νεκρῶν, ἐκ σπέρματος Δαυίδ is declared to be in accord with Paul's gospel (v. 8), for which he suffered (v. 9), and which leads to salvation (v. 10). While so brief a summary cannot be expected to be comprehensive, it apparently encapsulates what the author regards as key elements of Paul's gospel,[21] presumably in accord with his own theological outlook. Paraenetically, "It is the eschatological hope contained in the good news of Jesus' resurrection that undergirds the admonitions to suffer."[22] The "promise of life that is in Christ Jesus" (1:1) makes service worthwhile for both the minister (2:11b-12a) and those ministered to (2:10), and this promise may be trusted even in the face of death (4:6) because Christ was raised from death (2:8). Again, when the author seeks motivation for faithful, costly ministry, he finds it in his soteriology. Houlden's judgment that, "What we have here is no more than a slogan - no doctrinal use is made of the fact of Christ's resurrection,"[23] fails to recognize that it vouchsafes the "salvation that is in Christ Jesus with eternal glory" (v. 10) and is the basis for the promise of living and reigning together with Christ (vv. 11b-12a).

The resurrection reference also hints at the power/empowerment theme running through the letter. Timothy is to suffer κατὰ δύναμιν θεοῦ (1:8), of which the paradigmatic demonstration was the resurrection of Jesus (cf. Rom 1:4; 1 Cor 6:14; 2 Cor 13:4a; Phil 3:10; Eph 1:19-20). It may be that the perfect passive participle

---

19 Lock, 94-95; cf. Knight, 397; Spicq, 145.
20 By way of comparison, 1 Timothy has "Christ Jesus" 10x and "Jesus Christ" 3x; Titus, "Christ Jesus" 1x and "Jesus Christ" 3x; Romans, "Christ Jesus" 14x and "Jesus Christ" 18x. In the NT as a whole "Christ Jesus" occurs 83x and "Jesus Christ" 136x.
21 Cf. Barrett, 102: It is "evidently intended as a summary of the Pauline Gospel as understood by the author."
22 Bassler, 142.
23 Houlden, 118.

ἐγηγερμένος is preferred to the noun ἀνάστασις, because it highlights the action, indicating the operation of divine power. At the same time, the opponents' over-realized eschatology (v. 18) would be counteracted by the focus on the historical resurrection of Jesus,[24] and by the juxtaposition of ideas of resurrection and suffering.

12.2.5 "Of the Seed of David"

Why should ἐκ σπέρματος Δαυίδ,[25] follow the reference to the resurrection, contrary to the "more natural chronological sequence" in Rom 1:3-4?[26] A prior question is why it is mentioned at all.[27] Bassler surmises that it is cited as part of the received tradition, "but not contributing actively to the argument."[28] We should expect, however, that an author concerned for the transmission of Pauline tradition would ensure that in so concise a summary of Paul's gospel each phrase would count. Goulder suggests that it stresses Christ's humanity, as a "heavenly being incarnate."[29] Ignatius deploys that idea against docetic tendencies (Smyrn. 1:1; 2:1; cf. Trall. 9), but there, the thought moves chronologically from the Davidic reference to the resurrection. If Jesus' humanity were the main concern in 2 Timothy, the flow of thought would seem stinted: "Jesus Christ, risen from the dead, even though he was a human being!" His humanity could have been indicated by ἄνθρωπος (cf. 1 Tim 2:5) rather than ἐκ σπέρματος Δαυίδ, "a title of some dignity."[30]

Is it then a messianic identification? Despite objections that there is no such interest in the PE,[31] some concept of Christ's kingship is evident in 2 Timothy's references to reigning with Christ (2:12a) and Christ's kingdom (4:1, 18). It also accords with the continuity assumed between Israel's scriptures and Christian faith (e.g. 1:3, [32] 5;[33] 3:15-17) to describe the saviour (1:10) in terms of the hoped-for Davidic king. According to Lohse, בֶּן־דָּוִד was "constantly used by

---

24 See Towner, Goal, 102.
25 The expression appears in the NT only in 2 Tim 2:8; Rom 1:3; John 7:42; and Acts 13:22-23.
26 Towner, Goal, 102.
27 Kelly thinks it "irrelevant in the context." (177)
28 Bassler, 142.
29 Goulder, "Wolves," 153.
30 Marshall, "Christology of the Pastoral Epistles", 166.
31 E.g. Bassler, 142.
32 Spicq remarks, "elles implique la continuité et l'homogénéité de la foi dans les deux étapes de l'économie du salut." (702)
33 See e.g., Easton, 39; Fee, 222-23; Hinson, 339; Lock, 84.

the Rabb. as a messianic designation,"[34] and Longenecker describes a "settled conviction" in Judaism that the messiah would be of Davidic descent.[35] The utilization of this theme in early Christian preaching is illustrated in Acts (e.g. 2:25-36; 13:22-23, 32-39). Did it hold any significance for the author of 2 Timothy?

At this point it may be helpful to return to Luke's representation of Paul's preaching in Acts 13:16-41. The crux of the sermon is that Jesus is the promised descendant of David through whom salvation would come to Israel. The key to that identification is the resurrection, exploiting the double significance of ἐγείρω, raising up from the dead and exalting to kingship. God "gave" (ἔδωκεν) the judges and Saul to Israel (Acts 13:20, 21), but "raised up" (ἤγειρεν) David (v. 22). Similarly, God "raised up" Jesus from the dead (v. 30). David, however, suffered decay after death (v. 36), but "the one whom God raised up" did not (v. 37).[36] The absence of ἐκ νεκρῶν in v. 37 facilitates the double reference. Jesus was "raised up" both from the dead and to the ultimate Davidic kingship.[37] It makes good sense to see both aspects in 2 Tim 2:8. When the qualifying clause ἐκ σπέρματος Δαυίδ is referred to the participle ἐγηγερμένος rather than directly to Ἰησοῦς Χριστός or to an implied verb such as "descended" (NIV) or "born" (NEB), the statement reads, "Jesus Christ, raised up from the dead [and] out of David's seed." The order is not unprecedented. In Acts both Peter (Acts 2:14-39) and Paul (13:16-41) first proclaim Jesus' resurrection (2:24; 13:30-31), then on that basis identify him as the fulfilment of Davidic expectations (2:25-36; 13:32-39).[38] The order in 2 Tim 2:8 encapsulates the same argument: "Jesus Christ - raised up from the dead and thus demonstrated to be the one raised up out of David's descendants in whom God's salvific promises are fulfilled."

---

34 E. Lohse, "υἱὸς Δαυίδ," *TDNT* 8:478-88, 481.
35 R. N. Longenecker, *The Christology of Early Jewish Christianity* (Grand Rapids: Baker, 1970), 109.
36 In Acts, deliverance from decay (διαφθόρα) demonstrates Jesus' messianic identity (Acts 2:27, 31; 13:34, 35, 36, 37; citing LXX Ps 15:10 [16:10]). Sir 47:22 celebrates the divine preservation of the Davidic line from διαφθόρα. In 2 Tim 1:10 Jesus manifests the cognate ἀφθαρσία, freedom from decay.
37 Bruce, *Acts*, 260 (also 259-60, n. 79 on the double sense of ἀνίστημι); cf. Marshall, *Acts*, 226-27, n. 2.
38 Cf. Acts 17:3 (see Marshall, "Christology of the Pastoral Epistles", 166-67).

12.3 Paul's Suffering (vv. 9-10)

12.3.1 The Character of the Suffering

Kelly finds here (and in Col 1:24) the notion of "a predetermined amount of suffering which the Messianic community must undergo before the End can come." By his enduring, Paul reduces what others must suffer, and hastens the End.[39] Hanson objects that this concept of "completing what is lacking in Christ's afflictions" is absent from the PE, and (comparing Phil 1:12-18) thinks it more likely that the value of Paul's suffering lies in its exemplary function.[40] Bassler tries to resist importing an interpretation from elsewhere, and seeks a reading "consistent with the emphasis of the letter." This leads her to identify the crucial role of the gospel and its ministry, and explain the suffering as "a call to work hard for the gospel."[41] This is part of its purpose, but further explication is possible. The verbs κακοπαθέω (v. 9) and ὑπομένω (v. 10) may indicate something of the character of this suffering, and the concept is elaborated by four prepositional clauses, ἐν ᾧ (v. 9) qualifying κακοπαθέω, and διὰ τοῦτο, διὰ τοὺς ἐκλεκτούς and ἵνα . . . τύχωσιν (v. 10) relating to ὑπομένω.

a. κακοπαθέω

The verbs κακοπαθέω, "bear hardship patiently" (2:9; 4:5),[42] and συγκακοπαθέω (1:8; 2:3),[43] are in the NT almost unique to 2 Timothy,[44] but they are central to the letter's paraenetic purpose. Timothy is exhorted, συγκακοπάθησον τῷ εὐαγγελίῳ κατὰ δύναμιν θεοῦ (1:8); συγκακοπάθησον ὡς καλὸς στρατιώτης Χριστοῦ Ἰησοῦ (2:3); and in the final appeal, σὺ δὲ νῆφε ἐν πᾶσιν, κακοπάθησον, ἔργον ποίησον εὐαγγελιστοῦ, τὴν διακονίαν πληροφόρησον (4:5). The expression ἐν ᾧ κακοπαθῶ (2:9) belongs in this series. Since Paul models that to which Timothy is called, the idea in 2:9 could be related to the suffering required of Timothy, which is "in the gospel" (1:8), accompanying the task of teaching (2:1-3) and preaching (4:5; cf. v. 2). Accordingly, although a link to

---

39 Kelly, 178.
40 Hanson, *Epistles*, 131. In relation to Christ's suffering, however, the ideas of following his example and participating in his sufferings are not mutually exclusive (see e.g. Phil 2:5-11; 3:10-11; 1Pet 2:21; 4:13).
41 Bassler, 143.
42 BAGD, 397.
43 Possibly the author's coinage (see W. Michaelis, "πάσχω, κτλ.," *TDNT* 5:904-39, 936).
44 James 5:13 has κακοπαθέω (cf. κακοπάθεια, 5:10).

Christ is grammatically possible,⁴⁵ the relative pronoun in 2:9 should probably be referred to "my gospel" (2:8),⁴⁶ indicating suffering endured by Paul while exercising his ministry.

The phrase μέχρι δεσμῶν specifies the extent of this suffering,⁴⁷ with perhaps a faint echo of the suffering μέχρι θανάτου characteristic of the martyrs in 4 Maccabees (for the Law in 6:21, 30; 7:8, 15:10; for εὐσέβεια in 7:16; 13:27; 17:7; see also 13:1; 16:1; 17:10; cf. 2 Macc 13:14; 3 Macc 7:1), or even of Christ's obedience μέχρι θανάτου in Phil 2:8. The expression ὡς κακοῦργος recalls that in 2 Timothy Paul's chains were potentially a source of shame (1:8, 16). Interestingly, κακοῦργος occurs elsewhere in the NT only in Luke 23:32, 33, 39, representing the criminals with whom Jesus was crucified. For Luke, to be evaluated as a lawbreaker was part of Jesus' messianic suffering (Luke 22:37; Isa 53:12),⁴⁸ and potentially that of his followers.⁴⁹ To that extent, the suffering of Christ's messenger in 2 Tim 2:9 reflects that of Christ himself.

b. ὑπομένω

In vv. 9-10 ideas of suffering (κακοπαθῶ) and enduring (ὑπομένω) are combined.⁵⁰ Again, 4 Maccabees provides a parallel: "For we, through this severe suffering (κακοπάθεια) and endurance (ὑπομονή), shall have the prize of virtue and shall be with God, on whose account we suffer" (4 Macc 9:8). In the Hellenistic environment ὑπομονή was associated with the virtue of courage, standing firm under attack,⁵¹ as displayed in the heroic endurance of the martyrs in 4 Maccabees (1:11; 5:23; 6:9; 7:9, 22; 9:6, 22, 30; 13:12; 15:30, 31, 32; 16:1, 8, 17, 19, 21; 17:7, 10, 12, 17, 23). In 2 Timothy Paul models courageous ὑπομονή in the face of hostility (τοῖς διωγμοῖς, τοῖς παθήμασιν, 3:10-11).⁵² Young reads 2 Timothy as an attempt

---

45 Hanson cites Holtz, "Jesus Christ, in whom I suffer" (*Epistles*, 131); cf. Simpson, 133.
46 So Oberlinner, *2.Timotheusbrief*, 79.
47 Heb 11:36 also describes suffering "to the extent of (ἔτι) imprisonment," linked to attaining (τυγχάνω) a soteriological outcome (v. 35; cf. 2 Tim 2:10).
48 Cf. the scribal addition to Mark 15:28, μετὰ ἀνόμων ἐλογίσθη.
49 See Marshall, *Luke*, 823-27; cf. 1 Pet 2:21-23.
50 Cf. Heb 10:32, ὑπεμείνατε παθημάτων; 1 Pet 2:20-22, πάσχοντες ὑπομενεῖτε; in James 5:10-11, κακοπαθία and μακροθυμία are exhibited by οἱ ὑπομείναντες.
51 See F. Hauck, "μένω, κτλ.," *TDNT* 4:574-88.
52 Cf. *1 Clem.* 5.5-7: Παῦλος ὑπομονῆς βραβεῖον ὑπέδειξεν . . . ὑπομονῆς γενόμενος μέγιστος ὑπογραμμός.

"to create a model of the martyr living out the Pauline gospel grounded in the death and resurrection of Christ."[53] For early Christianity, a martyrological model was to hand in the Maccabean literature, presenting heroes suffering for the faith and rewarded with immortality. Paul the sufferer in 2 Timothy exhibits marked similarities to these martyrs. To consider just one episode, the ordeal of the eldest brother in 4 Maccabees ch. 9: both the brother and Paul follow their πρόγονοι (4 Macc 9:1-2; 2 Tim 1:3), are unjustly treated as wrongdoers (4 Macc 9:10, 15; 2 Tim 2:9), expect ἀφθαρσία (4 Macc 9:22; 2 Tim 1:10), serve as examples (4 Macc 9:23; 2 Tim 3:10-11), and call others to the struggle (4 Macc 9:24; 2 Tim 2:3-4). In each case condemnation by a human authority contrasts with divine vindication (4 Macc 9:24; 2 Tim 4:8). In this tradition suffering is ennobled, but not celebrated for its own sake: it is both purposeful and expectant, endured for the sake of εὐσέβεια (4 Macc 9:6; 13:12; 16:17), God (16:19, 21), etc., and in anticipation of the personal reward of life with God (9:22; 18:23) and benefit for the nation (6:27-30).[54] To hear 2 Timothy in the context of this tradition accentuates the nobility of Paul's suffering, countering any suggestion of shame, suggests purposefulness and underlines its exemplary function.

In addition to this martyrological connotation, ὑπομονή, associated with eschatological hope in the LXX prophets (e.g. Mic 7:7; Hab 2:3; Zep 3:8), has an apocalyptic colouring in parts of the NT. Revelation requires ὑπομονή of "the saints" (Rev 1:9; 2:2, 3, 19; 3:10; 13:10; 14:12) and in the Synoptics, ὁ δὲ ὑπομείνας εἰς τέλος οὗτος σωθήσεται (Matt 10:22; 24:13; Mark 13:13).[55] 2 Timothy shares with the Synoptic apocalyptic material features such as deception and going astray in the last days (3:1-9; 4:3-4; cf. Matt 24:4, 11, 24), enduring (2:10, 12a; cf. Matt 24:13) evangelizing the nations (4:17; cf. Matt 24:14), coming judgment (1:12, 18; 4:1, 8; cf. Matt 25:31-46), future glory (2:10; cf. Matt 24:30; 25:31) and kingdom (2:12a; 4:18; cf. Matt 25:34). In this setting Paul's enduring in 2:10 acquires the character of an End Time phenomenon.

---

53 Young, *Theology*, 127.
54 The frequency with which 4 Maccabees qualifies suffering with a purpose clause is striking. See also 6:30; 7:22; 9:8; 10:10; cf. 2 Tim 1:12; 1 Pet 3:14, 17, 18.
55 Hauck, *TDNT* 4:586 describes ὑπομονή in Paul as "a basic Christian virtue and attitude," but cf. the more nuanced survey in U. Falkenroth, C. Brown, "ὑπομένω," *NIDNTT* 2:772-76. Romans associates ὑπομονή with ἐλπίζω and ἀπεκδέχομαι (8:17-25) and urges eschatologically orientated endurance in tribulation (12:12; cf. 13:11-13).

12.3.2 The Motive for the Suffering

Three qualifying clauses attach meaning to Paul's suffering.

a. διὰ τοῦτο

Διὰ τοῦτο could be referred either retrospectively to the statement about the word of God (v. 9b), or prospectively to what is said about the elect and their attaining to salvation (v. 10).[56] Paul endures either "because of his confidence in the gospel,"[57] or "in view of the priceless benefits to be obtained by those who receive the message."[58] Hanson retorts that, "Therefore must not be pressed; it is more in the nature of a link-word than a part of a carefully reasoned argument."[59] Nonetheless, a retrospective reference does allow a coherent flow of thought to be traced. Moving from Christ (v. 8) to Paul's gospel about Christ (v. 8c) to suffering in the work of the gospel (v. 9a), it arrives at Paul's imprisonment (v. 9a). Then the tide turns.[60] Unlike its minister, the word of God is not shackled (v. 9c), and on that basis Paul perseveres in his ministry, accepting the suffering, confident that the word of God will achieve its saving purpose.

b. ὁ λόγος τοῦ θεοῦ

The expression ὁ λόγος τοῦ θεοῦ (v. 9b) is often taken as an exact equivalent of τὸ εὐαγγέλιον (v. 8b),[61] missing a possible nuance.[62]

---

56 Surveying all NT uses of διὰ τοῦτο, Moo identifies four categories: 1. (most common) διά as causal and τοῦτο as retrospective, "because of what has just been said"; 2. διά as causal and τοῦτο as prospective, "because of what is about to be said, namely that"; 3. διά denoting final clause and τοῦτο as prospective, "for this reason, namely, with the purpose that"; and 4. διά denoting final clause as causal and τοῦτο as retrospective, "in order to accomplish what we have just said." He tentatively places 2 Tim 2:10 in category 3. (Moo, *Romans*, 317-18, n. 17)
57 Hinson, 345; cf. Hendricksen, 252.
58 Guthrie, 144; cf. Spicq, 747; Knight, 398-99; Kelly, 178.
59 Hanson, *Epistles*, 131.
60 Signalled by the adversative ἀλλά (Mounce, 514).
61 E.g. Barrett, 103; Dibelius-Conzelmann, 108; Fee, 247; Guthrie, 144; Hendricksen, 251; Houlden, 118; Kelly, 177.
62 2 Timothy employs several expressions for that which is proclaimed: τὸ μαρτύριον τοῦ κυρίου ἡμῶν (1:8); τὸ εὐαγγέλιον (1:10; 2:8); ἡ παραθήκη (1:12, 14); ὁ λόγος τοῦ θεοῦ (2:9); ὁ λόγος τῆς ἀληθείας (2:15); ὁ λόγος (4:2); οἱ ἡμέτεροι λόγοι (4:15); ἡ διδασκαλία (3:10); ἡ ὑγιαίνουσα διδασκαλία (4:3); ἡ ἀλήθεια (4:4); τὸ κήρυγμα (4:17). The meanings overlap, but each has some distinctive aspect that may explain its

The thought may be simply that the message gets out despite Paul's imprisonment (cf. Phil 1:12-18),[63] but ὁ λόγος τοῦ θεοῦ here seems "almost personified."[64] Rarely remarked in this connection is the series of summary statements in Acts announcing the progress of the λόγος τοῦ θεοῦ/τοῦ κυρίου, often despite opposition (6:7; 12:24; 13:49; 19:20). 2 Timothy shares this confidence that though the messenger be opposed, the message will still be effective. Perhaps it echoes the defiant assertion of the OT prophets that whatever opposition they personally suffered, the דְּבַר־יְהוָה would be fulfilled.[65] With this accenting, the statement that ὁ λόγος τοῦ θεου οὐ δέδεται would express the conviction that God's saving purpose (1:9) articulated in the gospel (1:10; cf. 1:1) would certainly be achieved. Spicq emphasizes the power contained within the word of God,[66] Hasler, the fixed course determined by God's providence.[67] In fact divine power and purpose are complementary aspects of a word that is effective because it declares and effectuates God's decision. This understanding is consistent with the salvation-historical framework that has been glimpsed in the exegesis. The divine promise of life has been made operative in the raising of Jesus from death as the royal messiah (2:8). The evangelist may therefore labour, confident that salvation-history is running its course and "the elect" will be saved. The "word of God" is not only the message but the activated decision of God.

c. διὰ τοὺς ἐκλεκτούς

The soteriological setting makes the general meaning of ἐκλεκτός, "choice,"[68] unlikely here, but is the author proposing a doctrine of predestination,[69] appropriating OT language for the NT people of God,[70] or merely employing "a fairly conventional term for believing Christians"?[71] In v. 10 it identifies those who are to receive salvation, with a term that in the LXX (along with non-theological uses)

---

choice in a specific instance.
63 So Guthrie, 144.
64 Marshall, 736; cf. Dibelius-Conzelmann, 108; Hinson, 135; Kelly, 177; Lock, 95; Spicq, 747. Cf. 1 Thess 2:13; 2 Thess 3:1.
65 E.g. Isa 1:20; 22:25; 24:3; 25:8; 40:5; 58:18; Jer 13:5; Joel 3:8; Obad 1:18. Cf. Isa 55:11.
66 Spicq, 747, citing Isa 40:8; 55:11.
67 Hasler, 65.
68 See G. Schrenck, "ἐκλέκτος," TDNT 4:181-92, 181.
69 E.g. Kelly, 178; Hinson, 345; Hendrickson, 253-54.
70 E.g. Bassler, 143; Fee, 247; Easton, 52.
71 Hanson, *Epistles*, 131.

characterizes Israel as God's covenant people, the special objects of his saving and blessing (e.g. 1 Chron 16:13; Pss 104:6, 43 [105:6, 43]; 105:5, 23 [106:5, 23]; Isa 42:1; 43:20; 45:4; 65:9, 23; Tob 8:15; 2 Macc 1:25; Wis 3:9; 4:15; Sir 46:1; 47:22).⁷² Development in the concept of "the elect" can be traced in intertestamental apocalyptic writing,⁷³ and seen in the Synoptic apocalyptic passages, where many of the NT occurrences of the term ἐκλεκτός are found (Matt 22:14; Matt 24:22, 24, 31, par. Mark 13:20, 22, 27; Luke 18:7; cf. Rev 17:14). With this apocalyptic colouring, which we have already noted in 2 Timothy,⁷⁴ οἱ ἐκλεκτοί indicates the beneficiaries of God's unfolding saving intervention.

The question remains whether the treatment of election in Romans should influence the interpretation here. The term ἐκλεκτός is very rare in Paul,⁷⁵ but it appears in Rom 8:33 at the climax of the argument with the challenge, τίς ἐγκαλέσει κατὰ ἐκλεκτῶν θεοῦ ; θεὸς ὁ δικαιῶν.⁷⁶ The ἐκλεκτοί are those who love God (οἱ ἀγαπῶντες τὸν θεόν), who are called according to his purpose (οἱ κατὰ πρόθεσιν κλητοὶ ὄντες), whom God foreknew (προέγνω), predestined (προώρισεν) to be conformed to the likeness of his Son, called (ἐκάλεσεν), justified (ἐδικαίωσεν) and glorified (ἐδόξασεν) (vv. 28-30); they are those on whose behalf God acts (θεὸς ὑπὲρ ἡμῶν), for whom he gave (παρέδωκεν) his Son and will give (χαρίσεται) all things (vv. 31-32); God himself justifies them, the exalted Christ pleads in their defence (vv. 33-34), and in all conceivable circumstances they remain inseparably bound to God's love that is theirs in Christ Jesus (35-39). Certain of these features appear in 2 Timothy. Salvation is referred to God's purpose and grace and explicated in terms of God's calling (1:9, with aorist tense, as in Romans). Final salvation is painted in colours of glory (2:10; cf. 4:18), and the gifts of salvation are received "in Christ" (1:1, 9, 13; 2:1, 10) through faith (3:15). The two letters, however, address different concerns. In Romans, the question of who constitutes the elect, "a central element in Jewish self-understanding,"⁷⁷ is of major

---

72 Ps 104 [105] links the deliverance of the ἐκλεκτοί (vv. 6, 43) to the fulfilment of God's λόγος (covenant promise to the seed of Abraham, vv. 8, 19, 42), and pictures Joseph, tested in prison until in time the λόγος came to pass (v. 19). Similarly, 2 Tim 2:9-10 presents the prisoner Paul, tested but enduring in confidence that God's word of promise would indeed be fulfilled.
73 See Schrenck, *TDNT* 4:183-85.
74 See above on ὑπομονή (pp. 143-44 and n. 55).
75 Rom 8:33; 16:13; Col 3:12.
76 See Schrenck on "ἐκλεκτός in Paul," *TDNT* 4:189-90.
77 Dunn, *Romans* 1:502.

importance. 2 Timothy is more concerned with the minister's task. In that connection, the identity of οἱ ἐκλεκτοί is not the primary issue. The point is first that it is worthwhile persevering in ministry because there are those who will be saved, and then that the recipients of Christian salvation enjoy the blessings assigned in the OT to "God's elect." The internal evidence of the letter is insufficient either to demonstrate or disallow a definition of οἱ ἐκλεκτοί in 2:10 as "those whom God's eternal predestination has chosen to receive salvation."[78]

Acts 13:16-52 offers a further point of comparison. After the preaching of ὁ λόγος τοῦ κυρίου/θεοῦ to Gentiles (vv. 44, 46), some believe, specifically, ὅσοι ἦσαν τεταγμένοι εἰς ζωὴν αἰώνιον (v. 48). The meaning of this expression is debated,[79] but it must at least indicate that the coming to faith of these Gentiles was in God's purpose, as confirmed by the citation of Isa 49:6 in v. 47. In 2 Tim 2:10 the term οἱ ἐκλεκτοί similarly has the effect of colouring mention of the response to the gospel with the suggestion of God's intention and initiative.

12.4 Salvation (v. 10b)

The anarthrous noun σωτηρία is qualified by the phrase [ἡ] ἐν Χριστῷ Ἰησοῦ and its extension, μετὰ δόξης αἰωνίου (v. 10).

12.4.1 "In Christ Jesus"

This first expression unambiguously defines salvation christologically, but its precise significance is more elusive.[80] Ἐν Χριστῷ formulae seem to be a Pauline coinage,[81] expressing various ideas. Harris identifies seven: incorporative union, sphere of reference, agency or instrumentality, cause, mode, location, and authoritative basis.[82] 2 Timothy has seven examples (1:1, 9, 13; 2:1, 10; 3:12, 15), all in the form, ἐν Χριστῷ Ἰησοῦ,[83] and, except for 3:12, as a predicate with the article. Both spatial and instrumental aspects

---

78 Kelly, 178.
79 See e.g. Barrett, *Acts* 1:658-59 and Bruce, *Acts*, 267-68, n. 111, both inclining to the Jewish concept of enrolment in the Book of Life.
80 See above on 1 Tim 1:14 (pp. 46-47 and n. 60); also on 2 Tim 1:9 (pp. 119-20).
81 A. Oepke, "ἐν," *TDNT* 2:537-43, 541.
82 Harris, "Prepositions," 1192.
83 Romans and 1 Corinthians have the forms ἐν Χριστῷ Ἰησοῦ, ἐν Χριστῷ, and ἐν Χριστῷ Ἰησοῦ τῷ κυρίῳ ἡμῶν. 2 Corinthians, however, uses only, ἐν Χριστῷ (7x).

are found. "In Christ Jesus," as the one risen from the dead (2:8a; cf. 1:10), resides the power to deliver from death and corruption; in and through him, as the focal point of salvation history (2:8b), God's saving purpose (1:9) and promise (1:1) are fulfilled; and through the message about him, the gospel (2:8c-9; cf. 1:10), hearers come into relation with him and receive this salvation. In 2:10, the article refers the characterization ἐν Χριστῷ Ἰησοῦ specifically to σωτηρία: it is not those saved (at least not directly) but salvation that is "in Christ."[84] Here spatial and instrumental aspects coalesce, and there is also a temporal implication. As Marshall observes, since salvation is "in Christ Jesus" now, "the effects of the saving event, the death and resurrection of Christ, continue to be operative,"[85] in the present age.

12.4.2 "With Eternal Glory"

For Hanson, this second qualifying clause is merely "thrown in as a makeweight,"[86] but the letter's soteriological horizon does extend beyond the present age (e.g. 1:10, 12, 18; 4:1, 8),[87] and "eternal glory" reappears together with the "heavenly kingdom" in 4:18. In 2:10, the effect of connecting σωτηρία with δόξα αἰώνιος is to lift the thought from the present, with its suffering, to a glorious future.[88] A similar association of God's deliverance with everlasting glory is found in the Greek LXX. Σοφία rescues Joseph and gives him δόξα αἰώνιος (Wis 10:14), and in Bar 4:24 σωτηρία is promised to Zion μετὰ δόξης μεγάλης καὶ λαμπρότητος τοῦ αἰωνίου ("with great glory and with the splendour of the Everlasting") by the agency of ὁ αἰώνιος σωτὴρ ὑμῶν (v. 22), bringing ἡ αἰώνιος εὐσοφρύνη μετὰ τῆς σωτηρίας ὑμῶν ("everlasting joy with your salvation," v. 29). In the NT the prospect of eternal glory in contrast to temporal affliction encourages endurance (e.g. 2 Cor 4:17; 1 Pet 5:10). Since 2 Timothy ch. 2 implies an eternal saviour (v. 8) and envisages living and reigning with Christ (vv. 11-13), there seems no reason to dispute that, "salvation is primarily an eschatological reality: it comes with

---

84 This does not preclude the saved also being "in Christ." Romans speaks both of people in Christ (8:1) and redemption (3:24) and love (8:39) in Christ. In Paul, that which is in Christ is the possession of those who are in Christ.
85 Marshall, "Christology of the Pastoral Epistles", 167.
86 Hanson, *Epistles*, 131.
87 See on "life and immortality" in 2 Tim 1:10 above (pp. 125-26).
88 Spicq notes the paraenetic impact of the "Émouvant contraste entre κακοῦργος et δόξα." (747)

eternal glory."[89]

12.4.3 ἵνα . . . τύχωσιν

The verb τύγχανω denote the attaining of salvation. In the NT its usual transitive use signifies the obtaining of some benefit.[90] Only two contexts are soteriological, and in each the reference is to attaining resurrection (τυχεῖν καὶ τῆς ἀναστάσεως τῆς ἐκ νεκρῶν, Luke 20:35; ἵνα κρείττονος ἀναστάσεως τύχωσιν, Heb 11:35). Although not explicit in 2 Tim 2:10, a resurrection connotation would be consonant with the "eternal glory" (v. 10) and the references to Christ's resurrection (v. 8) and eschatological life (vv. 11-13).

The aorist subjunctive τύχωσιν could suggest a degree of provisionality. The ἵνα clause expresses a purpose, which, however secure, is yet to be attained, and Paul and others must contribute to its realization. Ignatius employs the same ἵνα + τύχωσιν construction to urge ministers to persevere so that others might "attain to God" (*Eph.* 10), and slaves to endure in order to "attain to a greater freedom from God" (*Pol.* 4.3).[91] This sense of a goal yet to be reached applies in 2 Tim 2:10. Towner comments, "it is on the eschatological (unfinished) character of salvation . . . that the accent falls here."[92]

12.5 Overview of vv. 8-10

Bringing together the results of this exegesis, various soteriological ideas may be traced chiastically through vv. 8-10 yielding a chain of ideas in the form of a parabola (see table below). From the idea of life associated with Christ, the thought moves to God's salvation-historical purpose and to the message and the cost of its ministry, reaching its nadir with the reference to Paul's chains. At this point ἀλλά reverses the downward movement and the apostle's chains are answered by the unchained word of God, leading to the costly but purposeful ministry for the sake of those who in God's salvation-historical purpose will gain eternal glory in Christ. (Note that the order of the predicates of Christ in v. 8 fits this structure.)

---

89   Fee, 248.
90   See Luke 20:35; Acts 24:2; 26:22; 27:3; Heb 8:6; 11:35. It occurs in the *Hauptbriefe* only in 1 Cor 14:10; 15:37; 16:6, in non-theological usages.
91   Cf. *Smyrn.* 9.2 (these and other references in O. Bauernfiend, "τυγχάνω, κτλ.," *TDNT* 8:238-45, 242).
92   Towner, *Goal*, 103.

vv. 8a-9b	main idea	vv. 9c-10b
Ἰησοῦς Χριστὸς ἐγηγερμένος ἐκ νεκρῶν (8a) ↓	Jesus Christ and life and salvation	ἵνα καὶ αὐτοὶ σωτηρίας τύχωσιν τῆς ἐν Χριστῷ Ἰησοῦ μετὰ δόξης αἰωνίου (10c) ↑
ἐκ σπέρματος Δαυίδ (8b) ↓	God's purpose in salvation history	διὰ τοὺς ἐκλεκτούς (10b) ↑
κατὰ τὸ εὐαγγέλιον μου, ἐν ᾧ κακοπαθῶ (8c-9a) ↓	Costly ministry of the gospel	διὰ τοῦτο πάντα ὑπομένω (10a) ↑
μέχρι δεσμῶν ὡς κακοῦργος (9b) →	Chains (bind messenger but not message)	ἀλλὰ ὁ λόγος τοῦ θεοῦ οὐ δέδεται (9c)

12.6 The Hymn (vv. 11-13)

Introduced by πιστὸς ὁ λόγος (v. 11), this piece "gains its authority through being a summary of traditional, received statements."[93] Attempts to isolate the quotation and derive the author's viewpoint from his additions are hampered by disagreement on how far the author's hand may be detected.[94] The approach open to us is to ask why the author chose to include this material and how he intended it to contribute to his argument.

The piece is clearly intended to support the preceding paraenesis, and Fee may be right to refer the γάρ (v. 11b) back to the whole appeal to accept suffering and keep in mind the risen Lord (vv. 1-

---

[93] Marshall, 739. Cf. Knight, 400-01, and *Faithful Sayings*, 112-15.
[94] Hanson extends the quotation through vv. 11-13a with a final gloss, ἀρνήσασθαι γὰρ ἑαυτὸν οὐ δύναται (*Epistles*, 132; cf. Kelly, 179; Towner, *Goal*, 103). Easton limits it to the first two couplets (52); Donelson (*Pseudepigraphy*, 149-50) and Fee (249) attribute the whole piece to the author. Houlden suggests Rom 6:8 as a source (119; cf. Knight, 408).

10).⁹⁵ More specifically, several ideas from vv. 8-10, such as enduring and Jesus' risen life, recur in vv. 11-13.⁹⁶

12.6.1 Dying and Living (v. 11b)

a. The συν- Prefix

A striking feature of this piece is the reiteration of συν- compounds (συναπεθάνομεν, συζήσομεν, συμβασιλεύσομεν). In 1:8 and 2:3 συγκακοπαθέω envisages sharing between human subjects, but such a reading ("If we die together we shall live together"; cf. 2 Cor 7:3) is unlikely here where the exhortation is related to the dying, living and reigning of Christ (vv. 8, 10). The question is whether the συν- implies similarity of experience or some more mystical union.

b. εἰ γὰρ συναπεθάνομεν

This "dying" has been variously interpreted as baptism, conversion or martyrdom. Beasley-Murray insists that the aorist tense fixes it firmly in the past, concluding, "it is the death with Christ in baptism, according to the teaching of Rom. 6.1ff, that is solely in view."⁹⁷ Dunn also locates it in the past, but as "the death with Christ experienced at conversion-initiation."⁹⁸ Others combine the two as conversion-expressed-in-baptism.⁹⁹ On the other hand, the aorist may indicate a condition that, from the standpoint of the reader, has yet to be fulfilled. Roloff reads it as a call to martyrdom, as radical obedience to Christ.¹⁰⁰ The problem with this is that the piece progresses from dying to enduring, the reverse of what might be expected if martyrdom were in view.

---

95 Fee, 248.
96 See Towner, *Goal*, 103.
97 G. R. Beasley-Murray, *Baptism in the New Testament* (London: Macmillan, 1963), 208; cf. Hanson, *Epistles*, 132. The aorist may not be quite as decisive as Beasley-Murray suggests. On popular usage see B. G. Mandilaras, "Confusion of Aorist and Perfect in the Language of the Non-Literary Greek Papyri," in *Akten des XIII. Internationalen Papyrologenkongresses* (ed. E. Kießling and H.-A. Ruprecht, Munich, 1974), 251-62.
98 J. D. G. Dunn, *Baptism in the Holy Spirit* (Philadelphia: Westminster, 1970), 169-70.
99 Cf. Towner, *Goal*, 104; Barrett, 104; Fee, 249.
100 J. Roloff, "Der Weg Jesu als Lebensnorm (2 Tim 2,8-13): Ein Beitrag zur Christologie der Pastoralbriefe," in *Anfänge der Christologie* (ed. C. Breytenbach and H. Paulsen; Göttingen: Vandenhoeck & Ruprecht, 1991), 155-67, 164-65.

These various allusions need not, however, be mutually exclusive. The Pauline corpus relates the death of the believer to the death of Christ in a variety of ways. In Phil 3:10-11 Paul speaks of a κοινωνία παθημάτων αὐτοῦ [of Christ], συμμορφιζόμενος τῷ θανάτῳ αὐτοῦ, suggesting that in his suffering Paul is following the example of and becoming increasingly identified with Christ, envisaging resurrection life as the ultimate outcome (cf. 2:9). "Becoming like him in his death" includes both the present reality of suffering and the future possibility of literal physical death. In 2 Cor 4:10-11 Paul speaks of carrying around the death of Jesus in his body and continually being given over to death for the sake of Jesus. This "death" is again a present reality. Elsewhere the concept of a past death of the believer with Christ to the powers governing the old aeon, namely sin (Rom 6:2, 7), the Law (Rom 7:4; Gal 2:19) or the στοιχεῖα τοῦ κόσμου (Col 2:8, 20) is the ontological indicative upon which is grounded both the present ethical imperative and the future eschatological promise of life (Rom 6:1-14; Gal 2:19-20; Col 2:11-12, 20; 3:1-11). The past "death," explicitly associated with baptism (Rom 6:3-4; Col 2:12), does not preclude the need to "put to death" sinful behaviour (Rom 8:13; Col 3:5, 8). This brief survey has yielded examples of past, present and future "death," representing leaving the old sphere of existence, suffering for Christ, or getting rid of sin.[101] The Synoptics add the possibility of a literal dying with Christ: ἐὰν δέῃ με συναποθανεῖν σοι, οὐ μή σε ἀπαρνήσομαι (Mark 14:31; cf. Matt 26:35).

In 2 Tim 2:11, a conversion-baptism reference would give good sense, but in the wider paraenesis concerning faithful service, the thought of costly ministry may resonate (v. 10). In this connection, an allusion to martyrdom is not impossible. Hanson sees only "a looking back at Paul's martyrdom" from a less hazardous age.[102] There are no internal grounds, however, for distancing 2 Timothy from any real possibility of persecution.[103] Marshall captures the range of significance, in "a past death to self which may involve readiness even for martyrdom."[104]

c. καὶ συζήσομεν

If the "dying" is literal, this "living" with Christ must represent an

---

[101] In addition, the believer's literal death is "in Christ," guaranteeing resurrection life (1 Thess 4:13-16).
[102] Hanson, *Epistles*, 132.
[103] Cf. Barrett, 104: "the saying . . . is doubtless quoted here because of the possibility of death in persecution."
[104] Marshall, 739.

eschatologically realized existence, while if "dying with Christ" refers to baptism, conversion or suffering in ministry, some present experience of life with Christ may be intended. In the context, as in many of the Pauline contexts of Christ-related death cited above, both future and present aspects could support the paraenesis: the offer of present life shared with Christ would strengthen the reader for service and the assurance of future life would inspire to sacrifice. Both aspects are found in 2 Timothy. The resources for present ministry and godly living are received "in Christ Jesus" (1:13-14; 2:1; 3:12), while eschatological reward (4:8) and postmortem saving into "his heavenly kingdom" (4:18) are also anticipated (cf. 2:10). A promise of life with Christ that is both the source of present empowerment and the content of future hope would agree with the letter's outlook and meet its paraenetic requirements, encouraging "dying" in the sense of the abnegation of self in costly ministry.

12.6.2 Enduring and Reigning (v. 12a)

a. εἰ ὑπομένομεν

In 2 Timothy endurance is a characteristic of Paul's ministry (2:10; 3:10). Even if the material is traditional, in its setting here it must pick up these connotations of the endurance in faithful service which Paul exemplifies.[105]

b. καὶ συμβασιλεύσομεν

In its only other NT occurrence (1 Cor 4:8), συμβασιλεύω expressess Paul's ironical wish that he could reign together with the Corinthians, who, according to their over-realized eschatology, had already come into their kingdom.[106] The prospect of reigning is not denied (cf. 1 Cor 6:2), but confined to the future; the present demands endurance (1 Cor 4:12).[107] Again, however, it is in the apocalyptic passages of the Synoptics and in Revelation that the NT references closest in atmosphere to 2 Tim 2:12 are found. The Synoptics anticipate that, having paid the price of following him, Jesus' apostles would "sit on thrones judging the twelve tribes of Israel" (Luke 22:28-30; Matt 19:28). In Revelation the believer who overcomes (an idea associated with eschatological endurance in, e.g.

---

105 See e.g. Mounce, 516.
106 See C. K. Barrett, *A Commentary on the First Epistle to the Corinthians* (BNTC; 2nd ed., London: A&C Black, 1971), 108. K. L. Schmidt, "συμβασιλεύω," *TDNT* 1:591, assumes that σὺν Χριστῷ is implied.
107 Knight, 405.

3:10-12) will share Christ's throne (3:21; cf. 11:16; 20:4). The martyrs will reign with Christ (ἐβασίλευσαν μετὰ Χριστοῦ/αὐτοῦ, 20:4, 6), and the servants of the Lamb will reign forever (βασιλεύσουσιν εἰς τοὺς αἰῶνας τῶν αἰώνων, 22:5). In 2 Timothy ch. 2 these apocalyptic connotations would reinforce the kairological framework that we are detecting. Enduring is necessary in these difficult days preceding the End, but believers are sustained by the vision of reigning with Christ in the coming age.

12.6.3 Denying and being Denied (v. 12b)

This line is constructed, according to Beasley-Murray, "in manifest dependence on Mt. 10.33."[108] It may well echo the dominical saying, but what specifically is the author of 2 Timothy warning against, and how is the consequence to be interpreted?

a. εἰ ἀρνησόμεθα

Read against the letter's implied setting, Towner suggests that "'denial' takes its meaning from the apostasy (from the apostolic faith) that was troubling Ephesus."[109] Hymenaeus and Phyletus serve as examples of church leaders once true to the faith who now deny it, and the warning extends to those embroiled in doctrinal disputes.[110] Towner follows Schlier's judgment that "ἀρνεῖσθαι implies a previous relationship of obedience and fidelity. It can take place only where there has first been acknowledgment and commitment."[111] At first sight this definition fails to account for its uses in Acts for the Jewish rejection of Jesus (3:13) and the Israelites' refusal to accept Moses as their ruler (7:35), but even there the implication may be that in rejecting his agents, the people have broken their relationship with God. In 1 John 2:22, 23 "denying" is the opposite of "confessing" Christ (ὁμολογέω), indicating apostasy from orthodox Christian commitment.

This sense of turning away from an earlier faith commitment fits the context in 2 Tim 2:12. The first person plural form of the verb draws in both writer and reader, implying that the warning is pertinent even to Christian teachers, and if the piece had baptismal associations that would reinforce the idea of reneging on a pledge. Of what might such a failure consist? In the Synoptics it represents

---

108 Beasley-Murray, *Baptism*, 208.
109 Towner, *Goal*, 106.
110 Towner, *Goal*, 106.
111 H. Schlier, "ἀρνέομαι," *TDNT* 1:469-71, 470 (cited by Towner, *Goal*, 289, n. 176).

failure in the face of persecution to maintain open allegiance to Christ (Matt 10:33; Luke 12:9; illustrated by Peter's denial of Christ, Matt 26:70, 72; Mark 14:68, 70; Luke 22:57; cf. John 13:38; 18:25,27). This is also the context in Revelation, where those churches are commended which have not denied in spite of persecution (Rev 2:13; 3:8). 2 Peter and Jude, however, use ἀρνέομαι to characterize the activity of false teachers (2 Pet 2:1; Jude 4) and in 1 Timothy and Titus ungodly actions are said to constitute a denial of God or the faith (1 Tim 5:8; Titus 1:16). In 2 Tim 2:11-13 the echo of the dominical saying and possible suggestions of martyrdom make a warning against failing to confess allegiance to Christ under threat plausible. In the implied setting of Paul's imprisonment, a reader might be expected to contrast such denial with Paul's faithful perseverance in his testimony (4:16-18).

The context of paraenesis to teachers, however (2:14; cf. 2:2), might allow the widening of the concept to include denial in the sense of failing to adhere to the true doctrine under the pressures of the age (3:1-9; 4:1-5). In this connection 3:5 speaks of some "denying" (ἠρνημένοι) the power of godliness, which is linked with opposing the truth and failing with regard to the faith (3:8). As in the Synoptics, the concepts of "denying" and "being ashamed" overlap (see 1:8, 16; cf. Mark 8:38; Luke 9:26).[112] In summary, the author utilizes material which may carry connotations of faithful witness under threat, but in the context of teachers straying from the truth, the idea of denial could well include failure to remain faithful to the apostolic message.

b. κἀκεῖνος ἀρνήσεται ἡμᾶς

The Synoptic reference to Christ's denying of those who deny him "brings out the vital significance of people's attitude to Jesus here and now in view of the coming judgment."[113] Since that judgment is prominent in 2 Timothy, it is reasonable to see an eschatological reference in 2:12. To be denied by Christ on "that day" will presumably mean to be refused the mercy (1:18), reward (4:8) and welcome into the heavenly kingdom (4:18) that are anticipated for the faithful. This serves as motivation for faithful service. Again, the paraenetic strategy of the author is to set greater value on eschatological than temporal conditions, regarding Christ's future judgment as more important than the estimate of contemporaries (4:1; cf. 4:3).

---

112 Cf. Houlden, 119.
113 Marshall, *Luke*, 516.

12.6.4 Our Faithlessness, His Faithfulness (v. 13)

This final couplet seems to some scholars to be quite out of step with the letter's perspective, explicable only as part of the traditional material,[114] while for others it is "one of the most important concepts in the Pastorals,"[115] so distinctive that it may be the author's own addition.[116] These judgments depend of course on a decision about its meaning. Does it reinforce the threat in v. 12b or balance it with a promise? To what, or whom, is God faithful - himself, the threat, his purpose, or the unfaithful person? And does ἀπιστοῦμεν represent the failing already expressed by ἀρνησόμεθα (v. 12b) or something different in content or degree?

A positive outcome might seem to upset the balance of the piece, which would otherwise comprise a pair of positive (vv. 11b-12a) followed by a pair of negative statements (vv. 12b-13a).[117] On the other hand a twist in the tail is as familiar a literary technique as the setting of equivalent ideas in parallel. A weightier objection is that a positive interpretation would produce an internal inconsistency: if it has just been asserted that those who deny Christ will themselves be denied by him, how can it now be claimed that this will not transpire? On this basis, Stott explains, "So he will deny us, as the earlier epigram asserts. Indeed, if he did not deny us (in faithfulness to his plain warnings), he would then deny himself."[118]

This is to assume, however, that the two protatic conditions (εἰ ἀρνησόμεθα and εἰ ἀπιστοῦμεν) are identical, whereas it is possible to make a distinction between a definitive denial of Christ and lapses in faith or faithfulness.[119] Furthermore, while it is technically possible that an affirmation of God's faithfulness could refer to his consistency in carrying through his threats, in the overwhelming majority of cases in the NT such affirmations are made in order to bolster confidence rather than to warn,[120] and often with eschatological salvation in view.[121] Thus we find Paul expressing

---

114 E.g., Dibelius-Conzelmann, 109.
115 Donelson, *Pseudepigraphy*, 150.
116 E.g Hanson, *Epistles*, 133.
117 See e.g. Hendriksen, 259-60.
118 Stott, *2 Timothy*, 64. Cf. Matthew Henry *in loc.*, "If we be false to him, he will be faithful to his threatenings."
119 Towner, *Goal*, 107.
120 Knight notes the "strikingly uniform" references to the faithfulness of God and Christ (407).
121 Cf. Knight: "[In Paul] The faithfulness of God is intimately related to the final salvation of believers, indeed it is the assurance that God will confirm them to that end" (*Faithful Sayings*, 128-29).

confidence with regard to the status of Christians on the Day of Christ, because, πιστὸς ὁ θεὸς δι' οὗ ἐκλήθητε εἰς κοινωνίαν τοῦ υἱοῦ αὐτοῦ Ἰησοῦ Χριστοῦ τοῦ κυρίου ἡμῶν (1 Cor 1:9).[122]

God's faithfulness is also invoked as the ground of the hope that Christians would be preserved from sin and evil in this life (1 Cor 10:13; cf. 2 Thess 3:3; se also 2 Cor 1:18). For the writer of Hebrews, faith includes the judgment that God will be faithful to his promises (Heb 11:11). In the Johannine literature, assurance of forgiveness is based upon the faithfulness of God (1 John 1:9). While 2 Timothy could be an exception to the rule, this weight of NT usage suggests that in early Christianity a declaration of the faithfulness of God or Christ is more likely to be making a positive than a negative point.[123] A solemn warning would not be inconceivable in a letter which retains a degree of conditionality in relation to Christ's judgements on "that day," but the reiteration of the confidence of v. 9 would serve the paraenetic purpose well. In the ministry context, these closing lines could be heard as a declaration that even though his servants falter in faith and are "unbelieving,"[124] Christ will prove himself faithful to his word.

12.7 Summary

This paraenetic passage, urging the acceptance of suffering in the cause of the gospel, establishes a link between costly ministry and the effecting of God's saving purpose. As in the Lukan tradition of Pauline preaching, The primary datum of the gospel is the resurrection of Jesus, which confirms his messianic identity. The "of the seed of David" reference, allusions to God's purpose (implicit in ὁ λόγος) and the description of those who will be saved as "the elect" are consistent with a salvation-historical framework, although Christ's suffering also serves an exemplary purpose, as does the endurance of Paul himself. There are overtones of the martyr tradition of Hellenistic Judaism (particularly in 4 Maccabees) in the presentation of Paul, colouring the characterization of the ministry which is urged. The passage invites would-be servants of the gospel to identify with Christ in his death and suffering, life and reign. The

---

122 See also 1 Thess 5:23-24; cf. Heb 10:23.
123 See, e.g., Beasley-Murray, *Baptism*, 209 n. 1; Dibelius-Conzelmann, 109; Hanson, *Epistles*, 133. J. M. Bassler argues that the final line affirms God's faithfulness in, "'He remains faithful' (2 Tim 2:13a)," in *Theology and Ethics in Paul and is Interpreters* (ed. E. H. Lowering Jr. and J. E. Sumney; Nashville: Abingdon, 1996), 173-83.
124 Cf. John 20:27, μὴ γίνου ἄπιστος ἀλλὰ πιστός.

prospect of an apocalyptic final judgement issuing in eternal life with Christ motivates to eschatological endurance and continuing faithfulness, but, somewhat in tension with that, the final word is of confidence in Christ's faithfulness specifically in the fulfilment of his saving purpose.

CHAPTER 13

2 Timothy 3:14-17

Σὺ δὲ μένε ἐν οἷς ἔμαθες καὶ ἐπιστώθης, εἰδὼς παρὰ τίνων ἔμαθες, καὶ ὅτι ἀπὸ βρέφους [τὰ] ἱερὰ γράμματα οἶδας, τὰ δυνάμενά σε σοφίσαι εἰς σωτηρίαν διὰ πίστεως τῆς ἐν Χριστῷ Ἰησοῦ. πᾶσα γραφὴ θεόπνευστος καὶ ὠφέλιμος πρὸς διδασκαλίαν, πρὸς ἐλεγμόν, πρὸς ἐπανόρθωσιν, πρὸς παιδείαν τὴν ἐν δικαιοσύνῃ, ἵνα ἄρτιος ᾖ ὁ τοῦ θεοῦ ἄνθρωπος, πρὸς πᾶν ἔργον ἀγαθὸν ἐξηρτισμένος.

We have here one of the clearest and fullest statements in the NT of the significance of the OT.[1] Intriguing for the purposes of this study is the link postulated between these "sacred writings" and a salvation that is "through faith in Christ Jesus." What are these "sacred writings," and in what sense do they contain soteriological power? What is suggested about the author's concept of faith and its relation to salvation?

13.1 Context

Again, paraenesis concerning the exercise of ministry provides the context for a soteriological statement.[2] The σὺ δέ in v. 14 sets Timothy and his task in sharp contrast to the opponents and their activities described in v. 13. While they "go on" (προκόψουσιν, v. 13), Timothy "remains" (μένω . . .),"[3] remaining in what he has learned and known since childhood. The opponents deal in deceit that will ultimately fail its adherents, but Timothy's resources are sure and will lead to salvation.

In the larger context of 2:14-4:8 a sustained contrast is developed between Paul and Timothy and their opponents in which the paramount theme is the truth. The false teachers have "swerved from the truth" (περὶ τὴν ἀλήθειαν ἠστόχησαν, 2:18) and "oppose

---

1   B. Kowalski, "Zur Funktion und Bedeutung der alttestamentlichen Zitate und Anspielungen in den Pastoralbriefen," *SNTSU* 19 (1994): 45-68, 66.
2   Cf. 1:9-11; 2:8-13.
3   Spicq, 784.

the truth" (ἀντίστανται τῇ ἀληθείᾳ, 3:8); their followers are "never able to come to a knowledge of the truth" (μηδέποτε εἰς ἐπίγνωσιν ἀληθείας ἐλθεῖν δυνάμενα, 3:7) and "turn away from listening to the truth" (ἀπὸ . . . τῆς ἀληθείας τὴν ἀκοὴν ἀποστρέψουσιν, 4:4); the urgent need of such teachers is for "repentance into a knowledge of the truth" (μετάνοια εἰς ἐπίγνωσιν ἀληθείας, 2:25). Forsaking the truth, they are characterized by "wrangling about words" (λογομαχεῖν, 2:14), "godless chatter" (βέβηλοι κενοφωνίαι, 2:16), "stupid and senseless controversies" which provoke "quarrels" (μωροὶ καὶ ἀπαίδευτοι ζητήσεις . . . μάχαι, 2:23) and "myths" (μῦθοι, 4:4); they live "deceiving and being deceived" (πλανῶντες καὶ πλανώμενοι, 3:13). This serves to accentuate the place of truth in Timothy's ministry. He is to deal in a straightforward manner with "the word of truth" (ὀρθοτομῶν τὸν λόγον τῆς ἀληθείας, 2:15) which is the content of his teaching (specified as ὁ λόγος, 4:2, and ἡ ὑγιαινούσῃ διδασκαλία, 4:3). When Timothy is directed to the "sacred writings" in such a context, the implication is that, in marked contrast to the "myths" that provide material for the opponents (4:2), they are a source of that truth. If rightly handled (2:14-15) and continued in (3:14), they will yield the benefits listed in 3:15-17.

In contrast to the ruinous ministry of the opponents (2:14), Paul's ministry has already been presented as salvific in effect (2:10). This consideration provides motivation to persevere in ministry. Now Timothy is encouraged to continue in a ministry which, similarly, will bring about salvation. The linking of the sacred writings to salvation is therefore part of the larger argument that ministry, rightly exercised, results in the salvation of others. Timothy is being directed towards the resources for this soteriologically effective ministry.

13.2 The Sacred Writings and Salvation (v. 15a, b)

13.2.1 "The Sacred Writings"

What the term ἱερὰ γράμματα represents for this author is debated, and the textual issue of the integrity of the article adds a further twist.[4] There is ample evidence, however, of the use of the phrase in Hellenistic Judaism to refer to the books of the Hebrew canon,[5] and according to Schrenk, "The lack of the article makes no difference in

---

4 See Knight, 443.
5 See examples in G. Schrenk, "γράμμα," *TDNT* 1:761-69, 763-64; cf. Dibelius-Conzelmann, 119-20 and n. 6.

what is clearly a technical term."⁶ Hasler wants to extend it to the apostolic writings and even the PE themselves, so that, "So wird V.16 zu einer Selbstempfehlung," but this is highly speculative and requires a particular view of the date and provenance of the PE. Hanson concludes, "The phrase, with or without the article, means the OT, and nothing else."⁷

13.2.2 "Are Able"

The participle δυνάμενά "affirms that the ἱερὰ γράμματα have a certain innate ability, which is specified in the following infinitive clauses."⁸ This contrasts with the teaching of the opponents whose followers are "powerless" to attain knowledge of the truth (μηδέποτε εἰς ἐπίγνωσιν ἀληθείαν ἐλθεῖν δυνάμενα, 3:7). The δυνάμενά also places this statement in the chain of "power" terms running through the letter which explicates the exhortation to Timothy, συγκακοπάθησον τῷ εὐαγγελίῳ κατὰ δύναμιν θεοῦ (1:8).⁹ As this theme unfolds, it is in connection with that power that the scriptures appear.

13.2.3 "To Make Wise for Salvation"

The verb σοφίζω could carry connotations of human cleverness or its display,¹⁰ but the LXX illustrates positive uses, specifically of instruction in the Law of God making one wise.¹¹ This "wisdom" is not so much an innate quality of good judgment as knowledge and understanding that is learned. In Sirach, for example, becoming wise is possible only for one who is free from other work (38:24-25) and able to devote himself to study of the Law and the wisdom of the ancients (38:34b-39:11). Wilckens judges that, "The author adopts this usage and transfers it without a break to Christian instruction in the OT, by knowledge of which a man attains to salvation in Christian faith."¹²

---

6 Schrenk, *TDNT* 1:765 (examples in n. 13).
7 See also Oberlinner, *2.Timotheusbrief*, 145.
8 Knight, 443-44. Cf. Heb 4:12, where the word of God is ἐνεργής.
9 See above, pp. 113-14.
10 E.g. Sir 7:5; 10:26; 32:4; cf. examples in "σοφίζω,"1b, 2 in BAGD, 760; also 2 Pet 1:16, the only other NT occurrence.
11 See e.g. LXX Ps 18:8 [19:7]; 118:98 [119:98]. Fee sees Ps 19:7 reflected in 2 Tim 3:15 (279).
12 U. Wilckens, "σοφίζω," *TDNT* 8:527-28, 527.

The content of this "salvation" is not elaborated here, and must therefore be sought elsewhere in the letter.¹³ Here the concern is with the attaining of salvation, and the sacred scriptures as a means to that end. But what is the nature of their contribution? Is it to instruct in the sort of living that leads to salvation, or to point to Christ and thus promote saving faith? The former approach appeals to the behavioural outcomes listed in vv. 16-17. In Hasler's view, the author regards the OT as a handbook of Christian piety that points the way to salvation through the practice of the virtues.¹⁴ To stress the "ostensive ability to produce virtue,"¹⁵ however, may underestimate the christological specificity of a salvation that is expressly "through faith that is in Christ Jesus" (v. 15).¹⁶ We might compare Ignatius's use of σοφίζω in *Smyrn.* 1.1: Δοξάζω Ἰησοῦν Χριστὸν τὸν θεὸν τὸν οὕτως ὑμᾶς σοφίσαντα. Here the outcome is to be established in faith, which has christological content. To be "made wise" is therefore to have become persuaded of certain items of belief with reference to Christ, from his Davidic descent (1.1) to his resurrection (1.2). There is no mention of the role of the OT in this passage from Ignatius, but the pertinent point is that the force of the verb σοφίζω is cognitive rather than behavioural.¹⁷

When 2 Tim 3:15 is read in that way, the emphasis falls on the knowledge about Christ and salvation that the sacred writings, as interpreted by the apostle and his successors, can provide. According to the testimony of Acts, it was in the OT that early Christian preaching found ways of interpreting Christ's Davidic descent and his resurrection, constructing a soteriological explication of the Christ event from OT components (see e.g. Acts 13:16-41). Since precisely those items of belief have already been highlighted in 2 Tim 2:8, it is reasonable to attribute to this author the conviction that the cognitive content of faith may be supplied by the OT as

---

13 Knight's generalisation that "σωτηρία is used in the NT of the spiritual deliverance from bondage to sin that Christ brings" (444) cannot serve for every instance. The contexts must be allowed to ellucidate the range of significances.
14 Hasler, 75.
15 Donelson, *Pseudepigraphy*, 191.
16 Cf. Kowalski, "Zitate", 66:"Vielmehr konnte eine den Glauben an Christus vorbereitende und das AT hochschätzende Bedeutung aus im Zusammenhang mit dem Hinweis auf die jüdischen Vorfahren herausgearbeitet werden."; cf. Merkel, 76.
17 By locating σοφίζω within the technical vocabulary of Jewish *paideia* as he understands it Spicq perhaps underestimates the cognitive aspect in the present context (786).

applied to Christ, and that in this sense these writings are able to make wise for salvation.

13.3 Faith and Salvation (v. 15c)

As we have already noted, it is characteristic of 2 Timothy to qualify an idea by the article with the predicative phrase ἐν Χριστῷ Ἰησοῦ (1:1, 13; 2:1, 10; 3:15). As Barrett insists, this is no "mere pendant, added almost absent-mindedly."[18] At the very least it must indicate a consistent impulse on the part of the author to characterize significant ideas christologically. The effect in 3:15 is to affirm that, "The salvation to which the Old Testament points is not independent of Christ."[19] But how is this faith to be understood? For Knight, it has "the active sense of 'believing' or 'trusting' in Christ as one's Lord and thus as one's Savior," as in Rom 10:9.[20] Hasler, on the other hand, sees not Pauline justification by faith but the attaining of salvation by piety and adhering to the correct faith of the church.[21] Wallis, bringing his own understanding of "the faith of Jesus" in the PE, argues,

> Once again, Christ cannot be abstracted from faith and considered the object of belief; rather, the faith which appropriates salvation is one which has its source and substance in the faith of Christ Jesus himself.[22]

Perhaps comparison with the other "that is/are in Christ Jesus" references could suggest a way forward. Paul's apostleship concerns "life that is in Christ Jesus" (1:1); Timothy is to minister in "faith and love that are in Christ Jesus" (1:13), finding strength in "the grace that is in Christ Jesus (2:1); and the elect will obtain "salvation that is in Christ Jesus" (2:10). As in 2:10, it is helpful to consider both spatial and instrumental aspects of the usage.[23] Life, faith, love, grace and salvation have their source in Christ and flow from him to those who adhere to him, recognising him to be God's agent of salvation and living according to their allegiance to him. By analogy, the "faith

---

18 Barrett, 114, *contra* such as Dibelius-Conzelmann who evidently regard it as unworthy of comment in any of its five occurrences in 2 Timothy.
19 Barrett, 114.
20 Knight, 444.
21 Hasler, 75 ("Frömigkeit und die kirkliche Rechtgläubigkeit"); cf. Oberlinner, *2.Timotheusbrief*, 146.
22 I. G. Wallis, *The Faith of Jesus Christ in Early Christian Tradition* (SNTSMS 84; Cambridge: Cambridge University Press, 1995), 142 (on PE see 135-44).
23 See above (pp. 148-49).

that is in Christ Jesus" in 3:15 is part of that complex of salvation realities given by God through Christ (cf. 1:9) and appropriated as individuals learn about and put their trust in this salvation through Christ that is the content of the gospel and shape their lives accordingly. The function of the sacred writings is to instruct people in the appropriation of that gift which produces the twin outcomes of salvation and service.[24] This πίστις is therefore neither Jesus's own faith in the sense that Wallis suggests nor is it only human belief directed towards Christ. There is no hint of Hasler's "ecclesiastical piety."[25] Rather, it is part of the existence into which those who are on the way to salvation enter. There are cognitive and behavioural aspects, and the OT is recommended to Timothy as his primary resource for the cultivation of both.

13.4 Summary

The attribution of salvific power to the OT scriptures is to be understood in terms of two emphases of this letter, the soteriological outcome of ministry rightly exercised and the continuity between the faith of Judaism and the Christian Gospel. From the author's theological perspective the OT directs those taught by it to faith in Christ and a life of righteousness, and hence to salvation.

---

24 In the context of Timothy's ministry, the four uses of scripture in v. 16 all relate to teaching: διδασκαλία, ἐλεγμός, ἐπανόρθωσις, and παιδεία. The third of these, a NT hapax, is found in a suggestive context in Philodemus's treatise *On the Good King According to Homer* where he says that he has taken from Homer ἀφ[ορμῶν] . . . εἰς ἐπανόρθωσιν δυνα[σ]τε[ιῶν] ("starting points . . . for the correction of exercises of power", PHerc. 1507 col. 43.16-19), an example of a Hellenistic philosopher exegeting his "sacred texts" in search of practical guidance. Cf. Epictetus, *Diatr.* 3.21.15, where it is said that the mysteries are established ἐπὶ παιδείᾳ καὶ ἐπανορθώσει τοῦ βίου (cited by Barrett, 115). Philo speaks of the Jewish scriptures, given εἰς ἐπανόρθωσιν βίου ("for the rectifying of life," *Mos.* 2.28-36).
25 Marshall, 790 n. 68.

Chapter 14

2 Timothy 4:16-18

Ἐν τῇ πρώτῃ μου ἀπολογίᾳ οὐδείς μοι παρεγένετο, ἀλλὰ πάντες με ἐγκατέλιπον· μὴ αὐτοῖς λογισθείη· ὁ δὲ κύριός μοι παρέστη καὶ ἐνεδυνάμωσέν με, ἵνα δι' ἐμοῦ τὸ κήρυγμα πληροφορηθῇ καὶ ἀκούσωσιν πάντα τὰ ἔθνη, καὶ ἐρρύσθην ἐκ στόματος λέοντος. ῥύσεταί με ὁ κύριος ἀπὸ παντὸς ἔργου πονηροῦ καὶ σώσει εἰς τὴν βασιλείαν αὐτοῦ τὴν ἐπουράνιον· ᾧ ἡ δόξα εἰς τοὺς αἰῶνας τῶν αἰώνων, ἀμήν.

This passage depicts two acts of saving: an experience of temporal deliverance is recalled and a final saving anticipated. Both are significant for the soteriological outlook of this letter, the former because a soteriological purpose is discerned in it and the latter because it suggests something of the author's vision of ultimate salvation.

14.1 Context

In the letter's paraenesis this episode functions as a final illustration of that faithful, empowered witness to which Timothy is summoned. Two courtroom scenes provide the backcloth. The most obvious is that of Paul's "first defence" (4:16a). His witness and ministry are also interpreted, however, from the perspective of eschatological judgment. The exhortation appeals to Christ's coming judgment (4:1), Paul himself looks beyond natural death to the Lord's verdict (4:8) and there is a further allusion to eschatological accounting in Paul's prayer that the failure of his friends might not be held against them (4:16b). The force of the paraenesis depends on the premise that the decision of the eschatological judge counts for more than the opinion of the historical one, and a place in the coming kingdom makes the forfeit of temporal honour, freedom and even life worthwhile. We glimpse here elements of the soteriological framework assumed by the author, on the basis of which he urges the faithful exercise of ministry and acceptance of its cost in the present age.

14.2 The Past Rescue (v. 17)

14.2.1 *The Reference*

The πρώτη ἀπολογία refered to in v. 16 may be either a trial associated with an earlier imprisonment or the first stage of the judicial process within which 2 Timothy sets Paul. The arguments are inconclusive,[1] but the issue scarcely affects the presentation of salvation. Whichever the occasion, the event is spoken of in terms of a saving whose outcome is interpreted in a broader soteriological context.

14.2.2 *The Character and Content of This Rescue*

The saving that Paul experienced on that occasion is described in two ways: ὁ δὲ κύριός μοι παρέστη καὶ ἐνεδυνάμωσέν με, and ἐρρύσθην ἐκ στόματος λέοντος. The first claim is that the Lord had stood alongside Paul. Most commentators assume "the Lord" in this statement to be Christ, but Hinson takes the referent to be God, on the grounds that the piece concludes with a doxology that would most naturally be ascribed to God (v. 18).[2] In this letter, however, most of the fifteen occurences of the term κύριος (1:2, 8, 16, 18; 2:7, 19 (2x), 22, 24; 3:11; 4:8, 14, 17, 18, 22) refer to Christ. The opening greeting distinguishes "Christ Jesus our Lord" from "God our Father" (1:2). On four occasions the term identifies the eschatological judge, who is clearly Christ (4:8; cf. 1:16, 18; 4;14), and Christ is also in view in the references to "the testimony of our Lord" (1:8) and "the Lord's servant" (2:24). The account of Korah's rebellion in Numbers ch. 16 refers of course to the God of Israel, but two observations suggest that the author of 2 Timothy intends Christ to be the subject of the statements that he utilizes in 2:19. First, in the citation from Num 16:5, Ἔγνω κύριος τοὺς ὄντας αὐτοῦ, κύριος is preferred to the LXX's ὁ θεός. Secondly, v. 19b, which appears to be a "generalized summary of the exhortation in Nu. 16:26 that uses language found elsewhere in the OT,"[3] draws on Joel 3:5, a text cited by Paul in Rom 10:13 in relation to his preaching of Christ. It seems that both Paul and the author of 2 Timothy are willing to refer OT statements about Yahweh to Christ as Lord.[4] To take 4:17 as another

---

1   See Knight, 468-69 and 17-20.
2   Hinson, 359.
3   Knight, 416.
4   See Dunn on the application of a *Kyrios Yahweh* reference to *Kyrios Jesus* in Rom 10:9 (*Romans*, 2:607-08), and on the use in Rom 10:13 of Joel 3:5, which he thinks was "probably more widely used in early Christian self-

reference to Christ would place it in a series of references to Christ as κύριος describing his past rescuing and future judging and saving (3:11; 4:8, 14, 17, 18).

There is no means of deciding whether the statement, ὁ δὲ κύριός μοι παρέστη, claims some mystical experience (cf. the testimony of the Lukan Paul in Acts 27:23, παρέστη γάρ μοι . . . ἄγγελος), or simply affirms figuratively that the Lord had not abandoned Paul.[5] The paraenetic concern is to demonstrate that the Lord's servants who seek to maintain a faithful witness in the face of opposition do not stand alone, because the Lord himself is with them. Along with the supporting presence of the Lord came an embuing with power, taking up the theme of empowerment for witness that runs through this letter (e.g. 1:8; 2:1).[6] "Paul's experience thus offers an object lesson for Timothy, who was earlier urged to rely on the power and strength of God."[7]

14.2.3 The Purpose of this Strengthening

The strengthening of Paul has the specific purpose, ἵνα δι' ἐμοῦ τὸ κήρυγμα πληροφορηθῇ καὶ ἀκούσωσιν πάντα τὰ ἔθνη (v. 17). In the terse phrasing, the close link between the κήρυγμα and Paul its herald is established by the instrumental δι' ἐμοῦ, placed prominently at the beginning. The passive form πληροφορηθῇ allows an implication of divine purpose. At the same time, it echoes the call to Timothy to fulfil his ministry (4:5c) against a background of present opposition (4:2-4) and coming judgment (4:1). Again, Paul serves as a model. This is even clearer if τὸ κήρυγμα represents not only the message's content but also the activity of proclaiming it. Hendriksen's "the heralded message" attempts to capture the double reference in English.[8]

---

understanding" (citing Acts 2:17-21, 39; Rom 5:5; Titus 3:6; Mark 13:24 pars.; Rev 6:12) (611).
5   Fee understands it as "not necessarily the language of religious mysticism," but certainly an indication of a subjective awareness of Christ's presence (297).
6   Davies remarks that 4:17 "recalls the earlier teaching that only God's power could help people to remain faithful during persecution" (89).
7   Bassler, 177.
8   Hendriksen, 326. It is easier to accomplish in some other languages. The revised Almeida Portuguese translation (Sociedade Bíblica do Brasil, 1969), for example, has "a pregação fosse plenamente cumprida," where "a pregação" can be either the activity of preaching or that which was preached.

Introduced by an epexegetical καί,⁹ the phrase ἀκούσωσιν τὰ ἔθνη supplies further explication of this "fulfilling." Whatever the historical reference,¹⁰ the theological point is that the help given to Paul has served a larger purpose than the apostle's personal benefit. God intends that all nations should hear the message, and to that end he enables his messengers to do their part. The primary soteriological significance of this "deliverance," then, is not so much that God preserves his servants from affliction but rather (as in 2:9-10) that his saving purpose for the world through the gospel will not be thwarted by human opposition.

14.2.4 The Metaphor

This rescue is further described as, ἐρρύσθην ἐκ στόματος λέοντος. Some scholars read this as a metaphor for deliverance in general,¹¹ but most attempt a more specific identification. If the rescue is construed as the deliverance of Paul from martyrdom or suffering, the "lion" may be a literal threat in the Roman amphitheatre, or a figurative reference to some authoritative figure or perhaps even the Roman Empire itself.¹² Another possibility is an allusion to the devil's opposition (cf. 1 Peter 5:8),¹³ of which 2 Timothy has already warned (2:26). Lightfoot's comment on the σωτηρία anticipated in Phil 1:19-20 might then apply here: "[Paul's] personal safety cannot be intended . . . for the σωτηρία of which he speaks, will be gained equally whether he lives or dies."¹⁴ On the other hand, if the fear of failing Christ is prominent, then empowering for witness might itself be regarded as a deliverance.¹⁵

---

9   See e.g. Knight, 470; Oberlinner, *2.Timotheusbrief*, 178 n. 44; Spicq, 820.
10 Among many proposals, Guthrie suggests that Paul's preaching to a "cosmoplitan" audience in Rome represents a fulfilment of his mission (176-77), while Hanson understands it to refer to the spread of the gospel in the pagan world subsequent to Paul's martyrdom (*Epistles*, 161).
11 E.g. Davies, 89.
12 See Dibelius-Conzelmann (124 and n. 16), who cite Josephus's reference to the death of Tiberius, "the lion is dead" (*Ant.* 18.228), and Ignatius's description of soldiers as leapards (Ign. *Rom.* 5.1); cf. Fee, 297; Guthrie, 176; Knight, 471.
13 The context of 1 Peter's reference to the devil as a "roaring lion" is also an exhortation to ministers to remain faithful despite opposition, anticipating the crown of life (5:1-11).
14 J. B. Lightfoot, *St. Paul's Epistle to the Philippians* (Classic Commentary Library; Grand Rapids: Zondervan, 1953; repr. from original ed., London: Macmillan & Co., 1913), 91.
15 Cf. Barrett, 123. Bassler cites Phil 1:12-14 as a parallel example of witness

Perhaps, however, the author's choice of metaphor owes more to the characterization of the one rescued than to the particular type of peril. Points of contact are often noted between this passage and Psalm 22 [LXX Ps 21].[16] This does not mean, however, that the deliverance in 2 Tim 4:17 must be the same as that of which the Psalm speaks.[17] Rather, the principal correspondence might be between the two sufferers. If, with the Synoptics, the author relates Ps 22 to Christ's suffering on the cross,[18] then the allusion to the Psalm may be intended to tint Paul's suffering with evocations of the suffering of Christ.[19]

The paradigmatic biblical rescue from the lion's mouth is, however, that of Daniel (Dan 6:16-27). This is presented both as a demonstration of the saving power of the living God (vv. 26-27) and as vindication of Daniel's faithfulness to God (vv. 16, 20) and his innocence before the king (v. 22). In 1 Maccabees' litany of "the deeds of the ancestors," it is the vindication of Daniel's innocence that is emphasized: "Daniel, because of his innocence, was delivered from the mouth of the lions" (Δανιηλ ἐν τῇ ἁπλότητι αὐτοῦ ἐρρύσθη ἐκ στόματος λεόντων, 1 Macc 2:60). This reinforces the conclusion that, "none of those who put their trust in him will lack strength" (v. 61). In the OT, particularly in the Psalms, deliverance and vindication are often closely linked (e.g. Pss 17:2 [LXX 16:2]; 24:5 [23:5]; 43:1 [42:1]; 54:1 [53:3]; Isa 62:1; 63:1; cf. Luke 18:7). With this colouring, the rescue from lions image in 2 Tim 4:17 would place Paul in that succession, revered in Judaism, of faithful servants of the Lord who were vindicated by him.[20] Additionally, the outcome of Daniel's deliverance in Dan 6:25-27, as of Paul's in 2 Tim 4:17, was that the nations heard and were summoned to worship this living and saving God. Both accounts see a larger purpose in the deliverance than the rescue of one individual; it serves to extend the knowledge of God throughout the world.

---

borne despite imprisonment (177).

16 Listed by, e.g., Hanson, *Epistles*, 162; Towner, 211-12; see also Spicq, 821; Fee, 296-98, 299.
17 As Hendriksen, 327, apparently followed by Fee, 298, deduces.
18 See Matt 27:29, 39, 43, 46; Mark 15:34.
19 Cf. P. H. Towner, *1-2 Timothy & Titus* (IVPNTC; Downers Grove: IVP, 1994), 211.
20 In the speech of Mattathias in 1 Macc 2:50-68, as in 2 Timothy, Jewish ancestors are considered worthy of imitation in respect to their service for God (1 Macc 2:56; 2 Tim 1:3). Several of the qualities listed by Mattathias correspond to attributes which the writer of 2 Timothy commends.

14.3 The Future Rescue (v. 18)

14.3.1 The Shift in Focus

From the past experience of Paul a more general lesson is drawn, with the focus now on the ultimate outcome of the Lord's rescuing and saving.[21] The verbs ῥύομαι and σῴζω are both in the future tense. It would be unwise to force too precise a distinction between the two, especially as they are parallel terms in LXX Ps 21:9, 21-22, but it is possible that the latter verb and its cognates carry particular associations in this letter with final salvation or at least with salvation as a specifically religious category (cf. the verb in 1:9; the noun σωτηρία in 2:10 and 3:15; and the title σωτήρ in 1:10), whereas ῥύομαι, as in the preceding verse, can be used of temporal rescue.[22] Prior takes v. 18 as witness that Paul was "very hopeful of the outcome of his case" and anticipating further missionary activity.[23] Most scholars, however, would agree with Bassler that the statement has in view "a rescue for the heavenly kingdom, not a rescue for life 'in the flesh' (cf. Phil 1:22-26)."[24] Paul could then be said to be "saved" even if he was not rescued from physical death.[25]

14.3.2 πᾶν ἔργον πονηρόν

That from which rescue is assured is encapsulated in the phrase, πᾶν ἔργον πονηρόν. The context requires more than a straightforward moral understanding of this "evil." The particular instance from which this generalization is construed is the persecution which had threatened to obstruct the fulfilling of Paul's commission (v. 17). It is "evil" in that it opposes Christ, his servants and the *kerygma*. Elsewhere in the letter, persecutions are associated with πονηροὶ ἄνθρωποι, whose iniquity can be expected to increase as they continue πλανῶντες καὶ πλανώμενοι (3:13). Such people and conditions are characteristic of the "last days" (3:1) which furnish the context for the ministry to which 2 Timothy summons the successors of the apostle. The term πονηρός, then, resonates with religious and eschatological connotations.[26] The evil deeds from which Christ's

---

21 "Das Bekenntnis zum Beistand des Kyrios von V 17 erhält mit V 18 eine eschatologisch gewendete Abrundung." (Oberlinner, *2.Timotheusbrief*, 180.)
22 In Knight's view, σώσει is selected as appropriate to ultimate deliverance (472).
23 Prior, *Letter-Writer*, 163. He fails, however, to explain (or even mention) the reference to the "heavenly kingdom."
24 Bassler, 178.
25 Cf. Towner, 212.
26 G. Harder comments on the ἡμέραι πονηραί of Eph 5:16: "The days are

servants may expect deliverance are those which form part of the opposition to Christ and his gospel in this age of proclamation which precedes the coming of Christ and his kingdom. Although some find the key to the "evil" in v. 18 in the final petition of the Lord's Prayer,[27] it is more helpful to understand it against the wider background of the evil intrinsic to the last days.[28] From this perspective, rescue is effected when servants of Christ are preserved from failure to fulfil their commission, as exemplified by Paul (v. 17).

14.3.3 εἰς τὴν βασιλείαν αὐτοῦ τὴν ἐπουράνιον

For the servant himself, however, there is the prospect of a final saving εἰς τὴν βασιλείαν αὐτοῦ τὴν ἐπουράνιον. According to Barrett, "the text seems to imply the belief that Paul will survive till the *parousia*."[29] The the prospect of Paul's imminent death (ἀνάλυσις, 4:6), however, does not negate his confidence that he will participate in the parousia (ἐν ἐκείνῃ τῇ ἡμέρᾳ, 4:8). Indeed, the letter states explicitly that both living and dead will encounter Christ at his coming (4:1). The reference here is to "salut plénier, par la mort."[30] God's saving extends to carrying Paul safely into (εἰς) "his heavenly kingdom."[31] The letter conjoins the kingdom's realization to the appearing of Christ (4:1) on "that day" (1:12, 18; 4:8). Christ's coming as judge will require a final accounting of all who have lived, from which mercy is hoped and rewards anticipated (4:1; cf. 1:12, 18; 4:8). Participation in the coming kingdom can be described as sharing in Christ's reign, which is promised to those who have endured (2:11-12). It involves eternal life, which is a sharing in Christ's resurrection life (2:8, 11; 1:10, cf. 1:1).

Such an understanding is quite in accord with the concept of the heavenly kingdom in other NT writings. In Matthew's Gospel it is ἡ βασιλεία τῶν οὐρανῶν that Jesus proclaims and that seekers hope to enter (e.g. Matt 18:3; 19:23).[32] More specifically, Paul uses the term

---

evil ... because they are part of the last time" ("πονηρός, πονηρία," TDNT 6:546-66, 554). Note also the eschatological flavour of the αἰὼν τὸ πονηρόν in Gal 1:4 and the πονηροὶ ἄνθρωποι and τὸ πονηρόν of 2 Thess 3:2-3.

27 Knight describes it as a Pauline adaptation of that petition (472); cf. Guthrie, 177.
28 Cf. Oberlinner, *2.Timotheusbrief*, 180.
29 Barrett, 124; cf. Hanson, *Epistles*, 161-62.
30 Spicq, 821; cf. Hendriksen, "In the past Paul had been rescued *from* death. Now he will be rescued *by means of* death" (327).
31 2 Tim 4:18 is cited as an example of a pregnant construction in "εἰς," 7, BAGD 230.
32 The phrase is exclusive to Matthew in the NT, usually as reverent

ἐπουράνιος in 1 Corinthians ch. 15 to characterize existence in the kingdom of God. Christ himself, raised from the dead, is ὁ ἐπουράνιος (vv. 47, 48) and the adjective is also applied to those who will inherit the kingdom (v. 48) and their bodies (v. 40), in antithetical contrast to that which is "earthly" (ἐπίγειος, v. 40) or "of dust" (χοϊκός, vv. 48, 49) and hence moribund and outside of Christ. The "heavenly" state described is of post-mortem resurrected life with Christ. 2 Timothy shares with the Synoptics the goal of entry into the heavenly kingdom, and what may be glimpsed of the concept of kingdom does not conflicts with that delineated in 1 Corinthians.

To anticipate a saving into (or unto, or for[33]) the Lord's heavenly kingdom therefore suggests a concept of salvation that is Christologically determined, future in orientation, and involves the transcending of mortality. Since entry into the kingdom depends upon the verdict of Christ the judge, this salvation also requires the granting of mercy. The expression of confidence in that outcome implies that the saving into the kingdom includes a preserving from anything that might disqualify one from entry.

14.3.4 The Doxology

The idea of eternal glory has already been linked with salvation and with the resurrected Christ in 2:10. Here the configuration is that of a doxology.[34] As Oberlinner remarks, the question of whether praise is here offered to God or to Christ cannot be conclusively resolved, such is their interconnectedness from the salvation-historical perspective of this letter.[35] The effect is to keep the focus on the divine, the eternal and the glorious, strengthening the impression that it is to a salvation beyond the temporal and the moribund that the author aspires. As Guthrie comments, "His mind is clearly centred more on eternal realitites than any hopes of further release."[36]

---

periphrasis for ἡ βασιλεία τοῦ θεοῦ.
33 See Fee, 298.
34 Cf. Gal 1:5; Rom 9:5; and 1 Tim 1:17: in each case the ascription of glory is prompted by mention of God's saving in Christ. In Phil 4:20 a similar doxology follows an assurance of God's provision "according to his riches in glory in Christ Jesus."
35 Oberlinner, 2.Timotheusbrief, 181.
36 Guthrie, 178.

14.4 Summary

The first of the two savings to which this passage testifies illustrates the letter's conviction that in fulfilment of God's saving purpose he will ensure that his message reaches its destination, specifically the Gentile world. To that end God has preserved and empowered his messenger. The presentation alludes to the intertestamental theme of God's vindication of his servants, though they suffer at the hands of human authorities, and suggests an apocalyptic, End Time setting for Paul's witness. The second, anticipated, saving envisages an eschatological vindication issuing in acceptance into the eternal heavenly kingdom that Christ will establish at his coming.

CHAPTER 15

Summary of Salvation in 2 Timothy

15.1 General Observations

The personal and urgent tone that permeates this letter also colours the treatment of salvation. Prominent, and poignant in the setting of Paul's imminent death, is the theme of life beyond physical death. Such life depends upon Christ, who is himself raised from the dead (2:8; cf. 2:11). He has abolished death and brought this immortal life to light (1:10); it will be enjoyed by those who are saved by Christ into his heavenly kingdom (4:18), having received mercy from him when he appears as judge "on that day" (4:1, 8; cf. 1:18; 4:14). The promise of this life gives to Paul's apostleship its content and purpose (1:1). The concept of salvation in this letter therefore stretches beyond the present age, which is grimly characterized by opposition and persecution for those who want to teach and live by the message of Christ (1:15; 2:8-10, 14-18, 23-26; 3:1-13; 4:2-5, 16-18). It steps outside the present order to embrace not only a post-temporal but also a pre-temporal reality, for the saving has been in one sense achieved and given before historic time (1:9). Here is a kairological framework within which the present age is seen to be the opportune time for the making known of that saving and its outcome, immortal life, which God has given. The full benefits of salvation are, however, eschatological, awaiting Christ's final appearing (4:1) and a future resurrection (2:18).

The ministry of Paul, Timothy and their successors (2:2) has a crucial role as the means whereby that revelation, contained in the deposit of healthy teaching (1:13-14; 4:3) which is also the gospel (1:10-12; 2:8), the "word of God" (2:9), "word of truth" (2:15; cf. 2:25; 3:7), and the *kerygma* (4:17), is communicated. Real as the pressures are to be ashamed of this testimony and the suffering that accompanies it (1:8), those called to the ministry of the gospel (1:9) must serve courageously (1:7; 4:2, 5), accepting suffering (1:8; 2:3) and drawing on the spiritual resources of power and grace that are available to them through God, Christ and the Holy Spirit (1:7, 8-9, 14; 2:1-2; 3:11; 4:16-18). They have the example of Paul himself, and his confidence that through this costly ministry God's purpose is being accomplished (2:9) and salvation is being received (2:10). They must also, however, have a concern for their own ultimate salvation, and be sure to endure and keep the faith so as to receive the "crown of righteousness" at the final reckoning (4:6-8).

With this concept of salvation as a divine project that stretches from before time to beyond time, continuity is assumed between God's activity and message contained in the OT scriptures and the salvation now revealed in Christ (3:14-17; cf. possibly 1:5). Those who suffer in the service of this saving message stand in line with those who have served God faithfully in the past within Judaism (1:3), with Moses (3:8) and with the martyrs of more recent Jewish history (see discussion of 2:8-13). The opposition envisaged in this letter has no particular Jewish flavour, coming rather from "wicked people and imposters" who propagate error and empty ideas, stir up controversy and create their own followings within the Christian community (2:14-18, 23-26; 3:2-9, 12-13; 4:3-4). Nonetheless, the message of salvation is still expressly for "the nations" of the whole Roman world (4:17).

15.2 Specific Aspects of the Presentation of Salvation

15.2.1 The Benefits of Salvation

The benefits of salvation in 2 Timothy are focused upon the future. Christ our saviour "abolished death and brought life and immortality to light" (1:10), and it is the promise of that life that gives content and motivation to Paul's ministry (1:1). The "salvation that is in Christ Jesus" is associated with "eternal glory" (2:10), in a life described as living and reigning with Christ (2:11-12). There are experiences of saving in this life, but these are interpreted as preserving in order that ministry might be fulfilled (4:17). The definitive saving is that which issues in life in the Lord's heavenly kingdom (4:18). Entry into that life depends upon acquittal at the final judgment (1:12, 15, 18; 4:8, 14; cf. 4:1). The benefits of salvation therefore include the receiving of mercy and "the crown of righteousness" on "that day" (4:16, 18; 4:8).

15.2.2 God and Christ in Relation to Salvation

Important for this letter is a sense of the overarching purpose of God. It is he who "saved us . . . according to his own purpose and grace" (1:9a), giving that grace in Christ before time (1:9b). A confidence that God has a saving purpose, and it will succeed, is evident in the statement that God's word is not subject to the restrictions that its proclaimers may have to endure (2:9), the

Summary of Salvation in 2 Timothy 177

determination that "the elect" will obtain salvation (2:10), and the certainty that "God's firm foundation stands," and he knows who are his (2:19). It is God who inspired the sacred scriptures which are able to make wise for salvation through faith in Christ (3:15-17), and repentance and coming to know the truth is for God to grant (2:15). God's general providential care, so prominent in 1 Timothy, is not a feature of this letter. Rather, the focus is eschatological salvation, rooted in God's pretemporal gracious purpose, revealed through the Christ event and now declared by his servants, and on its way to fruition despite present opposition.

This eschatological salvation is in almost every case referred clearly to Christ. The "promise of life" and "salvation" are both described as "in Christ Jesus" (1:1; 2:10), and salvation comes through faith in Christ Jesus (3:15). The role of Christ in the achievement of this salvation is indicated at various points along a salvation-historical continuum to which the OT scriptures bear witness (3:15). It was in him that grace was given before time (1:9). He came into human history as "the descendant of David," a messianic identity that aligned him with the saving promises of God (2:8). In his appearing as saviour his death and resurrection accomplished the defeat of death and the bringing to light of immortality (1:10), making available a salvation into eternal life for those who are identified with him in his death and endurance (2:11-12). In the present age believers experience Christ's grace (2:1), faith and love (1:13), as they seek to εὐσεβῶς ζῆν ἐν Χριστῷ Ἰησοῦ (3:12), and his servants have his presence now to strengthen and preserve them while there remains a task of witness for them to perform (4:17-18a). Christ will appear again, this time as judge of all (4:1), and in that capacity it will be for him to show mercy (1:18) or to pay back wrongdoers (4:14), and to award "the crown of righteousness" to faithful servants and all whose lives are oriented in faith and hope towards that day (4:8), who depend upon him to convey them safely in due course into his heavenly kingdom (4:18b). While there is a degree of conditionality about the final verdict "on that day," the tone is one of confidence, since Christ's faithfulness will endure even if that of his servants falls short (2:13).

15.2.3 Paul and Salvation

Paul's apostleship is defined as "for the sake of the promise of life that is in Christ Jesus" (1:1). His role and calling, given by God in Christ before time (1:9), is to proclaim the gospel that has been entrusted to him, accepting the suffering that results (1:8, 11-12). This letter has Paul describe as "my gospel" the simple testimony,

"Jesus Christ, raised from the dead, descendant of David" (2:8), encapsulating the witness to the resurrection with its interpretation in OT messianic terms. For this witness he is not only called but also strengthened by the Lord in the face of opposition, "so that through me the message might be fully proclaimed and all the Gentiles might hear it" (4:17). Paul's ministry is salvific in that through it, with its suffering, the elect "obtain the salvation that is in Christ Jesus" (2:10). The prominence of the dimension of suffering imbues his ministry with something of a sacrificial character ("poured out as a libation," 4:6), but when his ministry has been fulfilled, there awaits the award of the crown of righteousness (4:6-8) and the safe entry into the heavenly kingdom.

Again, it is not Paul alone who exercises this salvific ministry of witness with suffering. Timothy is regarded as saved for it and called to it along with Paul (1:9) and he too is entrusted with the "good treasure" (1:14) and is challenged to fulfil his ministry (4:5 and indeed the letter as a whole). Paul has declared the message, Timothy has received it, and now it is for him to pass it on to others who in turn will teach others again (2:1).

15.2.4 Those Who are Saved

In 2 Timothy, with its focus upon final salvation into life in the heavenly kingdom, certain individuals and groups are spoken of in ways that indicate that they are or will be recipients of this salvation. Paul is one whom God has saved (1:9) and the Lord will save (4:18), Timothy, with Paul, has been saved (1:9), and it is anticipated that Onesiphorus will receive mercy at the eschaton (1:18). Two categories of people who will be saved in this final sense are mentioned, "the elect" (2:10) and "all who have longed for his appearing" (4:8), a phrase that suggests an attitude of faith and orientation of life founded upon the message about Christ.

The faithful saying in 2:11-13 depicts salvation as a sharing in the life of Christ in his kingdom and also specifies qualifications for this future, namely dying and enduring with Christ, and not denying him. This accords with the costly, martyrological witness exemplified by Paul (1:8, 11-12; 2:8-10; 3:10-12; 4:6-8, 16-18), to which Timothy is also called (1:8; 2:3; 4:1-5). Salvation awaits Paul, who has "fought the good fight," "finished the race" and "kept the faith" (4:8). Eschatological mercy is sought for Onesiphorus because he "was not ashamed" of Paul (1:16), and by implication of the gospel for which he suffered (cf. the two ideas together in 1:8). With the theme of witness to the fore it is especially faithful witnesses who are shown to receive salvation.

More generally, salvation is "through faith in Christ Jesus" (3:15). Again, a cognitive dimension may be discerned, in the references to the "word of God" through which saving is effected, the teaching of the scriptures that "instruct . . . for salvation" (3:15) and the hope that some presently in error may "repent and come to know the truth" (2:25). Alongside the emphasis on human responsibility and faithfulness in connection with the witness are found references to God's initiative and intervention in the saving of individuals. The saving and calling of Paul and Timothy are ascribed to God's eternal purpose and grace (1:9-10), and the reference to "the elect" (2:10), though not explicated, indicates at least a confidence that, in God's economy of salvation there are those in whom his saving will be realized as his unchained word goes out (2:9). It is significant that Paul is specifically enabled by God to bring the message to the Gentiles (4:17).

In the face of apparent success on the part of the opponents, the letter finds comfort in the assurance that "the Lord knows those who are his" (2:19), and if there are among the opponents those who will turn back to the truth, it will be because God grants to them the gift of repentance and escape from the devil's grasp (2:25-26). From one perspective, salvation is for those who hear the Christian message, receive it as truth and live faithfully for Christ, maintaining their witness in spite of opposition; from another, those who are saved were already the objects of God's saving purpose and gracious call before time, they have now by his generous intervention come to repentance and faith, and they will be kept by him through the perils of this life (4:18; cf. 2:20) and ushered into the eternal kingdom. 2 Timothy owns both the conditionality of the former, with its warning, and the confidence of the latter, with its reassurance.

In common with 1 Timothy, this letter indicates that it is possible to go astray in relation to the faith, embracing erroneous teaching (2:16-18), being ensnared by the devil (2:26) and by ones own corrupt desires (3:1-8), deceived by imposters (3:13) and wandering from the truth to myths (4:3-4). While there are those who proclaim the message of Christ, others vigorously oppose it (4:14-15). This sombre backcloth serves to accentuate the importance for 2 Timothy not only of the activity of proclamation but of the content of the message proclaimed and taught, the "truth" (2:15, 18, 25; 3:7, 8; 4:4), for the attaining of salvation.

PART 4

SALVATION IN TITUS

"The grace of God ... bringing salvation"

CHAPTER 16

Introduction to Salvation in Titus

Though it shares significant items of vocabulary and subject matter with 1 Timothy (and to a markedly lesser degree with 2 Timothy), the letter to Titus has its own distinctive features and character which any satisfactory reading must take into account.

16.1 Situation and Tone

The addressee is different. Whether "Titus" is the historical colleague of Paul (2 Cor 2:13; 7:6, 13; 8:6, 16, 23) or a "typical figure," representing "what the continuing Pauline apostolate is and does,"[1] the stated recipient of the letter and his implied relationship to the sender constitute a significant part of the interpretive framework. The Titus of the *Hauptbriefe* is a trusted co-worker who features in a critical moment of self-definition of Pauline Christianity, the dispute over circumcision of Gentile converts. Paul refused to have the Gentile Titus circumcised, ἵνα ἡ ἀλήθεια τοῦ εὐαγγελίου διαμείνῃ πρὸς ὑμᾶς (Gal 2:5). By contrast, Acts informs us that Paul had Timothy circumcised, διὰ τοὺς Ἰουδαίους . . . ᾔδεισαν γὰρ ἅπαντες ὅτι Ἕλλην ὁ πατὴρ αὐτοῦ ὑπῆρχεν (Acts 16:3). If the author was aware of the significance of Titus in relation to this issue in Paul's churches, it could have coloured the presentation of the situation faced by his implied addressee.

In comparison with the letters to Timothy, Titus seems to accent the confrontation between a Gentile Pauline leader and Judaizing opposition. Only here do the opponents specifically include οἱ ἐκ τῆς περιτομῆς (1:10). While the usage may be more general (as in Rom 2:25-27), Dunn discerns in the same same expression in Gal 2:12 "an identity determined by or focused in the act and fact of circumcision - hence the metonymy 'the circumcision,' not 'the circumcised'," indicating a specific faction within Judaism.[2] In Titus 1:10 the adverb μάλιστα seems to specify οἱ ἐκ τῆς περιτομῆς as a

---

1 Quinn, *Titus*, 14, 15.
2 J. D. G. Dunn, "Echoes of Intra-Jewish Polemic in Paul's Letter to the Galatians," *JBL* 112 (1993): 459-77, 461.

particular group among the many ἀνυπότακτοι, ματαιολόγοι καὶ φρεναπάται who threaten the church.³ rather than the general μῦθοι in 1 Timothy (1:4; 4:7) and 2 Timothy (4:4), Ἰουδαϊκοὶ μῦθοι are encountered by Titus (1:14), and he is warned against "quarrels about the law" (3:14). Nonetheless, Fee's assessment is fair: "False teachers are indeed in evidence . . ., but the letter as a whole is not dominated by their presence." ⁴ The less urgent tone is perhaps partly explained by the absence of the problem addressed in 1 Timothy of heterodox teaching actually within the existing church leadership (e.g. 1 Tim 1:3-7).⁵

The ecclesiastical structure assumed appears simpler than that in 1 Timothy (2 Timothy has little to judge by). Whereas 1 Timothy advises on ἐπίσκοποι (3:1-7), διάκονοι (3:8-13), γυναῖκες (3:11), χῆραι (5:3-16), and πρεσβύτεροι (5:17-19), some of whom apparently exercised a specialised teaching function (5:17b-18), Titus mentions only the appointment of πρεσβύτεροι (1:5-9), listing qualities required in an ἐπίσκοπος in a way that suggests that both terms refer to the one function (1:7-9).⁶ A less elaborate structure would fit the earlier stage of ecclesiastical development implied in the letter, comparable to the period of consolidation after initial evangelisation in Galatia described in Acts 14:21-23. Suitable leaders are to be identified, steps taken to counter rival teachers, and instruction given for converts whose life context is still largely that of the surrounding culture.

Unlike 1 and 2 Timothy, directed to the major city of Ephesus, the destination implied in Titus is the Mediterranean island of Crete, where new Christian communities are emerging in some of the island's many towns. The letter accurately represents Cretan conditions in several ways, in particular the rather archaic social organisation built around male age groups age groups.⁷ Roman

---

3   On μάλιστα see Campbell, "ΜΑΛΙΣΤΑ"; Skeat, "Especially"; and above on 1 Tim 4:10.
4   Fee, 11.
5   Couser suggests that the approach is preventative rather than corrective ("God and Christian Existence", 134).
6   Quinn concludes, "For the purposes of the author at this point they were practically synonymous" (*Titus*, 85).
7   Athenaeus, *Deipnosophistae* 4.142-43; see description in R. F. Willetts (ed.), *The Law Code of Gortyn*, Berlin: Walter de Gruyton, 1967, 10-11.

Crete had a significant Jewish population,[8] with links to the Jewish community in Alexandria.[9]

16.2 The Presentation of Salvation

Explicit soteriological statements in Titus are restricted to three Greek sentences, but these are rich in content and strategically deployed in the letter's argument to relate both Paul's apostleship (1:1-3) (and by extension Titus's role (1:4)) and the letter's practical instruction (2:1-10; 3:1, 8-14) to "God our Saviour" and his saving purpose and activity (1:1-4; 2:11-14; 3:3-7). They also supply the content of "healthy" and "profitable" teaching (2:1; 3:8; cf. 1:9), in contrast to the "empty talk" and "unprofitable and worthless" disputes of the opponents (1:10; 3:9).

Three distinctive soteriological features may be noted at this point. First there is the unusual incidence of the term σωτήρ. With six occurrences (out of 10 in the PE, 24 in the NT) this relatively short letter uses the term more than any other NT writing. An additional feature, almost unparalleled in the NT, is the ascription of the term to both God and Christ.[10] The pairing of references seems intentional: "God our Saviour" (1:3) with "Christ Jesus our Saviour" (1:4); "God our Saviour" (2:10) with "our Saviour, Jesus Christ" (2:13); "God our Saviour" (3:4) with "Jesus Christ our Saviour" (3:6). A second feature is the pervasive interest in "good deeds." Whereas the false teachers are πρὸς πᾶν ἔργον ἀγαθὸν ἀδόκιμοι (1:16) believers are to be πρὸς πᾶν ἔργον ἀγαθὸν ἕτοιμοι (3:1); Titus himself is to be a τύπος καλῶν ἔργων (2:7); the Saviour's self-giving is to produce a people ζηλωτὴς καλῶν ἔργων (2:14); Christians must learn καλῶν ἔργων προΐστασθαι (3:8, 14). Fee takes this to be "the dominant theme of the letter - good works with exemplary behavior, with a concern for what outsiders think."[11] We must ask how this "dominant theme" relates to the author's soteriology. Thirdly, the three soteriological statements all contain language that seems to echo in more than one sounding chamber! The presence of

---

8 Josephus *Ant.* 17.327; *B.J.* 2.103; *Vita* 76 (describing his third wife as a Jew from a notable Cretan family); Philo *Legat.* 282. See also 1 Macc 15:23 and Acts 2:11.
9 S. V. Spyridakis, *Ptolemaic Itanos and Hellenistic Crete* (University of California Publications in History 82; Berkeley: University of California Press, 1970) 102 n. 169.
10 Elsewhere in the NT only Luke's Gospel predicates σωτήρ of both God (1:47) and Christ (2:11).
11 Fee, 173.

Hellenistic Benefactor terminology and philosophical terms has been noted;[12] at the same time much of the language seems "conspicuously Septuagintal"[13] and there are expressions "reminiscent of the genuine Pauline epistles."[14] Is this to be explained as an indiscriminate mingling of sources, or is there authorial purpose in the utilisation of particular terms and their conceptual backgrounds? The question is significant for an exploration of how the author understood and communicated his ideas of salvation.

---

12 See Mott, "Greek Ethics."
13 Quinn, *Titus*, 171.
14 Dibelius-Conzelmann, 150.

Chapter 17

Titus 1:1-4

Παῦλος δοῦλος θεοῦ, ἀπόστολος δὲ Ἰησοῦ Χριστοῦ κατὰ πίστιν ἐκλεκτῶν θεοῦ καὶ ἐπίγνωσιν ἀληθείας τῆς κατ' εὐσέβειαν ἐπ' ἐλπίδι ζωῆς αἰωνίου, ἣν ἐπηγγείλατο ὁ ἀψευδὴς θεὸς πρὸ χρόνων αἰωνίων, ἐφανέρωσεν δὲ καιροῖς ἰδίοις τὸν λόγον αὐτοῦ ἐν κηρύγματι, ὃ ἐπιστεύθην ἐγὼ κατ' ἐπιταγὴν τοῦ σωτῆρος ἡμῶν θεοῦ, Τίτῳ γνησίῳ τέκνῳ κατὰ κοινὴν πίστιν, χάρις καὶ εἰρήνη ἀπὸ θεοῦ πατρὸς καὶ Χριστοῦ Ἰησοῦ τοῦ σωτῆρος ἡμῶν.

17.1 Context

For a short letter this is such a full opening that Quinn believes it was intended to introduce the whole PE corpus.[1] While this is impossible to demonstrate,[2] it certainly forms a rich and suggestive overture to the letter to Titus,[3] announcing several of its key themes and terms.[4] This being so, it is significant for the present study that it exhibits an "overall soteriological focus."[5] This appears in the double predication of the title σωτήρ to God (v. 3) and to Christ Jesus (v. 4), the first of three such pairings (2:10, 13; 3: 4, 6),[6] which link Christ to

---

1 Quinn, *Titus*, 50.
2 Marshall finds "nothing in Tit. 1.1-4 that suggests it bears this relationship to 1 and 2 Tim." (112)
3 Offering "an advance summary of the letter" (R. J. Karris, *The Pastoral Epistles* (New Testament Message 17; Wilmington, Del.: Michael Glazier, 1979), 105); cf. Houlden, 139-40.
4 "The terms *faith, truth, godliness, promise, hope, eternal life*, along with the notion that these truths are now revealed in the gospel, are the key concepts in the author's theology." (Donelson, *Pseudepigraphy*, 171). Couser finds "no themes left untreated" ("God and Christian Existence", 138)
5 Couser, "God and Christian Existence", 152. Cf. Marshall, 112.
6 In 1:3, 4 a reference to Christ as σωτήρ (v. 4b) is set in proximity to a formulation applying the title to God (v. 3). In 2:10, 13 a reference to God as σωτήρ (v. 10) appears alongside an ascription of the title to Christ (v. 13). The tradition history of the third example (3:4, 6) is disputed (see Marshall, 306-7) but even if it is traditional, the pairing of σωτήρ referents accords with the author's predilection. Cf. Kelly, 229.

Israel's "God our Saviour" in his saving character and work.[7] The roles of Paul and Titus are introduced in overt relation to this saviour God and saviour Christ. A chain of authorization tracks the instructions given to Titus back to the salvific purpose of God.

17.2 What God has Done

Each of the three verbs in this introductory section, two active and one passive, describes an action of God. He has promised eternal life (v. 2), manifested his word (v. 3), and entrusted its proclamation to Paul (v.3). Since God is σωτήρ (v. 3), these are soterially significant actions, presenting eternal life as the goal of salvation and the revealing of God's message, extended through the commissioning of a messenger, as the means by which it is to be attained.

17.2.1 God Promised Eternal Life Before Time

Does the phrase ἐπηγγείλατο ὁ θεός refer to some specific pronouncement,[8] or, as Spicq prefers, "sans précision de temps, mais en référence au décret salvifique immuable de Dieu"?[9] The issue arises because, uniquely in the NT, this statement combines the concepts of promise, implying communication, and pretemporality, which makes the idea of communication problematic.

a. ἐπηγγείλατο

Although Spicq objects that the OT does not, strictly speaking, promise eternal life,[10] the question is whether it would have been possible for the author to find this hope in the OT. Paul certainly does. It is the promise, not the law, that is δυνάμενος ζῳοποιῆσαι (Gal 3:21-22), and the promise that Abraham would be "the father of many nations" called for faith in θεὸς ὁ ζῳοποιοῦν τοὺς νεκρούς (Rom 4:18), which Paul connects with Christian faith ἐπὶ τὸν ἐγείραντα Ἰησοῦν τὸν κύριον ἡμῶν ἐκ νεκρῶν (Rom 4:24), issuing in ζωὴ αἰώνιος (Rom 5:21). Acts claims that "what God promised to our ancestors he has fulfilled for us, their children, by raising Jesus from the dead" (13:32-33), and Hebrews urges perseverance in order

---

7   On possible backgrounds for the use of σωτήρ see above, pp. 19-26.
8   According to Scott, "it is plain from the context that the allusion is not to God's eternal plan, but to a promise he made in the distant past." (150) He sees in the term σωτήρ (v. 3), however, "the God who had purposed from the beginning to save His elect people." (151)
9   Spicq, 593; Brox, 280.
10 Spicq, 593.

to be "imitators of those who through faith and patience inherit the promises" (6:12; cf. 6:13-7:6; 11:8-9).[11] As G. H. Guthrie remarks, "The promises made to Abraham form not only the foundation of Israel's history but also the foundation of the NT theology of promise."[12] The use of ἐπηγείλατο in Titus 1:2 could suggest an identification of gospel hope with OT promises (cf. προεπηγγείλατο, Rom 1:1-6; προφῆται οἱ περὶ τῆς ὑμᾶς χάριτος προφητεύσαντες, 1 Pet 1:10-12), consonant with the appropriation in Titus of other OT concepts (e.g. λαὸς περιούσιος, 2:14; κληρονόμοι, 3:7).

b. πρὸ χρόνων αἰωνίων

On the other hand, the expression πρὸ χρόνων αἰωνίων aligns the text with the NT's "once hidden/now revealed" statements.[13] The puzzling feature is how something could be "promised" outside of time rather than within human history. The main options for English translators faced with πρὸ χρόνων αἰωνίων are illustrated by RSV's "ages ago" (in the distant past but within time) and NRSV's "before the ages began" (outside of historical time). Taking the latter option, H. P. Griffin Jr. considers that "the clarity of the phrase, 'before the beginning of time'" resolves the issue: "God's original intention before creation was for people to enjoy eternal life."[14] This may verge, however, on an anachronistic concept of time! This "clarity" supposes a sharper distinction between two distant pasts than an ancient author might have recognised.[15] Bruce Malina argues that the modern concept of abstract time would have been completely alien to the first century Mediterranean world,[16] for which time was

---

11 Hebrews discovers Christian eschatological hope in the Abrahamic promise (Gen 22:16-17; Heb 6:14), an exhortation to Israel (Ps 95:7-11; Heb 3:7-11), and Jeremiah's new covenant (Jer 33:31-34; Heb 8:8-12; cf. 4:1; 6:9-12, 17-18; 9:15; 10:36; 11:39-40).
12 G. H. Guthrie, "Promise," *DLNTD* 967-70, 968. Cf. J. Schniewind, G. Friedrich, "ἐπαγγέλλω, κτλ.," *TDNT* 2:576-86 (including eschatological interpretations of the Abrahamic promises in intertestamental Judaism, 579-81).
13 See above, pp. 120-21.
14 T. D. Lea and H. P. Griffin Jr., *1,2 Timothy, Titus* (NAC 34; Nashville: Broadman, 1992), 270-71.
15 Quinn reports the Cullmann-Barr debate on biblical language about time (*Titus*, 65-66). With Barr, he reads πρὸ χρόνων αἰωνίων as "the timeless order in which God himself lives" as distinct from χρόνοι αἰώνιοι, "the countless ages through which his creatures have come and gone."
16 B. J. Malina, "The Question of Time as First-Century Mediterranean Value," in *The Social World of Jesus and the Gospels*, London: Routledge, 1996, 177-214.

divided into "experienced time" (the concrete present, of variable and often long duration, depending upon the reality being experienced), [17] and "imaginary time" ("the sphere falling outside the horizon of the experienced world").[18] This latter sphere includes both remote past and as yet unrealized future, both closed to human beings. "Only God could know that imaginary period, and hence only God could reveal it through his prophets."[19] From this perspective, the purpose of the expression πρὸ χρόνων αἰωνίων is not to distinguish a time period pre- as opposed to post-creation, but to indicate that sphere outside human experience, known only to God and to human beings insofar as God reveals it. The once hidden/now revealed statements in the NT employ a variety of expressions to indicate this "imaginary time."[20] They do not so much "date" a divine event as relate it to God's eternal existence.[21]

It could also be the case that as Christian thought developed, the concept of promise retained its potency as an expression of God's self-commitment to save,[22] while the need to relate Christian hope to specific Jewish aspirations diminished.

c. ὁ ἀψευδὴς θεός

In 1:2 God is described as ἀψευδής, in polemical contrast to the deceitfulness lamented in the letter (1:10, 12, 14). Quinn assumes a Hellenistic background, suggesting "a prophetic knowledge that only a divinity could give, a truth that was beyond simply human verification."[23] Also significant, however, could be the OT affirmations that God would, indeed could, not lie. Balaam confesses, "God is not a human being, that he should lie" (Num

---

He moves beyond the Culmann-Barr debate, drawing on sociological insights.
17 Malina, *Social World*, 189.
18 Malina, *Social World*, 192.
19 Malina, *Social World*, 193.
20 Reference may again be made to the table on pp. 119-20 above.
21 Cf. distant past references in the OT. God exists מִן־הָעוֹלָם וְעַד הָעֹלָם (LXX: ἀπὸ τοῦ αἰῶνος καὶ τοῦ αἰῶνος) (1Chr 16:36; 29:10; Neh 9:5; Pss 40:14 [41:13]; 89:2 [90:2]; 102:17 [103:17]; 105:48 [106:48]); cf. God's gift of the land to Israel ἐξ/ἀπ' αἰῶνος καὶ ἕως αἰῶνος (Jer 7:7; 25:5). The LXX lacks πρὸ χρόνων αἰωνίων, but God is enthroned πρὸ τῶν αἰώνων (Ps 54:20 [55:19]) and works salvation πρὸ αἰῶνος (Ps 73:12 [74:12]). Wisdom, created ἐν ἀρχῇ/ἀπ' ἀρχῆς, existed πρὸ τοῦ αἰῶνος (Prov 8:23; Sir 24:9). In Tob 6:18 Tobias's marriage was determined ἀπὸ τοῦ αἰῶνος.
22 As "a statement of intent by God for his own sake" (Marshall, 126).
23 Quinn, *Titus*, 67; see also 54-55.

23:19) and Ps 89:35 (LXX 88:36) has God declare, "Once and for all I have sworn in my holiness; I will not lie to David!" (εἰ τῷ Δαυιδ ψεύσομαι). In the NT, Heb 6:18 cites God's promise and oath as two things in which "it is impossible that God would prove false" (ἀδύνατον ψεύσασθαι [τὸν] θεόν). In both Hebrews and Titus the considerations that buttressed OT faith in God's promises now support a faith that interprets them in Christian terms (Titus 3:6; Heb 6:11-12, 17).

17.2.2 God has Manifested His Word

a. ἐφανέρωσεν . . . ἐν κηρύγματι

The chain of prepositional clauses explicating Paul's apostleship is interrupted by the verb ἐφανέρωσεν. The focus has shifted to God and his activity with the statement, ἐπηγγείλατο ὁ ἀψευδὴς θεὸς πρὸ χρόνων αἰωνίων, combining a divine action with a time reference. This is balanced by a second such combination, ἐφανέρωσεν δὲ καιροῖς ἰδίοις τὸν λόγον αὐτοῦ, to which is appended a further phrase, ἐν κηρύγματι, indicating that this divine action of disclosure has been realized through the preaching. At this point the apostle comes again into view.

b. τὸν λόγον αὐτοῦ

The object of φανερόω - and hence the content of the κήρυγμα by which it is made known - is God's λόγος, most naturally understood here as the message about the aforementioned promise.[24] Arguing that "l'aoriste ponctuel évoque un moment historique précis," Spicq locates the moment of manifestation in Jesus' own preaching.[25] This may be more precise than the author intends. The λόγος is specifically the content of Paul's κήρυγμα, which is also the message of the church. In 2:5 the behaviour of converts must not compromise ὁ λόγος τοῦ θεοῦ, the church's message, which is also described as ἡ διδασκαλία τοῦ σωτῆρος ἡμῶν θεοῦ (2:10) and should probably be identified with ὁ κατὰ τὴν διδαχὴν πιστὸς λόγος that overseers should grasp (1:9).[26] In this context, the "word" is the message taught by the church, whose proclamation constitutes the "moment" in which God's word is manifested. The phrase ἐν κηρύγματι

---

24 Jerome (reported by Ellicott, 189; cf. E. Walder, cited by Towner, 220) finds the pre-existent Logos here, but this sits awkwardly with the qualifying phrase (Kelly, 228).
25 Spicq, 594.
26 Cf. Marshall, 167.

confirms this reading. As in the *Hauptbriefe*, the κήρυγμα may be understood as the activity of preaching together with its content (1 Cor 1:21; 2:4; 15:14; cf. Rom 16:25; see also 2 Tim 4:17).[27] Paul's ministry is therefore the locus of God's revelation.

c. καιροῖς ἰδίοις

The phrase καιροῖς ἰδίοις that qualifies ἐφανέρωσεν is found in the NT only here and in 1 Tim 2:6 and 6:15.[28] In 1 Timothy it conveys a sense of appropriateness and hence (divine) intentionality about the time at which something takes place. Here it characterises the present time as of salvific significance, because it is God's intended time for his message to be declared.

17.3 Paul and Titus in Relation to Salvation

17.3.1 Paul, δοῦλος θεοῦ

The statements about God's activity as saviour set the context within which Paul and Titus are introduced. Paul is characterised as a δοῦλος θεοῦ,[29] acting κατ' ἐπιταγὴν τοῦ σωτῆρος ἡμῶν θεοῦ (v. 3). He serves the saviour God's purposes. This "servant of God" predication may carry OT connotations. While the phrase δοῦλος θεοῦ is relatively infrequent in the LXX,[30] the "Servant of the LORD" (עֶבֶד יְהוָה) is a significant OT concept. It is referred to temple ministers (Pss 113:1; 134:1; 135:1), prophets or worshippers of the Lord (2 Kgs 9:7; 10:23), Joshua (Josh 24:29; Jdg 2:8), David (in the titles of Psalms 18 and 36), and the Servant in Isaiah (Isa 42:19; cf. 54:17). It is especially, however, a title of Moses (Deut 34:5; Josh 1:1, 13, 15; 8:31, 33; 11:12; 12:6; 13:8; 14:7; 18:7; 22:2, 4, 5; 2 Kgs 18:12; 2 Chr 1:3; 24:6),[31] who is also ὁ δοῦλος τοῦ θεοῦ in Rev 15:3.

This OT background may contribute to the willingness in early Christian discourse to use language that was perhaps considered

---

27 Outside the Pauline corpus the only NT occurrence is the Synoptic reference to Jonah's preaching (Matt 12:41 par. Luke 11:32), reflecting the rare κήρυγμα in LXX Jonah 3:2.

28 See above, pp. 66-67. Cf. two related references, both eschatologically accented, in Acts 1:7 and Gal 6:9.

29 Although the self-introductions in the Pauline corpus usually relate his ministry to both Christ and God (e.g. Rom 1:1; 1 Cor 1:1; 2 Cor 1:1) and he can be δοῦλος Χριστοῦ Ἰησοῦ (Rom 1:1; Phil 1:1), only here is Paul δοῦλος θεοῦ (but cf. Jas 1:1; Jude 1). See Quinn, *Titus*, 51-52.

30 References in Marshall, 117 n. 10; also Neh 10:30 (Moses).

31 See P. D. Miller Jr., "'Moses My Servant.' The Deuteronomic Picture of Moses," *Int* 41 (1987): 245-55.

demeaning in some religious circles.³² More specifically the example of Moses, whose teaching had authority precisely because of his status as God's servant, would be pertinent to the situation implied in Titus where instructions are for the life of God's people are being communicated. In Joshua, the new leader and עֶבֶד יְהוָה, Joshua (Josh 24:29; cf. Judg 2:8), repeatedly derives his authorization from what "Moses the servant of the LORD commanded" (Josh 1:13; 8:31, 33; 11:12; 22:2, 5). Titus envisages a successor who is required to lead and instruct, but whose authorization derives from the teaching of Paul, which carries divine authority because Paul, too, spoke as the servant of God.³³ While there is no explicit mention of the Moses-Joshua succession in Titus 1:1-4, it offers a natural paradigm of delegated authority and the author is certainly concerned to establish the "chain of command" from God to his servant Paul and thence to Titus.

17.3.2 Paul, ἀπόστολος Ἰησοῦ Χριστοῦ

Paul is next designated an apostle of Jesus Christ. Like God, Christ is σωτήρ (v. 4), so the work of his agent may be expected to relate to salvation. The apostleship is explicated by two prepositional clauses, κατὰ πίστιν ἐκλεκτῶν θεοῦ and ἐπ' ἐλπίδι ζωῆς αἰωνίου. Each of these elements is elaborated, the idea of the faith extended with καὶ ἐπίγνωσιν ἀληθείας τῆς κατ' εὐσέβειαν and the hope of eternal life described as formerly promised and now manifested in the preaching entrusted to Paul.

a. κατὰ πίστιν ἐκλεκτῶν θεοῦ

There are three questions here: Who are the ἐκλεκτοί θεοῦ, what is meant by their πίστις, and how does the preposition κατά relate this faith to Paul's apostleship? The concept of the ἐκλεκτοί in Judaism and early Christianity has already been discussed in relation to 2 Tim 2:10. In the context in Titus 1:1-4, the ἐκλεκτοί are those who have faith, expect eternal life and benefit from Paul's apostolic ministry. As in 2 Tim 2:10, Ps 105 (LXX 104) offers possible

---

32 See R. Tuente, "δοῦλος," *NIDNTT* 3:592-98, especially on the Greek environment (592-93). Interestingly the LXX seems reticent to refer δοῦλος to Moses, often preferring παῖς κυρίου for עֶבֶד יְהוָה in his case (e.g. Josh 1:13; 11:12; 12:6; 13:8; 18:7; 22:2, 5; 2 Chr 1:3).
33 Compare Miller's Moses with Paul in the PE: "Moses' work is truly done. The people have now the word of the Lord which Moses taught, and that will be their guide in the land that the Lord has promised." ("Moses My Servant", 254-55).

points of contact. The Psalm recounts God's promise to the patriarchs (vv. 7-11) and the deliverance of his chosen ones (οἱ ἐκλεκτοὶ αὐτοῦ, v. 43) through his servant Moses (ὁ δοῦλος αὐτοῦ, v. 26),[34] having remembered his "holy word" (λόγος, v. 42). The pattern thus rehearsed in Israel's worship is that God fulfils an ancient promise when for the sake of his chosen ones he sends his servant and effects word. This closely matches the shape of Paul's apostleship as sketched in Titus 1:1-4. The promise made in the past is manifested as a message (λόγος) effected through God's servant (δοῦλος) as one sent (ἀπόστολος) for the benefit of the inheritors of the promise (οἱ ἐκλεκτοί). The pretemporal choice of people to inherit eternal life is not ruled out by the context, but nor is it demanded. The interest, as in the reference to the λαὸς περιούσιος in 2:14, seems to lie in appropriating for the Christian community aspects of the self-understanding of the OT people of God.

The relation of Paul's apostleship to the πίστις ἐκλεκτῶν θεοῦ is indicated by κατά with the accusative. The versatility of this preposition (used four times in vv. 1-4) allows several possible interpretations,[35] but the main approaches take it to express either correspondence or purpose. The former makes sense in the phrase κατὰ κοινὴν πίστιν in v. 4, but Quinn argues that in v. 1 the verbal force of ἀπόστολος suggests movement,[36] inclining towards an expression of purpose. Set within the dynamic of God's activity, promising, revealing, and entrusting in the fulfilment of his promise, Paul's ministry must be understood in terms of God's purpose. This being so, even if the preposition were restricted to a general sense such as "in relation to," the context itself would impart purposive impetus to the relationship between Paul's apostleship and the faith of God's people.[37]

Various nuances of meaning of the term πίστις are represented in its six occurrences in Titus (1:1, 4, 13; 2:2, 10; 3:15). Again the context must guide the interpretation. The aspect of Paul's task specified in this section is preaching, in which God's message is manifested. As an outcome of such ministry, faith could be conceived as having both objective and subjective dimensions, with a specific content to which must answer believing trust and faithful obedience. Both dimensions are elaborated in the ensuing phrase.

---

34 God "sent" (ἐξαπέστειλεν) Moses (v. 26).
35 For options and discussion see Marshall, 119-20; Quinn, *Titus*, 62-63.
36 Quinn, *Titus*, 63.
37 Fee, 168; Marshall, 120; Mounce, 379.

b. καὶ ἐπίγνωσιν ἀληθείας τῆς κατ' εὐσέβειαν

Rather than taking this as an additional outcome distinct from πίστις it is better to understand the καί exepegetically, so that the phrase amplifies the idea of faith. In 1 Tim 2:4 the expression εἰς ἐπίγνωσιν ἀληθείας ἐλθεῖν could represent conversion,[38] but there are no *prima facie* grounds for so limiting it here.[39] In Titus, faith develops (e.g. 1:13), teaching and learning continue (1:9; 2:1,15; 3:8, 14), and grace exercises a training function (2:12). This knowledge of truth is in turn related to εὐσέβεια which characterises the manner of life in the present age of those who have put their hope in God's promised future (2:12-13). Again, κατά establishes the relationship. Correspondence is possible,[40] but an attitudinal and behavioural outcome of teaching truth would fit the paraenetic goals of the letter as a whole.[41] The faith promoted by Paul's ministry therefore contrasts with a defective faith marked by rejection of the truth and corrupt lives (1:13-16).

c. ἐπ' ἐλπίδι ζωῆς αἰωνίου

While ζωὴ αἰώνιος need not be exclusively future in orientation, this letter does present a future hope.[42] In 3:7 the phrase ἐλπίς ζωῆς αἰωνίου gives content to the benefits which "heirs" (κληρονόμοι) anticipate from Christ's saving work. The "blessed hope" is realized not in the present age but upon the awaited epiphany of Christ (2:12-13). Within this framework the eternal life that is hoped for remains principally future,[43] although it is also the lodestar by which the present life finds direction.

The relationship of this hope to Paul's ministry depends on how the syntax is read. If hope comprises a final item in the chain of outcomes of ministry, εὐσέβεια could seem to be a means to eternal life (cf. 1 Tim 6:7-8), a possibility NIV tries to avoid with the

---

38 See above, pp. 55-57.
39 See Fee, who also interprets κατὰ πίστιν as "coming to faith" (168).
40 E.g. "truth that is appropriate to godliness" (W. L. Liefeld, *1 & 2 Timothy/Titus* (NIVAC; Grand Rapids: Zondervan, 1999), 310).
41 Mounce translates, "truth that produces godliness" (377).
42 Cf. Marshall, on αἰώνιος in the PE: "Through its association with God and with the world to come, the word gains a stronger meaning; eternal life is not only everlasting but also shares the qualities of the life of God himself, its indestructibility and its joy." (125). See on 1 Tim 1:16 above (pp. 36-38); also, for ἐλπίς, see on 1 Tim 1:1 (pp. 28-33).
43 Mounce writes, "ζωή, 'life,' is more than physical existence; it is a fullness of life available now through Christ, which reaches its climax on the other side of the Lord's return." (380)

syntactically awkward rendering, "for the faith of God's elect and the knowledge of the truth that leads to godliness – a faith and knowledge resting on the hope of eternal life." This is not impossible if both τῆς κατ' εὐσέβειαν and ἐπ' ἐλπίδι ζωῆς αἰωνίου are subordinate clauses modifying the composite idea of faith and knowledge of truth.[44] Alternatively, ἐπ' ἐλπίδι ζωῆς αἰωνίου could be attached directly to ἀπόστολος, making eternal life (for himself and/or his hearers) a motive for Paul's work.[45] It is more satisfactory, however, to maintain the integrity of the chain of ideas, so that eternal life sums up the goal of both Paul's ministry and the faith and life that he taught.

17.3.3 Titus, γνήσιον τέκνον κατὰ κοινὴν πίστιν

Finally, Titus is related to Paul on the twin planes of linear continuity (γνήσιον τέκνον) and confessional identity (κατὰ κοινὴν πίστιν). The salvific character and divine authorization which mark Paul's ministry are thus extended to Titus's service. Just as Paul's ministry derives from both God and Christ (v. 1) Titus is referred to God and Christ together for the resources of grace and peace (v. 4).

17.4 Summary

Significant aspects of the author's idea of salvation emerge in this opening section. The soterial character of both God and Christ and, by derivation, the ministries of Paul and Titus are established. Christian salvation, whose content is eternal life, represents the fulfilment of God's eternal purpose expressed in OT promises. The present age is the time set for the manifesting of this salvation. Those who embrace the hope, hold to the faith and cultivate a godly life in accordance with the apostolic teaching can be regarded as God's elect, to whom accrue the status and blessings of the OT people of God.

---

44 See Fee's comments on the NIV text, 169.
45 E.g. Hinson, 362; Knight, 283-84.

CHAPTER 18

Titus 2:11-14

Ἐπεφάνη γὰρ ἡ χάρις τοῦ θεοῦ σωτήριος πᾶσιν ἀνθρώποις παιδεύουσα ἡμᾶς, ἵνα ἀρνησάμενοι τὴν ἀσέβειαν καὶ τὰς κοσμικὰς ἐπιθυμίας σωφρόνως καὶ δικαίως καὶ εὐσεβῶς ζήσωμεν ἐν τῷ νῦν αἰῶνι, προσδεχόμενοι τὴν μακαρίαν ἐλπίδα καὶ ἐπιφάνειαν τῆς δόξης τοῦ μεγάλου θεοῦ καὶ σωτῆρος ἡμῶν Ἰησοῦ Χριστοῦ, ὃς ἔδωκεν ἑαυτὸν ὑπὲρ ἡμῶν, ἵνα λυτρώσηται ἡμᾶς ἀπὸ πάσης ἀνομίας καὶ καθαρίσῃ ἑαυτῷ λαὸν περιούσιον, ζηλωτὴν καλῶν ἔργων.

In Spicq's view, this sentence is the very heart of the letter, and provides a summary of Pauline theology.[1] In it Taylor finds "the proposition, or theme, of the three letters," from which their whole witness may be summarised.[2] More modestly, it certainly provides "the basis for the preceding instruction on Christian living."[3] Highlighting appearances of salvific grace and the saviour Jesus Christ, this basis is strongly soteriological.

18.1 Context

The conjunction γάρ connects the passage with the preceding paraenesis, at least from 2:1 (σὺ δὲ λάλει ἃ πρέπει τῆς ὑγιαινούσῃ διδασκαλίᾳ),[4] providing a rationale for that activity. The reiteration of the command at the end of the section (ταῦτα λάλει καὶ παρακάλει, 2:15) confirms the connection. In addition, however, the theological passage may supply something of the content of that

---

1 Spicq, 635: "est le cœur même de l' Épître et un résumé de la théologie paulinienne."
2 W. F. Taylor Jr., "1-2 Timothy, Titus," in *The Deutero-Pauline Letters: Ephesians, Colossians, 2 Thessalonians, 1-2 Timothy, Titus* (ed. G. Krodel; rev. ed.; Proclamation Commentaries; Minneapolis: Fortress, 1993), 59-93, 89. Following unpublished work by W. Beckwith, Taylor describes an Aristotelian structure of argumentation in the PE, whereby Titus argues from *ethos*, 1 Timothy from *logos*, and 2 Timothy from *pathos* (78-79).
3 Marshall, 263; cf. Towner, *Goal*, 108.
4 Fee takes it back to 1:10 (193).

teaching.⁵ The ὑγιαινούσῃ διδασκαλία that Titus is to teach (2:1) is specifically ἡ διδασκαλία ἡ τοῦ σωτῆρος ἡμῶν θεοῦ (2:10). This corresponds to the theme of God's soterial goals and activity expounded in 2:11-14.⁶ Although the ταῦτα λάλει of v. 15 includes the practical instructions in chapter 2 and possibly chapter 3,⁷ it would be arbitrary to exclude the theological content. The goal of this teaching is not only that specific behaviours are learned but also that doctrinal tenets are grasped. Both are necessary for the self-understanding and continuing life of the community.

18.2 Grace Appeared so that We Might Live

2:11-14 consists of one sentence in two balanced parts, each with a subject, a main verb describing what that subject has done, and a complex purpose clause identifying the goal of that action. When other explicatory material is pared away, two essential ideas emerge: ἐπεφάνη ἡ χάρις . . . ἵνα ζήσωμεν (grace appeared so that we might live, vv. 11-13), and Ἰησοῦς Χριστὸς . . . ἔδωκεν ἑαυτὸν ἵνα λυτρώσηται ἡμᾶς (Jesus Christ gave himself in order to redeem us, v. 14). As each element is elaborated, an illuminating profile of soteriological activity and its outcome emerges.

18.2.1 Overview

The χάρις that appeared is salvific in character. It is τοῦ θεοῦ, emanating from the God who is ὁ σωτὴρ ἡμῶν (v. 10). The verb ἐπεφάνη is also soteriologically defined by the term σωτήριος. This may be read as a nominative adjective qualifying χάρις,⁸ as in KJV's "the grace of God that bringeth salvation."⁹ Being anarthrous, however, it belongs more naturally with the verb, ¹⁰ "a predicate nominative functioning adverbially, describing the effects of the appearing."¹¹ The phrase πᾶσιν ἀνθρώποις extends this idea by indicating the scope of its effectiveness, giving the sense, "The grace of God has made an appearance in a way that is salvific for all

---

5 Marshall, 262.
6 Cf. Läger: "Mit den Stichworten σωτήριος (V.11) und σωτήρ (V.13) ist ein Bezug zum vorausgehenden V.10 hergestellt, in dem Gott als σωτὴρ ἡμῶν bezeichnet wird." (*Christologie*, 93)
7 See Mounce, 432; cf. Quinn, *Titus*, 77-78.
8 Knight, 319; Towner, 244.
9 Cf. Spicq's exposition of "la grâce salvatrice," 635-37.
10 Marshall, 267 n. 95.
11 Mounce, 422 and 420 n. a.

people."[12] It is not that all have witnessed the epiphany, but its efficacy is directed towards all.[13] The activity of grace is represented by the present participle παιδεύουσα, signifying a continuing educative function, in contrast to the punctiliar aorist ἐπεφάνη. It's object is ἡμᾶς, the distinct group ("us," v. 8; associated with the Christian message, v. 5) presupposed by the community guidance in vv. 2-10, rather than the preceding πάντες ἄνθρωποι. It is upon the Christian community that training grace operates.

The purpose of the appearing of grace and its on-going training is ἵνα ζήσωμεν, that "we" (the Christian community) should "live." The character of this living is delineated in two participial clauses, a group of three adverbs and a time reference. A specific action (aorist participle ἀρνησάμενοι) clears the way for a life of a particular quality (adverbs σωφρόνως, δικαίως, and εὐσεβῶς). Though located temporally ἐν τῷ νῦν αἰῶνι, this life is consciously oriented (present participle προσδεχόμενοι) towards a specific object of hope, Christ's future ἐπιφάνεια. The purpose, then, of the manifesting of God's grace and its educative activity is to produce lives free from the domination of worldly desires, well ordered and virtuous, lived in anticipation of Christ's final saving. The chain of ideas culminates in "our saviour Jesus Christ," who then becomes the subject of the remaining part of the unit (v. 14).

18.2.2 ἐπεφάνη ἡ χάρις τοῦ θεοῦ

What - or who - is the "grace" that appeared? Mott contends that here and in 3:4 characteristics of God are personified,[14] in the way that Philo depicts God's virtues as active powers (δυνάμεις) and envisages ethical change as an outcome of manifestations of God, mediated through teaching.[15] Lau, on the other hand, appeals to the "emphatic placement of the aorist ejpefavnh," and takes it to refer to the specific historical manifestation of God's grace in "the whole earthly appearance of Christ, thus embracing his birth, life, death

---

12 Simpson illustrates the construction σωτήριος + dative in classical Greek (170).
13 Cf. D. Dawson-Walker, *Colossians and Titus* (The Devotional Commentary; London: The Religious Tract Society, n.d.), 253.
14 Mott, "Greek Ethics," 37; cf. Davies, 102; Kelly, 245; Spicq, 635; Stott, *1 Timothy & Titus*, 193. Dibelius identified it as a hypostatisation of the divine quality of grace, but Conzelmann disagrees (Dibelius-Conzelmann, 142 and n. 7; cf. Marshall, 267).
15 Mott, "Greek Ethics," 38-39.

and resurrection."[16]

Neither of these readings is entirely satisfactory. Mott's view underplays the clear Christological perspective of a passage which refers explicitly to both the future appearing and the past self-giving of Christ.[17] He allows that the author "retains" the expectation of an eschatological epiphany, but considers this to be in tension with the emphasis on ethical transformation ἐν τῷ νῦν αἰῶνι.[18] Although he defines the unit as 2:11-14, Mott omits v. 14 and the *Hingabemotif* from his discussion. The problem with Lau's interpretation is that, as he concedes, the subject of the verb in v. 11 is χάρις, "instead of Christ, as one would expect."[19] This betrays a prior decision attributing to the author a special use of ἐπιφαίνω which is then preferred even when it is not the most natural reading in the context.

A third possibility is that the reference is to the making known of God's gracious saving in the proclaiming of the gospel. The strength of this reading is that it agrees with what the author has already said: the good news of God's promise of eternal life became known when, ἐφανέρωσεν δὲ καιροῖς ἰδίοις τὸν λόγον αὐτοῦ ἐν κηρύγματι (1:3).[20] Χάρις would then stand here for the message of grace.[21] It functions similarly in Col 1:6, ἠκούσατε καὶ ἐπέγνωτε τὴν χάριν τοῦ θεοῦ ἐν ἀληθείᾳ. Luke's Paul also refers to the "message of [God's] grace" (ὁ λόγος τῆς χάριτας αὐτοῦ, Acts 20:32; cf. τὸ εὐαγγέλιον τῆς χάριτος τοῦ θεοῦ, v. 24).[22] The "appearing" would then be the on-going act whereby the knowledge of God's grace becomes available to humankind. Insofar as this revelation concerns Christ and came through him, Christ's historical appearing may be considered an epiphany of grace, but the expression ἐπεφάνη ἡ χάρις is better widened to include the missionary proclamation of that grace.[23]

---

16 Lau, *Manifest*, 156. Cf. Kelly, 244; Liefeld, 336. Houlden refers it to Christ's first coming (149). Donelson, speaking of "Jesus' first epiphany" (*Pseudepigraphy*, 141-46), seems to identify χάρις with Jesus, who is then the subject of παιδεύειν (145).
17 See Mounce, 422.
18 Mott, "Greek Ethics," 30.
19 Lau, *Manifest*, 156.
20 Cf. 2 Tim 1:9-10.
21 Cf. Scott: "Here [χάρις] is used to denote the whole Christian message, as conveyed through the life and death of Christ and everything He had taught. This constituted a single revelation of God's grace, which was intended to save the whole human family, not merely some favoured race or class." (167-68).
22 Cf. the message of 1 Peter, described as ἀληθὴς χάρις τοῦ θεοῦ (5:12).
23 Brox sees grace manifest in Christ's first appearing but continually

Fee considers (without accepting) a more specific reference to an historical preaching of Paul and Titus on Crete,[24] but it is difficult to accommodate πᾶσιν ἀνθρώποις in this suggestion.

18.2.3 σωτήριος πᾶσιν ἀνθρώποις

Grace appeared "soterially." The unusual term σωτήριος connects this appearing of grace to the two σωτήρ references (vv. 10, 13) and hence to the saving character and activity of both God and Christ. Many interpretations of the phrase πᾶσιν ἀνθρώποις have been offered,[25] but since it is most satisfactorily understood grammatically to belong with σωτήριος,[26] constituting an adverbial clause, those interpretations may be set aside which separate the two elements. In what sense, however, has grace appeared "soterially for all people"? It is evident from the context that not all have in fact received salvation: grace operates upon and Christ's self-giving has been effective for "us" rather than "all" (vv. 12, 14),[27] producing a particular group (the λαὸς περιούσιος, v. 14) distinct from others who do not share their faith (2:5, 8, 10). It has been suggested that the "all" might indicate all types of people, exemplified by the different ages, genders and socio-economic levels found in 2:2-10.[28] This would certainly connect the statement closely with the preceding instructions, but another possibility is suggested by the Judaizing character of the opposition in the letter (1;10, 14; 3:9). Against such, the πᾶσιν ανθρώποις would declare the universality of God's saving activity.[29] Quinn adduces the Lukan Paul's claims that God "commands all people everywhere to repent" (Acts 17:30),[30] and that he is a witness "to all people" (22:15).[31] In neither

---

actualised in the preaching of the word of grace (297-98); cf. Marshall, citing by way of analogy 2 Cor 5:18-21 (266).
24 Fee, 194.
25 Liefeld lists seven: grace has appeared to all people, or all kinds of people, or all believers; grace brings salvation to all people, or all kinds of people, or all believers; grace brings the *potential* of salvation to an unrestricted number of people, many of whom accept it. (337-38) Cf. discussion above on 1 Tim 2:4 and 4:10.
26 Marshall, 268; Ellicott, 205.
27 Cf. Towner, *Goal*, 109; Knight, 319.
28 E.g. Hendrickson, 370-71; cf. Kelly, 244-45; Knight, 319 (citing Lock); Stott, *1 Timothy & Titus*, 193.
29 Marshall allows that one effect of πᾶσιν ἀνθρώποις is to extend salvation beyond Jews (268).
30 Repentance is commanded "now," in contrast to "the times of ignorance," suggesting a once hidden/now revealed framework.

case is it conceivable that every individual is meant; rather, the universal applicability of the Christian gospel is declared.

The sometimes hyperbolic nature of confessional affirmations must also be recognised. In Col 1:6, cited above, the message of God's grace is said to be bearing fruit ἐν παντὶ κόσμῳ. The intent is not to supply accurate geographical data but to testify to the Christian movement's experience of wide and rapid growth, while also indicating the universal scope of the salvation it preached. Perhaps Titus 2:11 is best understood in a similar way, expressing the missionary conviction that the soterial significance of the appearing of grace is universally applicable (with some polemical distinction from a more exclusivist understanding), and reflecting the self-perception of the Christian movement as a world-wide phenomenon in first century Mediterranean terms.

18.2.4 παιδεύουσα ἡμᾶς

The soterial efficacy of this appearing of grace is explicated by the clause, παιδεύουσα ἡμᾶς. "The means by which χάρις delivers is παιδεία."[32] Dibelius-Conzelmann distinguish between ideas of παιδεία as discipline in the LXX and education in the general Hellenistic environment,[33] but this can be overplayed.[34] The ideas overlap in, e.g., an earlier statement of the universality of God's gracious training in Sir 18:13-14:

> ἔλεος δὲ κυρίου ἐπὶ πᾶσαν σάρκα·
> ἐλέγχων καὶ παιδεύων καὶ διδάσκων
> καὶ ἐπιστρέφων ὡς ποιμὴν τὸ ποίμνιον αὐτοῦ. τοὺς ἐκδεχομένους παιδείαν ἐλεᾷ
> καὶ τοὺς κατασπεύδοντας ἐπὶ τὰ κρίματα αὐτοῦ.

> The compassion of the Lord is for every living thing.
> He rebukes and trains and teaches them,
> and turns them back, as a shepherd his flock.
> He has compassion on those who accept his discipline and who are eager for his precepts.

Just how the appearing of grace accomplishes the training becomes comprehensible if ἐπεφάνη ἡ χάρις refers to the manifesting of the message of grace in Christ. This message,

---

31 Quinn, *Titus*, 181.
32 Mott, "Greek Ethics," 35.
33 Dibelius-Conzelmann, 142-43; cf. Houlden, 150.
34 See Mounce, 423-24; Fee, 198-99; Quinn, *Titus*, 163-64.

propagated through the health-giving teaching offered by Titus (2:1-10, 15; 3:1, 8) and church leaders (1:9), directs those trained by it into the life described in v. 12.[35]

18.2.5 ἵνα . . . ζήσωμεν

Four qualifications fill out the picture of life shaped by this παιδεία.

a. ἐν τῷ νῦν αἰῶνι

A time phrase, ἐν τῷ νῦν αἰῶνι, locates this life firmly in the present age, whose extent and character is indicated elsewhere in the letter. Prior to it, God's promise of eternal life was pledged (1:2); at the awaited epiphany of Christ it will give way to a different order (2:13); and between these two periods lies this present age, in which God's eternal will to save is revealed (1:1-3) and rescue from sin (2:14) may be realized existentially as ethical transformation (2:11-12; 3:3-7), in anticipation of Christ's ultimate triumph (2:13).

The expression τὸ νῦν αἰών is restricted in the NT to the PE (1 Tim 6:17; 2 Tim 4:10; Titus 2:12), although the idea is found elsewhere.[36] In Titus the present age is not expressly denounced as evil, although it "stands in contrast with the future age which is characterised by the appearing of the Saviour. Hence there is a certain negative quality about it." [37] Its primary significance in 2:12 is that it constitutes the realm in which the practical effects of training by grace are to be lived out.

b. ἀρνησάμενοι

Two singularities mark a starting point and an end point for the grace-trained life. The former is expressed by the aorist participle ἀρνησάμενοι. The verb occurs 30x in the NT, always carrying negative overtones,[38] with three significant exceptions in which the renunciation represents a choice of God's promised future over present gain. In Luke 9:23 (cf. ἀπαρνέομαι in pars. Matt 16:24; Mark 8:34) would-be disciples must deny self, take up the cross and follow

---

35 Cf. Hasler, 94: "Konkret verwirklichen die mit der Verkündigung, Belehrung und Zurechtweisung beauftragten Gemeindeleiter diese Heilspädogogik am Volk des Herrn."
36 E.g. Mark 10:30 (νῦν ἐν τῷ καιρῷ τούτῳ); Gal 1:4, where Christ rescues ἐκ τοῦ αἰῶνος τοῦ ἐνεστῶτος πονηροῦ; and Eph 2:2 (Satan works νῦν, in τὸ αἰών τοῦ κόσμου τούτου).
37 Marshall, 272.
38 See Schlier, TDNT 1:469-71.

Christ. Heb 11:24-25 has Moses renouncing his privileged status in Egypt with the "fleeting pleasures of sin" to share ill-treatment with God's people. Titus 2:11-14 shares this perspective, but is perhaps closer in atmosphere to the considered life-choice of Hebrews than to the radical self-denying summons of the dominical saying. Bruce writes, "Moses weighed the issues in his mind, and decided that the temporal wealth of Egypt was far less valuable than 'the stigma that rests on God's Anointed' (NEB)."[39] Like Moses in Hebrews, those trained by grace in Titus ch. 2 say no to this world's pleasures (v. 12; cf. Heb 11:25b) and yes to membership of the people of God (v. 14; cf. Heb 11:25a), embracing a future-oriented Christ-focused faith (v. 13; cf. Heb 11:26, where Moses' faith involves identification with the Christ).[40]

Kelly suggests that the "once-for-all act" represented by the aorist ἀρνησάμενοι refers to baptism, "when they turned their back on their pagan life and accepted Christ." [41] While baptism would be an appropriate expression of this renunciation, it is the inner attitude rather than a sacramental act that is primarily in view. The present participle παιδεύουσα indicates an on-going training, and the instructions in chapter 2 must require a continual choosing of those behaviours that are commended over others that are disapproved, whereby that general renunciation is particularised in specific situations. There is here the recurring NT tension between singularity and continuity in Christian transformation (cf. Rom 6:1-14).

That which must be renounced is encapsulated in the terms ἀσέβεια and κοσμικαὶ ἐπιθυμίαι (v. 12). Kelly understands these as "false conceptions of God" and "purely this-world inclinations."[42] In the context, however, it is the behavioural rather than the cognitive aspect of ἀσέβεια that comes to the fore, especially in contrast to the idea of εὐσέβεια (εὐσεβῶς) in the same verse.[43] Foerster asks whether, "ἀσέβεια does not denote wilful transgression of the orders, while the 'worldly lusts' are the avarice of the adversaries."[44] It is unhelpful, however, to narrow the reference to a characterisation of the opponents. The whole Christian community

---

39 F. F. Bruce, *The Epistle to the Hebrews* (London: Marshall, Morgan & Scott, 1965), 320.
40 Bruce discusses Moses' faith in *Hebrews*, 316-24.
41 Kelly, 245; cf. Brox, 298; Hinson, 369; Karris, 116; but see Mounce, 424.
42 Kelly, 245.
43 Cf. Fee, 194; Marshall, 270.
44 *TDNT* 7:190.

(2:1-10) is being exhorted to move from the "before" represented in these terms to the "after" of the grace-trained life.

The term ἐπιθυμίαι is not intrinsically negative, but "a growing tendency to use the word, as here, of bad desires, temptations, including sexual desire" may be discerned.[45] This is so in 3:3, where the pre-Christian condition includes δουλεύοντες ἐπιθυμίαις καὶ ἡδοναῖς ποικίλαις. These ἐπιθυμίαι act upon people, engendering attitudes and behaviours antithetical to the ideal presented in the letter. For the attainment of the grace-trained life, not only renunciation of them (2:12) but also rescue from them (3:3-7) is necessary. These desires are specifically κοσμικαί, "worldly." A similar association appears in 2 Pet 1:3-4, where divine power enables escape from "the corruption that is in the world because of lust" (ἡ ἐν τῷ κόσμῳ ἐν ἐπιθυμίᾳ φθορά. Cf. 2 Pet 2:20) into a life of εὐσέβεια.[46] Knight relates the κοσμικαὶ ἐπιθυμίαι to πᾶσα ἀνομία in v. 14, "with 'the world' considered as the realm of disobedience to God and of sin," finding a Pauline counterpart in Gal. 6:14 (ἐμοὶ κόσμος ἐσταύρωται κἀγὼ κόσμῳ).[47] The antithesis is, however, less sharply drawn in Titus. The emphasis here is less on eschatological escape from the world than on ethical deliverance from worldliness ἐν τῷ νῦν αἰῶνι (v. 12; cf. 3:1-8).

c. προσδεχόμενοι

The second singularity is a future ἐπιφάνεια that will terminate the present age. It is part of the function of the saving manifestation of grace to create in believers the attitude of conscious anticipation expressed by προσδεχόμενοι.[48] The future epiphany will be a manifestation of the σωτήρ. Were it not for the identification of this figure with Jesus Christ, this expression of hope could belong among the range of perspectives of Hellenistic Judaism. In Luke προσδέχομαι represents the waiting in hope that characterises the righteous of Israel such as Simeon (Luke 2:25), Anna (Luke 2:38) and Joseph of Arimathea (Luke 23:51; cf. Mark 15:43), who await respectively the consolation of Israel, the redemption of Jerusalem and the kingdom of God.[49] Luke places Paul in this company,

---

45 Marshall, 270 (references in n. 104).
46 Cf. 1 John 2:15-17, where carnal ἐπιθυμίαι belong to the κόσμος which is passing away.
47 Knight, 320.
48 Described by Spicq, 639, as "un état, une attitude, l'ensemble d'une conduite finalisée par une événement futur (*Lc.* ii, 25, 38; xxiii, 51) qui est la raison de vivre."
49 See E. Hoffmann, "ἀποκαραδοκία," NIDNTT 2:244-46, esp. p. 245. The

identifying his Christian hope of resurrection and judgment with Jewish expectation (e.g. Acts 23:6; 24:14-15; 28:20). The link in Titus 2:12-13 between waiting for the coming kingdom and living righteously in readiness for it is also in harmony with that form of Jewish piety so favourably portrayed by Luke.[50]

The focus of this expectancy is ἡ μακαρία ἐλπίδα καὶ ἐπιφάνειαν τῆς δόξης τοῦ μεγάλου θεοῦ καὶ σωτῆρος ἡμῶν 'Ιησοῦ Χριστου. This cascade of ideas – blessedness, hope, epiphany, glory, majesty, God, saviour, Jesus Christ – exhibits more impressionistic artistry than grammatical exactitude. The effect is to paint the parousia as a manifestation of divine glory bringing blessing and salvation through Christ for those who have put their hope in God.[51] The juxtaposition of ideas of epiphany and majesty (μέγας) is noteworthy. It appears frequently in 2 and 3 Maccabees where μέγας and various compounds tint the notion of divine manifestation (ἐπιφάνεια, ἐπιφαίνω) with colours of majesty (e.g. 2 Macc 3:24; 3 Macc 2:9; 5:8; 6:18, 39. Cf. 2 Sam 7:23). The exact relationships between the elements in v. 13 are, however, elusive. In particular, who or what will appear? Various solutions are syntactically possible:

a) a glorious-appearing of <u>the-great-God</u> *and* of <u>our-saviour-Jesus-Christ</u>;

b) a glorious-appearing of <u>our-great-God-and-saviour</u> (who is Jesus Christ);

c) an appearing of <u>the-glory-of-the-great-God</u> *and* of <u>our-saviour-Jesus-Christ</u>;

d) an appearing of <u>the-glory-of-the-great-God</u> (personified in our-saviour-Jesus-Christ);

e) an appearing of <u>the-glory-of-our-great-God-and-saviour</u> (who is Jesus Christ).[52]

---

general sense of receiving or expecting is also found (e.g. Luke 15:2; Acts 23:21; Rom 16:2; Phil 2:29; Heb 10:34; 11:35).

50 See J. L. Green, *The Gospel of Luke* (NICNT; Grand Rapids: Eerdmans, 1997), 142-46; Marshall, *Luke*, 118; J. Nolland, *Luke* (3 vols.; WBC 35A-C; Dallas: Word, 1989-93), 1:118.

51 Cf. Dawson-Walker: "It suggests to us the transcendent and ineffable splendour, the overwhelming greatness of the Coming for which we look." (259)

52 See M. J. Harris, "Our Great God and Savior (Titus 2:13)," in *Jesus as God. The New Testament Use of* Theos *in Reference to Jesus* (Grand Rapids: Baker, 1992), 173-85.

From his thorough examination of the linguistic, grammatical and theological issues, Harris concludes that "it seems highly probable that in Titus 2:13 Jesus Christ is called 'our great God and Savior'," claiming the support of "almost all grammarians and lexicographers, many commentators, and many writers on NT theology or Christology."[53] If so, the awaited epiphany is of Christ as the saving God in his divine glory.

While this is clearly of great christological interest,[54] our focus must be on the soteriological contribution. It indicates a perspective in which the final saving intervention of God and Christ's future appearing coalesce into a single hope. What is experienced "in the present age" may be salvific but it does not exhaust salvation; a consummate divine saving event is still awaited. This waiting suggests a concept of faith that, as for Luke's righteous Israel, combines adherence to certain beliefs about God and the world with obedience to their ethical implications to create a cognitive-behavioural identity by which the community of the faithful may be known. For this author, both faith and identity are focused upon Christ.

d. σωφρόνως καὶ δικαίως καὶ εὐσεβῶς

Qualifying ζήσωμεν, these adverbs depict the grace-trained life. Mott points out the affinity of this ideal and its expression with the four cardinal virtues of Greek ethics, φρόνησις, δικαιοσύνη, ἀνδρεία, and σωφροσύνη,[55] particularly as utilised by Philo. From this perspective he finds in Titus 2:11-12 a shift from earlier Christian understandings of salvation: "The end of salvation now at least includes the goal of virtue in Greek ethical philosophy. Conversion is the transfer from the control of the vices to the exercise of virtue in its highest forms."[56] Again, however, Mott's reading fails to account for the quite distinctive Christian content of the material, in respect to which Mounce retorts, "Apart from the words used, this is about as far from Hellenistic philosophy as one can get."[57] Mott's work does confirm that the language of 2:11-13 would have been familiar to a Hellenistic Jewish reader. To such a reader, however, the most striking features may well have been not the familiar elements, which could be taken for granted, but those

---

53 Harris, *Jesus as God*, 185. Sharing his conclusion are Knight, 321-26; Liefeld, 339-41; Marshall, 272-82; Mounce, 425-31; and Towner, 246-48.
54 See, e.g., Läger, *Christologie*, 94; Lau, *Manifest*, 247.
55 Mott, "Greek Ethics".
56 Mott, "Greek Ethics", 30.
57 Mounce, 422.

Christian distinctives which come into sharper profile when set alongside Hellenistic Jewish writings. 4 Maccabees, for example, favours the triad, σωφροσύνη, δικαιοσύνη, and ἀνδρεία (1:3-4; 1:6; 1:18; 5:23-24; cf. 4:23; 15:10). According to Mott this is a standard grouping representing the canon of virtues. He argues that it could be varied by substituting εὐσέβεια for one of the three, thus explaining the absence of ἀνδρεία in Titus 2:12.[58] The great contrast between the two writings, however, consists not in the choice of representative virtues but in how they are produced and how the enemies of virtue, the ἐπιθυμίαι, are overcome. In 4 Maccabees this is achieved through training in the law;[59] in Titus it is through training by grace.

18.3 Jesus Christ Gave Himself in Order to Redeem Us

The statement, ἔδωκεν ἑαυτὸν ἵνα λυτρώσηται, describes an action of Jesus and its purpose. Both elements are then elaborated. The self-giving was specifically ὑπὲρ ἡμῶν (the Christian community which continues in view in the successive clauses). The redeeming has specific beneficiaries (again, "us"), and its content is explicated first negatively (ἀπὸ πάσης ἀνομίας) then positively (καθαρίσῃ, attached to λυτρώσεται by the epexegetical καί) The idea of "purify" is also extended. A direct object, λαὸν περιούσιον, identifies those who are both objects and outcome of the action, and they are further characterised by the quality, ζηλοτὴς καλῶν ἔργων. The indirect object ἑαυτῷ indicates that this is achieved for the sake of the verb's subject, Jesus.

18.3.1 ὃς ἔδωκεν ἑαυτὸν ὑπὲρ ἡμῶν

This *Hingabemotiv* appears elsewhere in the NT:

καὶ γὰρ ὁ υἱὸς τοῦ ἀνθρώπου οὐκ ἦλθεν διακονηθῆναι ἀλλὰ διακονῆσαι καὶ δοῦναι τὴν ψυχὴν αὐτοῦ λύτρον ἀντὶ πολλῶν
(Mark 10:45 par. Matt 20:28)

[κυρίου ᾽Ιησοῦ Χριστοῦ] τοῦ δόντος ἑαυτὸν ὑπὲρ τῶν ἁμαρτιῶν ἡμῶν
(Gal 1:4)

---

58 Mott, "Greek Ethics", 25.
59 E.g. 4 Macc 1:17; 13:24.

ὃ δὲ νῦν ζῶ ἐν σαρκί, ἐν πίστει ζῶ τῇ τοῦ υἱοῦ τοῦ θεοῦ τοῦ ἀγαπήσαντός με καὶ παραδόντος ἑαυτὸν ὑπὲρ ἐμοῦ

(Gal 2:20)

[ἄνθρωπος Χριστὸς Ἰησοῦς] ὁ δοὺς ἑαυτὸν ἀντίλυτρον ὑπὲρ πάντων

(1 Tim 2:6)

Marshall identifies four common elements: (a) a verb "to give/hand over"; (b) "himself/his soul"; (c) a preposition "on behalf of/instead of"; (d) "me/us/many/all."[60] The conviction that Christ gave himself for others was evidently a commonplace in early Christianity that found expression in various forms. It would therefore be unwise to assume that Titus 2:14a represents a conscious redaction of the Markan form. Its significance for the author must be discovered in the role it plays in its context.

In this setting, it confirms that the "God and saviour" whose glorious epiphany is awaited (v. 13) is the same Jesus Christ who participated in human history and suffered death (v. 14). As saviour he will appear in glory as saviour, and as saviour he gave himself. The concept of Christ's saving therefore embraces both his earthly ministry and eschatological victory. Although the universal scope of the soterial manifestation is affirmed (v. 11), the *Hingabemotiv* continues the chain of first person plural forms (παιδεύουσα ἡμᾶς . . . ζήσωμεν . . . σωτῆρος ἡμῶν . . . ὑπὲρ ἡμῶν . . . λυτρώσεται ἡμᾶς) identifying the Christian community as its effectual beneficiaries. No conflict need be inferred between this ὑπὲρ ἡμῶν (v. 14) and the ὑπὲρ πάντων of 1 Tim 2:6. The paraenetic purpose is different. The latter counters an exclusivist attitude, whereas the goal in Titus 2:14, appropriate to emerging congregations, is to strengthen community through a consciousness of distinctive identity.

18.3.2 ἵνα λυτρώσηται ἡμᾶς ἀπὸ πάσης ἀνομίας καὶ καθαρίσῃ ἑαυτῷ λαὸν περιούσιον, ζηλωτὴν καλῶν ἔργων

To the *Hingabemotiv* is appended a purpose clause replete with OT language and concepts, specifically those pertaining to Israel's self-understanding as God's people. Evocations of redemption (λυτρόω), deliverance from sin (ἀνομία), cleansing (καθαρίζω), the special people (λαὸς περιούσιος), and zeal (ζηλωτής) ring out in "a

---

60 Marshall, 282-83.

concatenation of ideas from [LXX] Ps 129.8 . . . and Ezek 37.23."⁶¹ Other possible OT backgrounds include the references to Israel as the λαὸς περιούσιος (e.g. Exod 19:5; Deut 7:6; 14:2; 26:18; cf. LXX Ps 134:4 [135:4], ὅτι τὸν Ιακωβ ἐξελέξατο ἑαυτῷ ὁ κύριος Ισραηλ εἰς περιουσιασμὸν αὐτου), and as the people whom God has redeemed (e.g. Exod 15:13; 1 Chron 17:21).⁶² The relating of redemption to the removal of sin is found in, e.g., Isa 44:22, but Lau detects echoes of 2 Sam 7:23:

> καὶ τίς ὡς ὁ λαός σου Ισραηλ ἔθνος ἄλλο ἐν τῇ γῇ; ὡς ὡδήγησεν αὐτὸν ὁ θεὸς τοῦ λυτρώσασθαι αὐτῷ λαὸν τοῦ θέσθαι σε ὄνομα τοῦ ποιῆσαι μεγαλωσύνην καὶ ἐπιφάνειαν τοῦ ἐκβαλεῖν σε ἐκ προσώπου τοῦ λαοῦ σου, οὗ ἐλυτρώσω σεαυτῷ ἐξ Αἰγύπτου, ἔθνη καὶ σκηνώματα.
>
> Who is like your people, like Israel? Is there another nation on earth whose God went to redeem it as a people, and to make a name for himself, doing great and awesome things for them, by driving out before your people, whom you redeemed for yourself from Egypt, nations and its gods?
>
> (NRSV mg.)

If correct, this would be a suggestive background, as 2 Samuel ch. 7 has been described as "the central theological manifesto of Yhwh's benevolence toward the dynasty of David and toward Israel,"⁶³ and a text which "had the power of engendering a national identity."⁶⁴

Titus 2:14, then, appropriates a framework from the thought world of Israel for its depiction of the benefits of God's saving for the Christian community. In one respect, however, a distinction is made. Israel demonstrated her participation in the privileged relationship with God by zeal for God's law (1 Macc 2:26, 27, 50, 58; 2 Macc 4:2; 4 Macc 16:16; Acts 21:20; cf. Acts 22:3; Phil 3:6) or for the traditions of Judaism (2 Macc 2:21; 14:38; Gal 1:14). In Titus this becomes simply zeal for doing good (cf. 1 Pet 3:13). Being "zealous for the good" is not unprecedented in Jewish literature (ἐζήλωσα τὸ ἀγαθόν, Sir 51:18), and it is difficult to estimate whether the motive might be polemical. What is clear is that the author recognises that, as for Israel, with the privilege of being the people of God comes the

---

61 Towner, *Goal*, 109 (Ps 130:8 in ETr).
62 See, e.g., Lau, *Manifest*, 150-54; Marshall, 283-86; Quinn, *Titus*, 158-61.
63 A. Laato, "2 Samuel 7 and Ancient Near Eastern Royal Ideology", *CBQ* 59 (1997): 244-69, 269.
64 W. M. Schniedewind, cited by A. Fitzpatrick-McKinley, review of W. M. Schniedewind, *Society and the Promise to David: The Reception History of 2 Samuel 7:1-17*, *RRT* 7 (2000): 282-84.

responsibility to live according to God's way. For him that takes the form of "good deeds" (2:7, 14; 3:1, 8, 14). These contribute to the church's witness, but are also of considerable importance in relation to Christian identity. "Our people" (οἱ ἡμέτεροι) are discipled into the vigorous pursuit of good works (3:14), whereas to be "unfit for any good work" exposes others as "corrupt and unbelieving," whatever they profess (1:15-16).

How, then, could the church come to define itself by Israel's claims upon God? For this author the key is the self-giving of Christ, understood according to OT texts which "supply him with the theological categories to interpret the event of salvation." [65] These include redemption from sin, cleansing and setting apart for God, and the forming of a particular people who are to live according to his ways. As with the elect and the promise in 1:1-3, there is no overt defence of the transfer of concepts from Israel to the church. Despite the judaising threat (1:10, 14), it seems that the author may assume rather than having to establish the validity of this appropriation.

18.4 The Language of the Unit

A feature of this unit is the juxtaposition of the "griechische Offensbarungsschema" [66] in vv. 11-13 with language that is "consciously Septuagintal"[67] in v. 14. Quinn suggests that it "may indicate here a contribution from the prophetic order within the Jewish-Christian community envisioned in Titus, a contribution that aimed to give a memorable form, intelligible to Hellenistic believers, to the apocalyptic content of the old Palestinian *didache*."[68] While his "prophetic order" is speculative, Quinn may be correct in discerning an intentional translation of primitive Christian teaching into thought forms accessible to a Hellenistic audience. This impression is strengthened when it is observed that certain key ideas seem to appear in two different forms, with a degree of parallelism,[69] as follows:

---

65 Karris, 117.
66 Hasler, 94.
67 Quinn, *Titus*, 171; cf. Hanson, *Epistles*, 185.
68 Quinn, *Titus*, 177. Cf. Dibelius-Conzelmann, 143
69 Marshall sees v. 14 as "broadly parallel with vv. 11f." (282).

Concept familiar to Hellenistic popular philosophy	Essential religious idea	Primitive Christian formulation, derived from OT ideas
Ἐπεφάνη γὰρ ἡ χάρις τοῦ θεοῦ σωτήριος πᾶσιν ἀνθρώποις	Entry of divine gift	Ἰησοῦ Χριστοῦ, ὃς ἔδωκεν ἑαυτὸν ὑπὲρ ἡμῶν
παιδεύουσα ἡμᾶς, ἵνα ἀρνησάμενοι τὴν ἀσέβειαν καὶ τὰς κοσμικὰς ἐπιθυμίας	Release from immoral state	ἵνα λυτρώσηται ἡμᾶς ἀπὸ πάσης ἀνομίας
σωφρόνως καὶ δικαίως καὶ εὐσεβῶς ζήσωμεν ἐν τῷ νῦν αἰῶνι	New, ethically attractive way of life	ζηλωτὴν καλῶν ἔργων
προσδεχόμενοι τὴν μακαρίαν ἐλπίδα καὶ ἐπιφάνειαν τῆς δόξης τοῦ μεγάλου θεοῦ καὶ σωτῆρος ἡμῶν Ἰησοῦ Χριστου	Self-awareness as a group oriented towards God	καὶ καθαρίσῃ ἑαυτῷ λαὸν περιούσιον

The letter presents itself as a missionary text and it is entirely plausible that in the context of early Christianity's Gentile mission language and concepts should have been made sought whereby a Jewish messianic faith could answer the aspirations of the wider Hellenistic world.

18.5 Summary

The understanding of salvation that emerges from this unit both draws upon the theological categories of a Jewish salvation-historical perspective, fulfilled in the Christian story, and opens itself to the Hellenistic environment. Just as it is the reference to Christ that serves as the hinge of this little salvation dyptich, creating a unity out of its two separate parts, it is the author's understanding of the Christ event that enables him to relate it soteriologically both to the Jewish faith tradition and to the ideals of the Hellenistic world. A sense of identity is thus created that is specifically Christocentric, in conscious contradistinction to other religious expressions both Jewish and Greek.

Salvation awaits its completion when Jesus appears as the divine saviour, but in this present world God's grace, soterial in its intent, effects moral transformation in individuals, thus creating a community after the OT pattern of a people purified and devoted to God. The doing good which results commends the teaching about God and salvation, in line with the missionary interest evident in the insistence that this salvific grace is revealed for all people. While the transfer from *Unheil* to *Heil* may be depicted as a process effected by the training operation of God's grace, it is also understood forensically as the accomplished outcome of Christ's sacrificial self-giving, which deals with the consequences of ἀνομία and establishes his ownership of the redeemed people.

CHAPTER 19

Titus 3:1-8

Ὑπομίμνησκε αὐτοὺς ἀρχαῖς ἐξουσίαις ὑποτάσσεσθαι, πειθαρχεῖν, πρὸς πᾶν ἔργον ἀγαθὸν ἑτοίμους εἶναι, μηδένα βλασφημεῖν, ἀμάχους εἶναι, ἐπιεικεῖς, πᾶσαν ἐνδεικνυμένους πραΰτητα πρὸς πάντας ἀνθρώπους. Ἦμεν γάρ ποτε καὶ ἡμεῖς ἀνόητοι, ἀπειθεῖς, πλανώμενοι, δουλεύοντες ἐπιθυμίαις καὶ ἡδοναῖς ποικίλαις, ἐν κακίᾳ καὶ φθόνῳ διάγοντες, στυγητοί, μισοῦντες ἀλλήλους. ὅτε δὲ ἡ χρηστότης καὶ ἡ φιλανθρωπία ἐπεφάνη τοῦ σωτῆρος ἡμῶν θεοῦ, οὐκ ἐξ ἔργων τῶν ἐν δικαιοσύνῃ ἃ ἐποιήσαμεν ἡμεῖς ἀλλὰ κατὰ τὸ αὐτοῦ ἔλεος ἔσωσεν ἡμᾶς διὰ λουτροῦ παλιγγενεσίας καὶ ἀνακαινώσεως πνεύματος ἁγίου, οὗ ἐξέχεεν ἐφ' ἡμᾶς πλουσίως διὰ Ἰησοῦ Χριστοῦ τοῦ σωτῆρος ἡμῶν, ἵνα δικαιωθέντες τῇ ἐκείνου χάριτι κληρονόμοι γενηθῶμεν κατ' ἐλπίδα ζωῆς αἰωνίου. Πιστὸς ὁ λόγος· καὶ περὶ τούτων βούλομαί σε διαβεβαιοῦσθαι, ἵνα φροντίζωσιν καλῶν ἔργων προΐστασθαι οἱ πεπιστευκότες θεῷ· ταῦτά ἐστιν καλὰ καὶ ὠφέλιμα τοῖς ἀνθρώποις.

The cascade of soteriologically accented images in Titus 3:3-7 comprises "perhaps the fullest statement of salvation in the New Testament."[1] Fee regards it as "an early creedal formulation that presents Pauline soteriology . . . in a highly condensed form,"[2] and Guthrie finds a "characteristic Pauline flavour" in content such as δικαιωθέντες τῇ ἐκείνου χάριτι (v. 7).[3] The same phrase, however, "has given rise to dark suspicions among Protestant editors that the author is not being true to Pauline doctrine,"[4] and it cannot be assumed that terms familiar from the *Hauptbriefe* have an identical meaning here. An appreciation of how the unit functions in the letter's argument may suggest something of the author's intention.

---

1   Stott, *1 Timothy & Titus*, 201.
2   Fee, 203.
3   Guthrie, 206; cf. Kelly, 253; Mounce, 448.
4   Hanson, *Epistles*, 192.

19.1 Context

The formula πιστὸς ὁ λόγος (v. 8), found only here in Titus, probably identifies at least part of the preceding material as a formulation recognised in the author's community. Whether the saying comprises all of vv. 3-7 or some part of it is difficult to determine,[5] and in any case, as Marshall writes, "we may ask whether the writer has so adapted it to his own purposes here that the task of identifying a traditional basis will be fruitless."[6] Rather than attempting to isolate the saying, then, it will be more helpful to track the flow of thought through the unit as a whole.

The theological statement is framed by two mandates to teach (vv. 1-2 and 8), and deal authoritatively with opposition (2:15; 3:9-11). In each case the express goal is that members of the community should do good, for the benefit of all (πρὸς πάντας ἀνθρώπους, v. 2; καλὰ καὶ ὠφέλιμα τοῖς ἀνθρώποις, v. 8), including non-Christians.[7] The soteriological material itself exhibits a striking arrangement. If the instructions set its outer parameters, the centre is the statement, ἔσωσεν ἡμᾶς (v. 5), "the main subject and verb of the whole sentence."[8] Immediately preceding and following this affirmation are prepositional clauses supplying the ground and means of the saving: depending οὐκ ἐξ ἔργων τῶν ἐν δικαιοσύνῃ ἃ ἐποιήσαμεν ἡμεῖς ἀλλὰ κατὰ τὸ αὐτοῦ ἔλεος (v. 5a), it is achieved διὰ λουτροῦ παλιγγενεσίας καὶ ἀνακαινώσεως πνεύματος ἁγίου, οὗ ἐξέχεεν ἐφ' ἡμᾶς πλουσίως (v. 5b). Moving further out from the centre are references to the one who saves, ὁ σωτὴρ ἡμῶν, both God (v. 4) and Jesus Christ (v. 6). Next are phrases tracing this saving to the gracious character of God: ὅτε δὲ ἡ χρηστότης καὶ ἡ φιλανθρωπία ἐπεφάνη (v. 4) and δικαιωθέντες τῇ ἐκείνου χάριτι (v. 7). Finally, there are depictions of those upon whom this saving operates, first as they were (ἦμεν γάρ ποτε καὶ ἡμεῖς ἀνόητοι, ἀπειθεῖς, πλανώμενοι, δουλεύοντες ἐπιθυμίαις καὶ ἡδοναῖς ποικίλαις, ἐν κακίᾳ καὶ φθόνῳ διάγοντες, στυγητοί, μισοῦντες ἀλλήλους, v. 3) and then as they have become (κληρονόμοι γενηθῶμεν κατ' ἐλπίδα ζωῆς αἰωνίου, v. 7). This is a chiastic arrangement, as set out below:

---

5   See Knight, 347-49.
6   Marshall, 307; cf. Kelly, 254.
7   See Knight, 352.
8   See, 203; cf. Mounce: "The main thought is ἔσωσεν ἡμᾶς, 'he saved us,' and the rest of the creed is explanatory." (438)

A	**MANDATE (2:15-3:2)**	
1	Deal authoritatively with opposition	
	μηδείς σου περιφρονείτω (2:15)	
2	Teach Christians to do good, bringing benefit to people	
	Ὑπομίμνησκε αὐτοὺς ἀρχαῖς ἐξουσίαις ὑποτάσσεσθαι, πειθαρχεῖν, πρὸς πᾶν ἔργον ἀγαθὸν ἑτοίμους εἶναι, μηδένα βλασφημεῖν, ἀμάχους εἶναι, ἐπιεικεῖς, πᾶσαν ἐνδεικνυμένους πραΰτητα πρὸς πάντας ἀνθρώπους (1-2)	

B	**SALVATION TEACHING (3:3-7)**	
1	The condition out of which we are saved	
	Ἦμεν γάρ ποτε καὶ ἡμεῖς ἀνόητοι, ἀπειθεῖς, πλανώμενοι, δουλεύοντες ἐπιθυμίαις καὶ ἡδοναῖς ποικίλαις, ἐν κακίᾳ καὶ φθόνῳ διάγοντες, στυγητοί, μισοῦντες ἀλλήλους (3)	
2	The source of salvation: operation of God's graciousness	
	ὅτε δὲ ἡ χρηστότης καὶ ἡ φιλανθρωπία ἐπεφάνη (4a)	
3	The saviour: God	
	τοῦ σωτῆρος ἡμῶν θεοῦ (4b)	
4		Explanation of salvation: why?
		οὐκ ἐξ ἔργων τῶν ἐν δικαιοσύνῃ ἃ ἐποιήσαμεν ἡμεῖς ἀλλὰ κατὰ τὸ αὐτοῦ ἔλεος (5a)
5		The saving act
		ἔσωσεν ἡμᾶς (5)
4^1		Explanation of salvation: how?
		διὰ λουτροῦ παλιγγενεσίας καὶ ἀνακαινώσεως πνεύματος ἁγίου, οὗ ἐξέχεεν ἐφ' ἡμᾶς πλουσίως (5b-6a)
3^1	The saviour: Jesus Christ	
	διὰ Ἰησοῦ Χριστοῦ τοῦ σωτῆρος ἡμῶν (6b)	
2^1	The source of salvation: operation of God's grace	
	ἵνα δικαιωθέντες τῇ ἐκείνου χάριτι (7a)	
1^1	The condition into which we are saved	
	κληρονόμοι γενηθῶμεν κατ' ἐλπίδα ζωῆς αἰωνίου (7b)	

A¹	**MANDATE (3:8-11)**
2¹	**Teach Christians to do good, bringing benefit to people** Πιστὸς ὁ λόγος· καὶ περὶ τούτων βούλομαί σε διαβεβαιοῦσθαι, ἵνα φροντίζωσιν καλῶν ἔργων προΐστασθαι οἱ πεπιστευκότες θεῷ· ταῦτά ἐστιν καλὰ καὶ ὠφέλιμα τοῖς ἀνθρώποις (8)
1¹	**Deal authoritatively with opposition** μωρὰς δὲ ζητήσεις καὶ γενεαλογίας καὶ ἔρεις καὶ μάχας νομικὰς περιΐστασο· εἰσὶν γὰρ ἀνωφελεῖς καὶ μάταιοι. αἱρετικὸν ἄνθρωπον μετὰ μίαν καὶ δευτέραν νουθεσίαν παραιτοῦ, εἰδὼς ὅτι ἐξέστραπται ὁ τοιοῦτος καὶ ἁμαρτάνει ὢν αὐτοκατάκριτος (9-11)

This outline illustrates how the salvation teaching (vv. 3-7) has been worked into the paraenesis (2:15-3:2; 3:8-11). Other devices, such as the contrast between the seven-fold depiction of desirable behaviour in vv. 1-2 and the catalogue of seven vices in v. 3,[9] help to weave the materials into a unit.

Regarding salvation, one observation may already be made. The author proposes ethical transformation as the tangible outcome of the soterial operation of God upon sinful people, and he believes that the message of this salvation, in contrast to the esoteric offerings of the opponents (v. 9), will promote a virtuous life. We turn now to examine this teaching in more detail.

19.2 Then and Now (vv. 3, 7)

The catalogue of reprehensible characteristics (v. 3) is introduced by ἦμεν γάρ ποτε καὶ ἡμεῖς, displaying two significant soteriological convictions. First, the now of salvation is distinct from a former time when salvation had not been experienced. Salvation is not intrinsic to the human condition, but introduces a change in it. Second, the phrase καὶ ἡμεῖς distinguishes those now in a state of salvation from others not in that condition: at one time "we" were as "they" now are. Notwithstanding the epiphany of grace that is σωτήριος πᾶσιν ἀνθρώποις (2:11), the salvation of 3:3-7 has evidently not been actualized in all people, just as at one time it had not been actualized in those now said to have been saved.

---

9   See Stott, *1 Timothy & Titus*, 202; cf. Liefeld, 350; Spicq, 649. Quinn claims to find an "elaborate chiasmus" in v. 3 (*Titus*, 201), but it is rather forced and fails to convince (see Marshall, 309 n. 23).

Some similarities between the vice list in v. 3 and characterisations of the opponents (e.g. ἀπειθεῖς, 1:16) raise the possibility that "Paul is presenting the false teachers, who have been troubling these communities, as living illustrations of life outside of Christ."[10] The failings are, however, more general,[11] portraying the human condition of *Unheil* in terms of individual and corporate life soured by folly, disobedience, delusion, and enslavement to lusts. This condition carries culpability. To be ἀπειθεῖς is to be like the rebellious of Israel (e.g. LXX Num 20:10; Sir 16:6; 47:21; Zech 7:12; Isa 30:9; Jer 5:23; cf. ἀπειθέω in Exod 23:21; Lev 26:15; Num 11:20; 14:43; Deut 1:26; 9:7, 23, 24; 32:51; Josh 5:6; Neh 9:29; Hos 9:15; Zech 7:11; Isa 1:23, 25; 3:8; 30:12; 36:5; 59:13; 63:10; 65:2; Jer 13:25; Bar 1:18, 19). In comparison with other NT catalogues of evil behaviour such as Rom 1:29-31, Gal 5:19-21, or 1 Cor 6:9-10, however, the subjects in Titus 3:3 appear as much victims as perpetrators of their condition. They are foolish in need of training, deceived in need of enlightenment, and enslaved in need of deliverance. In the train of thought this characterisation prepares for the announcement of God's saving intervention (v. 4) by showing that to be effective it must provide both illumination and moral deliverance. Rhetorically it perhaps also encourages an attitude of compassion rather than condemnation towards such people.[12] The underlining of God's χρηστότης καὶ φιλανθρωπία (v. 4) also suggests that the author favours a gracious approach to those still outside salvation.

Ποτέ (v. 3) and ὅτε (v. 4) set the thought in a temporal framework. In contrast to the imperfect ἦμεν indicating that the condition ascribed to "then" was a continuous state, ὅτε introduces a string of aorists, ἐπεφάνη . . . ἔσωσεν . . . ἐξέχεεν, which suggest particular events. The outcome of these is expressed in terms ("heirs," "hope," "eternal life") that suggest a state not yet fully realized. The thought thus moves from a continuous past state through particular points of time to a new condition of being which is now inaugurated but awaits future completion. The passage thus takes its place among several in the NT where a then-now schema is employed to contrast existence within and outside Christian salvation (e.g. Rom 6:17-23; 7:5-6; 11:30; 1 Cor 6:9-11; Gal 3:23-29; 4:3-

---

10 Towner, 253-54.
11 See Fee, 202. Quinn allows some situational specificity, commenting that, "The items of this vice catalog are not vices as such; they are adjectival of persons." (*Titus*, 200-01).
12 Cf. the tone of Wis 9-19, where pagan behaviour is on the one hand condemned but on the other attributed to ignorance, and God's benevolence is repeatedly affirmed. Cf. 1 Tim 1:13.

7; 8-9; Eph 2:1-10; 11-22; 4:17-24; 5:6-11; Col 1:21-22; 3:1-11; 1 Pet 2:10; 4:1-6).

The difficulty with this construction, however, is that at first sight the then-now comparison in Titus 3:3-7 is not of like with like. Unlike the more direct contrast between the way of life recommended in vv. 1-2 and that deplored in v. 3, the former condition is described in behavioural terms, the latter in theological. Yet, notwithstanding the disparate categories, the author clearly intends to set the two in antithesis. The implication must be that the benefits of v. 7 are not enjoyed by people whose way of life matches v. 3, and conversely v. 3 can no longer describe one to whom v. 7 applies. The underlying assumption is that found in Paul, that οἱ τὰ τοιαῦτα πράσσοντες βασιλείαν θεοῦ οὐ κληρονομήσουσιν (Gal 5:21), a conviction also stated in 1 Cor 6:9-11, which provides an instructive parallel to our text.[13] There, as here, the "then" takes the form of a vice list and the "now" is a set of theological affirmations, but the contrast works because the behaviours belonging to "then" render those who exhibit them ineligible for the theological status of heirs of God, whereas those who are now heirs have become so through a divine intervention that has altered not only their theological status but also their ethical condition.

19.3 What Appeared? (v. 4)

Pivotal alike to the structure of the unit and the transformation described is what happened, ὅτε δὲ ἡ χρηστότης καὶ ἡ φιλανθρωπία ἐπεφάνη τοῦ σωτῆρος ἡμῶν θεου (v. 4). For the third time in Titus epiphany language describes a decisive soteriological moment (cf. 2:11, 13). If "ἐπιφαίνειν, 'to appear,' is always used in the NT of Jesus' appearing," then "Jesus as the embodiment of God the Father's goodness and philanthropy" must be in view here.[14] That reading of the verb has, however, already been disputed.[15] If the reference is to the making known of the gracious and benevolent character of God it is still possible to view Christ's earthly appearing as the focal point of that revelation without taking v. 4 as an oblique way of speaking about the incarnation. The paraenetic interest of the context is well served by describing God's saving intervention in this way. After the deepening ugliness of v. 2, culminating in μισοῦντες ἀλλήλους, the sudden introduction of χρηστότης and φιλανθρωπία offers the potential for a new reality. It is on these aspects of God's

---

13 See Beasley-Murray, *Baptism*, 213-16.
14 Mounce, 447. Cf. Towner, 254.
15 See discussion on 2:11 above (pp. 198-200).

character that Christian attitudes to others are founded.[16]

In the Christ event and its continuing telling, then, the essential goodness and generosity of God is revealed. As in 2:11-14, however, this goodness is not only declared, it is operative in the world. Correspondingly, believers may not only imitate God's graciousness but also be energised by it for that challenge.

19.4 The Saviour (vv. 4, 6)

In v. 4 God is σωτήρ specifically in his χρηστότης and φιλανθρωπία.[17] This portrayal fits comfortably with Hellenistic ideals of benefaction, suggesting to some commentators conscious opposition to the Imperial cult.[18] Even if the title σωτήρ may have invited comparison with other Graeco-Roman benefactors, however, the content of the saving in vv. 5-7 is distinctive, drawn from the religious traditions of Judaism and early Christianity. Again, references to God (v. 4) and Christ (v. 6) as σωτήρ are juxtaposed. For this author, the term is appropriate to the nature and activity of both. If a distinction must be made, God, in his grace and mercy, is viewed as the originator of salvation (vv. 4-5) and Jesus as the one through whom it is effected (v. 6).[19]

19.5 "He Saved Us" (v. 5)

The chiastic structuring of the material in 3:3-7 marshals the thought first towards and then out from the central affirmation, ἔσωσεν ἡμᾶς (v. 5), so that, "all that leads up to the verb and flows from it enters into the understanding of what is intended by it."[20] To save (v. 5) is thus to effect transformation from one state (v. 3) to another (v. 7). Why and how God achieves this is elaborated in vv. 4-6.

The subject of the verb ἔσωσεν is God (v. 4),[21] specifically as ὁ σωτήρ ἡμῶν. The verb therefore represents a divine action. This sharpens the idea of God as σωτήρ: he has performed a specific action on the basis of which the predication is appropriate. The

---

16 Cf. Bassler, 207; Spicq, 651. For Spicq, however, φιλανθρωπία still evokes the incarnation. (652)
17 Cf. Läger, *Christologie*, 100: "Die Güte und Menschenfreundlichkeit Gottes erweisen ihn als σωτήρ (V.4), sie charakterisieren sein rettendes Handeln."
18 See Hanson, *Epistles*, 186-88; Mounce, 455.
19 Cf. Brox, 309.
20 Knight, 341.
21 Cf. Quinn: "For the PE the action of saving is ultimately an act of God as *ho theos*, the Father." (*Titus*, 305)

concept is further specified by the object, ἡμᾶς. Tracking the unit's first person plural forms it transpires that those whom God has saved (v. 5) were once reprehensible (v. 3) and did nothing to merit salvation (v. 5a), but have received a life-engendering infusion of the Spirit (vv. 5b-6) and consequently anticipate eternal life as God's heirs (v. 7). Reading on, we find that it is those who have put their faith in God (v. 8) for whom these statements are true. This passage therefore describes God's saving of a particular set of people, "us," producing not only individual transformation but also a community, conscious of being saved, whose identifying feature is to be an ethically attractive way of life. This goal in v. 8, ἵνα φροντίζωσιν καλῶν ἔργων προΐστασθαι οἱ πεπιστευκότες θεῷ, recurs as the concluding thought of the letter, μανθανέτωσαν δὲ καὶ οἱ ἡμέτεροι καλῶν ἔργων προΐστασθαι (3:14). Again, a particular community (οἱ ἡμέτεροι, "our people," who are οἱ πεπιστευκότες θεῷ, v. 8) is to be identified by specific behaviour (καλῶν ἔργων προΐστασθαι). In actualizing this ideal, teaching plays a crucial role (μανθανέτωσαν, cf. φροντίζωσιν, v. 8).

The aorist tense of σῴζω might suggest that salvation is considered to be a completed reality.[22] Aspects of salvation, however, still await realization: believers are "heirs" with the "hope of eternal life" (v. 7; cf. 1:2; 2:13). This creates some degree of eschatological tension.[23] We could compare Rom 8:24, τῇ γὰρ ἐλπίδι ἐσώθημεν, where an aorist form of σῴζω and the notion of hope combine.[24] In both Rom 8 and Titus 3 the possession of this hope is itself an outcome of divine saving (cf. Eph 2:12, where the state of *Unheil* includes ἐλπίδα μὴ ἔχοντες, in contrast to the blessing of ἡ ἐλπὶς τῆς κλήσεως αὐτοῦ, 1:18). In these texts, to have been transferred from the bulk of humanity without hope of sharing in the inheritance of God's people into that privileged group who enjoy this hope is already to have experienced rescue, even if complete salvation lies in the future (cf. Rom 13:11). 1 Peter displays a similar pattern of past saving action, present life in hope and future inheritance (1:3-5, 18-21). Again, this present status carries ethical obligations, underlined by then-now contrasts (1:14-16; 2:10-12; cf. 4:1-4). In common with these writers, the author of Titus exhibits an understanding of salvation shaped by the OT scriptures and the religious history and aspirations of Israel. Within this inherited

---

22 As, e.g., Knight, 341.
23 Cf. Bassler: "the author retains the eschatological tension of Paul's thought, for, though 'saved,' the believer possesses only the *hope* of eternal life" (208).
24 See e.g. Houlden, 153; Marshall, 316; also comments on Rom 8:24 in *NIDNTT* 3:205-16, 214. Cf. 2 Tim 1:9.

framework they can use salvation language both of past acts of God and of awaited eschatological consummation without inconsistency.

A matter of debate is whether the verb ἔσωσεν refers to "a specific intervention . . . in the historical lives of those who had come to believe,"[25] or more generally to "the possibility of salvation accomplished by Christ's coming, his death, and resurrection."[26] The personal pronouns in vv. 5b-6 could suggest the former, but against this Mounce argues that the ἔσωσεν (v. 5) should be considered concurrent with ἐπεφάνη (v. 4) so that in his view it "centers not on the individual's appropriation of salvation but on God's overall plan of salvation actualized in the Christ event."[27] In his eagerness to resist any over-individualising of the saving and particularly the possibility of a baptismal reference, Mounce opposes the objective "God's provision in Christ for his people" to a subjective "individual experience." This antithesis is too sharply drawn. The Christ event is not unambiguously depicted, and it is arbitrary to disallow any reference to the believer's personal experience on the grounds of "the corporate nature of the creed." Haykin argues to the contrary that the author "wishes to present the pneumatological position of the credal affirmation as his own," and that the material could appropriately describe individual experience.[28] The corporate and the individual are not, however, mutually incompatible.[29] It is a function of confessional language that by it worshippers both declare the faith of their community and affirm it as their own, interpreting their personal experience in terms of their church's metanarrative of salvation.

19.6 The Grounds of Salvation (v. 5a)

The explanation for God's saving is offered first negatively and then positively in two prepositional clauses (οὐκ ἐξ ἔργων τῶν ἐν δικαιοσύνῃ ἃ ἐποιήσαμεν ἡμεῖς and κατὰ τὸ αὐτοῦ ἔλεος) set in antithesis by the adversative ἀλλά. There is a contrast between human and divine subjects (ἐποιήσαμεν, first person plural, "we";

---

25 Quinn, *Titus*, 217; cf. Marshall: "the reference is to personal experience of salvation rather than to God's action at the cross" (316 and nn. 51 and 52).
26 Mounce, 438.
27 Mounce, 438.
28 M. A. G. Haykin, "The Fading Vision? The Spirit and Freedom in the Pastoral Epistles," *EvQ* 57 (1985): 291-305, 304.
29 Here, as in 2:11-14, Marshall sees references both to God's saving and to individual experience, the former emphasised in ch. 2 and the latter in ch. 3 (305).

ἔσωσεν, third person singular, "he"), and between the righteous acts of the former and the mercy of the latter. The extent to which this corresponds to the Pauline antithesis between Law and grace is much debated,[30] but its contribution here is to establish God and his nature as the basis for salvation. The author is perhaps cautioning against self-congratulation in the way that Deuteronomy ch. 9 reminds the people of Israel that the inheritance they enjoy is not owed to their own δικαιοσύνη (Deut 9: 4, 5, 6); on the contrary, they had been ἀπειθοῦντες (v. 7). The readers of Titus, though now κληρονόμοι (v. 7), had been ἀπειθεῖς (v. 3) and must not imagine that they had merited God's gift. The verbal link between δικαιοσύνη (v. 5) and δικαιωθέντες (v. 7) underscores the atithesis between their works and God's grace.

In these verses, then, to be saved is to become an inheritor of God's promise of eternal life. The qualifying condition of righteousness is not something that people achieve (active verb ἐποιήσαμεν) but is the outcome of something done to them (passive verb δικαιωθέντες); it is due not to "us" (ἡμεῖς) but to God (ἐκείνου); it is not of works (ἐξ ἔργων) but by grace (τῇ χάριτι). While this assertion would serve to refute claims of nomistic righteousness, the law is not specified and in the context Kelly correctly judges that "upright moral conduct in general" is in view.[31] This letter commends righteous living (2:12), but presents it as an outcome of the operation of God's grace (2:11; 3:7).

The positive ground of God's saving is his ἔλεος, which represents חֶסֶד in the Hebrew Bible, that loving kindness of God that is the basis of the covenant relationship of Israel with Yahweh. In the LXX, especially in the Psalms, ἔλεος is frequently associated with God's saving (e.g., with σῴζω and cognates, LXX Pss 6:5; 12:6; 16:7; 17:51; 30:17; 56:4; 68:14; 84:8; 97:3; 108:26; 118:41; cf. Isa 56:1), sometimes appearing in parallel as equivalent ideas (e.g. δεῖξον ἡμῖν κύριε τὸ ἔλεός σου καὶ τὸ σωτήριόν σου δῴης ἡμῖν, LXX Ps 84:8; cf. 118:41). Mercy is opposed to that which people deserve, as in the pasalmist's plea to be treated not according to his sins and ignorance but according to God's ἔλεος and χρηστότης (LXX Ps 24:7). A similar antithesis to that in Titus ch. 3 is found in Daniel 9:18: οὐ γὰρ ἐπὶ ταῖς δικαιοσύναις ἡμῶν ἡμεῖς δεόμεθα ἐν ταῖς προσευχαῖς ἡμῶν ἐνώπιόν σου ἀλλὰ διὰ τὸ σὸν ἔλεος (for it is not on the ground of our deeds of righteousness that we present our prayers before you, but because of your mercy. Cf. Bar 2:19). In

---

30 See Marshall, 313-16.
31 Kelly, 251, commenting that Paul's polemic against works in Romans also extends beyond the law.

neither case is it entirely clear whether the thought is that no truly righteous deeds have been performed or that the righteous deeds that have been achieved are insufficient basis for any claim on God. The essential point is that access to the benefits of God's saving is an unmerited gift explicable only in terms of God's mercy.

19.7 The Means of Saving (vv. 5b-6)

The saving is said to be achieved διὰ λουτροῦ παλιγγενεσίας καὶ ἀνακαινώσεως πνεύματος ἁγίου, οὗ ἐξέχεεν ἐφ' ἡμᾶς πλουσίως διὰ Ἰησοῦ Χριστοῦ τοῦ σωτῆρος ἡμῶν. To determine the significance here of terms such as λουτρόν, παλιγγενεσία, and ἀνακαίνωσις would itself be challenging, but in addition the syntax is capable of a variety of interpretations. Bassler contents herself with the impression that this "string of words, linked together too loosely to permit any rigorous analysis of their logical connection, associates the act of salvation with water . . ., rebirth, renewal, and the Holy Spirit."[32] Different relationships between the ideas could, however, yield different soteriological nuances, and we must therefore attempt to trace the connections.

Several readings are grammatically possible, as below:

a	διὰ	God saved by means of <u>two elements</u>:
	λουτροῦ παλιγγενεσίας	*washing-of-regeneration*
	καὶ	+
	ἀνακαινώσεως πνεύματος ἁγίου, οὗ ἐξέχεεν ἐφ' ὑμᾶς	*renewal-of-Holy-Spirit-that-he-poured-out-upon-us.*
b	διὰ	God saved by <u>one element</u>:
	λουτροῦ	*washing,*
		which effects <u>two results</u>:
	παλιγγενεσίας	*regeneration*
	καὶ	+
	ἀνακαινώσεως πνεύματος ἁγίου, οὗ ἐξέχεεν ἐφ' ὑμᾶς	*renewal-of-Holy-Spirit-that-he-poured-out-upon-us.*

---

32 Bassler, 208.

c	διὰ	God saved by <u>one element</u>:
	λουτροῦ ... πνεύματος ἁγίου, οὗ ἐξέχεεν ἐφ' ὑμᾶς	washing ... of Holy-Spirit-that-he-poured-out-upon-us.
		It effects <u>one result</u>:
	παλιγγενεσίας καὶ ἀνακαινώσεως	regeneration-and-renewal.
d	διὰ	God saved by <u>one element</u>:
	λουτροῦ ... οὗ ἐξέχεεν ἐφ' ὑμᾶς	washing ... that-he-poured-out-upon-us.
		It effects <u>two results</u>:
	παλιγγενεσίας	regeneration
	καὶ	+
	ἀνακαινώσεως πνεύματος ἁγίου	renewal-of-Holy-Spirit.
e	διὰ	God saved by <u>one element</u>:
	λουτροῦ ... οὗ ἐξέχεεν ἐφ' ὑμᾶς	washing, that-he-poured-out-upon-us.
		It effects <u>one result</u>:
	παλιγγενεσίας καὶ ἀνακαινώσεως πνεύματος ἁγίου	regeneration-and-renewal (which is all) of-Holy-Spirit.

One issue is whether παλιγγενεσία καὶ ἀνακαίνωσις represents one reality or two. For Spicq, the term παλιγγενεσία evokes the Stoic doctrine of periodic renewal of the cosmos after destruction by conflagration, serving in Titus ch. 3 to relate individual regeneration to cosmic renewal inaugurated by Christ.[33] There are, however, other possible references.[34] Josephus uses it for both the resurrection (*Ap.* 2.218) and the post-exilic revival of national life (*Ant.* 11. 66).[35] F. W. Burnett finds considerable variety in Philo's usage, but concludes

---

33 Spicq, 652-53.
34 See J. Guhrt, "παλιγγενεσία," *NIDNTT* 1:184-86; J. D. M. Derrett, "Palingenesia," *JTS* ns 20 (1984): 51-58; C. P. Thiede, "A Pagan Reading of 2 Peter. Cosmic Conflagration in 2 Peter 3 and the Octavius of Minucius Felix," *JSNT* 26 (1986): 79-96.
35 Cited in *NIDNTT* 1:185.

that he rejected the Stoic understanding and "seems to have reserved the term for the soul's rebirth after physical death."[36]

Elsewhere in the NT the term occurs only in Matt 19:28, which Burnett has also examined. Again he discounts any specific Stoic background, finding no indication in Matthew's Gospel of the concept of cosmic conflagration.[37] D. C. Sim, however, cites Matt 5:18 and 24:35 as evidence for a belief in the earth's destruction at the eschaton, with παλιγγενεσία representing a re-created cosmic order.[38] Michel connects it to the eschatological reign of the Son of Man.[39] All that can be said with confidence is that παλιγγενεσία communicates an image of rebirth, whether of the world, a nation or an individual.[40]

Rather than assuming some specific background to the term, therefore, it may be more fruitful for an understanding of the concept in Titus ch. 3 to explore the idea of rebirth in early Christianity, as, e.g., in John 3:3-8 and 1 Pet 1:3-5. Mounce objects that, "παλιγγενεσία, regeneration, is not technically rebirth, and therefore references to John 3 and 1 Peter are irrelevant."[41] This is unnecessarily pedantic. The expressions παλιγγενεσία, ἀναγεννάω (1 Pet 1:3, 23), and ἄνωθεν γεννάω (John 3:3) all combine the root idea of begetting (γεννάω, γένεσις) with a qualifier (πάλιν, ἀνά, ἄνωθεν) indicating that this is a second or subsequent begetting.

In John 3:3-8, this new birth, described as "of the Spirit" (v. 8; cf. v. 34), is a prerequisite for entering the kingdom of God. In 1 Pet 1:3-5, the re-generating is credited to God's mercy (v. 3) and it qualifies its object for an eschatological inheritance (vv. 4-5). In v. 23 it is a fruit of the living word of God, associated with obedience to the truth and mutual love (v. 22). Although terms and details differ, John ch. 3 and 1 Peter ch. 1 share a similar framework. The natural human condition is of exclusion from the eternal life of God; by his grace and power God generates new life in individuals who thereby become heirs of his eternal kingdom. The context in Titus 3:3-7 would support such content and, without ruling out additional

---

36 F. W. Burnett, "Philo on Immortality: A Thematic Study of Philo's Concept of παλιγγενεσία," *CBQ* 46 (1984) 447-70, 456.
37 F. W. Burnett, "Παλιγγενεσία in Matthew 19:28: A Window on the Matthean Community?" *JSNT* 17 (1983) 60-72, 62.
38 D. C. Sim, "The Meaning of παλιγγενεσία in Matthew 19.28," *JSNT* 50 (1993) 3-12.
39 O. Michel, "ὁ υἱὸς τοῦ ἀνθρώπου," *NIDNTT* 3:613-34, 629.
40 Cf. Burnett, "Matt 19:28", 65.
41 Mounce, 448.

connotations, it is reasonable to understand παλιγγενεσία in that sense here.

In contrast to the range of possible backgrounds for παλιγγενεσία, ἀνακαινώσις is a "Pauline hapax."[42] In Rom 12:2 it represents the renewal of mind by which the believer's way of life is transformed. The new condition of believers is described in terms of a then-now contrast, countering their former disobedience by God's mercy: ποτε ἠπειθώσατε . . . νῦν δὲ ἠλεήθητε (Rom 11:30; cf. God's χρηστότης, 11:22-23). In 2 Cor 4:16 this inner renewing is an on-going experience of believers, an aspect of the transformation (μεταμορφούμεθα, 3:18) effected by the Spirit (3:3, 8, 17, 18), whose work now is the guarantee of eschatological life (5:5). The apostle can both declare the "new creation" to be a completed act (5:17) and speak of renewing as a continuing process (4:16). Col 3:10 paints a similar picture of on-going renewal (present passive participle of ἀνακαιόω) alongside a then-now contrast (3:7-8) which assumes change from the old life to the new to have already occurred (3:1, 3, 9, 10), while, again, final consummation awaits Christ's appearing (3:4).

These examples witness to a consistent pattern in the Pauline tradition of a continual process of renewing, associated with the Holy Spirit, that effects moral transformation in the present lives of those who can already be said to have entered into new life.[43]

To read ἀνακαίνωσις as a continuing process of moral renewal would be congruent with the pervasive emphasis on training in Titus. The rebirth rebirth imagery of παλιγγενεσία, however, suggests a singular event. To read the terms as synonyms, then, is perhaps to underplay the particular colouring of each.[44] As in the other NT contexts just explored, it is quite possible that both punctiliar and present continuous aspects of the effect of God's saving could be in view.

Mounce insists that, "The context in Titus 3:5 requires that it be a once-for-all renewal because salvation is seen as an accomplished fact,"[45] but this presses the language too far. In such terse phrasing the use of the aorist ἔσωσεν to ascribe the whole saving action to God need not restrict the idea of ἀνακαίνωσις to a single point in

---

42 Fee, 205; cf. H. Haarbeck, H.-G. Link, C. Brown, "καινός," NIDNTT 2:670-73.
43 Cf. Eph 4:23-24, with pres. passive ἀνανεόω.
44 Towner reads them as synonyms for the one event while still distinguishing two effects, rebirth and renewal (256-57); cf. Spicq, 653; Marshall, 321.
45 Mounce, 449.

time. Despite reading the καί as copulative not epexegetical,[46] Mounce excludes any notion of process in ἀνακαίνωσις, which must therefore be "positional sanctification" bestowed at the moment of conversion.[47] This he considers to be Pauline doctrine, but in Paul's uses of ἀνακαίνωσις and ἀνακαινίζω surveyed above a process is clearly in view. In agreement with that Pauline tradition, Titus ch. 3 understands salvation to encompass a decisive entry point, a continuing process, and a final consummation.

If the terms παλιγγενεσία and ἀνακαίνωσις are conceptually distinguishable, there remains the question of their syntactical relationship to the modifiers διὰ λουτροῦ and πνεύματος ἁγίου. Do they belong together as the result of the washing and the Holy Spirit's work, or is washing associated with rebirth and the Spirit with renewal? Or does the washing effect both rebirth and Holy Spirit renewal?

A chiastic movement of thought may be detected:

    A an action . . . ἔσωσεν ἡμᾶς

      B a means . . . διὰ λουτροῦ

        C an outcome . . . παλιγγενεσίας

        C¹ an outcome . . . καὶ ἀνακαίνωσις

      B¹ a means . . . πνεύματος ἁγίου

    A¹ an action . . . οὗ ἐξέχεεν ἐφ' ἡμᾶς πλουσίως

This would yield two connected actions, "he saved us" and "he poured out upon us richly," two means, washing and the Holy Spirit, and two outcomes, regeneration and renewal, giving the sense, "He saved us by pouring out upon us richly a washing of the Holy Spirit that produces regeneration and renewal."[48] This could help to explain what at first sight is the strangely muted contribution of Christ. If the expression διὰ Ἰησοῦ Χριστοῦ τοῦ σωτῆρος ἡμῶν attaches only to its preceding clause, Christ's part in the saving seems limited to being the channel through whom God poured the Holy Spirit. If, on the other hand, it qualifies the whole unit which explicates the statement ἔσωσεν ἡμᾶς, the thought would be that

---

46 Mounce, 449.

47 Mounce, 450.

48 Beasley-Murray notes the "apparent . . . parallelism of the two lines," but objects to distinguishing παλιγγενεσία and ἀνακαίνωσις because "It is misleading to imply that regeneration is effected by the washing but renewal by the Holy Spirit" (*Baptism*, 210-11). The reading offered here avoids that difficulty by combining washing and the Holy Spirit as the means by which both regeneration and renewal are effected.

God our saviour saved us in the manner described in vv. 5-6a through Jesus Christ our saviour: Christ is the agent through whom God saves.

Apart from any possible chiastic patterning, which is admittedly tentative, the image of outpouring (ἐξέχεεν) is appropriate to both washing and the Holy Spirit. Applied to both it would picture a washing by the poured out Holy Spirit, echoing the OT promise of cleansing and renewal through God's Spirit (Ezek 36:25-27).[49]

Although this picture of washing, especially when associated with the Holy Spirit, is a natural metaphor for spiritual cleansing,[50] it is often read more specifically as a reference to baptism.[51] This is not so self-evident as is sometimes assumed.[52] The term λουτρόν does not necessarily represent baptism. It appears only rarely in Biblical texts (3x LXX, 2x NT). In Sir 34:25 the reference is to ritual cleansing after touching a dead body, paralleling βαπτίζω. In Song 4:2 and 6:6, however, the λουτρόν is a sheep dip! About half of the occurrences of the cognate verb λούω in the LXX refer to cultic washing, often in preparation for priestly ministry (Lev 14:8, 9; 15:5, 6, 7, 8, 10, 11, 13, 16, 18, 21, 22, 27; 16:4, 24, 26, 28; 17:15, 16; 22:6; cf. Exod 29:4; 40:10; Num 19:7, 8, 19; Deut 23:12). This Levitical practice provides the background for the idea of washing in Heb 10:22 (λούω) and possibly in Eph 5:26, the other NT example of λουτρόν. In these NT references, as in Titus ch. 3, washing could serve as a metaphor for the spiritual effects of Christ's saving independently of any reference to baptism, and even if a baptismal allusion is present, it could be illustrative rather than constitutive of the saving process.

Neither the term λουτρόν nor the image of washing, then, compels us to find in Titus 3:5 "un sacrement de seconde naissance."[53] Quinn acknowledges that to describe the text as sacramental is to use "the terminology of a later age,"[54] but the

---

49 See Knight, 343-44.
50 See e.g. Marshall, 318; Mounce, 439-40; Towner, 257.
51 E.g. R. E. O. White, *The Biblical Doctrine of Initiation* (London: Hodder & Stoughton, 1960), 202; O. Culmann, *Baptism in the New Testament* (trans. J. K. S. Reid, Studies in Biblical Theology 1; London: SCM, 1950), 48; Beasley-Murray, *Baptism*, 209-16; NIDNTT 1:185, 290.
52 See Towner, *Goal*, 117; also J. A. T. Robinson, "The One Baptism as a Category of New Testament Soteriology," *SJT* 6 (1953): 257-74, 269, although his own understanding of the washing as "the whole ministry of Jesus from Jordan to Pentecost, conceived as the great Baptism whereby 'he saved us'" is not persuasive.
53 Spicq, 652-53. Scott's discovery of a baptism "efficacious in itself" (176) is roundly dismissed by, e.g., Beasley-Murray, *Baptism*, 213; Mounce, 439.
54 Quinn, *Titus*, 217.

ideology as well as the terminology is anachronistic. The evident concern in Titus is not for the sacraments but for knowledge of truth (1:1), preaching (1:3) and teaching (1:9; 2:1, 3, 7, 10, 15; 3:1, 8).[55] Even where cleansing is mentioned in 2:14, there is no explicit indication of baptism. The emphasis is rather on Christ's self-giving as the means of cleansing and on its ethical outcome, a people ζηλωτὴν καλῶν ἔργων.

This brings into question Donelson's reading of Titus 3:4-7, which goes to the heart of his system, representing "the real key to understanding the cosmological and salvific forces which have been unleashed."[56] He finds here salvation by good deeds, enabled by "reception of a spirit" through baptism, which gives to cultic leaders the power to admit to salvation or not.[57] Leaving aside the explicit denial in the text that righteous acts earn salvation (v. 5), it might be expected that if the author's intention were to bolster human authority figures he would have made more of their role and the supposed cultic act in this key depiction of the endowment of salvation.

Instead, as Haykin comments, "the major emphasis of the clause is patent, namely, the saving work of the Spirit."[58] The chiastic scheme pairs the ideas of λουτρόν and πνεῦμα ἅγιον to represent the means of saving. The association of moral cleansing with God's Spirit is found in the OT (e.g. Ps 51:10 [LXX 50:12]; Exek 36:25-27) and elsewhere in the NT. In Acts 15:7-11, for example, the extending of salvation to the Gentiles includes their hearing and believing the gospel (v. 7), receiving God's gift of the Holy Spirit (v. 8) and having hearts purified by faith (v. 9): these elements constitute being "saved (aorist σωθῆναι) through the grace of the Lord Jesus" (v. 11). In 1 Cor 6:9-11, washing, along with sanctification and justification, is accomplished, ἐν τῷ ὀνόματι τοῦ κυρίου Ἰησοῦ Χριστοῦ καὶ ἐν τῷ πνεύματι τοῦ θεοῦ ἡμῶν (v. 11).

Distinctive to Titus, however, is the use of the verb ἐκχέω in such a context (3:6). It suggests abundant generosity, [59] which could in itself explain its choice, but the fact that it is the term used in Acts of the outpouring of the Spirit (Acts 2:17, 18; 10:45; cf. Joel 3:1, 2) by the

---

55 Cf. White, *Initiation*, 202 n. 7.
56 Donelson, *Pseudepigraphy*, 143.
57 Donelson, *Pseudepigraphy*, 143.
58 Haykin, "Fading Vision", 303.
59 Marshall, 322. Cf. the statement in Sir 18:11: διὰ τοῦτο ἐμακροθύμησεν κύριος ἐπ' αὐτοῖς καὶ ἐξέχεεν ἐπ' αὐτοὺς τὸ ἔλεος αὐτοῦ. That is why the Lord is patient with them and pours out his mercy upon them.

exalted Christ (2:33) suggests an allusion to Pentecost.⁶⁰ A further connotation should also be considered. In the LXX ἐκχέω depicts the pouring out of sacrificial blood (e.g. Lev 4:7, 18, 25, etc.), reflected tellingly in the Synoptic saying, τοῦτό ἐστιν τὸ αἷμά μου τῆς διαθήκης τὸ ἐκχυννόμενον ὑπὲρ πολλῶν (Mark 14:24, par. Matt 26:28; Luke 22:20). In the context of saving διὰ 'Ιησοῦ Χριστοῦ τοῦ σωτῆρος ἡμῶν, it is not impossible that ἐξέχεεν could hint at Christ's sacrifice.

19.8 The Outcome of the Saving (v. 7)

The unit concludes with a ἵνα clause expressing purpose. The ἵνα could be refered to either ἐξέχεεν or ἔσωσεν, and there is the question of whether the participle δικαιωθέντες is to be read as part of the purpose or as a recapitulation of what accomplishes the purpose. Mounce rightly remarks that such questions are "more grammatical than theological" and do not fundamentally alter the import of the statement,⁶¹ but the various syntactical possibilities do produce slightly different nuances of meaning. If the ἵνα clause refers back to ἐξέχεεν, it describes the purpose of the outpouring of the Spirit; if it modifies ἔσωσεν then it presents the broader idea of God's purpose in saving. If the thought runs through the unit from each element to the next, the ἵνα clause would be most naturally related to ἐξέχεεν. The reading preferred here, however, sees the thought building up not by simple linear progression but by a chiastic patterning whereby the content of the central idea, "he saved us," is supplied by the rest of the material. The ἵνα clause expresses the purpose of the whole saving act, including not only the pouring out of the Spirit but also the regeneration and renewal that it effects.⁶²

Given that the ἵνα clause modifies the main verb ἔσωσεν, the status of δικαιωθέντες depends on where it is placed along the cause-effect continuum between ἔσωσεν ἡμᾶς and κληρονόμοι γενηθῶμεν. Is it part of the goal of the saving, so that people are saved in order to become justified, or an aspect of the saving action, so that people are saved by being justified in order to become heirs? It is most satisfactorily understood as extending the idea of the main

---

60 Marshall sees the individual's experience of the Spirit, "probably linked with the paradigmatic experience of the church at Pentecost." (321-22) Cf. Rom 5:5.
61 Mounce, 450-51.
62 Cf. Hinson, who refers ἵνα to both verbs, together representing the whole divine act (373-74).

verb.⁶³ The aorist passive participle δικαιωθέντες sums up from the viewpoint of its objects the saving that has already been described from the viewpoint of its subject by the two aorist active forms ἔσωσεν and ἐξέχεεν. God's saving and our being justified are two ways of expressing the same soteriological movement, whose goal is, ἵνα κληρονόμοι γενηθῶμεν.⁶⁴

Just as ἔσωσεν is due to τὸ αὐτοῦ ἔλεος (v. 5), δικαιωθέντες is attributed to τῇ ἐκείνου χάριτι (v. 7). Together with the reference to the χρηστότης and φιλανθρωπία of God (v. 4), these terms build a picture of salvation owed to the merciful, gracious and loving nature of God.⁶⁵ The contrast between ineffective human action ἐν δικαιοσύνῃ (v. 5) and effective divine action implied in the passive δικαιωθέντες (v. 7) sharpens the profile. Justifying results from divine action upon people whose own actions cannot bring them into that condition (cf. v. 3).⁶⁶ The goal of this saving-which-justifies is, "that we might become heirs according to the hope of eternal life" (cf. 1:2). In the Synoptics, to "inherit eternal life" is a religious aspiration (Matt 19:29; Mark 10:17; Luke 10:25; 18:18) equivalent to the idea of inheriting the kingdom of God (Matt 20:1; 25:34; Mark 10:23; Luke 18:17). The qualification is righteousness (Matt 5:20). Titus 3:3-7 makes good sense within this framework. The human condition is of unrighteousness, and consequently exclusion from eternal life; the achievements of human righteousness are not enough; God saves by making people righteous and thus qualifying them to share in eternal life. Further light is thrown on the concept by the description of these beneficiaries οἱ πεπιστευκότες θεῷ (v. 8). To ask whether this righteousness is forensic or moral is perhaps to posit an antithesis that the author would not recognise. The paraenetic purpose which the theological formulation supports is to encourage doing good (3:1-2, 8). The author contends that, while believers live in eschatological hope, ⁶⁷ God's saving produces an ethical reshaping of their present existence.

---

63 Cf. Guthrie, 206.
64 The verbal affinity between γενηθῶμεν and παλιγγενεσία may be intentional.
65 Klöpper argues that ἐκείνου must represent Christ, since the author would have used αὐτοῦ to indicate God's grace ("Soteriologie", 57-88, 65-66). The choice of pronoun is not decisive, however, and either referent is conceivable for this author, for whom both God and Christ are σωτήρ and the source of χάρις καὶ εἰρήνη (1:4).
66 Cf. 1 Cor 6:9-11. Sir 31:5 opposes δικαιόω to πλανάω.
67 See Bassler, 208.

19.9 Summary

In this paraenetically motivated section a rich fund of salvation material is utilized to persuade readers that the outcome of God's saving in those who have embraced the Christian message should be good lives that benefit others. Salvation is beyond human achievement. It is God's work, due to his essential goodness, effected through the self-giving of Christ and the influence of the Spirit. The trinity is glimpsed as a partnership in the saving enterprise. Again, both God and Jesus Christ are "our saviour." From the divine perspective, salvation has already been achieved, but for the recipient it involves a distinct point of change associated with coming to faith in God in response to the Christian message, a cleansing and generating of new life by the Spirit, and a continuing renewal of life also by the Spirit. The effect is to create a righteous condition, qualifying the beneficiaries for eternal life. This condition is visible now in behaviour that contrasts with their former lives outside this salvation.

CHAPTER 20

Summary of Salvation in Titus

20.1 General Observations

Salvation is presented in this letter principally in three passages (1:1-4; 2:11-14; 3:3-7) which show signs of careful literary and theological construction. A distinctive feature is the ascription of the title σωτήρ to both God and Jesus (1:3, 4; 2:10, 13; 3:4, 6), setting Jesus as saviour alongside the continued use of the OT-influenced "God our saviour." In the three main theological sections, OT soteriological categories are appropriated to describe aspects of God's saving and the Christian community that results from it. Alongside these, however, are found terms and concepts that relate to the Hellenistic religious and philosophical environment. There seems to be a concern to translate aspects of Christian faith that had their origin within Judaism into terms intelligible to a Hellenistic thought world.

In this letter the concept of revealing or manifesting plays a significant part. God's gracious saving character and his purpose and promise, rooted in the distant past, have been made known in this present age through the Christ event and its missionary proclamation. The historical elements of the Christ event are, however, more than a revelation of God's will to save. They are the means by which that saving has been made available, as is illustrated by references to two specific aspects, Christ's sacrificial self-giving (2:14) and his pouring out of the Spirit (3:5-6). Saving takes effect in individuals who respond with faith to this revelation through an experience of conversion and on-going ethical transformation, attributed to training in (the message of) God's grace and the influence of the Holy Spirit. Those individuals find themselves incorporated into a new community, conceptually modelled on the OT people of God, exhibiting distinctive behavioural norms.

The letter to Titus "identifies the salvation that comes through Jesus as the fulfilment of that promised by God."[1] Having begun in God's promise in the distant past (1:2), it will be completed in the

---

1 L. T. Johnson, *Letters to Paul's Delegates: 1 Timothy, 2 Timothy, Titus* (The New Testament in Context; Valley Forge: Trinity, 1996), 219.

future life (1:1; 3:7) that will be inaugurated by Christ's next appearing in glory (2:13). The paraenetic emphasis of this letter, however, lies on life in the present age which is for Christians both a response to the revelation of that past promise and an anticipation of that future hope. By such a life, Christian converts themselves contribute to the continuing revelation of God's saving in the world (2:10), illustrating the rescue from destructive behaviours and attitudes and the practical outcomes of moral and spiritual cleansing.

20.2 Specific Aspects of the Presentation of Salvation

20.2.1 The Benefits of Salvation

In the letter to Titus it is again eternal life that is identified as the benefit sought from God our saviour (1:2), and achieved for us by Jesus Christ our saviour (3:6-7). The realization of this blessing awaits the future glorious manifestation of Christ (2:14). Meantime there are benefits for those who have become the community of Christ (2:14), and heirs of this eternal life (3:7), in that God's grace (2:11-12) and the gift of the Holy Spirit (3:5-6) have an educative, liberating and renewing effect, issuing in a new quality of inner and relational life (2:12; 3:1-8).

20.2.2 God and Christ in Relation to Salvation

As in 1 Timothy, God is "our saviour" (1:3; 2:10; 3:4). He promised eternal life before the ages began (1:2) and has made it known through the preaching of his apostle (1:3). It is God who has "saved us" (3:5), justifying us in order to make us inheritors of this eternal life (3:7), an action utterly undeserved by its beneficiaries and due only to God's grace, kindness and mercy (2:11; 3:4, 5). The activity of God our saviour is not restricted, however, to a past promise and a future gift. The manifesting of his grace and the operation of his Spirit has an educative and ethical effect in the present age, producing moral and relational transformation (2:11-12; 3:1-8). The beneficiaries of this salvific process are "those who have come to believe in God" (3:8), and they are distinguished by their behaviour from those who "profess to know God, but deny him by their actions" (1:16).

Christ, along with God, is "our saviour" in the letter to Titus (1:4; 2:13; 3:6). While the predicate may have something of the function of a title (1:4), there are also three specific ways in which Christ acts as saviour. He has redeemed the beneficiaries of this saving from sin by the giving of himself, purifying and making of them a people for himself (2:14); it is through him that the Holy Spirit has been poured out to effect rebirth and renewal, which are the means whereby sinful people are justified and become heirs of eternal life (3:5-7); and he will one day be gloriously manifested as God and saviour (2:13), bringing the present age to its close and bestowing the promised eternal life.

20.2.3 Paul and Salvation

Paul's apostleship has as its goal the realization of the eternal life promised by God before time (1:2). His ministry contributes to that realization in that it consists in the proclamation by which God's promise is made known (1:3), and it is through responding to that revelation with the mutually associated elements of faith, knowledge of the truth and godly behaviour (1:1), that the hope of eternal life is embraced (1:2). After that initial statement of Paul's apostleship, its warrant and its purpose, there is no explicit mention of Paul, though his authority is implicit in the relationship envisaged between Paul as author and Titus as recipient of the letter. The rich salvation material in the letter (2:11-14; 3:3-7) is presented as what Titus is to teach (2:15; 3:1, 8), and the letter urges the appointment to church office of people who will be able to fulfil a teaching role (1:9), so although the authority for the teaching content derives ultimately from that which had been entrusted to Paul (1:3), its communication in the context of this letter is in the hands of other figures, both translocal and local, within the church.

20.2.4 Those Who are Saved

At the heart of the letter to Titus is the conviction that the grace of God appeared in a way that is soterially significant for all people (2:11). This could be read as an affirmation of the universal scope of God's saving over against some more exclusive, probably Judaising, viewpoint (see e.g. 1:10, 14-16). Elsewhere in the letter, however, salvation is consistently described in relation to "us." The grace that has appeared with salvific effect has operated upon "us" (2:12), it is "we" who live in anticipation of the parousia (2:12-13), and it was "for us" that Christ gave himself (2:14). God saved "us" (3:5), though "we ourselves" had formerly been deceived and entrapped in a sinful way of life (3:3); the Spirit who effects the rebirth and renewal has been poured out upon "us" (3:6) and it is "we" who, justified by his grace, are now heirs with the hope of eternal life (3:7). From the perspective of the implied author and addressee, those in whom all this can be considered to have taken place are now "our people" (οἱ ἡμέτεροι, 3:14). Salvation is therefore presented as the possession of the community of which Paul, Titus and the Christians on Crete are members. Terms such as "God's elect" (1:1), "a people of his own" (2:14) and "heirs" (3:7) are appropriated from the language in which Israel's self-consciousness as the OT people of God was expressed. For this letter, the beneficiaries of salvation are those who are incorporated into the new people of God, a community that interprets the Christ event as the means by which "God our saviour" has acted to bring his saving to effect. This community is characterized by "good works" (2:7, 14; 3:1, 8, 14) which are the visible evidence of the saving that has begun (see, negatively, 1:16) and thus confirm the community's message (2:5, 8, 10).

For all the emphasis on good works, there is no suggestion that these are the means by which salvation is attained; rather, it is those who have been saved and upon whom the Spirit has been poured out (3:5-6) who must "learn to devote themselves to good works" (3:14). It seems to be assumed that the saving operation of grace and the Spirit will create the conditions within which such learning is possible. Hence the letter exhibits a pervasive concern for the teaching of the community, urging the necessity for right teaching (1:9; 2:1, 3, 6, 7-8, 9-10, 15; 3:1, 8) and commanding the refuting and silencing of the wrong sort of teaching (1:9, 10-16; 3:9-11). "Healthy teaching" (1:9; 2:1) is that which promotes the lifestyle appropriate to the saved people of God.

Not only is this community shaped by a specific kind of teaching, but it is called into existence by a particular message. Paul's apostleship is regarded as being, "for the sake of God's elect and the knowledge of the truth that leads to godliness, in the hope of eternal life . . ." (1:1-2). His preaching is God our saviour's means of making known his promise of eternal life (1:3; explicated with specific reference to Christ and the Spirit in 3:4-7; cf. the Christ-referred future hope in 2:13-14), and the fruit of that preaching in those who receive it is faith and godliness (1:1). Thus the saved community addressed in the letter consists of people of faith, "those who have come to believe in God" (3:8a), and of godliness, because it is they who are able to learn to do good (3:8b). In Titus, the beneficiaries of salvation are those who have heard the apostolic gospel, responded with belief, and been incorporated into a Christian community committed to an ethically exemplary life. While the final benefit awaits the parousia, they are already experiencing salvation as the rescue from a godless life.

If those who are saved have come to a knowledge of the truth (1:1) and are evidencing ethical transformation (2:14; 3:3-8), they may be contrasted with deceiving teachers and their followers (1:10-16) who, rejecting the truth (1:14), exhibit corruption in conscience and behaviour (1:15-16; cf. 3:3). Again, the acceptance of healthy teaching is vital to entry into salvation.

Part 5

CONCLUSIONS

Chapter 21

Salvation in the Three Letters

21.1 Specific Aspects Compared

Summaries of certain aspects of the presentations of salvation in the three PE have already been offered in the final sections of the investigations of each letter. These may now be compared.

21.1.1 The Benefits of Salvation

All three letters envisage a final salvation comprising a future eternal life, together with present experiences of God's saving. It is in relation to the latter that they are most diverse. In 1 Timothy the faith in God which will bring entry into the life to come also enhances the enjoyment of much in the present life, as it is recognized and received with gratitude as the gift of a benevolent God. Titus also promises present benefit, in the ethical transformation which is the existential dimension of the cleansing that is central to God's saving intervention. In 2 Timothy, however, the focus is firmly on the hope of future salvation and present experiences of God's saving are primarily in the context of preserving and enabling for the fulfilment of ministry in a hostile environment.

21.1.2 God and Christ in Relation to Salvation

Each of the three letters exhibits its own distinctive emphases in its presentation of God and Christ in relation to salvation. 1 Timothy speaks of "God our saviour" in a manner reminiscent of the OT, but extends the scope of his saving beyond Israel to all, for whom he is the universal benefactor. It is also God's desire that all should attain eschatological salvation, but this is specifically in and through Christ, made available though his incarnation and priestly mediation, and realized at his return. In Christ grace and mercy are received by all who make him the object of their faith. In 2 Timothy God is revealed as the instigator and guarantor of eternal life which depends upon his mercy and grace and is coming to fruition as his eternal saving purpose unfolds. Central to that purpose is Christ, locus of the pretemporal gift of grace, Davidic messiah, and saviour by virtue of his victory over death which has opened the way to immortality for those who are identified with him. The risen Christ will return as eschatological judge with the authority to bestow life in his kingdom, and meantime his gracious and empowering presence is experienced by those who are on the way to eternal life. Titus claims "God our saviour" for the Christian community, for whom God and Christ, who is also "our God and saviour," are closely identified. Salvation will be consummated with the epiphany of Christ the divine saviour. Nonetheless there are functional specificities in the roles of God and Christ in relation to salvation. To God is ascribed the pretemporal promise of eternal life and the grace and mercy to which it is due, and it is achieved through Christ's historical self-giving to redeem and his channelling of cleansing and renewal by the Holy Spirit.

While there are differences of emphasis and detail, then, all three letters regard the historical Christ event as crucial to the provision of eschatological salvation, assume Christ's continuing gracious influence in the present age and envisage a future manifestation of Christ which will usher in final salvation. There is greater diversity in the presentations of God in relation to salvation, 1 Timothy universalising Israel's saviour God, 2 Timothy stressing God's eternal saving purpose realized in Christ, and Titus claiming God as the saviour specifically of the Christian community.

21.1.3 Paul and Salvation

With varying emphases, the three letters all present Paul as exercising a soteriologically significant ministry, specifically as one through whom the message of God's saving purpose and its realization through Christ is made known. His ministry has its source in God's commissioning and is related to the outcome of eternal life (1 Tim 1:1; 2 Tim 1:1; Titus 1:1-3). 1 Timothy stresses Paul's calling as a teacher of the Gentiles and understands Paul's ministry as part of the eschatological witness to the nations that belongs to the End Times. 2 Timothy refers Paul's ministry to the eternal purpose of God, on which grounds its success is assured. At the same time it has a martyrological character in that he must suffer for the sake of it and persevere in faithfulness, and through doing so he contributes to the salvation of others. In Titus Paul is the authorized proclaimer of the message of God's salvation who can declare what must be taught in the missionary congregations, and again this ministry is located at a divinely appointed and therefore soteriologically significant time. The differing emphases are in accord with the special interests of each letter, but all agree that Paul is a channel of God's revelation of his saving intent and means. Each letter also recognizes that other people – Timothy, Titus and those whom they will teach and appoint – also participate in the making known of what God has revealed, and the emphasis lies on the authoritative content of the message rather than the leadership status and authority of Paul.

21.1.4 Those Who are Saved

All three PE present salvation as the possession of those who accept and hold to the message of God's saving through Christ as proclaimed by Paul and other faithful messengers. All understand that faith to include right belief together with life choices and behaviour consistent with an orientation of life towards the final salvation anticipated. Again, however, each has its own distinctive emphases. 1 Timothy is concerned to stress, against exclusivist interpretations, that there is the possibility of salvation for "all," specifically including sinners, Gentiles and women. Urging perseverance in costly ministry, 2 Timothy highlights the outcome of salvation for faithful servants of Christ and those who benefit from their ministry (including Gentiles). There is a confidence that as they come to faith God's eternal saving purpose is unfolding. In Titus it is "we," the Christian community in a missionary context, who have been saved through accepting the health-giving teaching of the Pauline missionaries and learning to live distinctively as God's people.

21.2 Similarities and Differences

21.2.1 Shared Characteristics

The starting point for our exegetical investigation was the observation that certain salvation language, distinctive or unusual in the NT as a whole, is prominent in the PE. Part of its distinctiveness is a more Hellenistic character than is encountered in some parts of the NT, and in the course of our study of all three letters fruitful points of contact have been found with the literature of Hellenistic Judaism, suggesting a common milieu. Furthermore, all three letters make use of apparently pre-formed materials that relate in various ways to soteriological concerns. Beyond these formal similarities, our study of the content and function of the salvation material has identified certain conceptual features common to the presentation of salvation in all three letters. They share a kairological framework within which the origin of salvation is located in the pretemporal decision of God to which the OT scriptures bear witness, the execution of the saving plan has been begun in the historic Christ event and continues in the present age through gospel proclamation, and the goal of salvation will finally be realized upon Christ's appearing in glory and the entering into eternal life for those who have been saved. The three share convictions regarding the universal scope of salvation and an interest in the implications of salvation for life in the present age. All three have an interest in the revelation of salvation, affirming God's intention that it should be made known and highlighting the importance of the right content and faithful exercise of the teaching ministry by which the revealing continues to take place. The three stress the authenticity of the message proclaimed by Paul and the necessity for continuing ministry that is faithful to that tradition. The entering into the salvation of which these letters speak involves coming to a "knowledge of the truth," believing the message and living reverently in accordance with it. It may be confirmed, then, that the three PE exhibit aspects of a common soteriological perspective. There are also, however, particular features that give each letter its own distinctive profile in terms of its presentation of salvation.

21.2.2 Distinctive Features

The very terms whose occurrence in all three letters gives the initial appearance of similarity are not necessarily employed in identical ways across the correspondence. This may be illustrated by a summary of the findings in relation to the key terms σωτήρ, ἐπιφάνεια and εὐσέβεια.

a. σωτήρ

In 1 Timothy it is God who is σωτήρ (1:1; 2:3; 4:10), the OT "God our saviour" who this letter affirms to be the saviour of all. In 2 Timothy Christ is σωτήρ (1:10), and through his epiphany God's saving grace was revealed and its outcome, life and immortality, brought to light. Titus distinctively attributes the predicate "our saviour" to both God and Christ (1:3, 4; 2:10, 13; 3:4, 6), identifying the latter as the agent through whom God's saving is realized.

b. ἐπιφάνεια/ἐπιφαίνω

1 Timothy has only one instance of this vocabulary (6:14), where the noun signifies the future appearing of Christ. The incarnation of Christ is described in the phrase, "manifest in flesh" (3:15), but the verb here is the much more common φανερόω (48x in the NT). The

noun ἐπιφάνεια occurs 3x in 2 Timothy. Twice the reference is to the future appearing of Christ and on the other occasion it is the historic Christ event, as an appearing through which God's saving grace and the life and immortality that are its outcome were revealed (1:9-10). In Titus the noun depicts Christ's future appearing (2:13) whereas the verb describes the manifesting of God's saving grace (2:11) and of his goodness and love for humankind (3:4). While the Christ event is doubtless the key element in the making known of these aspects of God's nature and purpose, it is by no means self-evident that the intention is to describe the incarnation *per se* as an epiphany. Even in 2 Timothy 1:10, where the noun is used in relation to Christ, the focus seems to be not so much on Christ's coming into the world as on his resurrection, the basis for the claim that he had "abolished death and brought immortality and life to light through the gospel."

c. εὐσέβεια

1 Timothy presents εὐσέβεια in a very positive light as that which brings eschatological gain as well as temporal benefit (4:8; 6:6). Although "our" εὐσέβεια is determined by specific Christological beliefs (3:16), the term principally represents a religiously shaped way of living. As such it is the practical goal of the apostolic teaching (6:3) and should be cultivated by all Christians (2:2) and in particular by teachers such as Timothy (4:7). It is possible for false teachers to pursue it for the wrong motives (6:5). In contrast to 1 Timothy, the noun εὐσέβεια appears only once in Titus, where it is again an envisaged outcome of true teaching (1:1), but the idea recurs in the use of the adverbial form εὐσεβῶς to indicate an aspect of the mode of living produced by the παιδεία of grace (2:12). The references in 2 Timothy strike a different tone. False teachers can present an appearance of εὐσέβεια but deny its power (3:5), and far from being a way to benefit in this life, those who want to live εὐσεβῶς will have to suffer persecution (3:12).

21.2.3 The Three Presentations of Salvation and Their Purposes

Despite the sharing of certain special vocabulary, then, there are differences between the letters in the relative importance given to specific terms and in the way they are used. In relation, for example, to the use of epiphany language, recognition of the distinctiveness of each letter greatly reduces the support for the view that there is a developed and consistent two-epiphany schema that imposes a uniform content on epiphany terms across the letters.[1] It is preferable to allow that these letters have found epiphany language useful in more than one way in the communication of aspects of their soteriological schemas. Similarly, while it would be unwise to make too much of the single reference in 2 Timothy, both 1 Timothy and Titus clearly have particular and different purposes in their utilization of the σωτήρ predicate. An appreciation of the viewpoint of each in this regard is more satisfactorily achieved by evaluating their uses of the vocabulary separately rather than by attempting a synthesis of all three, and reading back the results of that synthesis into the usage of each letter.

When they are treated separately it emerges that the use of salvation language and concepts is in each case in agreement with what can be discovered from other features of that letter concerning its purpose and implied occasion. 1 Timothy, adopting a stance over against opponents who devalue the present, material world and limit access to salvation, presents God as the beneficent saviour of all through his providential ordering of the created world, who is also executing a plan of eschatological salvation for all who believe in Christ. On one level the saving that God offers, as "our saviour" and "the saviour of all," is enjoyed in the form of peace and provision and contentment by those who look to him in dependent prayer and trust and live reverently in his world. On another level, however, the saving that Christ came into the world to accomplish gives grace and love that enable erstwhile sinners and enemies of Christ to look beyond the present age to a qualitatively superior future existence to be inaugurated by Christ's appearing.

In 2 Timothy the tone is one of personal paraenesis, urging the faithful exercise of ministry in the face of opposition. Both the specific content of salvation that is emphasized and the presentation of ministry in salvific terms relate to this setting. Of the three PE, 2 Timothy presents the most sombre portrayal of the present age, a time of opposition for witnesses to the gospel, hardship for Christ's servants and persecution for all who want to live godly lives. While there is the expectation of rescue in this life from attacks that would prevent Christ's ministers completing the work he has given them to do, the focus of salvation in this context is eschatological, finding its content in immortal life in Christ's heavenly kingdom. The call is to faithfulness in ministry, and the salvation theme is deployed in support of this exhortation in two ways in particular. First, ministry is shown to contribute to salvation, in that it is a means by which

---

[1] See e.g. Lau, *Manifest*, and H. Stettler, *Die Christologie der Pastoralbriefe* (WUNT 2.105; Tübingen: J. C. B. Mohr, 1998).

God carries forward his saving purpose. The gospel through which life and immortality are brought to light (1:9-10) reaches people as it is proclaimed by those to whom it has been entrusted, namely, Paul (1:11), Timothy (1:13-14) and others (2:2). Through the minister's suffering the message reaches the elect, who obtain salvation (2:8-10). In addition, the minister's own salvation is held out as a goal to encourage perseverance. While confidence is ultimately in the Lord who will see his servant safely through into his heavenly kingdom, there is also a degree of conditionality in the linking of faithfulness in witness to that final outcome (2:11-13; 4:6-8), that carries the implication that for the sake of his own salvation as well as that of others, Timothy should fulfil his ministry.

Titus displays a particular interest in the continuing mission of the church in a non-Jewish environment, and to that end, alongside the articulation of significant salvation ideas in traditional language (2:14; 3:5-7) are found terms and concepts intelligible to a Hellenistic audience which establish points of contact with their symbolic world and provide for them a way into the understanding of those traditional soteriological affirmations (2:11-13; 3:3-4). This letter seems to have a particular concern for the content of teaching (see the reiterated instruction to teach, tell, etc. in 2:1, 3, 6, 9, 15; 3:1, 8, including the specific ταῦτά, 2:15; 3:8), and it is not implausible that the two elaborate soteriological pieces (2:11-14; 3:3-7) could have been intended to provide teaching material or serve as models for communication in a Hellenistic setting. The stress on the present outcome of salvation in ethically attractive lives (2:1-10; 3:1-2, 8, 14) accords with the stated concern to protect the reputation of the fledgling Christian community and its message (2:5, 8, 10). At the same time the indications of Judaizing opposition (1:10, 14) suggest that there could be a polemical purpose in the appropriation of OT People of God categories to give identity to the largely Gentile community that is the fruit of Christian mission (1:1; 2:14; 3:7).

CHAPTER 22

Implications for Understanding the PE

22.1 The Individual Coherence and Distinctiveness of the PE

First the general point may be made that the observations above weigh against the notion that the soteriological material in the PE is inserted haphazardly and with little reflection. In all three the use made of salvation concepts lends effective support to the paraenesis and the distinctive features of each presentation of salvation are in each case in accord with the general character and paraenetic goals of the letter in question. This adds to the growing body of evidence for the internal rhetorical and theological coherence of each of these letters.[1]

On the other hand the results of this study challenge the assumption that the three are most adequately understood as a single three-part work.[2] The three letters do exhibit aspects of a shared soteriological perspective, but this is also shared more widely within the NT. There is sufficient specificity about the application of soteriological material in each letter to support the view that each represents a distinct response to a particular occasion. Even terms commonly taken to be characteristic of the PE as a group have been found to be utilized in different ways in the three letters. Clearly there are implications here for the study of the PE. If each of these letters offers its own distinctive soteriological presentation, it must be asked whether each may not also have a unique contribution to make in other areas. The voice of each should be heard. Since interpretations of the PE commonly treat its themes by formulating syntheses of relevant material in the three letters and on that basis describing a single perspective or set of concerns, the findings of this investigation, if valid, will require a nuancing of those readings to take fuller account of differences between the letters. At the very least, there is a case for investigating whether different results are

---

1   In agreement with, e.g., Fiore, *Personal Example*; Towner, *Goal*; Harding, *Tradition and Rhetoric*; Tollefson, "Titus"; and *contra* Miller, *Composite Documents*.
2   Supporting Johnson's tentative suggestion in *1 & 2 Timothy*, 82.

obtained in relation to themes other than salvation when each letter is approached on its own terms as a discrete item of correspondence with its own internal coherence.³ The findings of our study also caution against assuming that the significance of a particular feature or expression in one of the letters must also hold for any occurrences in the other letters. Rather than explain terms in one letter according to their use elsewhere in the PE, the primary pointers to their significance should be sought first in the letter itself.

22.2 Re-evaluation of Some Current Interpretations of the PEs' Soteriological Perspective

In the light of our investigation, certain widely held perceptions of the soteriology of the PE may be evaluated, specifically that the main focus of salvation is life in the present age; that the presentation of salvation restricts salvation to the cult and is designed to bolster the power of cultic leaders; that the figure of Paul has been elevated to an exclusive place in the scheme of salvation; and that the theology of salvation found in the PE represents a decline or departure from Pauline soteriology.

22.2.1 Salvation as Good Citizenship in the Present Age?

In 1990 J. L. Houlden wrote, "Certain views have become almost *de rigeur* in the recent study of the Pastoral Epistles," among which he lists church life marked by institutionalization, salvation seen as something achieved in the past through Christ and appropriated through baptism, and that the PE represent "bourgeois Christianity," a desire to live respectably and comfortably but not provocatively in the world.⁴ He was in effect testifying to the influence that Dibelius-Conzelmann's *christliche Bürgerlichkeit* interpretation continued to hold in PE scholarship.⁵ The present study joins other recent work in finding Dibelius-Conzelmann's reading inadequate.⁶ While it is true that 1 Timothy and Titus

---

3   See e.g. Richards, *Difference and Distance*.
4   J. L. Houlden, review of Towner, *Goal*, *ExpTim* 101 (1990): 312-13.
5   See Dibelius-Conzelmann, 10. This approach still surfaces in general surveys, as e.g. in the description of the PE in D. L. Barr, *New Testament Story: An Introduction* (2nd. ed., Belmont: Wadsworth Publishing Company, 1995), 171-72: "Attention to the present has eclipsed concern for the future kingdom. Church as organization is replacing church as family. The desire to be well thought of by those outside has eroded freedom."
6   With, e.g., Schwarz, *Bürgerliches Christentum*; Towner, *Goal*; R. M. Kidd,

demonstrate an interest in Christian existence in the world (the observation is less valid for 2 Timothy), the explanation of this concern in terms of a soteriological perspective which lacks any real future dimension must be disputed. This view fails to appreciate that there is in 1 Timothy a recognition both of the general "saving" benefits that God in his universal benefactor role provides for the world and of the particular hope of eternal life that is made available through Christ. The latter hope focuses upon a future appearing of Christ, and although the present life is not disparaged it is the anticipated future that is the ὄντως ζωή (6:19). It is of Titus that it would be most valid to claim that the consciousness of salvation serves as the presupposition of an attitude of good citizenship (2:14; 3:1-5), but even here salvation is not complete until the coming of Christ in glory and the inheriting of eternal life. Moreover, the overt defensive or missionary concern must also be taken into account in explaining the behavioural exhortations. In 2 Timothy the more negative appraisal of the "last days" is the ground against which the figure of eschatological salvation is the more sharply delineated. In none of the PE has the prospect of future salvation disappeared. It remains a persuasive and powerful consideration that each letter is able to deploy rhetorically. The *christliche Bürgerlichkeit* perspective misses the mark most completely in relation to 2 Timothy, where salvation's eschatological horizon dominates.

22.2.2 Soteriology as an Ideological Stratagem?

Donelson's reading of the PE discerns a sophisticated soteriological schema deliberately constructed in order to place power in the hands of cultic leaders. According to this plan, "it is solely by way of virtue that God saves."[7] Jesus' saving consists in teaching the way of virtue and rewarding virtue at the final judgement.[8] This teaching has been handed down by Paul and taken over by cultic leaders, so that, "the effective power of Jesus' epiphany is mediated to believers by way of cultic leaders."[9] It is the spirit who enables the performance of those virtuous deeds which will save, but this too works in the interests of the leaders:

Wealth and Beneficence in the Pastoral Epistles: A "Bourgeois" Form of Early Christianity? (SBLDS 122; Atlanta: Scholars Press, 1990).

7   Donelson, *Pseudepigraphy*, 140; cf. 153, ". . . quiet virtues constitute the sole means of salvation."
8   Donelson, *Pseudepigraphy*, 139: "Thus Jesus saves, because virtues save."
9   Donelson, *Pseudepigraphy*, 142.

Part of God's management of this plan is the restriction of access to the spirit to the cultic act of baptism. Thus he places cosmological power into the hands of cultic leaders. In order to possess this spirit, one must appear before the church leaders and become subject to them.[10]

Despite Donelson's complaint that earlier interpreters had erred by trying to construct the author's theological system from statements plucked from their contexts in the PE, his own discussion of the evidence suffers from a high degree of selectivity of another sort. He privileges those passages that extol the virtuous life but sets aside or simply ignores other statements (e.g. Titus 3:5a and 2 Tim 1:9) which explicitly deny that people are saved because of meritorious accomplishment.

The cultic reading depends largely upon Titus 3:5b-7, which in the present study was judged to refer to baptism only in a secondary sense. Furthermore the assertion that to be baptized involves entering into subjection to the church leaders, an important part of Donelson's system, is not in the text at all. Presumably he assumes this to be the case on the basis of his reconstruction of the situation and purpose of the PE, but whereas his scheme requires that references to ministers or ministry in relation to salvation be understood as claims on behalf of church leaders for control over salvation, they may equally well be read as paraenesis directed towards leaders and teachers, encouraging them in their task by showing the contribution of right and faithful ministry to salvation.

22.2.3 *"Paulology" as a Soteriological Category?*

In her recent study of the Christology of the PE, K. Läger suggests that the PE present a "symbiotic unity" of Paul with his message of the saving work of Christ. Paul – and only Paul! - is the mediator of the message of the saving activity of God. Message and messenger are integrated to such an extent that Paul himself becomes a part of the message. It is "Paulology" rather than Christology that comes to the fore in the PE.[11]

This overstates the case. Certainly in each of these letters the message of salvation is expressly that which was entrusted to Paul. It is not, however, the person of Paul but the message and its faithful

---

10 Donelson, *Pseudepigraphy*, 143.
11 Läger, *Christologie*, especially in the sections on "Soteriologie, Christologie und 'Paulologie'," 175-80, and "Die soteriologische Funktion des Paulus," 128-30.

ministry which are the means by which salvation is mediated. Paul is presented as the authorized bearer of the former (1 Tim 1:11; 2:7; 2 Tim 1:11, 13; 2:2, 8; Titus 1:3) and the primary exemplar for the latter (in 1 Tim 1:1, 12-16; and especially in 2 Tim 1:1, 11-12; 2:8-10; 3:10-11; 4:6-18; this is not such a major emphasis in Titus, although it might be suggested in 1:1). The first is in keeping with the polemical aim of refuting opponents and the second supports the paraenetic goal of encouraging faithful ministry. To suggest, therefore, that the foundational axiom for this author is, *extra Paulum nostrum nulla salus*,[12] is to misrepresent him. He would perhaps rather affirm, *extra evangelium nostrum* (which we learned from Paul) *nulla salus*. Läger is correct, however, to stress the very significant place that each of these letters affords to the transmission of the message of salvation and the findings of our study confirm that the three letters share a conviction that faithful teaching of the authentic message issues in salvation and to that extent participates in the salvation process.

22.2.4 A Decline from Paul?

Some distance between these letters and the Paul of the *Hauptbriefe* is commonly estimated on the grounds of the absence of certain themes held to be central to Paul's understanding of the gospel, the presence of "non-Pauline" terms and of "Pauline" terms with altered significance, and a generally flatter, more static character with much emphasis on the gospel as a fixed body of beliefs. For this study of the soteriology of these letters the pertinent question is not that of authorship as such, but of the compatibility or otherwise of the picture or pictures of salvation that emerge in the PE with what is considered to be an authentic Pauline soteriology.

In the course of the exegesis that has formed the heart of this investigation, the sense of distance from Paul has diminished at a number of points. As well as specific points of correspondence with Paul noted in the exegesis there have been two general tendencies that have served to reduce the impression of otherness relative to the *Hauptbriefe*. One has been the recognition that in each letter the explicitly theological material is for the most part firmly integrated into the thought of that letter and contributes to its paraenetic purpose. On the one hand this requires that the ideas contained in these theological units should be taken seriously as indicative of the author's conceptual framework, which on occasions means crediting him with a "Pauline" thought! On the other, it underscores the occasionality of these letters and reminds the interpreter that the

---

12   Läger, *Christologie*, 177.

author has selected material and themes to support particular paraenetic or polemical objectives.[13] With this in mind, it would be methodologically unsafe to argue from the absence of particular features or themes that these have no place in the author's soteriology, when their omission could simply be due to the fact that other emphases better served his purpose in that particular letter. This recognition of the integration of the soteriological material, then, has given greater credence to the apparently Pauline aspects of thought in the theological pieces and to some extent lessened the force of the argument from the absence of significant Pauline themes.

The other general tendency towards a reduced sense of distance from Paul has come about through considering each letter separately before collating the results of the exegesis for the PE as a whole.[14] This has allowed each to stand independently alongside the Pauline corpus, and in the case of two out of the three at any rate the effect has been to lessen the distance relative to that which is sensed between Paul and a synthesis of the three PE. For 2 Timothy standing alone the distance seems very slight. Here is a concept of salvation that stretches from God's pretemporal purpose and grace to eschatological saving and reward, that focuses upon Jesus Christ, messiah and Lord, who in his death and resurrection destroyed death and opened the kingdom of heaven, and calls the elect to identify themselves with Christ in his death and, by his grace and Spirit, maintain their witness until they are finally saved into his heavenly kingdom.

The short letter of Titus, while employing some novel language, also moves from pretemporal promise to eschatological glory, finding the source of salvation in God's grace and mercy, its achievement in Christ's self-giving to redeem and the giving of new life by the Spirit. Again, when considered independently of the other PE, the language of "justified by grace" resonates with that of Paul and is not contradicted by the practical emphasis on good works as the proper *modus vivendi* of the community whose life is intended to authenticate its message.

---

13 The same pertains, of course, to the *Hauptbriefe*. As Mounce remarks, "A quick look at the acknowledged Pauline letters shows that frequently a theme that is common in one book is of considerably less significance in another, or is totally omitted" (lxxxix, with a table of examples and further discussion on pp. xc-xci).

14 Johnson makes the valid point that the picture is distorted by reading not only the PE but also the undisputed letters of Paul as "composite constructs" (*1 & 2 Timothy*, 82).

Of the three it is 1 Timothy, with its exposition of the general providence of God and the corresponding call to εὐσέβεια, that strikes the reader as the most distant from the Paul of the *Hauptbriefe*. Yet even here the insistence that "everything created by God is good" (1 Tim 4:4) sits comfortably, as Dunn recognizes, with "Paul's essentially Jewish conception of a cosmos which was created good," in which "nothing is unclean in itself" (Rom 14:14).[15] In addition, 1 Timothy, in agreement with Paul, speaks of a particular saving for eternal life that has been made possible by Christ's coming to save sinners, which involved his incarnation and self-giving as a ransom, and is received by those who put their faith in him. There may even be a glimpse, in 2:15, of a salvation-historical substructure that connects Christ's coming to save to the promise that mitigated Eve's curse in Gen 3:15.

While none of the letters provides a comprehensive exposition of Pauline soteriology, there is considerable agreement with Paul on those aspects of salvation that each does reveal.

Comparison at the other end of the time scale with the writings of the Apostolic Fathers has been limited in this study to a few points of detail. In the course of the exegesis of the soteriological passages in the PE, however, correspondences with other NT writings have generally been sufficient to suggest that there is no compelling reason to locate their understanding or presentation of salvation at a later point in time than such canonical books as Acts or 2 Peter. P. W. Barnett concludes his brief survey of salvation in the Apostolic Fathers with this assessment:

> The future salvation brought into the present by the death and resurrection of Jesus Christ, in fulfilment of the prophets, as mediated by the word of the gospel – ideas that are so powerfully stated or implied across the later as well as the earlier NT writings – are muted or absent in the postapostolic literature.[16]

On this criterion, the PE would certainly belong with the NT writings in which these ideas are decidedly present rather than the later literature from which they are absent.

22.3 Principal Exegetical Results and Some Implications

Alongside these general conclusions the detailed exegetical work

---

15 J. D. G. Dunn, *The Theology of Paul the Apostle* (Grand Rapids: Eerdmans, 1998), 39.
16 P. W. Barnett, "Salvation", *DLNTID*, 1072-75, 1075.

Implications for Understanding the PE

undertaken in chapters 2 – 4 has produced a number of findings in relation to particular points and issues. It may therefore be useful to set out some of the principal results of the exegesis, particularly where there are implications for the current scholarly discussion in relation to the understanding of salvation in the PE.

22.3.1 1 Tim 1:1

The relative restraint in the use of the title σωτήρ in early Christian texts, both in the NT and in the writings of the Apostolic Fathers, weighs against the idea that 1 Timothy simply reproduces what had become a stereotyped Christian expression. Here the pairing of θεὸς σωτήρ ἡμῶν with Χριστὸς Ἰησοῦς ἡ ἐλπίς ἡμῶν is found to reflect the rare (contra Spicq) combination of the terms σωτήρ and ἐλπίς in LXX Ps 64:6 [65:5]. This Psalm unusually extends the scope of God's function as Saviour beyond Israel to the ends of the Earth, supplying a background congenial to the author of 1 Timothy's own universalizing instinct.

The notion of ἐλπίς is explicated in terms of that stream of Jewish eschatological hope envisaging resurrection and future life that was claimed and defined christologically by the Lukan Paul in Acts.

Both of these findings challenge the reading of the PE represented by Dibelius-Conzelmann, Easton, Hanson, etc., according to which traditional terms, expressions and units of material that have been utilized in these letters may be regarded as of little account in assessing the author's theological outlook. They give more weight to the Jewish background than allowed by Hasler who understands the PE as expressions of a Hellenized Christianity and, against interpretations influenced by Dibelius-Conzelmann's *christliche Bürgerlichkeit* that stress the preoccupation of these letters with existence in the present world almost to the exclusion of future expectation, a clear eschatological horizon is affirmed.

22.3.2 1 Tim 1:12-17

The notion of Paul as a paradigm of a saved sinner is found to be not entirely satisfactory as a way of explaining the details of the portrait. Wolter's suggestion that Paul is presented here as "der bekherte Gottesfiend" is helpful in pointing the way to an alternative reading, and in the course of the exegesis a focus on Paul as a commissioned blasphemer is detected. Negatively, this cautions against the approach of Knight and others who relate each detail of Paul's story in this passage to the experience of salvation *per se*. Positively, it allows the passage to participate in the letter's strategy in relation to its primary practical concern with the activity of false teachers, modelling the restoration to fruitful Christian service of some presently categorized as blasphemers, faithless and ignorant.

This has the effect of softening the critique of scholars such as Houlden who draw a sharp distinction between the genuine Paul's concept of unmerited saving grace and this apparent mitigation of culpability on the grounds of ignorance.

Links are detected between the presentation of Paul and his experience of saving in 1:12-17 and the characterization in Acts of both Jews who in ignorance opposed Christ and "Gentile sinners."

This passage includes the first occurrence in this letter of the phrase ἐν Χριστῷ Ἰησοῦ. Allan's well known article on "The 'In Christ' Formula in the Pastoral Epistles" misreads this and other instances in the PE of the usage "which is in Christ Jesus" qualifying a noun by comparing it unfavourably with the more personal and ontologically accented "in Christ" expression in Paul. When, however, the usage in the PE is set alongside more similar expressions in the *Hauptbriefe*, Allan's proposed contrast between Paul's mystical union with Christ and the PEs' relating of the believer to abstract qualities loses much of its force.

22.3.3 1 Tim 2:1-7

This is a key text for Dibelius-Conzelmann's description of the general project of the PE as the promotion of a world-accommodating virtuous and quiet life. Philonic usage, however, illustrates a specific religious connotation of ἡσυχία that better fits the context, expressing the hope that rulers will so act that conditions are created for the reception of the Christian message. The suggestion is offered that the concern for εὐσέβεια may reflect particular political circumstances in which Roman *impietas* legislation is being used against Christian groups. Such considerations weigh on the side of finding in this passage a dynamic missionary impulse in engagement with the world in place of Dibelius-Conzelmann's quiet withdrawal.

Again, apparently traditional material is fully integrated into the argument (*contra* Houlden). The statement about God's will to save is explored not through the lens of later theological arguments about divine sovereignty but from the perspective of the Jewish conviction concerning the one true God, which is extended here to affirm that the one God over all is accordingly the one saviour to whom all should look.

Hanson's suggestion that the mediator figure in vv. 5-6 is drawn from the μεσίτης in LXX Job 9:33 is rejected as it fails to explain the link between the mediator idea in v. 5 and the *Hingabemotif* in v. 6. Comparison with Hebrews (supported again by Philonic references) yields a mediatorial concept that includes the priestly functions of sacrifice and intercession, which is judged more appropriate to the setting in 1 Tim 2:1-7.

With regard to the puzzling notion of "witness in its proper time" it is proposed that it should be understood in relation to the eschatological witness to the nations (and to their rulers) found in the apocalyptic tradition in the Synoptic Gospels which has rarely been brought into the discussion of this text. One effect is to invest the present age with specific salvation-historical significance as a time of witness through which the saving will of God was nearing its realization. Again, the atmosphere is of missionary expectancy rather than settled resignation.

22.3.4 1 Tim 2:15

On this much discussed text the suggestion is offered that, having embarked upon a *haggadic* excursus on the Genesis account of the Creation and Fall in response to issues occasioned by the activity and teaching of his opponents, the author resolves the discussion with the broad affirmation that salvation comes to those who continue in faith, lived out in love, holiness and decency. It may well be that he has woven into this concluding affirmation a "faithful word" on the theme of salvation that has application to people generally rather than women specifically.

The statement concerning the saving of the woman "through the childbearing" is referred neither to some activity related to childbearing performed by the women addressed by the author (as concluded by, e.g., Porter, Oberlinner and Marshall) nor to the bearing of the Messiah by Mary (preferred by, e.g., Knight and Stott). Instead the allusion to Genesis ch. 3 is carried over to suggest a reference to the childbearing implied in the promise to Eve in Gen 3:15 that it would be through her offspring (and hence through the now to be painful experience of childbearing) that ultimately the serpent would be defeated. This serves the author's polemical purpose of defending the activity of procreation against ascetic disapproval while also hinting at a salvation-historical framework.

This reading, then, explains the childbearing reference in terms of the continuing *haggadic* excursus and finds in the final conditional clause a much more conventional understanding of the way to salvation than is sometimes taken from this passage.

22.3.5 1 Tim 4:10

Despite the popularity of Skeat's proposal that the term μάλιστα may be taken as "that is" rather than "especially," so that God may be understood as saviour of one category of people, namely, believers, the reading adopted here reverts to the latter interpretation. It is consistent with the general outlook of 1 Timothy to present God as saviour of all in the sense that he is the one God from whom all good things come. Alongside this affirmation, however, lies the conviction that this God has made available an eschatological salvation into eternal life, and this is received by those who believe.

The concept of the "living God" is held to be significant, indicating a conceptual framework derived from the faith of Judaism and not only identifying the God of Israel as the only genuine deity but, especially in the phrase, ἐκκλησία θεοῦ ζῶντος (3:15), evoking OT images of the gathering of the People of God to worship and obey him. This heightens the inclusivist character of 1 Timothy, which is again found to extend the benefits and privileges of the OT People of God to Christian believers. Other hints are detected of links with the book of Deuteronomy and its setting of the instruction of the community by its leader prior to his departure. Again, 1 Timothy is discovered to move in a world shaped by the OT.

22.3.6 1 Tim 4:16

This statement begins with another Deuteronomic warning, "Watch yourself!" Against Easton, Hanson, Merkel and others who find the exhortation markedly un-Pauline, suggesting that it is within the power of a human being to "save", it is found that the stress lies on the message. The agent's task is to be faithful in communicating it so that both he and those who hear may through faith in it come to salvation. This accords with the missionary urgency already detected (supporting Ho's reading of the PE), and, as Oberlinner points out, the importance of the role of teaching and preaching in the church is underlined.

22.3.7 2 Tim 1:9-14

Although this and certain other passages are sometimes regarded as units of material that is more Pauline than the letter as a whole (see e.g. Bassler), the thought and language are thoroughly integrated with the rest of the letter and there is no reason to separate off its theological content. The exegesis demonstrates the paraenetic force of the material in its call to faithful and costly service.

The "calling", consonant with the calling of the servant of the Lord in Isaiah, is both to belong to God and to ministry. Hasler's reduction of the concept of grace to the condescension of a Hellenistic divine Benefactor is unnecessary and unjustified. The context establishes a strong antithesis between "works" and God's "purpose and grace" in a manner quite consistent with Paul.

The term "kairological" is suggested as descriptive of the time frame that emerges from the exegesis, encompassing the pre-temporal decision and gift of God, its manifestation in time and present proclamation. Elsewhere in 2 Timothy a further, future dimension that reaches beyond the present into a heavenly reality is presented.

The concept of *epiphany* both here and throughout the PE has been much studied. Against the consensus, the present study does not find a consistent epiphany Christology or two-epiphany schema in the PE. Rather, the exegesis of the various texts discovers that the epiphany language (ἐπιφάνεια, φαίνω) is used with differing connotations and referents. Here in 2 Tim 1:10 the most satisfactory explanation of the term seems to be in relation to Christ's post-resurrection appearances, declaring victory over death (supporting a little noticed suggestion by Spicq).

The role of the gospel in the continuing manifestation of this achievement and its results has been interpreted by some as an example of realized eschatology (e.g. Dibelius-Conzelmann). This, however, fails to take account of the letter's striking consciousness of a future dimension to the story of salvation (e.g. vv. 10b, 12).

The unit's paraenetic purpose is to urge unashamed and costly witness by the power of God. These are themes which run throughout this letter. The concept of shame is not as wholly Hellenistic as, e.g., Bassler would suggest, but picks up the OT conviction that those who put their trust in the Lord will not be put to shame. In this letter the concept receives an eschatological colouring.

22.3.8 2 Tim 2:8-13

The indication of the content of "my Gospel" invites comparison with Paul's summary in Rom 1:3-4. This study, however, draws into the discussion the representation of Paul's missionary preaching in Acts 13:16-41. Read alongside this material, 2 Tim 2:8 is seen to pick up the key points of the Lukan Paul's missionary message about

Christ, namely that his resurrection demonstrates that he is indeed Israel's promised messiah, of the line of David.

Again the Deuteronomic call to "remember" may be heard in the background of the charge to Timothy, suggesting a testamentary occasion within an OT conceptual framework.

As is the case with other formulaic material, the theological content of this unit has sometimes been relegated to "no more than a slogan" (Houlden). It is quite arbitrary, however, to pass over the indications in the letter that the resurrection of Christ played a significant role in the author's understanding of the Christian faith and in the personal paraenesis that appeals to it.

Here and in other parts of 2 Timothy connections may be drawn between the depictions of suffering and its outcomes and the endurance and achievement of the Maccabean martyrs, particularly in 4 Maccabees. This and other observations serve to root some of the terms, ideas and attitudes evident in this letter firmly within Judaism.

The exegesis of the hymn (vv. 11-13) decides in favour of a distinction between the last two protatic conditions (εἰ ἀρνησόμεθα and εἰ ἀπιστοῦμεν) allowing the final word to be of confidence in Christ's faithfulness, echoing the similar confidence expressed in 2:9-10.

22.3.9 2 Tim 3:14-17

Issue is taken here with Knight's characteristic assumption that the content of a theological term in the PE may be supplied from its use elsewhere in the NT. Nonetheless, in this instance, examination of σωτηρία in its context does yield an understanding of salvation consonant as far as may be discerned with a more general NT concept of salvation that is the outcome of faith in Christ. Hasler's reduction of the OT to a handbook of ecclesiastical piety does not do justice to this letter's depiction of a Christian belief system extended from but still in continuity with OT faith and aspirations, realized in the one who came of the seed of David.

22.3.10 2 Tim 4:16-18

In agreement with many commentators, the exegesis of this passage finds two "savings", one temporal and the other eternal. The temporal rescue, however, is seen to bear soteriological significance as an illustration of that empowerment for faithful and costly witness that reflects the paraenetic thrust of the letter as a whole. Various OT backgrounds to this passage have been suggested, but an exploration of Daniel's paradigmatic rescue from the lion's mouth as appropriated in 1 Maccabees uncovers further fresh evidence of the correspondence between the qualities commended in 2 Timothy with the thought world of Intertestamental Judaism.

The rescue from πᾶν ἔργον πονηρόν has been explained as an adaptation of the Lord's Prayer (e.g. by Knight, Guthrie), but it is read here against the more general background of the apocalyptic concept of the Last Days and their characteristic opposition to Christ and his servants.

There is no need to follow Barrett and Hanson in discovering in these verses a belief that Paul will survive until the *parousia*. The confidence declared is in a final saving that transcends death.

22.3.11 Titus 1:1-4

In the opening sentence of the letter to Titus the first of three pairings of σωτήρ predications of both God and Christ is encountered. Far from indicating indiscriminate use of traditional material this suggests an intentional identification of Christ with God in the realization of salvation.

The idea inherent in πρὸ χρόνων αἰωνίων has proved puzzling to commentators on account of the apparent juxtaposition of a promise (presumably given to someone within time) and its location before time. The exegesis draws on Malina's sociological description of the first century Mediterranean world's ideas of "experienced time" and "imaginary time" to cut the Gordian knot and understand the time reference as not so much "dating" a divine event as relating it to that sphere of existence known only to the eternal God.

With regard to the characterization of Paul as a "servant of God", Marshall correctly points out that the phrase δοῦλος θεοῦ is relatively rare in the LXX. A plausible OT background is found, however, in the designation of Moses in particular as the "Servant of the LORD" from whose teaching the younger successor, Joshua, derived his instructions and authorization. In this complex opening sentence of the letter to Titus there is scope for differing opinions on how exactly Paul's apostleship relates to the hope of eternal life. The most satisfactory reading of the syntactical chain of ideas, however, finds eternal life to be the goal of Paul's ministry and of the faith that he taught rather than his personal motivation (as preferred by, e.g., Hinson and Knight). By their derivation from both God and Christ as saviour, the salvific character of the ministries of Paul and Titus is established.

22.3.12 Titus 2:11-14

The soterial appearing of grace has attracted a range of interpretations from the personification of a divine quality (as in Mott's work) to the incarnation (e.g. Lau, Houlden, etc.). In the present study it is taken as the making known of the message of God's grace including the proclamation by Christ and the continuing teaching concerning him. Here agreement is found with Hasler who understands the training in v. 12 as the *Heilspädogogik* ministered by the church's teachers. the theme of right or health-giving teaching is of great importance in this letter.

The precise focus of hope in these verses is difficult to pin down, with several grammatical possibilities. The observation that in certain Hellenistic Jewish literature the language and ideas of epiphany and majesty are frequently juxtaposed prompts the suggestion that the language of this piece may be more pictorial than grammatically precise, creating an impression of glorious majesty. What is clear is that for this author salvation awaits eschatological completion.

Mott relates the triad of adverbs in v. 12 to the cardinal virtues of Hellenistic philosophy, finding a similar grouping in 4 Maccabees. At least as significant as this comparison, however, is the striking contrast: 4 Maccabees envisages the attaining of the virtues through training in the Law whereas Titus speaks of training by grace.

In the course of the exegesis it is discovered that several soteriological concepts appear twice in this unit, first in language and thought forms appropriate to the Hellenistic environment and then in formulations shaped by the OT ideas by which Christian convictions were first expressed. The proposal is made that this represents an intentional translation of the latter into the former in the context of missionary discourse, retaining primitive Christian affirmations while at the same time interpreting them for a non-Jewish audience by means of equivalent ideas intelligible within the general Hellenistic environment.

22.3.13 Titus 3:1-8

The detection of a chiastic structure aids the interpretation of this passage, with the thought centred on the affirmation, "he saved us" (v. 5). The chiasm begins (2:15-3:2) and ends (3:8-11) with practical exhortations to deal with opponents and to teach the Christian believers to live ethically attractive lives. The explication of salvation provides the basis for such teaching and its hope of success.

One matter of debate is whether the language of saving should be referred to individual experience (with, e.g., Haykin) or to the church as a corporate entity (as Mounce prefers). It is read in this study as confessional language that permits worshippers both to confess their community's faith and to interpret their individual experience in the same terms.

This passage is representative of the letter to Titus in its reiterated concern that the Christians should perform good works. Holding together the paraenetic with the confessional elements, however, it emerges that the author both shares Paul's conviction that salvation is an unmerited gift and sees the practical urgency of behavioural transformation in a setting of mission and witness.

22.4 Suggestions for Further Investigation

As argued above, the findings of this study suggest that it might prove fruitful to apply the same method, of hearing each letter on its own terms and interpreting its message within the framework set by its own internal coherence, to the study of other aspects of the theology and concerns of these letters. Could it be that when the particular voice of each has been more distinctly heard it will seem as unsatisfactory to make sweeping generalisations about "the Pastoral Epistles" as it would be to attempt a synthetic account of the content and purpose of "the Prison Epistles"? When a more distinct profile of each of the three PE emerges it may be time to revisit the question of the relationship of each separately to the Pauline corpus – or, more satisfactorily, to particular examples of the historical Paul's correspondence shaken loose from their absorption into the "composite construct" of the "undisputed Paulines." That will also be the appropriate point at which to explore afresh the points of contact and contrast between the three letters in relation to the items of shared vocabulary, the implied situations, the paraenetic goals and theological outlooks.

There is already a considerable body of work on the tradition histories of the various soteriological materials, to which it has been beyond the scope of this project to add. Certain features have emerged, however, which may repay further investigation. The two πιστοὶ λόγοι in 1 Timothy (1:15; 2:15-3:1) seem to be sayings about salvation that are woven into the argument of each passage. In each case a somewhat Johannine flavour was noticed, with the references to Christ coming into the κόσμος and salvation for those who remain (μένω) in faith. Was there perhaps a collection of sayings in circulation that, originating in a Johannine group, had now wider currency within early Christianity?[17] It is especially intriguing in view of the traditional association of both Johannine Christianity and 1 Timothy with Ephesus. There may be a hint here of a confluence of Pauline and Johannine streams suggesting a degree of intercommunication between various early Christian groups.[18] Further correspondences emerging in the exegesis that could be explored include those between the Pauline gospel as represented in 2 Timothy and the Lukan tradition of Paul's missionary preaching, and between 2 Timothy's depiction of Paul's suffering and the martyrological literature and ideals of the Maccabean tradition.

Finally, uncertainties about dating and provenance have made it difficult to relate these documents to specific historical and political settings, but they must nonetheless have been produced at particular points in the early history of the Christian movement. As such they will have been affected in some way by specific socio-political realities. One such dimension that has been relatively unexplored is the Roman Empire's *Impietas* legislation and its implications for the church at different points in time and in various parts of the Roman world. It was suggested in the study of 1 Tim 2:1-7 that this background may help to explain the differing stances taken in 1 Timothy and 2 Timothy with regard to εὐσέβεια (*pietas*). Further historical investigation might uncover more specific possibilities. With regard to Titus historical study of Roman Crete might allow the suggestion to be tested that aspects of the instruction contained in the letter might be related to a specific form of social organisation on the island. If that should prove to be the case the letter to Titus would provide material for a missiological study of an early Christian approach to mission in a particular and distinctive setting.[19] Along with Crete's social structure the link between Crete and Alexandria might be explored, particularly the place of Alexandrian Judaism in the social and religious context for Christian mission on Crete.

---

17 The issue of the common traditions in John and Luke may have a bearing on this wider question.
18 For a reconstruction drawing on evidence in the PE and the Johannine literature see Paul Trebilco, *The Early Christians in Ephesus from Paul to Ignatius* (WUNT 166, Tübingen: Mohr Siebeck, 2004).
19 For some intitial reflections on this topic see George M. Wieland, "Grace Manifest: Missional Church in the Letter to Titus", *Stimulus* 13.1 (2005): 8-11.

22.5 Concluding Summary

This study of salvation in the PE has confirmed the importance of this theme for each of these letters. Not only is salvation language prevalent, but in all three letters the concept of salvation plays a vital role in relation to the letter's purpose. The three share a soteriological outlook that exhibits to varying degrees a salvation-historical framework, in which salvation has its origin in the purpose of God, is implemented through the historic Christ-event, continues to be realized existentially through the proclamation of the message of salvation and a response of faith, and will reach its consummation in the gift of eternal life at Christ's return. They agree that this salvation is universally available but is received by those who believe the gospel and orientate their lives to its eschatological promise and present ethical demands.

Within this broad outline, however, each of the three letters makes its own use of soteriological concepts to address particular concerns and advance specific interests. In 1 Timothy the presentation has a polemical edge, countering heterodox teaching of an exclusivist, ascetic character that has gained a foothold in the church by stressing the universality of the scope of salvation, insisting that the saviour God of Israel is the one God and saviour of all, celebrating his benevolent provision of a good creation while pointing beyond the present age to a future of even greater worth for those who respond in faith to the message about Christ which is to be preached to all. The concern in 2 Timothy is paraenetic, urging the exercise of faithful, costly ministry in the face of harsh opposition which may even extend to physical death. In this context it is not the enjoyment of salvation here and now but the prospect of eschatological reward that is emphasized, together with the promise of grace and empowerment for faithfulness and the assurance that God himself is watching over his saving purpose and will fulfil it, whatever may happen to his servants in the present age. For Titus, the establishment of missionary congregations calls for the nurturing of a clear sense of Christian identity and community. This is found in the appropriation of OT soteriological categories for the Christian believers and an emphasis on the present ethical transformation that marks out these believers from both the general society of which they were once part and rival teachers and their followers. In this missionary context bold steps are taken to express in terms accessible to a non-Jewish Hellenistic audience salvation concepts that had their origin in Judaism.

In three distinct ways, then, the letters to Timothy and Titus address challenges facing the church and its mission by setting their various situations within a soteriological framework which, insofar as it can be uncovered from what is affirmed, expounded or seems to be assumed, is consistent in outline with that of the earlier Pauline letters. It is this framework that makes the paraenesis effective, as readers are urged on the basis of soteriological convictions to resist inward-looking, restrictive tendencies within the church and hold to a gospel universal in scope (1 Timothy), to continue faithful in the ministry of the gospel despite opposition and apparent set-backs (2 Timothy), and to nurture missionary communities whose lifestyle would serve as a demonstration of the saving efficacy of the message of God's grace (Titus).

The study has affirmed the internal coherence of each of the letters, specifically in the integration of soteriological material into their structures of argumentation in support of their paraenetic goals, while taking issue with the common assumption that the three letters are most satisfactorily read as a unified corpus. The *christliche Bürgerlichkeit* interpretation has again been found to be inadequate as an explanation of the perspective of the PE, and nor is there support for the notion of a soteriological schema that promotes salvation through the cult, as represented by an institutionalized church, its authorized leaders and its sacraments. Rather, those theological elements that may be discerned are in each case congruent with a Pauline perspective, and the particular emphases and form of each presentation are explicable in terms of three separate situations with their distinct pastoral and missiological challenges.

Bibliography

Primary Sources

Babbitt, F. C. *Plutarch*. LCL. London, 1962.
Boeckh, A., ed. *Corpus inscriptionum graecarum*. 4 vols. Berlin, 1828-77.
Cary, E. *Dionysius of Halicarnassus*. 7 vols. LCL. London, 1961.
Charlesworth, James H., ed. *The Old Testament Pseudepigrapha*. 2 vols. London: Dartman, Longman & Todd, 1983-85.
Clay, Diskin. *Lucretius and Epicurus*. New York: Cornell University Press, 1983.
Colson, F. H., G. H. Whittaker, and R. Marcus. *Philo*. 12 vols. LCL. London, 1929-62.
Gulick, C. B. *Athenaeus*. 7 vols. LCL. London, 1961.
Gummere, R. M. *Seneca: Ad Lucilium Epistulae Morales*. 3 vols. LCL. London, 1962.
Halbherr, Friedrich. *Inscriptiones Creticae: Opera et Consilio Friderici Halbherr Collectae*. 4 vols. Edited by Margherita Guarducci. Roma: Reale istituto di archeologia e storia dell'arte, 1935-50.
Hicks, R. D. *Diogenes Laertius*. 2 vols. LCL. London, 1965-66.
Hunt, A. S. and C. C. Edgar, *Select Papyri II. Non-Literary Papyri: Public Documents*. LCL, London, 1977.
Jones, H. L. *Strabo: The Geography*. 8 vols. LCL. London, 1959.
Klauck, Hans-Josef. *4 Makkabäerbuch*. Jüdische Schriften aus hellenistischer-römischer Zeit 3.6. Gütersloh: Gerd Mohn, 1989.
Lake, K. *The Apostolic Fathers*. 2 vols. LCL. London, 1912-13.
Oldfather, W. A. *Epictetus*. 2 vols. LCL. London, 1966-67.
Paton, W. R. *Polybius: The Histories*. 6 vols. LCL. London, 1922-27 (repr. 1960-67).
Rice, David G. and John E. Stambaugh. *Sources for the Study of Greek Religion*. Society of Biblical Literature Sources for Biblical Study 14. Missoula, Mont.: Scholars Press, 1979.
Tatum, James. *Apuleius and the Golden Ass*. Ithaca: Cornell University Press, 1979.
Thackeray, H. St. J. et al. *Josephus*. 10 vols. LCL. London, 1926-63.
Vanderlip, Vera Frederika. *The Four Greek Hymns of Isodorus and the Cult of Isis*. American Studies in Papyrology 12. Toronto: Hakkert, 1972.
Walton, F. R. *Diodorus of Sicily*. 12 vols. LCL. London, 1967.

Secondary Literature

Achtmeier, Paul J., Joel B. Green, and Marianne M. Thompson, eds. *Introducing the New Testament: its Literature and Theology*. Grand Rapids: Eerdmans, 2001.

Aland, K. *Vollständige Konkordanz zum griechischen Neuen Testament*. 3 vols. Berlin: de Gruyter, 1978-83.

Allan, John A. "The 'In Christ' Formula in the Pastoral Epistles." *New Testament Studies* 10 (1963): 115-121.

Allen, James. "The Skepticism of Sextus Empiricus." *ANRW* 36.4: 2582-2607. Part 2, *Principat*, 36.4. Edited by H. Temporini and W. Haase. Berlin: W. de Gruchy, 1990.

Anderson, H. "4 Maccabees: A New Translation and Introduction." Pages 531-64 in vol. 2 of *The Old Testament Pseudepigrapha*. 2 vols. Edited by James H. Charlesworth. London: Dartman, Longman & Todd, 1983-85.

Arnold, Clinton E. *Ephesians: Power and Magic: The Concept of Power in Ephesians in the Light of its Historical Setting*. Society for New Testament Study Monograph Series 63. Cambridge: Cambridge University Press, 1989

Asmis, Elizabeth. "Philodemus' Epicureanism." *ANRW* 36.4: 2369-2406. Part 2, *Principat*, 36.4. Edited by H. Temporini and W. Haase. Berlin: W. de Gruchy, 1990.

Aune, David E. "Hercules and Christ: Hercules Imagery in the Christology of Early Christianity." Pages 3-19 in *Greeks, Romans and Christians: Essays in Honor of Abraham J. Malherbe*. Edited by D. L. Balch, E. Ferguson, and W. A. Meeks. Minneapolis: Fortress, 1990.

Avotins, Ivars. "Training in Frugality in Epicurus and Seneca." *Phoenix* 31 (1977): 214-217.

Bagatti, Fr. Bellarmino, O.F.M. *The Church from the Circumcision: History and Archaeology of the Judeo-Christians*. Translated by Fr. Eugene Hoade, O.F.M. Publications of the Studium Biblicum Fanciscanum, Smaller Series 2. Jerusalem: Franciscan, 1971.

Bailey, Cyril. *Epicurus: The Extant Remains*. Oxford: Clarendon, 1926.

Balch, David L. "The Areopagus Speech. An Appeal to the Stoic Historian Posidonius against Later Stoics and the Epicureans." Pages 52-79 in *Greeks, Romans and Christians: Essays in Honor of Abraham J. Malherbe*. Edited by D. L. Balch, E. Ferguson, and W. A. Meeks. Minneapolis: Fortress, 1990.

- *Let Wives be Submissive: The Domestic Code in 1 Peter*. Society of Biblical Literature: Monograph Series 26. Atlanta, Ga: Scholars, 1981.
- Review of L. R. Donelson, *Pseudepigraphy and Ethical Argument in the Pastoral Epistles, Journal of Religion* 69 (1989): 235-7

Barnes, Jonathan. "Hellenistic Philosophy and Science." Pages 365-85 in

The Oxford History of the Classical World. Edited by John Boardman, Jasper Griffin, and Oswyn Murray. Oxford: Oxford University Press, 1986.

- "Pyrrhonism, Belief and Causation. Observations on the Scepticism of Sextus Empiricus." *ANRW* 36.4: 2608-2695. Part 2, *Principat*, 36.4. Edited by H. Temporini and W. Haase. Berlin: W. de Gruchy, 1990.

Barnett, P. W. "Salvation." Pages 1072-75 in *Dictionary of the Later New Testament and Its Developments*. Edited by Ralph P. Martin and Peter H. Davids. Downers Grove: IVP, 1997.

Barr, David L. *New Testament Story: An Introduction*. 2nd. ed., Belmont: Wadsworth Publishing Company, 1995.

Barrett, C. K. *The Acts of the Apostles*, vol. 1. International Critical Commentary. Edinburgh: T&T Clark, 1994.

- *A Commentary on the First Epistle to the Corinthians*. Black's New Testament Commentaries. 2nd ed., London: A&C Black, 1971.
- "Deuteropauline Ethics: Some Observations." Pages 161-72 in *Theology and Ethics in Paul and His Interpreters*. Edited by E. H. Lovering Jr., and J. L. Sumney. Nashville: Abingdon, 1996.
- "Jews and Judaizers in the Epistles of Ignatius." Pages 220-244 in *Jews, Greeks and Christians*. Studies in Judaism in Late Antiquity 21. Leiden: Brill, 1976.
- *The Pastoral Epistles*. New Clarendon Bible. Oxford: Clarendon, 1963.
- "Pauline Controversies in the Post-Pauline Period." *New Testament Studies 20 (1973-74): 229-45.*

Barth, Markus. *The People of God*. Journal for the Study of the New Testament Supplement Series 5. Sheffield: Sheffield Academic Press, 1983.

Bassler, Jouette M. *1 Timothy, 2 Timothy, Titus*. Abingdon New Testament Commentaries. Nashville: Abingdon, 1996.

- "'He remains faithful' (2 Tim 2:13a)." Pages 173-83 in *Theology and Ethics in Paul and His Interpreters*. Edited by E. H. Lovering Jr., and J. L. Sumney. Nashville: Abingdon, 1996.
- "The Widow's Tale: a Fresh Look at 1 Tim 5:3-16." *Journal of Biblical Literature* 103 (1984): 23-41.

Bauer, W., W. F. Arndt, F. W. Gingrich, and F. W. Danker. *Greek-English Lexicon of the New Testament and Other Early Christian Literature*. 2nd. ed. Chicago: University of Chicago Press, 1979.

Baugh, Steven M. "The Apostle among the Amazons." *Westminster Theological Journal* 56 (1994): 153-71.

- "'Savior of all people': 1 Tim. 4:10 in Context." *Westminster Theological Journal* 54 (1992): 331-40.

Bauman, Richard A. *Impietas in Principem: A Study of Treason against the Roman Emperor with Special Reference to the First Century A.D.* Münchener Beiträge zur Papyrusforschung und antiken

Rechtsgeschichte 67. München: C.H. Beck, 1974.
Beasley-Murray, George R. *Baptism in the New Testament*. London: Macmillan, 1963.
- *Jesus and the Kingdom of God*. Grand Rapids: Eerdmans, 1986.
Beker, J. Christiaan. *Heirs of Paul: Paul's Legacy in the New Testament and in the Church Today*. Minneapolis: Fortress, 1991.
- "The Pastoral Epistles: Paul and We." Pages 265-72 in *Text and Logos: The Humanistic Interpretation of the New Testament*. Edited by T. W. Jennings Jr. Atlanta: Scholars Press, 1990.
- "Paul the Theologian: Major Motifs in Pauline Theology." *Interpretation* 43 (1989): 352-65.
Bell, Richard H. "Rom 5.18-19 and universal Salvation." *New Testament Studies* 48 (2002): 417-32.
Bénétreau, S. *L'Épître aux Hébreux*. vol. 2. Vaux-sur-Seine: Édifac, 1990
Berger, Klaus and Carsten Colpe. *Religiongeschichtliches Textbuch zum Neuen Testament*. Das Neue Testament Deutsch: Textreihe 1. Göttingen: Vandenhoeck & Ruprecht, 1987.
Bickerman, Elias J. *The Jews in the Greek Age*. Cambridge, Mass.: Harvard University Press, 1988.
Boardman, John and N. G. L. Hammond, eds. *The Cambridge Ancient History*. Vol. 3.3. 2nd. ed. Cambridge: Cambridge University Press, 1982.
Boardman, John, Jasper Griffin, and Oswyn Murray, eds. *The Oxford History of the Classical World*. Oxford: Oxford University Press, 1986.
Boatwright, Mary T. "The Imperial Women of the Early 2nd Century AD." *American Journal of Philology* 112 (1991): 513-540.
Bockmuehl, Marcus. "'The trumpet shall sound': Shofar Symbolism and its Reception in Early Christianity." Pages 199-225 in *TEMPLUM AMICITAE: Essays on the Second Temple Presented to Ernst Bummel*. Edited by W. Horbury. Journal for the Study of the New Testament Supplement Series 48. Sheffield: Sheffield Academic Press, 1991.
de Boer, Martinus C. *The Defeat of Death: Apocalyptic Eschatology in 1 Corinthians 15 and Romans 5*. Journal for the Study of the New Testament Supplement Series 22. Shefield: Sheffield Academic Press, 1988.
- "Images of Paul in the Post-Apostolic Period." *Catholic Biblical Quarterly* 42 (1980): 359-80.
Borchert, G.L. "Light and Darkness." Pages 555-57 in *Dictionary of Paul and His Letters*. Edited by Gerald F. Hawthorne, and Ralph P. Martin. Downers Grove: IVP, 1993.
Borse, Udo. *1. und 2. Timotheusbrief/Titusbrief*. Stuttgarter Kleiner Kommentar Neues Testament 13. Stuttgart: Katholisches Bibelwerk, 1985.
Bowie, A. "Religion and Politics in Aeschylus' ORESTEIA." *The Classical*

Quarterly ns 43 (1993): 10-31.

Brandon, S. G. F., ed. *The Saviour God: Comparative Studies in the Concept of Salvation Presented to Edwin Oliver James*. Manchester: Manchester University Press, 1963.

Branick, Vincent. *The House Church in the Writings of Paul*. Zacchaeus Studies: New Testament. Wilmington, Del.: Michael Glazier, 1989.

Bratcher, Robert G. *A Translator's Guide to Paul's Letters to Timothy and to Titus*. London: United Bible Societies, 1983.

Brecher, Kenneth, and Michael Feirtag, eds. *Astronomy of the Ancients*. Cambridge, Mass.: MIT Press, 1979.

Breitenstein, Urs. *Beobachtungen zu Sprache, Stil und Gedankengt des Vierten Makkabäerbuchs*. Basel: Schwabe, 1976.

Bremner, J. "Paederasty," *Arethusa* 13 (1980): 279-98.

Brown, Colin, ed. *New International Dictionary of New Testament Theology*. 3 vols. Exeter: Paternoster, 1975-78.

Brown, Raymond E. *The Gospel According to John*. 2 vols. British ed. Anchor Bible 29-29A. London: Geoffrey Chapman, 1971 (New York: Doubleday, 1966-70).

Brox, Norbert. *Die Pastoralbriefe*. Regensburger Neues Testament 7. Regensburg: Friedrich Pustet, 1969.

Bruce, F. F. *The Book of Acts*. 2nd ed. New London Commentary. London: Marshall, Morgan & Scott, 1972.

- *The Epistle to the Hebrews*. London: Marshall, Morgan & Scott, 1965.
- *Galatians*. New International Greek Testament Commentary. Grand Rapids: Eerdmans, 1982.
- "'Our God and Saviour': a Recurring Biblical Pattern." Pages 51-66 in *The Saviour God: Comparative Studies in the Concept of Salvation Presented to Edwin Oliver James*. Edited by S. G. F. Brandon. Manchester: Manchester University Press, 1963.

Bultmann, R. *Theology of the New Testament*. Translated by K. Grobel. Vol. 2. London: SCM, 1955.

Burkert, Walter. *Ancient Mystery Cults*, Cambridge, Mass.: Harvard University Press, 1987.

- - - *Greek Religion, Archaic and Classical*. Translated by John Raffan. Oxford: Basil Blackwell, 1985.

Burnett, F.W. "Παλιγγενεσία in Matthew 19:28: A Window on the Matthean Community?" *Journal for the Study of the New Testament* 17 (1983): 60-72.

- "Philo on Immortality: A Thematic Study of Philo's Concept of παλιγγενεσία." *Catholic Biblical Quarterly* 46 (1984): 447-70.

Campbell, R. A. "Identifying the Faithful Sayings in the Pastoral Epistles." *Journal for the Study of the New Testament* 54 (1994): 73-86.

- "ΚΑΙ ΜΑΛΙΣΤΑ ΟΙΚΕΙΩΝ - a New Look at 1 Timothy 5:8." *New Testament Studies* 41 (1995): 157-160.

Cargal, T. B. "Seated in the Heavenlies: Cosmic Mediators in the Mysteries of Mithras and the Letter to the Ephesians." *Society of Biblical Literature Seminar Papers* 33 (1994): 804-21.

Carlson, R. P. "The Disputed Letters of Paul." Pages 110-20 in *The New Testament Today*. Edited by Mark A. Powell. Louisville Ky.: Westminster John Knox, 1999.

Caulley, T. S. "Fighting the Good Fight: The Pastoral Epistles in Canonical-Critical Perspective." *Society of Biblical Literature Seminar Papers* 26 (1987): 550-64.

Chae, Daniel J.-S. *Paul as Apostle to the Gentiles: His Apostolic Self-Awareness and its Influence on the Soteriological Argument in Romans*. Paternoster Biblical and Theological Monographs. Carlisle: Paternoster, 1997.

Charlesworth, James H. *The Pseudepigrapha and Modern Research*. Septuagint and Cognate Studies 7. Missoula, Mont.: Scholars Press, 1976.

Childs, B. S. *Exodus*. Old Testament Library. London: SCM, 1974.

Chilton, Bruce, and Jacob Neusner. *Judaism in the New Testament: Practices and Beliefs*. London: Routledge, 1995.

Clarke, Andrew D. and Bruce W. Winter, eds. *One God, One Lord in a World of Religious Pluralism*. Cambridge: Tyndale House, 1991.

Clay, Diskin. "The Philosophical Inscription of Diogenes of Oenoanda: New Discoveries 1969-1983." *ANRW* 36.4: 2446-2559. Part 2, *Principat*, 36.4. Edited by H. Temporini and W. Haase. Berlin: W. de Gruchy, 1990.

Clements, Ronald E. "'A Remnant Chosen by Grace' (Romans 11:5): The Old Testament Background and Origin of the Remnant Concept." Pages 106-21 in *Pauline Studies*. Edited by Donald A. Hagner, and Murray J. Harris. Exeter: Paternoster, 1980.

Collins, Raymond F. "The Image of Paul in the Pastorals." *Laval théologique et philosophique* 31 (1975): 147-73.

Colson, F. H. "'Myths and Genealogies' - A Note on the Polemic of the Pastoral Epistles." *Journal of Theological Studies* 19 (1917/18): 265-71.

Cook, David. "2 Timothy 4:6-8 and the Epistle to the Philippians." *Journal of Theological Studies* ns 33 (1982): 168-71.

- "The Pastoral Fragments Reconsidered." *Journal of Theological Studies* ns 35 (1984): 120-31.

Coupland, S. "Salvation Through Childbearing? The Riddle of 1 Timothy 2:15." *Expository Times* 119 (2001): 302-03.

Couser, Greg A. "God and Christian Existence in 1 and 2 Timothy and Titus." Ph.D. diss., University of Aberdeen, 1992.

- "'The testimony about our Lord', 'Borne by the Lord', or Both?", *Tyndale Bulletin* 55.2 (2004): 295-316.

Cranfield, C. E. B. *The Gospel According to Mark*. 3rd impression with

additional supplementary notes. Cambridge Greek Testament Commentary. Cambridge: Cambridge University Press, 1966, 1955.
Cullmann, O. *Baptism in the New Testament*. Translated by J. K. S. Reid. Studies in Biblical Theology 1. London: SCM, 1950.
Davies, Margaret. *The Pastoral Epistles*. Epworth Commentaries. London: Epworth, 1996.
- *The Pastoral Epistles*. New Testament Guides. Sheffield: Sheffield Academic Press, 1996.
Dawson-Walker, D. *The Epistle to the Colossians and the Epistle to Titus*, The Devotional Commentary. London: Religious Tract Society, n.d.
De Laix, Roger Alain. *Probouleusis at Athens: A Study of Political Decision-Making*. University of California Publications in History 83. Berkeley: University of California Press, 1973.
Derrett, J. D. M. "Palingenesia." *Journal of Theological Studies* ns 20 (1984): 51-58.
De Lestapis, S., S.J. *L'Énigme des Pastorales de Saint Paul*. Paris: Gabalda, 1976.
Detienne, Marcel, and Jean-Pierre Vernant. *Cunning Intelligence in Greek Culture and Society*. Translated by Janet Lloyd. Sussex: Harvester, 1978.
DeWitt, Norman Wentworth. *Epicurus and His Philosophy*. Minneapolis: University of Minnesota Press, 1954.
Dibelius, Martin, and Hans Conzelmann. *A Commentary on the Pastoral Epistles*. Translated by Philip Buttolph and Adela Yarbo. Hermeneia. Philadelphia: Fortress, 1972. Translation of Martin Dibelius. *Die Pastoralbriefe*. 4th rev. ed. By Hans Conzelmann. Handbuch zum Neuen Testament 13. Tübingen: J. C. B. Mohr, 1966.
Dillistone, F. W. *The Significance of the Cross*, London: Lutterworth, 1945.
Donelson, Lewis R. *Colossians, Ephesians, 1 and 2 Timothy, and Titus*. Westminster Bible Companion. Louisville, Ky.: Westminster John Knox, 1996.
- *Pseudepigraphy and Ethical Argument in the Pastoral Epistles*. Hermeneutische Untersuchungen zur Theologie 22. Tübingen: J. C. B. Mohr, 1986.
Dorandi, Tiziano. "Filodemo: gli orientamenti della ricerca attuale." *ANRW* 36.4: 2328-68. Part 2, *Principat*, 36.4. Edited by H. Temporini and W. Haase. Berlin: W. de Gruchy, 1990.
- "Filodemo storico del pensiero antico." *ANRW* 36.4: 2407-23. Part 2, *Principat*, 36.4. Edited by H. Temporini and W. Haase. Berlin: W. de Gruchy, 1990.
Dunn, J. D. G. *Baptism in the Holy Spirit*. Philadelphia: Westminster, 1970.
- "Echoes of Intra-Jewish Polemic in Paul's Letter to the Galatians." *Journal of Biblical Literature* 112 (1993): 459-477.

- *Jesus and the Spirit: A Study of the Religious and Charismatic Experience of Jesus and the First Christians as Reflected in the New Testament.* London: SCM, 1975.
- ed. *Jews and Christians: The Parting of the Ways A.D. 70-135.* 2nd Durham-Tübingen Research Symposium on Earliest Christianity and Judaism (Durham, 1989). Tübingen: J. C. B. Mohr, 1992.
- "Pauline Theology." Pages 100-09 in *The New Testament Today.* Edited by Mark A. Powell. Louisville Ky.: Westminster John Knox, 1999.
- *Romans.* 2 vols. Word Biblical Commentary 38A-B. Dallas: Word, 1988.
- "Romans, Letter to the." Pages 838-50 in *Dictionary of Paul and His Letters.* Edited by Gerald F. Hawthorne, and Ralph P. Martin. Downers Grove: IVP, 1993.
- *The Theology of Paul the Apostle.* Grand Rapids: Eerdmans, 1998.

Easton, B. S. *The Pastoral Epistles.* London: SCM, 1948.

Ellicott, C. J. *The Pastoral Epistles.* London: Parker & Son, 1866. Repr., Eugene Oreg.: Wipf and Stock, 1998.

Ellingworth, Paul. *The Epistle to the Hebrews.* New International Greek Testament Commentary. Grand Rapids : Eerdmans, 1993.

Elliott, J. K. *The Greek Text of the Epistles to Timothy and Titus.* Studies and Documents 36. Salt Lake City: University of Utah Press, 1968.

Ellis, E. Earle. "Pastoral Letters." Pages 658-66 in *Dictionary of Paul and His Letters.* Edited by Gerald F. Hawthorne, and Ralph P. Martin. Downers Grove: IVP, 1993.
- "The Pastorals and Paul." *Expository Times* 104 (1992): 45-47.
- *Paul's Use of the Old Testament.* London: Oliver & Boyd, 1957.
- "Traditions in the Pastoral Epistles." Pages 237-53 in *Early Jewish and Christian Exegesis. Studies in Memory of William Hugh Brownlee.* Edited by Craig A. Evans, and William F. Stinespring. Atlanta: Scholars Press, 1987.

Evans, Craig A. and Stanley Porter (eds.). *Dictionary of New Testament Background.* Downers Grove: IVP, 2000.

Everts, J. M. "Hope." Pages 415-17 in *Dictionary of Paul and His Letters.* Edited by G. F. Hawthorne and R. P. Martin. Downers Grove: IVP, 1993

Farrington, Benjamin. *The Faith of Epicurus.* London: Weidenfeld & Nicolson, 1967.

Fee, Gordon D. *1 and 2 Timothy, Titus.* New International Biblical Commentary 13. Peasbody, Mass.: Hendrickson, 1988.
- "Issues in Evangelical Hermeneutics, Part III: The Great Watershed - Intentionality and Particularity/Eternality: 1 Timothy 2:8-15 as a Test Case." *Crux* 36 (1990): 31-37.

Fenton, J. C. "Salvation." Pages 519-21 in *A New Dictionary of Christian*

Theology. Edited by Alan Richardson, and John Bowden. London: SCM, 1983.

Ferguson, E. "Τόπος in 1 Timothy 2:8." *Restoration Quarterly* 33 (1991-92): 65-73.

Ferguson, John. "Epicureanism under the Roman Empire." (Revised and supplemented by J.P. Hershbell.) Pages 2257-2327 in *ANRW* 36.4. Part 2, *Principat*, 36.4. Edited by H. Temporini and W. Haase. Berlin: W. de Gruchy, 1990.

Fiore, Benjamin. *The Function of Personal Example in the Socratic and Pastoral Epistles*. Analecta Biblica 105. Rome: Biblical Institute, 1986.

- "Passion in Paul and Plutarch. 1 Corinthians 5-6 and the Polemic against Epicureans." Pages 135-43 in *Greeks, Romans and Christians: Essays in Honor of Abraham J. Malherbe*. Edited by D. L. Balch, E. Ferguson, and W. A. Meeks. Minneapolis: Fortress, 1990.

Fitzmyer, Joseph A. "The Qumran Community: Essene or Sadducean?" *The Heythrop Journal* 36 (1995): 467-76.

Fitzpatrick-McKinley, A. Review of W. M. Schniedewind, *Society and the Promise to David: The Reception History of 2 Samuel 7:1-17*, *Reviews in Religion and Theology* 7 (2000): 282-84.

Foerster, W. "ΕΥΣΕΒΕΙΑ in den Pastoralbriefen." *New Testament Studies* 5 (1958-59): 213-18.

Fowl, Stephen E. *The Story of Christ in the Ethics of Paul: An Analysis of the Function of the Hymnic Material in the Pauline Corpus*. Journal for the Study of the New Testament Supplement Series 36. Sheffield: Sheffield Academic Press, 1990.

Fox, Robert Lane. "Hellenistic Culture and Literature." Pages 338-64 in *The Oxford History of the Classical World*. Edited by John Boardman, Jasper Griffin, and Oswyn Murray. Oxford: Oxford University Press, 1986.

Frischer, Benjamin. *The Sculpted Word: Epicureanism and Philosophical Recruitment in Ancient Greece*. Berkely: University of California Press, 1982.

Fung, Ronald Y.-K. "Justification by Faith in 1 & 2 Corinthians." Pages 246-61 in *Pauline Studies*. Edited by Donald A. Hagner, and Murray J. Harris. Exeter: Paternoster, 1980.

Gager, John G. "Marcion and Philosophy." *Vigiliae Christianae* 26 (1972): 53-59.

Garlington, Don B. *"The Obedience of Faith." A Pauline Phrase in Historical Context*. Wissenschaftliche Untersuchungen zum Alten und Neuen Testament 2.38. Tübingen: J. C. B. Mohr, 1991.

Garrett, Susan R. "The God of This World and the Afflictions of Paul. 2 Corinthians 4:1-12." Pages 99-117 in *Greeks, Romans and Christians: Essays in Honor of Abraham J. Malherbe*. Edited by D. L. Balch, E. Ferguson, and W. A. Meeks. Minneapolis: Fortress, 1990.

Gaventa, B.R. *From Darkness to Light. Aspects of Conversion in the New Testament*. Philadelphia: Fortress, 1986.

Gealy, Fred D. and Morgan P. Noyes. "The First and Second Epistles to Timothy and the Epistle to Titus, Introduction and Exegesis." Pages 341-551 in vol. 11 of *The Interpreter's Bible*. Nashville: Abingdon, 1955.

Gerber, Daniel. "1 Tm 1,15b : L'indice d'une sotériologie pensée prioritairement en lien avec la venue de Jésus?" *Revue d'histoire et de philosophie religieuses* 80 (2000): 463-77.

Gero, Stephen. "Christianity and Hellenism from the 1st to the 4th Century." *Didaskalos* 5 (1975-76): 123-135.

Giles, Kevin. "A Critique of the 'Novel' Contemporary Interpretation of 1 Timothy 2:9-15 Given in the Book, *Women in the Church*." *Evangelical Quarterly* 72 (2000): 151-67, 195-215.

- *What on Earth is the Church? A Biblical and Theological Inquiry*. London: SPCK, 1995.

Gill, David W. J. "Behind the Classical Façade: Local Religions of the Roman Empire." Pages 72-87 in *One God, One Lord in a World of Religious Pluralism*. Edited by A. D. Clarke, and B. W. Winter. Cambridge: Tyndale House, 1991.

Goodwin, Mark J. "The Pauline Background of the Living God as Interpretive Context for 1 Timothy 4.10." *Journal for the Study of the New Testament* 61 (1996): 65-85.

Goulder, Michael. "Colossians and Barbelo." *New Testament Studies* 41 (1995): 601-19.

- "The Pastor's Wolves. Jewish Christian Visionaries behind the Pastoral Epistles." *Novum Testamentum* 37 (1996): 242-56.

Grant, Robert. *Gods and the One God. Christian Theology in the Græco-Roman World*. London: SPCK, 1986.

Green, Joel B. "'Salvation to the End of the Earth' (Acts 13:47): God as Savior in the Acts of the Apostles." Pages 83-106 in *Witness to the Gospel: The Theology of Acts*. Edited by I. H. Marshall and D. G. Petersen. Grand Rapids: Eerdmans, 1998.

- *The Gospel of Luke*. New international Commentary on the New Testament. Grand Rapids: Eerdmans, 1997.

Green, Joel B., Scot McKnight and I. Howard Marshall (eds.). *Dictionaryu of Jesus and the Gospels*. Downers Grove: IVP, 1992.

Green, E. M. B. *Evangelism in the Early Church*. London: Hodder & Stoughton, 1970.

- *The Meaning of Salvation*. London: Hodder & Stoughton, 1965.

Greenberg, Moshe. "Job." Pages 283-304 in *The Literary Guide to the Bible*. Edited by Robert Alter and Frank Kermode. London: HarperCollins, 1989.

Grenz, Stanley J. with Denise Muir Kjesbo. *Women in the Church: A*

Biblical Theology of Women in Ministry. Downers Grove: IVP, 1995.

Gruenler, Royce Gordon. "The Mission-Lifestyle Setting of 1 Tim 2:8-15." *Journal of the Evangelical Theology Society* 41 (1998): 215-38.

Guthrie, Donald. *New Testament Introduction.* 3rd ed. London: IVP, 1970.

- *The Pastoral Epistles: An Introduction and Commentary.* Tyndale New Testament Commentaries. Leicester: Tyndale, 1957.

Guthrie, George H. "Promise." Pages 967-70 in *Dictionary of the Later New Testament and Its Developments.* Edited by Ralph P. Martin and Peter H. Davids. Downers Grove: IVP, 1997.

Hagner, Donald A. "Paul and Judaism - the Jewish Matrix of Early Christianity: Issues in the Current Debate." *Bulletin for Biblical Research* 3 (1993): 113-130.

Hahm, David E. "The Ethical Doxography of Arius Didymus." Pages 2935-3055 in *ANRW* 36.4. Part 2, *Principat,* 36.4. Edited by H. Temporini and W. Haase. Berlin: W. de Gruchy, 1990.

Hamilton, C. D. "Greek Rhetoric and History: the Case of Isocrates." Pages 290-98 in *Arktours: Hellenic Studies Presented to Bernard M. W. Knox on the Occasion of his Sixty-Fifth Birthday.* Edited by Glen W. Bowersock, Walter Burkert, and Michael C. J. Putnam. Berlin: de Gruyter, 1979.

Hanson, Anthony Tyrell. "The Domestication of Paul: A Study in the Development of Early Church Theology." *Bulletin of the John Rylands University Library of Manchester* 63 (1981): 402-418.

- *The Pastoral Epistles.* New Century Bible Commentary. London: Marshall Morgan & Scott, 1982.
- *The Pastoral Letters.* The Cambridge Bible Commentary. Cambridge: Cambridge University Press, 1968.
- Review of L. R. Donelson, *Pseudepigraphy and Ethical Argument in the Pastoral Epistles, Expository Times* 98 (1986): 84.
- *Studies in the Pastoral Epistles.* London: SPCK, 1968.

Harding, Mark. *Tradition and Rhetoric in the Pastoral Epistles.* Studies in Biblical Literature 3. New York: Peter Lang, 1998.

- *What Are They Saying about the Pastoral Epistles?* New York: Paulist, 2001.

Harris, Murray J. *Jesus as God: The New Testament Use of* Theos *in Reference to Jesus.* Grand Rapids: Baker, 1992.

- "Prepositions and Theology in the Greek New Testament." Pages 1171-1215 in vol. 3 of *The New International Dictionary of New Testament Theology.* Edited by Colin Brown. 3 vols. Exeter: Paternoster, 1975-78.
- "Titus 2:13 and the Deity of Christ." Pages 262-77 in *Pauline Studies.* Edited by Donald A. Hagner and Murray J. Harris. Exeter: Paternoster, 1980.

Harris, T. J. "Why Did Paul Mention Eve's Deception? A Critique of P.

W. Barnett's Interpretation of 1 Timothy 2." *Evangelical Quarterly* 62 (1990): 335-52.

Harrison, P. N. "Important Hypotheses Reconsidered, III. The Authorship of the Pastoral Epistles." *Expository Times* 67 (1955/56): 77-81.

- *The Problem of the Pastoral Epistles*. London: Oxford University Press, 1921.

Hartley, John E. "יָשַׁע." Pages 414-16 in *Theological Wordbook of the Old Testament*. Vol. 1. Edited by R. Laird Harris et al. Chicago: Moody Press, 1980.

Hasler, Victor. *Die Briefe an Timotheus und Titus (Pastoralbriefe)*. Zürcher Bibelkommentare zum Neuen Testament 12. Zürich: Theologischer, 1978.

Hatch, Edwin and Henry A. Redpath. *A Concordance to the Septuagint*. Oxford: Clarendon, 1897.

Hauerwas, Stanley and William Willimon. *Resident Aliens*. Nashville: Abingdon, 1989.

Häufe, Günter. "Gnostische Irrlehre und ihr Abwehr in den Pastoralbriefen." Pages 325-39 in *Gnosis und Neues Testament*. Edited by K.-W. Tröger. Gütersloh: Mohn, 1973.

Hawthorne, Gerald F., Ralph P. Martin and Daniel G. Reid (eds.). *Dictionary of Paul and His Letters*. Downers Grove: IVP, 1993.

Hay, David M. "Defining Allegory in Philo's Exegetical World." *Society of Biblical Literature Seminar Papers* 33 (1994): 55-68.

Haykin, M. A. G. "The Fading Vision? The Spirit and Freedom in the Pastoral Epistles." *Evangelical Quarterly* 57 (1985): 291-305.

Hays, Richard B. *Echoes of Scripture in the Letters of Paul*. New Haven: Yale University Press, 1989.

- Review of Philip H. Towner, *The Goal of our Instruction: The Structure of Theology and Ethics in the Pastoral Epistles*, *CBQ* 54 (1992): 177-78.

Heever, G. van den. "The Emergence of the Holy Man as μεσίτης." *Neotestamentica* 27 (1993): 419-35.

Hemer, Colin J. "Reflections on the Nature of New Testament Greek Vocabulary." *Tyndale Bulletin* 38 (1987): 65-92.

Hemphill, Kenneth S. *Spiritual Gifts: Empowering the New Testament Church*. Nashville: Broadman, 1988.

Hendriksen, William. *Commentary on 1 and 2 Timothy and Titus*. London: Banner of Truth, 1959.

Hengel, Martin. *The Zealots. Investigations into the Jewish Freedom Movement in the Period from Herod I until 70 A.D.* Translated by D. Smith. Edinburgh: T&T Clark, 1989. Translation of *Die Zeloten: Untersuchungen zur jüdischen Freiheitsbewegung in der Zeit von Herodes I bis 70 N.Chr.*, 2nd ed. Leiden: Brill, 1976.

Henry, Matthew. *An Exposition of the Old and New Testament*. Rev. ed. 6

vols. London: J. O. Robinson, 1836.

Heyworth, S. "Deceitful Crete: Aeneid 3.84 and the Hymns of Callimachus." *The Classical Review* ns 43 (1993): 255-257.

Hill, David. *Greek Words and Hebrew Meanings: Studies in the Semantics of Soteriological Terms*. Society for New Testament Studies: Monograph Series 5. Cambridge: Cambridge University Press, 1967.

Hinson, E. Glenn. "1 & 2 Timothy and Titus." Pages 299-376 in vol. 11 of *The Broadman Bible Commentary*, London: Marshall, Morgan & Scott, 1972.

Hitchcock, F. R. Montgomery. "Philo and the Pastorals." *Hermathena* 56 (1940): 113-35.

Ho, Chiao Ek, "Do the Work of an Evangelist: The Missionary Outlook of the Pastoral Epistles." Ph.D. diss., University of Aberdeen, 2000.

Hock, Ronald F. "A Dog in the Manger. The Cynic Cynulcus among Athenæus's Deipnosophists." Pages 20-37 in *Greeks, Romans and Christians. Essays in Honor of Abraham J. Malherbe*. Edited by D.L. Balch, E.Ferguson, and W. A. Meeks. Minneapolis: Fortress, 1990.

Holmes, J. M. *Text in a Whirlwind. A Critique of Four Exegetical Devices at 1 Timothy 2.9-15*. Journal for the Study of the New Testament Supplement Series 196. Sheffield: Sheffield Academic Press, 2000.

Holtz, Gottfried. *Die Pastoralbriefe*. 2nd ed. Theologischer Handkommentar zum Neuen Testament. Berlin: Evangelische Verlagsanstalt, 1972.

Hooker, Morna D. *Not Ashamed of the Gospel: New Testament Interpretations of the Death of Christ*. Didsbury Lectures. Carlisle: Paternoster, 1994.

Hopkins, Keith. *Conquerors and Slaves*. Sociological Studies in Roman History 1. Cambridge: Cambridge University Press, 1978.

- *Death and Renewal*. Sociological Studies in Roman History 2. Cambridge: Cambridge University Press, 1983.

Hopkinson, N. "Callimachus' Hymn to Zeus." *Classical Quarterly* ns 34 (1984): 139-148.

Horrell, David. "Converging Ideologies: Beyer and Luckmann and the Pastoral Epistles." *Journal for the Study of the New Testament* 50 (1993): 85-103.

Houlden, J. Leslie. *The Pastoral Epistles*. Penguin New Testament Commentary. Handsworth: Penguin, 1976. Repr., London: SCM, 1989.

- Review of Philip H. Towner, *The Goal of our Instruction: The Structure of Theology and Ethics in the Pastoral Epistles*, *Expository Times* 101 (1990): 312-13

Howard, George. *Paul: Crisis in Galatia: A Study in Early Christian*

Theology. Society for New Testament Studies: Monograph Series 35. Cambridge: Cambridge University Press, 1979.

Howell, Don N. Jr. "Pauline Eschatological Dualism and its Resulting Tensions." *Trinity Journal* New Series 14 (1993): 3-24.

Hultgren, Arland J. *New Testament Christology. A Critical Assessment and Annotated Bibliography*. Bibliographies and Indexes in Religious Studies 12. New York: Greenwood Press, 1988.

Hunt, S. A. "Light and Darkness." Pages 657-59 in *Dictionary of the Later New Testament and its Developments*. Edited by Ralph P. Martin and Peter H. Davids. Downer's Grove: IVP, 1997.

Isnardi Parente, Margherita. "Diogeniano, gli epicurei e la τύχη." *ANRW* 36.4: 2424-45. Part 2, *Principat*, 36.4. Edited by H. Temporini and W. Haase. Berlin: W. de Gruchy, 1990.

Jagt, Krijn A. van der. "Women are Saved through Bearing Children: A Sociological Approach to the Interpretation of 1 Tim 2:15." Pages 288-95 in *Issues in Bible Translation*. Edited by P. C. Stime. United Bible Societies Monograph Series 3. London: United Bible Societies, 1988. Repr. from *The Bible Translator* 39 (1988): 201-08.

Jebb, S. "A Suggested Interpretation of 1 Tim 2:15." *Expository Times* 81 (1969): 221-22.

Jervis, L. Ann. "Paul the Poet in First Timothy 1:11-17; 2:3B-7; 3:14-16." *Catholic Biblical Quarterly* 61 (1999): 695-712.

Johnson, Luke T. "II Timothy and the Polemic against False Teachers: a Re-examination." *Ohio Journal of Religious Studies* 6 (1978): 1-26.

- *Letters to Paul's Delegates: 1 Timothy, 2 Timothy, Titus*. The New Testament in Context. Valley Forge, Pa.: Trinity, 1996.
- *The First and Second Letters to Timothy: A New Translation with Introduction and Commentary*. Anchor Bible 35A. New York: Doubleday, 2001.
- "The New Testament's Anti-Jewish Slander and the Conventions of Ancient Polemic." *Journal of Biblical Literature* 108 (1989): 419-441.
- *The Writings of the New Testament: An Interpretation*. Rev. ed. Minneapolis: Fortress, 1999.

Jonge, M. de. "Jesus' Death for Others and the Death of the Maccabean Martyrs." Pages 142-51 in *Text and Testimony: Essays on the New Testament and Apocryphal Literature in Honor of A. F. J. Klijn*. Edited by T. Baarda *et al.* Kampen: Kok, 1988.

Karris, Robert J., O.F.M. "The Background and Significance of the Polemic of the PE." *Journal of Biblical Literature* 92 (1973): 549-564.

- "Pastoral Letters, The." Pages 573-76 in *The Oxford Companion to the Bible*. Edited by Bruce M. Metzger and Michael D. Coogan. Oxford: Oxford University Press, 1993.
- *The Pastoral Epistles*. New Testament Message 17. Wilmington, Del.: Michael Glazier, 1979.

Keck, Leander E. "Images of Paul in the New Testament." *Interpretation* 43 (1989): 341-51.
Keener, Craig S. "Man and Woman." Pages 583-92 in *Dictionary of Paul and His Letters*. Edited by Gerald F. Hawthorne, and Ralph P. Martin. Downers Grove: IVP, 1993.
- *Paul, Women & Wives: Marriage and Women's Ministry in the Letters of Paul*. Peabody, Mass.: Hendrickson, 1992.
Kelly, J. N. D. *The Epistles of Peter and Jude*. Black's New Testament Commentaries. London: A&C Black, 1969.
- *The Pastoral Epistles: I & II Timothy and Titus*. Black's New Testament Commentaries. London: A&C Black, 1963.
Kenny, Anthony. *A Stylometric Study of the New Testament*. Oxford: Clarendon, 1986.
Kidd, Reggie M. *Wealth and Beneficence in the Pastoral Epistles: A "Bourgeois" Form of Early Christianity?* Society of Biblical Literature Dissertation Series 122. Atlanta: Scholars Press, 1990.
Kittel, G., and G. Friedrich, eds. *Theological Dictionary of the New Testament*. Translated by G.W. Bromiley. 10 vols. Grand Rapids: Eerdmans, 1964-76.
Klauck, Hans-Josef. "Hellenistische Rhetorik im Diasporajudent. Das Exordium der vierter Makkabäerbuch (4 Makk. 1:1-12)." *New Testament Studies* 35 (1989): 451-465.
Kloppenborg, John S. "ΦΙΛΑΔΕΛΦΙΑ, ΘΕΟΔΙΔΑΚΤΟΣ and the Dioscuri: Rhetorical Engagement in 1 Thes. 4:9-12." *New Testament Studies* 39 (1993): 265-289.
Klöpper, A. "Zur Soteriologie der Pastoralbriefe (Tit. 3:4-7; 2 Tim. 1:9-11; Tit. 2:11-14)." *Zeitschrift für wissenschaftliche Theologie* 47 (1904): 57-88.
Knight, George W. III. *The Faithful Sayings in the Pastoral Epistles*. Kampen: Kok, 1968.
- *The Pastoral Epistles: A Commentary on the Greek Text*. New International Greek Testament Commentary. Grand Rapids: Eerdmans, 1992.
Kooij, Arie van der. "The Old Greek of Isaiah in relation to the Qumran Texts of Isaiah: Some General Comments." Pages 195-213 in *Septuagint, Scrolls and Cognate Writings*. Edited by G. J. Brooke and B. Lindars. Society for Biblical Literature Septuagint and Cognate Studies 33. Atlanta: Scholars Press, 1992.
Köstenberger, A. J. "Ascertaining Women's God-Ordained Roles: An Interpretation of 1 Timothy 2:15." *Bulletin for Biblical Research* 7 (1997): 107-44.
- "Syntactical Background Studies to 1 Timothy 2:12 in the New Testament and Extrabiblical Greek Literature." Pages 156-79 in *Discourse Analysis and Other Topics in Biblical Greek*. Journal for the

Study of the New Testament Supplement Series 113. Edited by S. E. Porter and D. A. Carson. Sheffield: Sheffield Academic Press, 1995.

Köstenberger, A. J., T. R. Schreiner, and H. S. Baldwin, eds. *Women in the Church: A Fresh Analysis of 1 Timothy 2:9-15*. Grand Rapids : Baker, 1995.

Kowalski, Beate. "Zur Funktion und Bedeutung der alttestamentlichen Zitate und Anspielungen in den Pastoralbriefen." *Studien zum Neuen Testament und seiner Umwelt* 19 (1994): 45-68.

Kretschmar, Georg. "The Early Church and Hellenistic Culture." *International Revew of Mission* lxxxiv 332/3 (Jan/Apr 1995) 33-46.

- "Der paulinische Glaube in den Pastoralbriefen." Pages 113-40 in *Glaube im Neuen Testament*. Edited by F. Hann, and H. Klein. Biblisch-theologische Studien 7. Vluyn: Neukirchener, 1982.

Kroeger, Richard Clark and Catherine Clark Kroeger. *I Suffer Not a Woman: Re-thinking 1 Timothy 2:11-15 in Light of Ancient Evidence*. Grand Rapids : Baker, 1993.

Kruse, C. G. "Virtues and Vices." Pages 962-63 in *Dictionary of Paul and His Letters*. Edited by Gerald F. Hawthorne, and Ralph P. Martin. Downers Grove: IVP, 1993.

Küchler, Max. *Schweigen, Schmuck und Schleier*. Novum Testamentum et Orbis Antiquus 1. Göttingen: Vandenhoeck & Ruprecht, 1986.

Kümmel, W. G. *Introduction to the New Testament*. Translated by H. C. Kee. London: SCM, 1975. Translation of *Einleitung in das Neue Testament*. 17th ed. Heidelberg: Quelle & Meyer, 1973.

Laato, A. "2 Samuel 7 and Ancient Near Eastern Royal Ideology," *Catholic Biblical Quarterly* 59 (1997): 244-69.

Läger, Karoline. *Die Christologie der Pastoralbriefe*. Hamburger Theologische Studien 12. Münster: Lit, 1996.

Lane, William L. "I Tim.iv.1-3. An Early Instance of Over-realized Eschatology." *New Testament Studies* 11 (1964): 164-67.

- *Hebrews 1-8*. Word Biblical Commentary 47A. Dallas: Word, 1991.

Lattimore, R. "Optatives of Consent and Refusal." Pages 208-18 in *Arktours: Hellenic Studies Presented to Bernard M. W. Knox on the Occasion of his Sixty-Fifth Birthday*. Edited by Glen W. Bowerstock, Walter Burkert, and Michael C. J. Putnam. Berlin: de Gruyter, 1979.

Lau, Andrew Yu-Yee. *Manifest in Flesh: the Epiphany Christology of the Pastoral Epistles*. Wissenschaftliche Untersuchungen zum Alten und Neuen Testament 2.86. Tübingen: J. C. B. Mohr, 1996.

Lauer, S. "*Eusebes Logismos* in IV Maccabees." *Journal of Jewish Studies* 6 (1955): 170-71.

Lea, T. D. and H. P. Griffin Jr. *1,2 Timothy, Titus*. New American Commentary 34. Nashville, Tenn.: Broadman, 1992.

Lee, G. M. "Epimenides in the Epistle to Titus." *Novum Testamentum* 22 (1980): 96.

Lentz, John Clayton Jr. *Luke's Portrait of Paul*. Society for New Testament Study Monograph Series 77. Cambridge: Cambridge University Press, 1993.
Levison, J. "Is Eve to Blame? A Contextual Analysis of Sirach 25:24." *Catholic Biblical Quarterly* 47 (1985): 617-23.
Liefeld, Walter L. *1 & 2 Timothy/Titus*. NIV Application Commentary. Grand Rapids : Zondervan, 1999.
Lightfoot, J. B. *St. Paul's Epistle to the Philippians*. Classic Commentary Library. Grand Rapids: Zondervan, 1953. Reprinted from original ed., London: Macmillan & Co., 1913.
Lips, Hermann von. *Glaube - Gemeinde - Amt*. Forschungen zur Religion und Literatur des Alten und Neuen Testaments 122. Göttingen: Vandenhoeck & Ruprecht, 1979.
- "Die Haustafel als 'Topos' im Rahmen der urchristlichen Paränese: Beobachtungen anhand des 1.Petrusbriefes und des Titusbriefes." *New Testament Studies* 40 (1994): 261-80.
Litfin, Duane. *St. Paul's Theology of Proclamation. 1 Corinthians 1-4 and Greco-Roman Rhetoric*. Society for New Testament Study Monograph Series 79. Cambridge: Cambridge University Press, 1994.
Lock, W. *A Critical and Exegetical Commentary on the Pastoral Epistles*. International Critical Commentary. Edinburgh: T&T Clark, 1924.
Lohfink, Gerhard. "Paulinische Theologie in der Rezeption der Pastoralbriefe." Pages 70-121 in *Paulus in den neutestamentlichen Spätschriften*. Quaestiones Disputatae 89. Edited by K. Kertlege. Freiburg: Herder, 1981.
Lohse, Eduard. "Changes of Thought in Pauline Theology? Some Reflections on Paul's Ethical Thinking in the Context of His Theology." Pages 146-60 in *Theology and Ethics in Paul and His Interpreters*. Edited by E. H. Lovering Jr., and J. L. Sumney. Nashville: Abingdon, 1996.
Longenecker, Richard N. *The Christology of Early Jewish Christianity*. Grand Rapids : Baker, 1970.
Longva, Anh Nga. "Kuwaiti Women at a Crossroads: Privileged Development and the Constraints of Ethnic Stratification." *International Journal of Middle Eastern Studies* 25 (1993): 443-56.
Lüdemann, Gerd. *Paul, Apostle to the Gentiles. Studies in Chronology*. Translated by F. Stanley Jones. London: SCM, 1984. Translation of *Studien zur Chronologie*. vol. 1 of *Paulus, der Heidenapostel*. Forschungen zur Religion und Literatur des Alten und Neuen Testaments 123. Göttingen: Vandenhoeck & Ruprecht, 1980.
Lührmann, Dieter. "The Beginnings of the Church at Thessalonica." Pages 237-49 in *Greeks, Romans and Christians: Essays in Honor of Abraham J. Malherbe*. Edited by D. L. Balch, E. Ferguson, and W. A. Meeks. Minneapolis: Fortress, 1990.

Luter, A. B. Jr. "Savior." Pages 867-69 in *Dictionary of Paul and His Letters*. Edited by Gerald F. Hawthorne, and Ralph P. Martin. Downers Grove: IVP, 1993.

Luz, Ulrich. "Rechtfertigung bei den Paulusschülern." Pages 365-83 in *Rechtfertigung: Festschrift für E. Käsemann*. Edited by J. Friedrich, W. Pöhlmann and P. Stuhlmacher. Tübingen: Mohr-Siebeck, 1976.

MacDonald, D. R. *The Legend and the Apostle: The Battle for Paul in Story and Canon*. Philadelphia: Westminster, 1983.

MacDonald, Margaret Y. *The Pauline Churches: A Socio-Historical Study of Institutionalization in the Pauline and Deutero-Pauline Writings*. Society for New Testament Study Monograph Series 60. Cambridge: Cambridge University Press, 1988.

MacMullen, Ramsay. *Paganism in the Roman Empire*, New Haven: Yale University Press, 1981.

Maile, J. F. "Exaltation and Enthronement." 275-78 in *Dictionary of Paul and His Letters*. Edited by Gerald F. Hawthorne, and Ralph P. Martin. Downers Grove: IVP, 1993.

Malherbe, Abraham J. "Hellenistic Moralists and the New Testament." *ANRW* 26.1: 267-333. Part 2, *Principat*, 26.1. Edited by H. Temporini and W. Haase. New York: de Gruyter, 1992.

- "'In Season and Out of Season': 2 Timothy 4:2." *Journal of Biblical Literature* 103 (1984): 235-43. Repr. pages 137-46 in *Paul and the Popular Philosophers*. Minneapolis: Fortress, 1989.
- "Medical Imagery in the Pastoral Epistles." Pages 19-35 in *Texts & Testaments: Critical Essays on the Bible and Early Church Fathers*. Edited by W. E. Marsh. San Antonio: Trinity University Press, 1980. Repr. pages 121-36 in *Paul and the Popular Philosophers*. Minneapolis: Fortress, 1989.
- *Paul and the Popular Philosophers*. Minneapolis: Fortress, 1989.
- *Paul and the Thessalonians: The Philosophic Tradition of Pastoral Care*. Philadelphia: Fortress, 1987.
- "Paulus Senex." *Restoration Quarterly* 36 (1994): 197-207.
- "Self-Definition among Epicureans and Cynics." Pages 46-59 in *Jewish and Christian Self-Definition*. vol. 3. Edited by Ben F. Meyer, and E. P. Sanders. London: SCM, 1982.
- *Social Aspects of Early Christianity*. 2nd ed. Philadelphia: Fortress, 1983.

Malina, Bruce J. *The New Testament World: Insights from Cultural Anthropology*. Rev. ed. Louisville, Ky.: Westminster John Knox, 1983.

- *The Social World of Jesus and the Gospels*. London: Routledge, 1996.

Mandilaras, Basil G. "Confusion of Aorist and Perfect in the Language of the Non-Literary Greek Papyri." Pages 251-62 in *Akten des XIII. Internationalen Papyrologenkongresses* (Marburg/Lahn, 2-6 August 1971). Edited by Emil Kießling and Hans-Albert Rupprecht. Munich,

1974.

Mansfeld, Jaap. "Doxography and Dialectic. The *Sitz im Leben* of the 'Placita'." *ANRW* 36.4: 3056-3229. Part 2, *Principat*, 36.4. Edited by H. Temporini and W. Haase. Berlin: W. de Gruchy, 1990.

- "Philosophy in the Service of Scripture: Philo's Exegetical Strategies." Pages 89-98 in *The Question of "Eclecticism": Studies in Later Greek Philosophy*. Edited by J. M. Dillon and A. A. Long. Berkeley: University of California Press, 1988.

Marshall, I. Howard. *The Acts of the Apostles*. Tyndale New Testament Commentaries. Leicester: IVP, 1980.

- "The Christology of Acts and the Pastoral Epistles." Pages 167-82 in *Crossing the Boundaries: Essays in Biblical Interpretation in Honour of Michael D. Goulder*. Edited by S. E. Porter, P. Joyce, and D. E. Orton. Biblical Interpretation Series 8. Leiden: Brill, 1994.
- "The Christology of the Pastoral Epistles." *Studien zum Neuen Testament und seiner Umwelt* 13 (1988): 157-77.
- "Faith and Works in the Pastoral Epistles." *Studien zum Neuen Testament und seiner Umwelt* 9 (1984): 203-18.
- *The Gospel of Luke: A Commentary on the Greek Text*. New International Greek Testament Commentary. Grand Rapids: Eerdmans, 1978.
- *I believe in the Historical Jesus*. London: Hodder & Stoughton, 1977.
- "Is Apocalyptic the Mother of Christian Theology?" Pages 33-41 in *Tradition and Interpretation in the New Testament: Essays in Honor of E. Earle Ellis*. Edited by Gerald F. Hawthorne, and Otto Betz. Grand Rapids: Eerdmans, 1987.
- *Jesus the Saviour: Studies in New Testament Theology*. Downers Grove: IVP, 1990.
- *Kept by the Power of God: A Study of Perseverance and Falling Away*. London: Epworth, 1969.
- "The Nature of Christian Salvation." *European Journal of Theology* 4 (1995): 29-43.
- *The Origins of New Testament Christology*. Issues in Contemporary Theology Series. Leicester: IVP, 1976.
- *The Pastoral Epistles*. International Critical Commentary. Edinburgh: T&T Clark, 1999.
- "Prospects for the Pastoral Epistles." Pages 137-55 in *Doing Theology for the People of God: Studies in Honor of J. I. Packer*. Edited by Donald Lewis, and Alister E. McGrath. Downers Grove Ill.: IVP, 1996.
- "Recent Study of the Pastoral Epistles." *Themelios* 23.1 (1997): 3-29.
- "Salvation, Grace and Works in the Later Writings in the Pauline Corpus." *New Testament Studies* 42 (1996): 339-58.
- "Salvation in the Pastoral Epistles." Pages 449-69 in *Frühes Christentum*. Edited by Hermann Lichtenberger. vol. 3 of *Geschichte-*

Tradition-Reflexion. Edited by Hubert Cancik, Hermann Lichtenberger, and Peter Schäfer. Tübingen: J. C. B. Mohr, 1996.
- "'Sometimes Only Orthodox' - Is there more to the Pastoral Epistles?" *Epworth Review* 20.3 (1993): 12-24.
- "Universal Grace and Atonement in the Pastoral Epistles." Pages 51-69 in *The Grace of God, the Will of Man*. Edited by C. Pinnock. Grand Rapids: Zondervan, 1989.

Martin, Luther H. *Hellenistic Religions. An Introduction*. Oxford: Oxford University Press, 1987.

Martin, Ralph P. *Colossians and Philemon*. rev. ed. New Century Bible. London: Marshall, Morgan & Scott, 1978.
- *Philippians*. Tyndale New Testament Commentaries. London: Tyndale, 1959.
- *Worship in the Early Church*. 2nd ed. Grand Rapids: Eerdmans, 1974.

Martin, Ralph P. and Peter H. Davids (eds.) *Dictionary of the Later New Testament and Its Developments*. Downers Grove: IVP, 1997.

Mayer, Günter. *Index Philoneus*. Berlin: de Gruyter, 1974.

McGrath, Alister E. *Christian Theology. An Introduction*. Oxford: Blackwell, 1994.

McIntyre, John. *The Shape of Soteriology: Studies in the Doctrine of the Death of Christ*. Edinburgh: T&T Clark, 1992.

McLean, Bradley H. "The Absence of an Atoning Sacrifice in Paul's Soteriology." *New Testament Studies* 38 (1992): 531-53.

Meeks, Wayne A. "The Circle of Reference in Pauline Morality." Pages 305-17 in *Greeks, Romans and Christians: Essays in Honor of Abraham J. Malherbe*. Edited by D. L. Balch, E. Ferguson, and W. A. Meeks. Minneapolis: Fortress, 1990.
- *The First Urban Christians. The Social World of the Apostle Paul*. New Haven: Yale University Press, 1983.
- *The Moral World of the First Christians*. London: SPCK, 1987.

Merkel, Helmut. *Die Pastoralbriefe*. Das Neue Testament Deutsch 9.1. Göttingen: Vandenhoeck & Ruprecht, 1991.

Metzger, Wolfgang. *Der Christushymnus 1.Timotheus 3,16: Fragment einer Homologie der paulinischen Gemeinden*. Arbeiten zur Theologie 62. Stuttgart: Calwer, 1979.

Michel, O. "Grundfragen der Pastoralbriefe." Pages 83-99 in *Auf dem Grunde der Apostel und Propheten*. Edited by M. Loeser. Stuttgart: Quell, 1948.

Miller, James D. *The Pastoral Letters as Composite Documents*. Society for New Testament Study Monograph Series 93. Cambridge: Cambridge University Press, 1997.

Miller, P. D. Jr. "'Moses My Servant.' The Deuteronomic Picture of Moses," *Interpretation* 41 (1987): 245-55.

Mitchell, Margaret M. "New Testament Envoys in the Context of

Græco-Roman Diplomatic and Epistolary Conventions: the Example of Timothy and Titus." *Journal of Biblical Literature* 111 (1992): 641-62.

Moffatt, James. *Grace in the New Testament.* London: Hodder & Stoughton, 1931.

Moo, Douglas J. "1 Tim 2:11-15: Meaning and Significance." *Trinity Journal* 1 (1980): 70-73.

- *The Epistle to the Romans.* New International Commentary on the New Testament. Grand Rapids: Eerdmans, 1996.
- "What Does It Mean Not to Teach or Have Authority Over Men? 1 Timothy 2.11-15." Pages 179-93 in *Recovering Biblical Manhood & Womanhood: A Response to Evangelical Feminism.* Edited by J. Piper and W. Grudem. Wheaton: Crossway, 1991.

Morgenthaler, Robert. *Statistik des neutestamentlichen Wortschatzes.* 3rd ed. Zürich: Gotthelf, 1982.

Moritz, Thorsten. "'Summing up all things': Religious Pluralism and Universalism in Ephesians." Pages 88-111 in *One God One Lord in a World of Religious Pluralism.* Edited by A. D. Clarke, and B. W. Winter. Cambridge: Tyndale House, 1991.

Morris, Leon *The Apostolic Preaching of the Cross.* 3rd ed. London: Tyndale, 1960.

- *The Cross in the New Testament.* Exeter: Paternoster, 1965.
- "Salvation." Pages 858-62 in *Dictionary of Paul and His Letters.* Edited by Gerald F. Hawthorne, and Ralph P. Martin. Downers Grove: IVP, 1993.

Mott, Stephen Charles. "Greek Ethics and Christian Conversion: The Philonic Background of Titus 2:10-14 and 3:3-7." *Novum Testamentum* 20 (1978): 22-48.

- "The Power of Giving and Receiving: Reciprocity in Hellenistic Benevolence." Pages 60-72 in *Current Issues in Biblical and Patristic Interpretation.* Edited by E. G. Hawthorne. Grand Rapids: Eerdmans, 1975.

Motyer, J. A. *The Prophecy of Isaiah.* Leicester: IVP, 1993.

Moule, C. F. D. *The Birth of the New Testament.* 2nd ed. London: A&C Black, 1966.

- "Influence of Circumstances on the Use of Eschatological Terms." Pages 184-99 in *Essays in New Testament Interpretation.* Cambridge: Cambridge University Press, 1982. Repr. from *Journal of Theological Studies* ns 15 (1964): 1-16.
- "The Problem of the Pastoral Epistles: A Re-appraisal." Pages 113-32 in *Essays in New Testament Interpretation.* Cambridge: Cambridge University Press, 1982. Repr. from *Bulletin of the John Rylands University Library of Manchester* 47 (1965): 430-52.

Moulton, J. H., W. F. Howard and N. Turner. *A Grammar of New Testament Greek.* Edinburgh: T&T Clark, 1906-76.

Mounce, William D. *Pastoral Epistles*. Word Biblical Commentary 46. Nashville: Thomas Nelson, 2000.

Murphy-O'Connor, Cormac and Mark Santer. *Salvation and the Church: An Agreed Statement by the Second Anglican - Roman Catholic International Commission*. London: Church House Publishing, 1987.

Murphy-O'Connor, Jerome. "2 Timothy Contrasted with 1 Timothy and Titus." *Revue biblique* 98 (1991): 403-18.

- *Paul, the Letter-Writer: His World, His Options, His Skills*. Good News Studies 41. Collegeville : Liturgical, 1995.

Murray, Oswyn. "Philodemus on the Good King according to Homer." *Journal of Roman Studies* 55 (1965): 161-82.

Myers, J. Wilson, Eleanor Emlen Myers, and Gerald Cadogan. *The Aerial Atlas of Ancient Crete*. London: Thames & Hudson, 1992.

Neumann, Kenneth J. *The Authenticity of the Pauline Epistles in the Light of Stylostatistical Analysis*. Society for Biblical Literature Dissertation Series 120. Atlanta: Scholars Press, 1990.

Neyrey, Jerome H. "Acts 17, Epicureans, and Theodicy. A Study in Stereotypes." Pages 118-34 in *Greeks, Romans and Christians: Essays in Honor of Abraham J. Malherbe*. Edited by D. L. Balch, E. Ferguson, and W. A. Meeks. Minneapolis: Fortress, 1990, 118-34.

Nickelsburg, George W. E. *Jewish Literature Between the Bible and the Mishnah: A Historical and Literary Introduction*. London: SCM, 1981.

- *Resurrection, Immortality and Eternal Life in Inter-Testamental Judaism*. Cambridge, Mass.: Harvard University Press, 1972.

Nisbet, Robin. "The Poets of the Late Republic." Pages 479-94 in *The Oxford History of the Classical World*. Edited by John Boardman, Jasper Griffin, and Oswyn Murray. Oxford: Oxford University Press, 1986.

Nolland, John. *Luke*. 3 vols. Word Biblical Commentary 35A-C. Dallas: Word, 1989-93.

North, J. Lionel. "'Human Speech' in Paul and the Paulines: the Investigation and Meaning of ἀνθρώπινος ὁ λόγος (1 Tim 3:1)." *Novum Testamentum* 37 (1995): 50-67.

Nussbaum, Martha C. *The Therapy of Desire. Theory and Practice in Hellenistic Ethics*. Martin Classical Lectures ns 2. Princeton: Princeton University Press, 1994.

Nygren, Anders. *Commentary on Romans*. Philadelphia: Fortress, 1949.

Oakes, Peter. "Epictetus (and the New Testament)." *Vox Evangelica* 23 (1993): 39-56.

Oberlinner, Lorenz. *Die Pastoralbriefe. Ersten Timotheusbrief*. Herders theologischer Kommentar zum Neuen Testament 11.2-1. Freiburg: Herder, 1994.

- *Die Pastoralbriefe. Zweiten Tomotheusbrief*. Herders theologischer Kommentar zum Neuen Testament 11.2-2. Freiburg: Herder, 1995.

- *Die Pastoralbriefe. Der Titusbrief.* Herders theologischer Kommentar zum Neuen Testament 11.2-3. Freiburg: Herder, 1996.
O'Brien, P. T. *Gospel and Mission in the Writings of Paul: An Exegetical and Theological Analysis.* Grand Rapids: Baker, 1993.
Oden, T. C. *First and Second Timothy and Titus.* Interpretation. Louisville: John Knox, 1989.
O'Hagan, Angelo. "The Martyr in the Fourth Book of Maccabees." *Studii Biblici Franciscani liber annus* 24 (1974): 94-120.
Packer, J. I. "What Did the Cross Achieve? The Logic of Penal Substitution." *Tyndale Bulletin* 25 (1974): 3-45.
Padgett, A. "Wealthy Women at Ephesus: 1 Tim 2:8-15 in Social Context." *Interpretation* 41 (1987): 19-31.
Page, Sydney. "Marital Expectations of Church Leaders in the Pastoral Epistles." *Journal for the Study of the New Testament* 50 (1993): 106-20.
Pak, James Yeong-Sik. *Paul as Missionary. A Comparative Study of Missionary Discourse in Paul's Epistles and Selected Contemporary Jewish Texts.* European University Studies Series 23, 410. Frankfurt: Peter Lang, 1991.
Parker, Robert. "Greek Religion." Pages 254-74 in *The Oxford History of the Classical World.* Edited by John Boardman, Jasper Griffin, and Oswyn Murray. Oxford: Oxford University Press, 1986.
Parrott, Douglas M. "Gnosticism and Egyptian Religion." *Novum Testamentum* 29 (1987): 73-93.
Payne, P. B. "Libertarian Women in Ephesus: A Response to Douglas J. Moo's Article, '1 Tim 2:11-15: Meaning and Significance'." *Trinity Journal* 2 (1981): 177-8.
- "Ms.88 as Evidence for a Text without 1 Cor 14.34-5." *New Testament Studies* 44 (1998): 152-58.
Perriman, A. C. "What Eve did; what women shouldn't do. The meaning of αὐθεντέω in 1 Timothy 2:12." *Tyndale Bulletin* 44 (1993): 129-42.
Pervo, Richard I. "Romancing an Oft-Neglected Stone: the Pastoral Epistles and the Epistolary Novel." *Journal of Higher Criticism* 1 (1994): 25-47.
Pierce, Ronald W. "Evangelicals and Gender Roles in the 1990s: 1 Tim 2:8-15: A Test Case." *Journal of the Evangelical Theology Society* 36 (1993): 343-56.
Porter, Stanley E. "What Does It Mean To Be 'Saved by Childbirth' (1 Tim 2:15)?" *Journal for the Study of the New Testament* 49 (1993): 87-102. Repr. pages 160-75 in *New Testament Text and Language: A Sheffield Reader.* Edited by S. E. Porter and C. A. Evans. Sheffield: Sheffield Academic Press, 1997.
Powell, Mark Allen. *What Is Narrative Criticism? A New Approach to the Bible.* Minneapolis: Fortress, 1990.

Pratscher, Wilhelm. "Die Stabilisierung der Kirche als Anliegen der Pastoralbriefe." *Studien zum Neuen Testament und seiner Umwelt* 18 (1993): 133-50.

Price, Simon. "The History of the Hellenistic Period." Pages 315-37 in *The Oxford History of the Classical World*. Edited by John Boardman, Jasper Griffin, and Oswyn Murray. Oxford: Oxford University Press, 1986.

Prior, Michael, C.M. *Paul the Letter-Writer and the Second Letter to Timothy*. Journal for the Study of the New Testament Supplement Series 23. Sheffield: Sheffield Academic Press, 1989.

Purcell, Nicholas. "The Arts of Government." Pages 560-91 in *The Oxford History of the Classical World*. Edited by John Boardman, Jasper Griffin, and Oswyn Murray. Oxford: Oxford University Press, 1986.

Quarles, Charles L. "The Soteriology of R. Akiba and E. P. Sanders' 'Paul and Palestinian Judaism'." *New Testament Studies* 42 (1996): 185-95.

Quinn, Jerome D. "The Holy Spirit in the Pastoral Epistles." Pages 345-68 in *Sin, Salvation and the Spirit: Commemorating the Fiftieth Year of the Liturgical Press*. Edited by D. Durken. Collegeville: Liturgical, 1979.

- "Jesus as Savior and Only Mediator (1 Tim 2:3-6): Linguistic Paradigms of Acculturation." Pages 249-60 in *Fede e Cultura/Foi et culture*. Turin: Elle di Ci, 1981.

- "The Last Volume of Luke: The Relation of Luke-Acts and the Pastoral Epistles." Pages 62-75 in *Perspectives on Luke-Acts*. Edited by C. H. Talbert, Macon, Ga: Mercer, 1978.

- "Ministry in the New Testament." Pages 130-60 in *Biblical Studies in Contemporary Thought*. Sommerville, Mass.: Grerno, Hadden, 1975.

- "On the Terminology for Faith, Truth, Teaching, and the Spirit in the Pastoral Epistles: A Summary." Pages 232-37 in *Teaching Authority and Infallibility in the Church: Lutherans and Catholics in Dialogue VI*. Edited by P. Empie, T. A. Murphy, and J. A. Burgess. Minneapolis: Augsburg, 1980.

- *The Letter to Titus. A New Translation with Notes and a Commentary and an Introduction to Titus, I and II Timothy, the Pastoral Epistles*. Anchor Bible 35. New York: Doubleday, 1990.

Quinn, J. D. and W. C. Wacker. *The First and Second Letters to Timothy: A New Translation with Notes and Commentary*. Grand Rapids : Eerdmans, 2000.

Redalié, Yann. *Paul après Paul. Le temps, le salut, la morale selon les épîtres à Timothée et à Tite*. Le Monde de la Bible 31. Genève: Labor et Fides, 1994.

Redekop, G. N. "Let the Women Learn: 1 Timothy 2:8-15 Reconsidered." *Studies in Religion* 19 (1990): 235-45.

Redditt, Paul L. "The Concept of *Nomos* in Fourth Maccabees." *Catholic Biblical Quarterly* 45 (1983): 269-80.
Renehan, Robert. "The Greek Philosophic Background of Fourth Maccabees." *Rheinisches Museum für Philologie* 115 (1972): 223-38.
Renna, Enrico. "Considerazioni sulla concezione antropomorfica degli dei net P.Herc.1055." Pages 447-51 in *Atti del XVII Congresso Internazionale di Papirologia* 2 (Napoli, 19-26 maggio 1983). Naples: Centro Internazionale per la Studio dei Papiri Ercolania, 1984.
Richards, E. Randolph. *The Secretary in the Letters of Paul*. Wissenschaftliche Untersuchungen zum Alten und Neuen Testament 2.42. Tübingen: J. C. B. Mohr, 1991.
Richards, William A. *Difference and Distance in Post-Pauline Christianity: An Epistolary Analysis of the Pastorals*. Studies in Biblical Literature 44. New York: Peter Lang, 2002.
Richardson, Alan. *An Introduction to the Theology of the New Testament*. London: SCM, 1958.
Rist, J. M. *Epicurus: An Introduction*. Cambridge: Cambridge University Press, 1972.
Robinson, J. A. T. "The One Baptism as a Category of New Testament Soteriology." *Scottish Journal of Theology* 6 (1953): 257-74.
Roetzel, Calvin J. *The World that Shaped the New Testament*. Atlanta: John Knox, 1985.
Roller, O. *Das Formular der paulinischen Briefe. Ein Beitrag zur Lehre vom antiken Briefe*. Beiträge zur Wissenschaft vom Alten und Neuen Testament 4.6. Stuttgart: Kohlhammer, 1933.
Roloff, Jürgen. *Der erste Brief an Timotheus*. Evangelisch-Katholischer Kommentar zum Neuen Testament 15. Zurich: Benziger, 1988.
- "Der Weg Jesu als Lebensnorm (2 Tim 2,8-13): Ein Beitrag zur Christologie der Pastoralbriefe." Pages 155-67 in *Anfänge der Christologie*. Edited by Cilliers Breytenbach and Henning Paulsen. Göttingen: Vandenhoeck & Ruprecht, 1991.
Rordorf, W. "Nochmals: Paulusakten und Pastoralbriefe." Pages 319-27 in *Tradition and Interpretation in the New Testament: Essays in Honor of E. Earle Ellis*. Edited by Gerald F. Hawthorne, and Otto Betz. Grand Rapids: Eerdmans, 1987.
Rowe, A. "Hermeneutics and 'Hard Passages' in the New Testament on the Role of Women in the Church: Issues from Recent Literature." *Epworth Review* 18.3 (1991): 82-88.
Russell, D. S. *Between the Testaments*. London: SCM. 1960.
Sanders, E. P. "The Covenant as a Soteriological Category and the Nature of Salvation in Palestinian and Hellenistic Judaism." Pages 11-44 in *Jews, Greeks and Christians: Religious Cultures in Late Antiquity*. Edited by R. Hamerton-Kelly, and R. Scroggs. Leiden: E. J. Brill, 1976.

- "Jesus in Historical Context." *Theology Today* 50 (1993): 429-48.
- *Judaism, Practice and Belief 63 B.C.E.-66 C.E.* London: SCM, 1992.
- *Paul.* Past Masters Series. Oxford: Oxford University Press, 1991.

Sanders, I. F. *Roman Crete: An Archaeological Survey and Gazetteer of Late Hellenistic, Roman and Early Byzantine Crete.* Warminster: Aris & Phillips, 1982.

Sandmel, Samuel. *A Jewish Understanding of the New Testament.* Aug. ed. London: SPCK, 1977.

Sawyer, John F. A. "יָשַׁע." Pages 441-63 in vol. 6 of *Theological Dictionary of the Old Testament.* Grand Rapids: Eerdmans. 1990. Translation of *Theologische Wörterbuch zum Alten Testament* 3.5-9. Edited by G. Botterweck and Helmer Ringgren. Stuttgart: Verlag W. Kohlhammer, 1982.

- *Semantics in Biblical Research. New Methods of Defining Hebrew Words for Salvation.* Studies in Biblical Theology New Series 24. London: SCM, 1972.

Schenk, W. "Die Briefe an Timotheus I und II und an Titus (Pastoralbriefe) in der neueren Forschung (1945-1985)." *ANRW* 25.4:3404-38. Part 2, *Principat*, 25.4. Edited by H. Temporini and W. Haase. Berlin: de Gruyter 1987.

Schlarb, Egbert. *Die gesunde Lehre: Häresie und Wahrheit im Spiegel der Pastoralbriefe.* Marburger Theologische Studien 28. Marburg: N. G. Elwert, 1990.

Schlatter, Adolph. *Die Briefe an die Thessalonischer, Philipper, Timotheus und Titus.* Erläuterungen zum Neuen Testament 8. Stuttgart: Calwer, 1987 (1964).

- *Die Kirche der Griechen im Urteil des Paulus: Eine Auslegung seiner Briefe an Timotheus und Titus.* Stuttgart: Calwer, 1983 (1936).

Schöllgen, Georg. "Die διπλῆ τιμή von 1.Tim.5,17," *Zeitschrift für die neutestamentliche Wissenschaft und die Kunde der älteren Kirche* 80 (1989): 232-39.

Schreiner, Thomas. "Did Paul Believe in Justification by Works? Another Look at Romans 2." *Bulletin for Biblical Research* 3 (1993): 131-56.

Schürer, E. *The History of the Jewish People in the Age of Jesus Christ.* 3 vols. Edited and revised by G. Vermes, F. Millar, and M. Black. Edinburgh: T&T Clark, 1973-87.

Schwarz, Roland. *Bürgerliches Christentum im Neuen Testament? Eine Studie zu Ethik, Amt und Recht in den Pastoralbriefen.* Österreichische biblische Studien 4. Klosterneuburg: Österreichisches Katholisches Bibelwerk, 1983.

Scott, E. F. *The Pastoral Epistles.* Moffatt New Testament Commentary. London: Hodder & Stoughton, 1936.

Scott, A. F. *The Roman Age: Every One a Witness.* London: White Lion,

1977.

Scott, J. J. Jr. "Immortality." Pages 431-33 in *Dictionary of Paul and His Letters*. Edited by Gerald F. Hawthorne, and Ralph P. Martin. Downers Grove: IVP, 1993.

- "Life and Death." Pages 553-55 in *Dictionary of Paul and His Letters*. Edited by Gerald F. Hawthorne, and Ralph P. Martin. Downers Grove: IVP, 1993.

Scott, James M. *Paul and the Nations: The Old Testament and Jewish Background of Paul's Mission to the Nations with Special Reference to the Destination of Galatians*. Wissenschaftliche Untersuchungen zum Alten und Neuen Testament 2.84. Tübingen: J. C. B. Mohr, 1995.

Seeley, David. *The Noble Death: Graeco-Roman Martyrdom and Paul's Concept of Salvation*. Journal for the Study of the New Testament Supplement Series 28. Sheffield: Sheffield Academic Press, 1990.

Segal, Alan F. "Paul's Thinking about Resurrection in Its Jewish Context." *New Testament Studies* 44 (1998): 400-19.

Seifrid, Mark A. "Blind Alleys in the Controversy over the Paul of History", *Tyndale Bulletin* 45 (1994): 73-95.

Sell, Jesse J. *The Knowledge of the Truth - Two Doctrines. The Book of Thomas the Contender and the False Teachers in the Pastoral Epistles*. European University Studies Series 23, Theology, 194. Frankfurt: Peter Lang, 1982.

Sim, D. C. "The Meaning of παλιγγενεσία in Matthew 19.28." *Journal for the Study of the New Testament* 50 (1993): 3-12.

Simpson, E. K. *The Pastoral Epistles: The Greek Text with Introduction and Commentary*. London: Tyndale, 1954.

Skeat, T. C. "Especially the Parchments: A Note on 2 Timothy 4:13." *Journal of Theological Studies* ns 30 (1979): 173-77.

Smallwood, E. Mary. *The Jews under Roman Rule from Pompey to Diocletian*. Studies in Judaism in Late Antiquity 20. Leiden: Brill, 1976.

Smith, Martin "Support from Oinoanda for a variant reading in Dionysius of Halicarnassus." *Hermes* 122 (1994): 503-4.

Smith, M. *Clement of Alexandria and a Secret Gospel of Mark*. Cambridge, Mass.: Harvard University Press, 1973.

Sparks, Irving Alan. *The Pastoral Epistles*. San Diego, Calif.: Institute of Biblical Studies, 1985.

Spicq, Ceslas. *Les Épitres Pastorales*. 2 vol. 4th ed. Paris: Gabalda, 1966.

Spyridakis, Stylianos. "Notes on the Jews of Gortyna and Crete," *Zeitschrift für Papyrologie und Epigraphik* 73 (1988): 171-5.

- *Ptolemaic Itanos and Hellenistic Crete*. University of California Publications in History 82. Berkeley: University of California Press, 1970.

Squires, John T. *The Plan of God in Luke-Acts*. Society for New Testament

Study Monograph Series 76. Cambridge: Cambridge University Press, 1993.

Staples, Peter. "The Unused Lever? A Study on the Possible Literary Influence of the Greek Maccabean Literature in the New Testament." *Modern Churchman* ns 9 (1966): 218-29.

Stenger, Werner. *Der Christushymnus 1Tim 3,16: Ein strukturanalytische Untersuchung*. Regensburger Studien zur Theologie 6. Frankfurt: Peter Lang, 1977.

Sterling, Gregory E. "'Wisdom among the Perfect': Creation Traditions in Alexandrian Judaism and Corinthian Christianity." *Novum Testamentum* 37 (1995): 355-84.

Stettler, Hanna. *Die Christologie der Pastoralbriefe*. Wissenschaftliche Untersuchungen zum Alten und Neuen Testament 2.105. Tübingen: J. C. B. Mohr, 1998.

Stibbe, Mark W. G. *John as Storyteller*. Society for New Testament Study Monograph Series 73. Cambridge: Cambridge University Press, 1992.

Stiefel, Jennifer H. "Women Deacons in 1 Timothy: a Linguistic and Literary Look at 'Women likewise . . .' (1 Tim 3:11)." *New Testament Studies* 41 (1995): 442-57.

Stone, Michael Edward, ed. *Jewish Writings of the Second Temple Period: Apocrypha, Pseudepigrapha, Qumran, sectarian writings, Philo, Josephus*. Philadelphia: Fortress, 1984.

- *Scriptures, Sects and Visions. A Profile of Judaism from Ezra to the Jewish Revolts*. Philadelphia: Fortress, 1980.

Stott, John R. W. *The Message of 1 Timothy & Titus*. The Bible Speaks Today. Leicester: IVP, 1996.

- *The Message of 2 Timothy*. The Bible Speaks Today. Leicester: IVP, 1973.

Stowers, Stanley K. *The Diatribe and Paul's Letter to the Romans*. Society for Biblical Literature Dissertation Series 57. Chico, Calif.: Scholars Press, 1981.

- *Letter Writing in Greco-Roman Antiquity*. Library of Early Christianity. Philadelpia: Westminster, 1986.

- "Paul on the Use and Abuse of Reason." Pages 253-86 in *Greeks, Romans and Christians: Essays in Honor of Abraham J. Malherbe*. Edited by D. L. Balch, E. Ferguson, and W. A. Meeks, Minneapolis: Fortress, 1990.

Stratton, B. J. "Eve through Several Lenses: Truth in 1 Timothy 2.8-15." Pages 258-73 in *A Feminist Companion to the Hebrew Bible in the New Testament*. Edited by A. Brenner. The Feminist Companion to the Bible 10. Sheffield: Sheffield Academic Press, 1996.

Sumney, Jerry. "'God Our Savior': The Theology of 1 Timothy." *Lexington Theological Quarterly* 33 (1998): 151-61.

Sweeney, Michael Leroy. "From God's Household to the Heavenly Chorus: a Comparison of the Church in the Pastoral Epistles with the Church in the Letters of Ignatius of Antioch." Ph.D. diss., Union Theological Seminary, Virginia, 1989.

Taylor, Walter F. Jr. "1-2 Timothy, Titus." Pages 59-93 in *The Deutero-Pauline Letters: Ephesians, Colossians, 2 Thessalonians, 1-2 Timothy, Titus.* Edited by Gerhard Krodel. Rev. ed. Proclamation Commentaries. Minneapolis: Fortress, 1993.

Tcherikover, Victor A., Alexander Fuks, and Menahem Stern, eds. *Corpus papyrorum judaicarum.* 3 vols. Cambridge, Mass.: Harvard University Press, 1957-64.

Thiede, C. P. "A Pagan Reading of 2 Peter. Cosmic Conflagration in 2 Peter 3 and the Octavius of Minucius Felix." *Journal for the Study of the New Testament* 26 (1986): 79-96.

Thiselton, Anthony C. "The Logical Role of the Liar Paradox in Titus 1:12,13. A Dissent from the Comentaries in the Light of Philosophical and Logical Analysis." *Biblical Interpretation* 2 (1994): 207-23.

Thompson, Michael B. Review of Philip H. Towner, *The Goal of our Instruction: The Structure of Theology and Ethics in the Pastoral Epistles. Evangelical Quarterly* 64 (1992): 358-59.

Tollefson, Kenneth D. "Titus: Epistle of Religious Revitalization." *Biblical Theology Bulletin* 30 (2000): 145-57.

Torrance, Thomas F. *The Doctrine of Grace in the Apostolic Fathers.* Edinburgh: Oliver & Boyd, 1948.

Torrey, C. "4 Maccabees." Pages 2882-86 in *Encyclopaedia Britannica* vol. 3, 1904.

Towner, Philip H. *1-2 Timothy & Titus.* IVP New Testament Commentary Series. Downers Grove: IVP, 1994.

- "Feminist Approaches to the New Testament: 1 Tim 2:8-15 as a Test Case." *Jian Dao* 7 (1997): 91-111.
- *The Goal of our Instruction: The Structure of Theology and Ethics in the Pastoral Epistles.* Journal for the Study of the New Testament Supplement Series 34. Sheffield: Sheffield Academic Press, 1989.
- "Gnosis and Realized Eschatology in Ephesus (of the Pastoral Epistles) and the Corinthian Enthusiasm." *Journal for the Study of the New Testament* 31 (1987): 95-124.
- "Pauline Theology or Pauline Tradition in the Pastoral Epistles: the Question of Method." *Tyndale Bulletin* 46 (1995) 287-314.
- "The Present Age in the Eschatology of the Pastoral Epistles." *New Testament Studies* 32 (1986): 427-48.

Trebilco, Paul. "What Shall We Call Each Other? Part One: The Issue of Self-designation in the Pastoral Epistles." *Tyndale Bulletin* 53.2

(2002): 239-58.
- *The Early Christians in Ephesus from Paul to Ignatius.* Wissenschaftliche Untersuchungen zum Neuen Testament 166. Tübingen: Mohr Siebeck, 2004.
Trites, A. A. "Witness." Pages 973-75 in *Dictionary of Paul and His Letters.* Edited by Gerald F. Hawthorne, and Ralph P. Martin. Downers Grove: IVP, 1993.
Trummer, Peter. *Die Paulustradition der Pastoralbriefe.* Beiträge zur biblischen Exegese und Theologie 8. Frankfurt: Peter Lang, 1978.
Turner, John D. "Ritual in Gnosticism." *Society for Biblical Literature Seminar Papers* 33 (1994): 136-81.
Turner, Nigel. *Grammatical Insights into the New Testament.* Edinburgh: T&T Clark, 1965.
Τζεδακης, Θεοδωρος Β. "Συντομος ιστορια της επισκοπης Κνωσους." *Κρητικη Χρονικα* ΚΑ (1969): 333-50.
Urmson, J. O. *The Greek Philosophical Vocabulary.* London: Duckworth, 1990.
van Bruggen, Jakob. *Die geschichtliche Einordnung der Pastoralbriefe.* Wuppertal: Brockhaus, 1981.
Verner, David C. *The Household of God: The Social World of the Pastoral Epistles.* Society for Biblical Literature Dissertation Series 71. Chico: Scholars Press, 1983.
Vorster, Willem S. "Stoics and Early Christians on Blessedness." Pages 38-51 in *Greeks, Romans and Christians: Essays in Honor of Abraham J. Malherbe.* Edited by D. L. Balch, E. Ferguson, and W. A. Meeks, Minneapolis: Fortress, 1990.
Waard, J. de. *A Comparative Study of the Old Testament Text in the Dead Sea Scrolls and in the New Testament.* Studies on the Texts of the Desert of Judah 4. Leiden: Brill, 1965.
Wainwright, Geoffrey. "Praying for Kings: The Place of Human Rulers in the Divine Plan of Salvation." *Ex Auditu* 2 (1986): 117-27.
Wainwright, John W. "*Eusebeia*: Syncretism or Conservative Contextualization?" *Evangelical Quarterly* 65 (1993): 211-24.
Wall, Robert W. "1 Timothy 2:9-15 Reconsidered (Again)", *Bulletin for Biblical Research* 14.1 (2004): 81-103.
Wallis, Ian G. *The Faith of Jesus Christ in Early Christian Tradition.* Society for New Testament Study Monograph Series 84. Cambridge: Cambridge University Press, 1995.
Walls, Andrew F. "Old Athens and New Jerusalem: Some Signposts for Christian Scholarship in the Early History of Mission Studies." *International Bulletin of Missionary Research* 21 (1996): 146-53.
Walters, G., and B. A. Milne. "Salvation." Pages 1271-75 in vol. 3 of *The Illustrated Bible Dictionary.* Edited by J. D. Douglas. Leicester: IVP, 1980.

Ward, Ronald A. *Commentary on 1 & 2 Timothy & Titus.* Waco, Tex.: Word Books, 1974.
- *Hidden Meaning in the New Testament: New Light from Old Greek.* London: Marshall, Morgan & Scott, 1969.
Ware, J. "The Thessalonians as a Missionary Congregation: 1 Thess 1:5-8." *Zeitschrift für die neutestamentliche Wissenschaft und die Kunde der älteren Kirche* 83 (1992): 126-31.
Waters, K.L. Sr, "Saved through Childbearing: Virtues as Children in 1 Timothy 2:11-15." *Journal of Biblical Literature* 123 (2004): 703-35.
Watson, Lindsay. *Arae: The Curse Poetry of Antiquity.* Arca, Classical and Medieval Texts, Papers and Monographs 26. Leeds: Francis Cairns, 1991.
Wedderburn, A. J. M. "The Soteriology of the Mysteries and Pauline Baptismal Theology." *Novum Testamentum* 29 (1987): 53-72.
Wells, David F. *The Search for Salvation.* Issues in Contemporary Theology. Leicester: IVP, 1978.
White, L. Michael. "Morality Between Two Worlds. A Paradigm of Friendship in Philippians." Pages 201-15 in *Greeks, Romans and Christians: Essays in Honor of Abraham J. Malherbe.* Edited by D. L. Balch, E. Ferguson, and W. A. Meeks, Minneapolis: Fortress, 1990.
White, R. E. O. *The Biblical Doctrine of Initiation.* London: Hodder & Stoughton, 1960.
Wiebe, B. "Two Texts on Women (1 Tim 2:11-15; Gal 3:26-29). A Test of Interpretation." *Horizons in Biblical Theology* 16 (1994): 54-85.
Wieland, George M. Review of Frances Young, *The Theology of the Pastoral Letters. Evangelical Quarterly* 68 (1996): 164-67.
- "Grace Manifest: Missional Church in the Letter to Titus", *Stimulus* 13.1 (2005): 8-11.
Wild, Robert A., S.J. "The Pastoral Letters." Pages 891-902 in *The New Jerome Biblical Commentary.* Edited by R. E. Brown, S.S., J. A. Fitzmyer, S.J., and R. E. Murphy, O.Carm. Student ed. London: Geoffrey Chapman, 1993 (1989).
Will, Frederic. "Notes from Crete." *Arion* 1 (1962): 74-83.
Willetts, Ronald F., ed. *The Law Code of Gortyn.* Berlin: Walter de Gruyton, 1967.
Williams, Sam K. *Jesus' Death as Saving Event. The Background and Origin of a Concept.* Harvard Dissertations in Religion 2. Missoula, Mont.: published by Scholars Press for Harvard Theological Review, 1975.
Williamson, Ronald. *Jews in the Hellenistic World: Philo.* Cambridge Comentary on Writings of the Jewish and Christian World 200 B.C. - 200 A.D. 1.2. Cambridge: Cambridge University Press, 1989.
Willis, Timothy M. "Gideon." Page 253 in *The Oxford Companion to the Bible.* Edited by Bruce M. Metzger and Michael D. Coogan. Oxford: Oxford University Press, 1993.

Wilson, Stephen G. *Luke and the Pastoral Epistles.* London: SPCK, 1979.
Wimbush, Vincent L. "The Ascetic Impulse in Ancient Christianity." *Theology Today* 50 (1993): 417-28.
Winter, Bruce W. "The 'New' Roman Wife and 1 Timothy 2:9-15: The Search for a *Sitz im Leben.*" *Tyndale Bulletin* 51 (2000): 285-94.
- "Providentia for the widows in 1 Tim 5:3-16." *Tyndale Bulletin* 39 (1988): 83-100.
Witherington, Ben, III. *Paul's Narrative Thought World: The Tapestry of Tragedy and Triumph,* Louisville, Ky.: Westminster, 1994.
- "Salvation and Health in Christian Antiquity: the Soteriology of Luke-Acts in its First Century Setting." Pages 145-66 in *Witness to the Gospel: The Theology of Acts.* Edited by I. H. Marshall and D. G. Petersen. Grand Rapids: Eerdmans, 1998.
- *Women in the Earliest Churches.* Cambridge: Cambridge University Press, 1988.
Witt, R. E. *Isis in the Graeco-Roman World.* London: Thames & Hudson, 1971.
Wolf, H. "Maccabees, Book of." Pages 8-22 in vol. 4 of *Zondervan Pictorial Encyclopaedia of the Bible.* Edited by M. C. Tenney. Grand Rapids: Zondervan, 1975.
Wolfe, B. P. "The Use of Scripture in the Pastoral Epistles." Ph.D. diss. University of Aberdeen, 1990.
Wolter, Michael. *Die Pastoralbriefe als Paulustradition.* Forschungen zur Religion und Literatur des Alten und Neuen Testaments 146. Göttingen: Vandenhoeck & Ruprecht, 1988.
- "Paulus, der bekehrte Gottesfiend. Zum Verständnis von 1.Tim. 1:13." *Novum Testamentum* 31 (1989): 48-66.
Wright, R. "How credible are Plato's Myths?" Pages 364-71 in *Arktours: Hellenic Studies Presented to Bernard M. W. Knox on the Occasion of his Sixty-Fifth Birthday.* Edited by Glen W. Bowerstock, Walter Burkert, and Michael C. J. Putnam. Berlin: de Gruyter, 1979.
Wright, N. T. *The New Testament and the People of God.* Minneapolis: Fortress, 1992.
Yamauchi, Edwin M. "Magic in the Biblical World." *Tyndale Bulletin* 34 (1983): 169-200.
- "Pre-Christian Gnosticism, the New Testament and Nag Hammadi in recent debate." *Themelios* 10 (1984): 22-7.
Young, Frances. Review of Philip H. Towner, *The Goal of our Instruction: The Structure of Theology and Ethics in the Pastoral Epistles. Journal of Theological Studies* ns 42 (1991): 256-58.
- "The Pastoral Epistles and the Ethics of Reading." *Journal for the Study of the New Testament* 45 (1992): 105-20.
- *The Theology of the Pastoral Letters.* New Testament Theology. Cambridge: Cambridge University Press, 1994.

Ziesler, John. *Paul's Letter to the Romans*. London: SCM, 1989.

INDEXES

Biblical and Other Ancient Literature

OLD TESTAMENT

Genesis

Chs 2-3	74, 80
Ch 3	257
3:15	80, 84, 254, 257
3:16	80
18:23	39
22:16-17	189
24:6	99

Exodus

10:28	99
15:13	210
19:5	210
19:12	99
23:21	99, 218
29:4	229
Ch 32	62
32:30	62
32:32	62
40:10	229

Leviticus

4:7	231
4:18	231
4:25	231
14:8	229
14:9	229
15:5	229
15:6	229
15:7	229
15:8	229
15:10	229
15:11	229
15:13	229
15:16	229
15:18	229
15:21	229
15:22	229
15:27	229
Chs 16-17	63
16:4	229
16:24	229
16:26	229
16:28	229
17:11	63
17:15	229
17:16	229
22:6	229
26:15	218

Numbers

11:20	218
14:43	218
15:22-31	41
Ch 16	167
16:15	167
16:26	167
19:7	229
19:8	229
19:19	229
20:10	218
23:19	190

Deuteronomy

Book	24, 94, 260
1:26	218
4:9	94
4:10	94
4:25-31	94
4:33	91, 94
5:26	91, 94
6:12	94
7:6	210
8:11	94
8:18	138
Ch 9	223
9:4	223
9:5	223
9:6	223
9:7	218, 223
9:10	94
9:11-21	61
9:23	218
9:24	218
9:25-29	61

11:16	94	**1 Samuel**	
12:13	94	**(1 Kingdoms)**	
12:19	94	Book	24
12:30	94	2:1	26
14:2	210	17:26	91
15:9	94	17:36	91
18:16	94	**2 Samuel**	
23:12	229	**(2 Kingdoms)**	
24:8	94	7:23	206, 210
26:18	210	**2 Kings**	
31:16-22	94	**(4 Kingdoms)**	
32:51	218	9:7	192
34:5	192	10:23	192
34:9	94	14:27	79
34:10	94	18:12	192
Joshua		19:4	91
1:1	192	19:16	91
1:13	192, 193	**1 Chronicles**	
1:15	192	16:13	147
3:10	91	16:35	25
5:6	218	16:36	190
8:31	192, 193	17:21	210
8:33	192, 193	29:10	190
10:6	23	**2 Chronicles**	
11:12	192, 193	1:3	192, 193
12:6	192, 193	24:6	192
13:8	192, 193	**Nehemiah**	
14:7	192	Book	24
18:7	192, 193	4:14	138
22:2	192, 193	9:5	190
22:4	192	9:27	23, 24
22:5	192, 193	9:29	218
24:29	192, 193	10:30	192
Judges		**Job**	
Book	24	9:33	58, 59, 256
2:8	192, 193	**Psalms**	
2:16	24	Book	24
3:9	23, 24	2:7	137
3:15	23, 24	6:4	223
Ch 6	45	6:11	111
6:14	24	7:1	28
6:34	45	13:3	128
6:36-37	24	13:5	28, 223
7:2	24	14:6-7	28
12:3	23, 24	16:9	30
		16:10	137, 141

Indexes

17:2	170	*69:6*	111
17:7	28, 223	*69:13*	223
18 Title	192	*70:2*	111
18:2	28	*71:1*	111
18:50	223	*71:4-5*	28
19:7	162	*74:12*	190
Ps 22	113, 170	*74:21*	111
22:4-5	113-14	*79:9*	25
22:5	111	Ps 84	92
22:8	28, 171	*84:2*	91
22:20-21	171	*85:5*	25
24:1	25	*85:7*	223
24:5	24, 25, 170	*86:13*	124
25:2	111	*89:35*	190
25:3	111	*90:2*	190
25:5	25, 25	*91:9*	28
25:7	223	*95:1*	25
25:20	111	*95:7-11*	189
27:1	25	*97:5*	25
27:9	25	*98:3*	223
31:1	111	*100:6*	89
31:16	223	*103:17*	190
31:17	111	*104:18*	28
33:16	79	Ps 105	147, 193
34:5	111	*105:6*	147
35:4	111	*105:7-11*	194
35:9	26	*105:8*	147
36 Title	192	*105:19*	147
37:19	111	*105:26*	194
40:14	111	*105:30*	63
41:13	190	*105:42*	147, 194
Ps 42	92	*105:43*	147, 194
42:2	91	*106:5*	147
43:1	170	*106:23*	61, 147
44:7	111	*106:46*	190
51:10	230	*109:26*	223
53:5	111	*113:1*	192
54:1	170	*119:31*	111
54:7	124	*119:41*	223
55:19	190	*119:46*	111
56:13	124	*119:80*	111
57:3	223	*119:98*	162
62:3	25	*119:116*	111
62:6	25	*127:5*	111
62:7	25, 28	*130:8*	210
62:9	28	*134:1*	192
65:5	25, 255	*135:1*	192
65:6	32	*135:4*	210

303

135:8	209	54:4-5	65
142:6	28	54:17	192

Proverbs

8:23	190	55:3	137
		55:4-5	68
		55:11	146

Song of Solomon

4:2	229	56:1	223
6:6	229	58:18	146
		59:13	218

Isaiah

Book	24	62:1	170
1:20	146	63:1	170
1:23	218	63:9	79
1:25	218	63:10	218
3:8	218	65:1	67
11:10	67	65:2	218
14:32	79	65:9	147
17:10	25	65:23	147
22:25	146		
24:3	146		
25:8	146		

Jeremiah

28:16	42, 43, 112	5:23	218
30:9	218	6:15	112
30:12	218	7:7	190
36:5	218	10:25	41
37:4	91	13:5	146
37:17	91	13:25	218
40:3-5	67	14:8	32
40:5	146	25:5	190
40:8	146	31:6	118
41:1	67	33:31-34	189

Ezekiel

41:8-10	118	3:16-21	100
42:1	118, 147	33:1-9	100
42:1-2	67	36:25-27	229, 230
42:5-9	118	37:23	210
42:19	192		
42:27	128		

Daniel

43:1-7	118	4:21	91
43:3	117	5:23	91
43:8-13	67	6:16-27	170
43:11	117	6:26	91
43:20	147	6:27	91
44:22	210	9:18	223
45:4	147	12:2	29, 36
45:15-16	67	12:7	91
45:21-22	65	12:13	29

Hosea

49:1	118	1:10	91, 92
49:6	30, 67, 118, 128, 137, 148	2:23	92
53:12	61, 63, 143	9:15	218

Joel
3:1-2	230
3:5	167
3:8	146

Obadiah
1:18	146

Jonah
3:2	192

Micah 24
7:7	25, 144

Habakkuk
1:18	26
2:3	144
3:18	25

Zephaniah
3:8	144

Zechariah
7:11	218
7:12	218

APOCRYPHA

Tobit
4:5	138
4:12	99
4:14	99
6:18	190
8:15	147

Judith
Book	24
12:10	118

Wisdom of Solomon
Book	15, 24, 125
1:15	125
2:23	125
3:4	29, 125
3:9	89, 147
3:18	29
4:1	125
4:15	147
4:20	29
5:14	29
6:17-20	125
6:18	125
6:19	125
8:13	125
8:17	125
Chs 9-19	218
10:4	79
10:14	149
11:23	25
12:1	125
15:3	125
16:7	25, 79
16:8	25
16:12	25
17:7	24
18:4	125

Sirach/Ecclesiasticus
Book	15, 24
7:5	162
10:26	162
16:6	218
17:30	125
18:11	230
18:13-14	202
24:9	190
24:22	112
25:24	75
29:20	100
31:5	232
32:4	162
34:13-14	32
34:25	229
36:1-22	65
38:24-25	162
38:34-39:11	162
41:17-42:1	112
42:1-8	112
46:1	147
47:21	218
47:22	141, 147
51:1	24
51:16-17	98
51:18	112, 210
51:29	112

Baruch
Book	24
1:18	218
1:19	218
2:19	223
4:22	24, 149
4:24	149
4:29	149

Susanna
60	29

Bel and the Dragon
Chs 5-6	91
Ch 24	91
Ch 25	91

1 Maccabees
Book	15, 24, 261
2:26	210
2:27	210
2:50	210
2:50-68	170
2:58	210
4:30	24
15:23	185

2 Maccabees
Book	15, 206
1:25	147
2:18	29
2:21	210
3:24	206
4:2	210
7:9	36
7:11	29
7:14	29
7:20	29
7:23	29
7:34-37	29
7:40	29
13:14	143
14:38	210

3 Maccabees
Book	15, 24, 158, 206
2:9	206
5:8	206
5:14	118
6:18	206
6:28	91
6:29	24
6:32	24
6:39	206
7:1	143
7:16	24

4 Maccabees
Book	15, 125, 207, 208, 260, 262
1:1	96
1:3-4	208
1:6	208
1:11	143
1:17	208
1:18	208
4:23	208
5:23	143
5:23-24	208
6:9	143
6:21	143
6:27-29	61
6:27-30	144
6:28	64
6:28-29	64
6:29	63
6:30	143, 144
6:31	96
7:3	125
7:8	143
7:9	143
7:16	96, 143
7:22	143, 144
Ch 9	144
9:1-2	144
9:6	143, 144
9:8	143, 144
9:10	144
9:15	144
9:22	38, 125, 143, 144
9:23	144
9:24	144
9:30	143
10:10	144
13:1	96, 143
13:12	143, 144
13:24	208
13:27	143
14:5	125
14:6	125

Indexes

15:2-3	36
15:10	143, 208
15:23	96
15:30	143
15:31	143
15:32	143
16:1	96, 143, 143
16:8	143
16:13	125
16:16	210
16:17	143, 144
16:19	143, 144
16:21	143, 144
17:7	143
17:10	143
17:12	38, 125, 143
17:18	29
17:21	64
17:22	64
17:23	143
18:2	96
18:23	29, 125, 144

NEW TESTAMENT

Matthew

1:21	35
4:21	118
5:9	39
5:18	226
5:20	232
8:25	35
9:11	39
9:13	39
9:21	35
9:22	35
10:13	155
10:18	66
10:22	35, 83, 144
10:33	156
11:19	39
12:17-21	67
12:41	192
14:30	35
16:16	91
16:24	203
16:25	35
18:3	172
19:16	36
19:17	36
19:21	37
19:23	172
19:23-24	36
19:25	35, 36
19:27	37
19:28	154, 226
19:28-29	37
19:29	232
20:1	232
20:28	208
22:14	147
24:4	144
24:4-5	67
24:11	67, 144
24:13	35, 83, 144
24:14	66, 144
24:22	147
24:23-24	67
24:24	144, 147
24:30	144
25:31	144, 147
25:31-46	144
25:34	36, 144, 232
24:35	226
25:46	36
26:28	231
26:35	153
26:63	91
26:70	156
26:72	156
26:75	138
27:29	170
27:39	170
27:40	35
27:42	35, 42
27:43	170
27:46	170

Mark

1:20	118
2:15	39
2:16	39

2:17	39	10:25	36, 232
5:28	35	10:28	36
5:34	35	11:32	192
6:56	35	12:1	100
8:34	203	12:9	156
8:35	35	14:7	99, 100
8:38	112, 156	15:1	39
10:17	36, 232	15:2	206
10:21	37	15:7	39
10:23	232	15:10	39
10:23-25	36	17:3	100
10:26	35, 36	18:7	147
10:28	37	18:9	40
10:30	36, 37, 203	18:13-14	40
10:45	60, 63, 208	18:17	232
11:21	138	18:18	36, 232
13:5-6	67	18:22	37
13:9-10	66	18:24	36
13:13	35, 83, 144	18:26	35, 36
13:20	147	18:28	37
13:22	67, 147	18:30	36, 37
13:24	168	18:42	35
14:24	231	20:35	150
14:31	153	21:8	67
14:68	156	21:12-13	66
14:70	156	21:19	83
15:28	143	21:34	100
15:30-31	35	22:20	231
15:34	170	22:28-30	154
15:43	205	22:37	143
		22:57	156

Luke

Book	264	23:32	143
1:47	21, 26, 185	23:33	143
2:11	26, 185	23:35	35
2:25	205	23:39	143
2:38	205	23:51	205
3:4-6	67	24:6	138
5:30	39	24:8	138
5:32	39	24:25	42
7:34	39		

John

7:48-50	35	Book	37, 264
8:11-12	35	1:9	43, 127
8:48	35	2:22	138
8:50	35	3:3	226
9:23	203	3:3-8	226
9:24	35	3:15	37, 42
9:26	112, 156	3:16	37

3:17	35, 43, 79	2:14-39	141
3:19	43	2:17	230
3:34	226	2:17-21	168
3:36	37	2:18	230
4:42	27	2:21	35
5:24	37	2:24	141
5:34	35	2:25-36	141
6:14	43	2:27	141
6:27	37	2:31	141
6:40	37	2:31-32	30
6:47	37	2:33	231
6:54	37	2:39	168
6:56	83	2:40	35
7:42	140	2:47	35
8:31	83	3:5	99, 100
8:32	56	3:13	155
9:16	40	3:17-19	42
9:24	40	4:9	35
9:25	40	4:33	66
9:31	40	5:31	26
9:39	43	5:35	100
10:36	43	6:7	146
11:25-26	37	7:35	155
12:16	138	9:3	128
12:25	37	9:3-6	128
12:46	43	9:5-6	118
12:47	35	9:15	67, 118
13:38	156	10:45	230
14:2-3	37	11:14	35
15:4	83	11:16	138
15:5	83	12:24	146
15:6	83	Ch 13	138
15:7	83	13:16-41	30, 137, 141, 163, 259
15:9	83	13:16-52	148
15:10	83	13:20	141
16:4	138	13:21	141
16:28	43	13:22	141
17:3	37	13:22-23	140
17:18	43	13:23	26
18:25	156	13:27	42
18:27	156	13:30	141
18:37	43	13:30-31	141
Acts		13:30-36	137
Book	40, 54, 254, 256	13:32-33	188
1:3	79	13:32-39	141
1:7	192	13:34	141
2:11	185	13:35	141
		13:36	141

13:37	141	*26:17-18*	30
13:38	42	*26:18*	128
13:44	137, 148	*26:20*	30
13:46	30, 137, 148	*26:22*	150
13:47	67, 128, 137, 148	*26:23*	30, 67, 128
13:48	137, 148	*27:3*	150
13:49	146	*27:20*	35
14:7	56	*17:23*	168
14:15-17	92, 102	*27:31*	35
14:21-23	184	*28:20*	206
15:1	35	*28:23*	30
15:7-11	230	*28:28*	30
15:11	35, 79	*28:31*	30
16:3	183	***Romans***	
16:30	35	*Letter*	37, 148, 223
16:31	35	*1:1*	192
17:3	141	*1:1-6*	189
17:23-28	102	*1:3*	140
17:30	42, 201	*1:3-4*	136, 140, 259
19:20	146	*1:4*	139
19:22	99, 100	*1:5*	46
20:24	200	*1:8-17*	115
20:26-27	100	*1:16*	112, 115
20:28	94, 100, 101	*1:23*	126
20:32	200	*1:29-31*	218
20:35	138	*2:6-7*	37, 126
21:20	210	*2:7*	125, 126
22:3	210	*2:24*	42, 48
22:6	128	*2:25-27*	183
22:6-11	128	*3:7*	40
22:9	128	*3:23*	61
22:11	128	*3:24*	47, 61, 149
22:14-16	118	*3:25*	48, 61
22:15	201	*3:29-30*	57
23-28	29-30	*4:16*	42
23:6	30, 206	*4:18*	188
23:21	206	*4:24*	188
24:2	150	*5:2*	30
24:14-15	30, 206	*5:5*	113, 168, 231
24:21	30	*5:8-10*	40
24:24	30	*5:9*	79
24:25	30	*5:12-21*	61
26:6	30	*5:17*	46
26:7	30	*5:18-19*	89
26:8	30	*5:19*	40
26:12-18	128	*5:20*	46
26:13	128	*5:21*	37, 46, 126, 188
26:15-18	118		

6:1	152	*11:25-36*	41
6:1-14	153, 204	*11:28*	42
6:2	153	*11:29*	117
6:3-4	153	*11:30*	218, 227
6:7	153	*11:30-32*	41, 43
6:8	151	*11:31*	42
6:9	124	*12:2*	227
6:11	47	*12:3*	119
6:15	46	*12:6*	119
6:17-23	218	*12:12*	144
6:23	37	*13:11*	88, 221
7:4	153	*13:11-13*	144
7:5-6	218	*14:14*	254
Ch 8	221	*15:12*	67
8:1	47, 149	*15:15*	119
8:13	153	*15:15-16*	46
8:15	115	*16:2*	206
8:16-25	30	*16:12*	97
8:17-25	144	*16:13*	147
8:24	117, 221	*16:25*	192
8:28-30	147	*16:25-26*	121
8:31-32	147	***1 Corinthians***	
8:33	147	*Letter*	148
8:33-34	147	*1:1*	192
8:34	61	*1:2*	94
8:35-39	147	*1:6-7*	67
8:39	47, 149	*1:9*	158
Chs 9-11	43	*1:21*	79, 192
9:1	52	*1:26*	117
9:5	173	*2:4*	192
9:15-18	43	*2:6*	124
9:22	48	*2:7-10*	121
9:23	43	*3:10*	46, 119
9:24	92	*3:15*	79
9:25-26	92	*4:8*	154
9:33	42, 112	*4:12*	154
10:2	41	*4:17*	47
10:2-3	43	*6:2*	154
10:3	41	*6:9-10*	218
10:8-17	42	*6:9-11*	218, 219, 230, 232
10:9	164, 167	*6:14*	139
10:11	42, 112	*7:11*	118
10:13	167	*7:20*	117
10:14	41	*7:25*	45
10:21	43	*9:22*	101
11:20	42, 67	*9:27*	101
11:22-23	227	*10:13*	158
11:23	42		

10:32	94	8:6	183
11:2	138	8:16	183
11:2-16	71	8:23	183
11:16	94	11:31	52
11:22	94	13:4	139
14:10	150	***Galatians***	
Ch 15	173	1:4	172, 203, 208
15:2	79, 83, 97	1:5	173
15:5-7	128	1:13	94
15:9	40, 49, 94	1:14	48, 210
15:14	192	1:15	120
15:26	122, 124	1:15-16	118
15:37	150	1:20	52
15:40	173	1:22	47
15:42	38, 125	2:5	183
15:47	173	2:9	46, 119
15:48	173	2:12	183
15:49	173	2:15	40
15:50	38, 125	2:19	153
15:52	126	2:19-20	153
15:53	38, 125	2:20	208
15:54	38, 125	3:15-22	61
15:55	115	3:19-20	61
16:6	150	3:21-22	188
2 Corinthians		3:23-29	218
Letter	148	4:3-7	218
1:1	94, 192	4:8-9	219
1:8-10	95	5:2-6	30
1:12	67	5:5	30
1:18	158	5:19-21	218
2:13	183	5:21	219
3:3	92, 227	6:8	37
3:8	227	6:9	192
3:17	227	6:14	205
3:18	227	***Ephesians***	
4:1	45	Letter	26
4:6	227	1:18	117, 221
4:10-11	153	1:19-20	139
4:16	227	2:1-10	219
4:17	149	2:2	203
5:5	227	2:5-9	115
5:17	227	2:8	79
5:18-21	200	2:11-22	219
6:16	92	2:12	31, 221
7:3	152	3:2	119
7:6	183	3:7	119
7:13	183	3:8	119

3:9-10	121	*3:5*	153
4:1	117	*3:7-8*	227
4:4	117	*3:8*	153
4:7	119	*3:9*	227
4:17-24	219	*3:10*	227
4:23-24	227	*3:12*	147
5:6-11	219		
5:14	127		
5:16	171		
5:23	26		
5:26	229		

Philippians

Letter	26
1:1	192
1:12-14	169
1:12-18	142, 146
1:19-20	169
1:22-26	171
2:5-11	142
2:8	143
2:16	100
2:29	206
3:6	48, 210
3:9	47
3:10	139
3:10-11	142, 153
3:14	117
3:20	26
4:20	173

Colossians

1:5-6	30
1:6	200, 202
1:16	56
1:21-22	219
1:23	30, 83
1:24	142
1:26	121
1:27	30, 97
1:29	87, 93
2:8	153
2:11-12	153
2:12	153
2:20	153
3:1	227
3:1-11	153, 219
3:3	227
3:4	227

1 Thessalonians

1:1	94
1:3	31
1:9	31, 92
1:10	31, 92
1:14	31
2:12	31
2:13	146
2:14	31, 94
4:5	41
4:7	118
4:13	31
4:13-16	153
5:23-24	158

2 Thessalonians

1:1	94, 117
1:4	94
1:8	66
1:10	66, 67
2:8	122
3:1	146
3:2-3	172
3:3	158

1 Timothy

1:1	19, **21-33**, 34, 95, 98, 99, 102, 103, 104, 195, 242, 244, 252, **255**
1:1-2	59
1:2	100
1:3	19, 21, 52
1:3-4	21, 70
1:3-7	71, 184
1:3-10	49
1:3-11	102
1:4	184
1:5	105
1:5-6	83
1:6	70, 109
1:8-11	65, 39
1:9	40
1:9-11	42

1:11	32, 104, 252	*3:1*	34, 79
1:12-16	82, 83, 99, 104, 118, 252	*3:1-7*	184
1:12-17	**34-50**, 52, **255-56**	*3:5*	94
1:13	68, 105, 218	*3:6*	57
1:14	79, 104, 119, 148	*3:8-13*	184
1:15	6, 19, 79, 87, 98, 102, 103, 104, 105, 263	*3:9*	105
		3:11	184
1:15-16	53, 56, 100, 103	*3:13*	47
1:15-17	9	*3:14*	85, 86, 98
1:16	19, 32, 52, 102, 104, 105, 195	*3:14-15*	86, 102
		3:14-16	86
1:17	104, 125, 173	*3:14-4:16*	85, 94
1:18	85, 100	*3:15*	56, 86, 90, 93, 94, 103, 244, 258
1:18-19	52		
1:18-20	102	*3:16*	6, 43, 54, 80, 85, 86, 90, 96, 98, 102, 104, 122, 245
1:19	83, 105, 109		
1:19-20	49, 52, 70, 105	*4:1*	71, 75, 83, 85, 86, 90, 97, 109
2:1-2	70, 103		
2:1-7	**51-68**, **256-57**, 264	*4:1-2*	67, 105
2:1-3:13	86	*4:1-3*	67, 70
2:2	96, 245	*4:1-4*	98
2:3	19, 26, 28, 98, 102, 244	*4:1-5*	85, 94
2:3-4	91, 103, 104	*4:1-16*	86
2:3-7	102, 104	*4:2*	57, 100, 105
2:4	19, 35, 79, 88, 90, 102, 105, 195, 201	*4:3*	56, 74, 90, 103, 105
		4:3-4	90, 95, 103
2:5	102, 103, 140	*4:3-5*	86, 102, 103
2:5-6	6, 19, 43, 90, 98, 102, 104	*4:4*	254
2:5-7	105	*4:4-5*	103, 104
2:6	44, 80, 102, 104, 105, 192, 209	*4:4-6*	98
		4:6	85, 86, 96, 97, 98, 99, 100, 102
2:7	70, 105, 252		
2:8	76	*4:6-8*	102
2:8-12	69, 70	*4:6-10*	38
2:8-15	74, 102	*4:6-16*	85
2:9	82, 83	*4:7*	54, 70, 86, 97, 184, 245
2:9-11	76	*4:7-8*	86, 96, 98
2:9-15	71	*4:7-10*	86, 105
2:11-15	71, 74	*4:8*	32, 54, 86, 87, 89, 90, 98, 103, 105, 245
2:12	72		
2:12-15	76	*4:9*	34, 87
2:13	77	**4:10**	19, 26, 28, 32, 56, 57, **85-97**, 98, 99, 100, 102, 103, 104, 105, 184, 201, 244, **258**
2:13-14	69, 70, 75		
2:13-15	71, 74, 76		
2:14	70, 77		
2:15	4, 11, 19, 35, **69-84**, 102, 103, 104, 105, 254, **257**	*4:11*	85, 98, 100
		4:12	90, 98, 99, 100
2:15-3:1	263	*4:13*	98, 99, 100

4:14	94, 99, 100	**2 Timothy**	
4:15	85, 96, 100	*1:1*	47, 123, 125, 127, 129, 139, 146, 148, 149, 164, 172, 175, 176, 177, 242, 252
4:15-16	98		
4:16	11, 19, 35, 94, **98-101**, 102, 105, **258**		
5:3-8	95	*1:2*	167
5:3-16	71, 184	*1:4*	119
5:4	54, 104	*1:3*	140, 176
5:5	103, 104	*1:3-12*	115, 116
5:7	85	*1:5*	116, 119, 140, 176
5:8	87, 156	*1:5-7*	116
5:11-13	70	*1:6*	119
5:11-15	71, 75	*1:6-14*	131
5:13	73	*1:7*	113, 116, 119, 175
5:14	74, 80	*1:8*	66, 110, 113, 119, 130, 131, 132, 133, 139, 142, 143, 145, 152, 156, 162, 167, 168, 175, 177, 178
5:15	70		
5:17	99, 100		
5:17-19	184		
5:21	59, 85	*1:9*	9, 47, 110, 113, 146, 147, 148, 149, 165, 171, 175, 176, 177, 178, 221, 251
6:2	85, 86		
6:3	54, 96, 245		
6:3-5	70	*1:9-10*	6, 179, 200, 245, 247
6:3-10	86	*1:9-11*	3, 127, 160
6:5	54, 56, 245	**1:9-14**	**115-33, 258-59**
6:6	54, 96, 105, 245	1:10	110, 140, 141, 144, 145, 146, 149, 171, 172, 175, 176, 177, 244
6:7	38, 103		
6:7-8	195		
6:9-10	70, 105	1:10-11	66
6:10	83, 109	1:10-12	175
6:11	54, 85, 86, 96, 105, 109	*1:11*	247, 252
6:12	19, 32, 38, 103, 105	*1:11-12*	177, 178, 252
6:12-14	105	*1:12*	110, 113, 144, 145, 149, 172, 176
6:13	59, 102, 103, 104		
6:13-15	102	*1:13*	47, 148, 164, 177, 252
6:14	122, 244	*1:13-14*	154, 175, 247
6:14-15	19, 38, 102, 104	*1:14*	145, 175, 178
6:15	66, 67, 104, 192	*1:15*	109, 175, 176
6:15-16	38	*1:16*	110, 143, 156, 167, 178
6:16	104	*1:18*	126, 131, 144, 149, 156, 167, 172, 176, 177, 178
6:17	70, 102, 103, 104, 203		
6:17-19	19, 32, 38, 95, 102, 105	*2:1*	47, 113, 119, 135, 148, 154, 164, 168, 177, 178
6:18-19	102, 103		
6:19	98, 103, 105, 250	*2:1-2*	130, 175
6:20	105, 130	*2:1-3*	142
6:20-21	70, 102, 105	*2:1-12*	138
6:21	83	*2:1-26*	135
6:25	109	*2:2*	130, 138, 156, 175, 247, 252

2:2-7	135	*3:8*	156, 161, 176
2:3	142, 152, 175, 178	*3:10*	109, 145, 154
2:3-4	144	*3:10-11*	143, 144, 252
2:7	167	*3:10-12*	178
2:8	111, 123, 131, 163, 172, 175, 177, 178, 252	*3:11*	167, 168, 175
		3:12	47, 54, 148, 154, 177, 245
2:8-10	127, 130, 175, 178, 247, 252	*3:12-13*	55, 176
		3:13	109, 160, 161, 171, 179
2:8-13	6, **135-59**, 160, 176, **259**	*3:14*	83, 109
2:9	130, 145, 175, 176, 179	**3:14-17**	**160-65**, 176, **260**
2:9-10	169	*3:15*	47, 110, 113, 147, 148, 171, 177, 179
2:10	47, 110, 125, 144, 148, 147, 161, 164, 171, 173, 175, 176, 177, 178, 179, 193	*3:15-17*	140, 177
		3:16	54, 111
		4:1	122, 140, 144, 149, 156, 166, 168, 172, 175, 176, 177
2:11	34, 123, 125, 175		
2:11-12	172, 176, 177	*4:1-5*	156, 178
2:11-13	124, 178, 247	*4:2*	145, 161, 175
2:12	144	*4:2-4*	168
2:13	113, 177	*4:2-5*	175
2:14	135, 156, 161	*4:3*	145, 156, 161, 175
2:14-15	161	*4:3-4*	109, 144, 176, 179
2:14-18	109, 175, 176	*4:4*	145, 161, 184
2:14-4:8	160	*4:5*	109, 142, 168, 175, 178
2:15	135, 145, 161, 175, 177, 179	*4:6*	123, 126, 139, 172, 178
		4:6-8	13, 176, 178, 247
2:16	161	*4:6-18*	252
2:16-18	179	*4:8*	122, 126, 131, 144, 149, 154, 156, 166, 167, 168, 172, 175, 176, 177, 178
2:16-19	135		
2:18	109, 126, 140, 160, 175		
2:19	167, 177, 179	*4:10*	109, 203
2:20	179	*4:13*	87
2:20-26	135	*4:14*	167, 168, 175, 176, 177
2:22	54, 167	*4:14-15*	109, 179
2:23	161	*4:15*	145
2:23-26	109, 175, 176	*4:16*	109, 176
2:24	167	**4:16-18**	67, 113, 127, 156, **166-74**, 175, 178, **260-61**
2:25	56, 161, 175		
2:25-26	179	*4:17*	113, 144, 175, 176, 178, 179, 192
2:26	169		
3:1	171	*4:17-18*	177
3:1-8	179	*4:18*	110, 113, 114, 117, 126, 140, 145, 154, 156, 175, 176, 178, 179
3:1-9	109, 144, 156		
3:1-13	175		
3:2-9	176		
3:5	54, 55, 113, 156, 245		
3:6-7	71		
3:7	55, 56, 113, 161, 162, 175		

Indexes 317

Titus
1:1	54, 55, 56, 230, 235, 236, 237, 245, 247, 252
1:1-2	237
1:1-3	121, 185, 203, 211, 242
1:1-4	185, **187-96**, 234, **261**
1:2	203, 221, 232, 234, 235, 236
1:3	26, 66, 185, 200, 230, 234, 235, 236, 237, 244, 252
1:4	43, 185, 234, 235, 244
1:5-9	184
1:7	43
1:9	34, 185, 191, 195, 203, 230, 237
1:10	183, 185, 190, 197, 201, 211, 236, 247
1:10-16	237
1:12	190
1:13	194, 195
1:13-16	195
1:14	184, 190, 201, 211, 237, 247
1:14-16	236
1:15-16	211, 238
1:16	156, 185, 218, 235, 237
2:1	185, 195, 197, 230, 237, 247
2:1-10	185, 203, 205, 247
2:2	194
2:2-10	199, 201
2:3	230, 237, 247
2:5	191, 199, 201, 237, 247
2:6	237, 247
2:7	185, 210, 230, 237
2:7-8	237
2:8	199, 201, 237, 247
2:9	247
2:9-10	237
2:10	26, 187, 191, 194, 198, 201, 230, 234, 235, 237, 244, 247
2:10-14	4
2:11	109, 217, 219, 223, 235, 236, 245
2:11-12	203, 235
2:11-13	247
2:11-14	3, 6, 185, **197-213**, 220, 222, 234, 236, 247, **262**
2:12	54, 55, 195, 223, 235, 236, 245
2:12-13	195, 236
2:13	11, 122, 185, 187, 219, 221, 234, 235, 236, 244, 245
2:13-14	237
2:14	185, 189, 194, 234, 235, 236, 237, 247, 250
2:15	195, 197, 198, 203, 215, 230, 236, 237, 247
2:15-3:2	216, 217, 262
Ch 3	198
3:1	185, 203, 210, 230, 236, 237
3:1-2	247
3:1-5	250
3:1-8	205, **214-33**, 235, **262**
3:3	205, 236, 238
3:3-4	247
3:3-7	4, 185, 203, 205, 234, 236, 247
3:3-8	237
	26, 185, 187, 199, 234, 235, 244, 245
3:4-7	3, 6, 11, 237
3:5	79, 235, 236, 251
3:5-6	234, 235, 237
3:5-7	9, 236, 247, 251
3:6	168, 187, 191, 234, 235, 244
3:6-7	235
3:7	189, 195, 223, 236, 237, 247
3:8	34, 185, 195, 203, 210, 230, 235, 236, 237, 247
3:8-11	217, 262
3:8-14	185
3:9	185, 201, 217
3:9-11	215, 237
3:14	184, 185, 195, 211, 221, 236, 237, 247
3:15	194

Hebrews
Letter	62
1:2	60
2:1-5	60
2:2	58
2:9	60
2:14	60
2:17	60
3:1	117
3:7-11	189
3:12	92
4:1	189
4:2	162
5:4	118
6:4	127
6:9-12	189
6:11-12	191
6:12	189
6:13-7:6	189
6:14	189
6:17	191
6:17-18	189
6:18	191
6:20	61
7:25	61
7:27	60
8:6	60, 150
8:8-12	189
9:11-28	60
9:12	60
9:14	60, 92
9:15	60, 189
9:24	61
9:26	60
10:5	43
10:10	60
10:22	229
10:23	158
10:26	56
10:31	92
10:32	127, 143
10:34	206
10:36	189
11:8-9	189
11:11	158
11:24-25	204
11:25	204
11:26	204
11:35	143, 150, 206
11:36	143
11:39-40	189
12:22	92
12:24	60
13:7	138

James
1:1	192
5:10	142
5:10-11	143
5:13	142
5:15	35

1 Peter
Letter	43
1:3	226
1:3-5	221, 226
1:4	125
1:10-12	189
1:14	43
1:14-16	221
1:18	43
1:18-21	221
1:19-20	122
1:21	121
1:22	43, 226
1:23	125, 226
2:6	42
2:10	43, 219
2:10-12	221
2:20-22	143
2:21	142
2:21-23	143
3:13	210
3:14	144
3:16	112
3:17	144
3:18	144
3:20	48
3:21	79
4:1-4	221
4:1-6	219
4:13	142
5:8	169
5:1-11	169
5:10	149
5:12	200

2 Peter
Letter	26, 27, 28, 54, 55, 254
1:1	27
1:2	27
1:3-4	205
1:11	27
1:16	162
2:1	156
2:20	27, 205
Ch 3	225
3:2	27, 138
3:9	48, 57
3:15	48
3:18	27

1 John
Letter	37
1:2	122
1:9	158
2:6	83
2:10	83
2:15-17	205
2:22	155
2:23	155
2:24	83
2:27	83
2:28	83
3:5	122
3:6	83
3:8	122
3:15	37
3:19	56
3:24	83
4:6	56
4:9	27, 43
4:13	83
4:14	27
4:15	83
4:16	83
4:22	27
4:25	27
4:29	27
5:13	37

2 John
1	56
19	83

Jude
1	192
4	156
5	35
25	21, 26

Revelation
1:9	144
2:2	144
2:3	144
2:13	156
2:19	144
3:8	156
3:10	144
3:10-12	155
3:21	155
6:12	168
7:2	91
11:16	155
13:10	144
14:12	144
15:3	192
17:14	89, 147
20:4	155
20:6	155
22:5	155

ANCIENT JEWISH WRITINGS

Odes of Solomon
Book	24

Psalms of Solomon
Book	24
5:11	32
15:1	28, 32

Testament of Benjamin
3:8	64

Testament of Dan
6:2	58

1QS
5:6	64
8:3-4	64

8:10	64
9:4	64

Philo
On the Life of Abraham
137	26
176	26

On the Confusion of Tongues
96	22

Against Flaccus
74.126	26

Who is the Heir?
206	61

On the Life of Joseph
195	26

Allegorical Interpretation
2.55-56	26
3.27	22, 26

On the Embassy to Gaius
22	26
282	185

On the Life of Moses
2.28	53
2.28-36	165
2.29-31	53-54
2.36	53
2.166	61, 62

On the Change of Names
76	96

On the Creation of the World
169	26
172	96

On Planting
70	96

On the Sacrifices of Cain and Abel
18	96
24	96

On the Special Laws
2.60-64	53

Josephus
Jewish Antiquities
11.66	225
17.327	185
18.228	169

Against Apion
2.218	225

Jewish War
2.103	185
3.459	26

The Life
76	185
244	26

GREEK AND LATIN WRITINGS

Athenaeus
Deipnosophistae
4.142-43	184

Apuleius
Metamorphoses
11.16	23

Cicero
De finibus
1.14	22

Diogenes Laertius
7.91	98

Epictetus
Diatribai
3.21.15	165

Isodorus
Hymns 22

Philodemus
PHerc 346
4	22
19	22

PHerc 1507
43.16-19	165

Plutarch
Moralia
2.102-21	23

Indexes

EARLY CHRISTIAN WRITINGS

1 Clement
2.4	36
5.5-7	143
58.2	36

Acts of Paul and Thecla
3:17	92
7:2	92
11:4-5	92

Acts of Peter
2.1.47	48

Barnabas
14.7	128
14.8	128
21.9	36

Gospel of Thomas
114	76

Hippolytus
Refutation of All Heresies
16.6.12-13 75

Ignatius
Letters	27, 31

To the Ephesians
1	31
5	31, 127
10	150
20	31, 126
21	31

To the Magnesians
8-9	31
10-11	31

To the Philadelphians
5	31
6	31
9	31, 126
11	31

To Polycarp
4.3	150

To the Romans
5.1	169

To the Smyrnaeans
1.1	140, 163
1.2	163
2.1	140
9.2	150

To the Trallians
Inscr.	31
2	31
9	140

Irenaeus
Against Heresies
1.30.7 75

Justin Martyr
Apology
61.12 127

Nag Hammadi Tractates
Hypostasis of the Archons 75
On the Origin of the World 75
Apocryphon of John 75

Origen
Fragments on Psalms
80.4 45

Modern Authors

Allan, J.A. 46, 47, 256
Anderson, H. 64
Baldwin, H.S. 69
Barnet, P.W. 77, 254
Barr, D.L. 249
Barrett, C.K. 38, 44, 46, 49, 57, 64, 72, 73, 88, 97, 117, 119, 121, 125, 137, 139, 145, 148, 152, 153, 154, 164, 165, 169, 172, 261
Bartsch, H.-W. 72
Bassler, J.M. 83, 87, 89, 90, 97, 99, 109, 110, 114, 115, 117, 125, 130, 131, 139, 140, 142, 146, 158, 168, 169, 171, 220, 221, 224, 232, 258, 259
Bauernfiend, O. 150
Baugh, S.M. 4, 88
Bauman, R.A. 54, 55
Beasley-Murray, G.R. 152, 155, 158, 219, 228, 229
Becker, O. 58
Beckwith, W. 197
Bell, R.H. 89
Bénétreau, S. 138
Bertram, G. 48, 49
Bockmuehl, M. 45
Boer, M.C. de 125
Brown, C. 21, 22, 35, 63, 144, 227
Brown, R.E. 27
Brox, N. 13, 44, 46, 48, 57, 58, 64, 73, 80, 81, 188, 200, 204, 220
Bruce, F.F. 4, 25, 40, 61, 101, 137, 141, 148, 204
Bultmann, R. 42, 56, 111, 112
Burnett, F.W. 225, 226
Büschel, F. 63
Campbell, R.A. 3, 34, 87, 184
Childs, B.S. 62
Chilton, B. 92
Coenen, L. 118
Conzelmann, H. 127
Coogan, M.D. 45
Cook, D. 13
Coupland, S. 4
Couser, G.A. 94, 184, 187

Cranfield, C.E.B. 66
Culmann, O. 229
Davies, M. 4, 44, 80, 117, 168, 169
Dawson-Walker, D. 199, 206
Derrett, J.D.M. 225
Dibelius-Conzelmann 5, 11, 12, 21, 22, 23, 28, 34, 42, 43, 44, 45, 46, 48, 51, 53, 59, 61, 64, 66, 87, 90, 91, 97, 115, 121, 122, 130, 133, 136, 145, 146, 157, 158, 161, 164, 169, 186, 199, 202, 211, 249, 255, 256, 259
Donelson, L.R. 9, 10, 11, 13, 21, 46, 49, 151, 157, 163, 187, 199, 230, 250, 251
Dunn, J.D.G. 126, 136, 147, 152, 167, 183, 254
Easton, B.S. 12, 44, 46, 58, 98, 101, 109, 117, 118, 122, 136, 140, 146, 151, 255, 258
Ellicott, C.J. 74, 127, 191, 201
Ellingworth, P. 127
Everts, J.M. 30
Falkenroth, U. 144
Fee, G.D. 4, 5, 19, 37, 41, 44, 49, 52, 54, 57, 61, 64, 70, 82, 87, 90, 97, 100, 114, 118, 121, 130, 131, 136, 140, 145, 146, 150, 151, 152, 168, 169, 170, 173, 184, 185, 194, 195, 196, 197, 201, 204, 212, 218, 227
Fiore, B. 13, 248
Fitzpatrick-McKinley, A. 210
Foerster, W. 21, 22, 25, 27, 35, 36, 54, 96, 204
Fohrer, G. 21, 22, 23, 24, 35
Fowl, S.E. 13
Friedrich, G. 189
Gealy, F.D. 12, 50
Gerber, D. 4, 44
Goodwin, M.J. 92, 93
Goulder, M. 62, 75, 136, 140
Green, J.L. 206
Greenberg, M. 59
Griffin, H.P. 189
Grudem, W. 70
Guhrt, J. 37, 225

Günther, W. 54
Guthrie, D. 41, 44, 46, 64, 69, 73, 80, 87, 88, 121, 125, 131, 145, 146, 169, 172, 173, 212, 232, 261
Guthrie, G.H. 189
Haarbeck, H. 227
Hamerton-Kelly, R. 67
Hanson, A.T. 12, 32, 33, 41, 54, 56, 57, 58, 59, 64, 65, 66, 71, 72, 74, 87, 98, 101, 120, 121, 126, 127, 129, 131, 142, 143, 145, 146, 149, 151, 152, 153, 157, 158, 169, 170, 172, 211, 212, 220, 255, 256, 258, 261
Harder, G. 171
Harding, M. 3, 13, 248
Harris, M.J. 42, 43, 53, 63, 77, 148, 206, 207
Hasler, V. 8, 9, 32, 38, 41, 44, 58, 59, 61, 65, 119, 127, 146, 162, 163, 164, 203, 211, 259, 260, 262
Hauck, F. 143, 144
Haykin, M.A.G. 222, 230, 263
Hendricksen, W. 44, 145, 146, 157, 168, 170, 172, 201
Henry, M. 157
Hinson, E.G. 46, 140, 145, 146, 167, 196, 204, 231, 261
Ho, C.E. 44, 55, 258
Hoffmann, E. 205
Holtz, G. 143
Horbury, W. 45
Horst, J. 47
Houlden, J.L. 38, 41, 47, 51, 53, 54, 57, 59, 64, 66, 69, 71, 82, 85,109, 121, 139, 145, 151, 156, 187, 199, 202, 221, 249, 255, 256, 260, 262
Howard, W.F. 42
Hunt, S.A. 128
Jagt, K.A. van der, 4, 69
Jebb, S. 72
Jeremias, J. 43
Johnson, L.T. 15, 16, 234, 248, 253
Karris, R.J. 49, 187, 204, 211
Keener, C.S. 71, 74
Kelly, J.N.D. 27, 28, 32, 38, 39, 45, 46, 47, 57, 64, 66, 67, 85, 118, 121, 125, 140, 142, 145, 146, 148, 151, 187, 191, 199, 201, 204, 212, 215, 223

Kenny, A. 15
Kidd, R.M. 249
Klöpper, A. 3, 232
Knight, G.W., III 37, 38, 39, 41, 42, 43, 45, 48, 49, 56, 65, 74, 79, 87, 88, 90, 98, 117, 130, 136, 139, 145, 151, 154, 157, 162, 163, 164, 167, 169, 171, 172, 196, 198, 201, 205, 207, 215, 220, 221, 229, 255, 257, 260, 261
Köstenberger, A. 69
Kowalski, B. 160, 163
Kroeger, R.C. & C.C. 58, 70, 74, 75, 76
Laato, A. 210
Läger, K. 8, 133, 198, 207, 220, 251, 252
Lake, K. 36
Lane, W.L. 127
Lau, A.Y.-Y. 69, 85, 115, 122, 131, 132, 136, 137, 199, 200, 207, 210, 246, 262
Lea, T.D. 189
Levison, J. 75
Liefeld, W.L. 195, 199, 201, 207, 217
Lightfoot, J.B. 169
Link, H.-G. 227
Lock, W. 31, 38, 46, 56, 57, 58, 114, 115, 139, 140, 146, 201
Lohse, E. 140, 141
Longenecker, R.N. 141
Luz, U. 115, 127
Malina, B.J. 189, 190, 261
Mandilaras, B.G. 152
Marshall, I.H. 3, 4, 5, 13, 15, 22, 23, 25, 34, 47, 48, 52, 54, 55, 56, 59, 63, 66, 73, 80, 87, 88, 99, 101, 116, 118, 130, 133, 140, 141, 143, 146, 149, 151, 153, 156, 165, 187, 190, 191, 192, 194, 195, 197, 198, 199, 200, 201, 203, 204, 205, 206, 207, 209, 210, 211, 215, 217, 221, 222, 223, 227, 229, 230, 231, 257, 261
Martin, R.P. 26, 30
Merkel, H. 6, 11, 45, 47, 48, 58, 81, 98, 121, 124, 133, 163, 258
Metzger, B.M. 45
Metzger, W. 12

Michaelis, W. 142
Michel, O. 81, 138, 226
Miller, J.D. 13, 14, 71, 72, 248
Miller, P.D. 192, 193
Moo, D.J. 70, 136, 145
Mott, S.C. 4, 186, 199, 200, 202, 207, 208, 262
Motyer, J.A. 65, 118
Moulton, J.H. 42
Mounce, W.D. 11, 15, 34, 40, 46, 48, 56, 57, 58, 61, 63, 65, 66, 69, 75, 88, 91, 123, 145, 154, 194, 195, 198, 200, 202, 204, 207, 212, 215, 219, 220, 222, 226, 227, 228, 229, 231, 253, 263
Mundle, W. 63
Murphy O'Connor, J. 15, 109
Neusner, J. 92
Nolland, J. 206
Noyes, M.P. 12
Nussbaum, M.C. 22
Nygren, A. 41
Oberlinner, L. 53, 56, 57, 59, 63, 65, 66, 72, 73, 80, 81, 87, 88, 89, 101, 109, 115, 126, 127, 129, 130, 136, 143, 162, 164, 169, 171, 172, 173, 257, 258
Oepke, A. 58, 59, 148
Packer, J.I. 123
Payne, P.B. 69
Peterson, D.G. 23
Pierce, R.W. 73
Piper, J. 70
Porter, S.E. 4, 69, 73, 79, 257
Prior, M. 15, 109, 171
Procksch, O. 63
Quinn, J.D. 3, 4, 8, 15, 24, 34, 35, 43, 44, 47, 54, 85, 125, 126, 130, 183, 184, 186, 187, 189, 190, 192, 194, 198, 201, 202, 210, 211, 217, 218, 220, 222, 229
Rengstorf, K.H. 39
Richards, W.A. 16, 249
Robinson, J.A.T. 229
Roloff, J. 7, 15, 32, 39, 42, 43, 47, 48, 49, 54, 56, 65, 66, 81, 85, 88, 152
Russell, D.S. 29
Sanders, E.P. 67

Sasse, H. 38, 43
Schenk, W. 3
Schlier, H. 155, 203
Schmidt, K.L. 117, 154
Schneider, J. 21, 22, 35
Schniedewind, W.M. 210
Schniewind, J. 189
Schreiner, T.R. 69
Schrenk, G. 57, 146, 147, 161, 162
Schwarz, R. 54, 249
Scott, E.F. 47, 122, 127, 188, 200, 217, 229
Scroggs, R. 67
Segal, A. 128, 129
Sim, D.C. 226
Simpson, E.K. 41, 55, 143, 198
Skeat, T.C. 87, 88, 184, 258
Spicq, C. 3, 6, 7, 32, 36, 38, 43, 47, 48, 49, 54, 57, 62, 64, 69, 87, 88, 118, 123, 127, 129, 130, 139, 140, 145, 146, 149, 160, 163, 170, 172, 188, 191, 197, 198, 199, 205, 217, 220, 227, 229
Spyridakis, S.V. 185
Sterling, G.E. 75
Stettler, H. 246
Stott, J.R.W. 63, 74, 87, 125, 138, 157, 199, 201, 212, 257
Strathmann, H. 64, 65
Sumney, J. 4
Taylor, W.F. Jr. 197
Thiede, C.P. 225
Tollefson, K.D. 14, 248
Towner, P.H. 6, 13, 43, 63, 69, 75, 87, 115, 117, 127, 129, 136, 140, 150, 151, 152, 155, 157, 170, 171, 191, 197, 198, 201, 207, 209, 218, 219, 227, 229, 248, 249
Trebilco, P. 90, 264
Trummer, P. 6, 136, 137
Tuente, R. 193
Turner, N. 42
Vanderlip, V.F. 22
Verner, D.C. 94
Wacker, W.C. 47, 85, 130
Wainwright, G. 4
Walder, E. 191
Wallis, I.G. 164, 165

Waters, K.L. 73, 74
White, R.E.O. 229, 230
Wieland, G.M. 264
Wilkens, U. 162
Willetts, R.F. 184
Willis, T.M. 45
Wilson, S.G. 137

Winter, B.W. 71
Witherington, B. III 23
Wolter, M. 8, 48, 130, 255
Young, F. 3, 4, 13, 14, 15, 34, 45, 48, 79, 87, 109, 121, 143, 144
Ziesler, J. 92

Hebrew Terms

אִיִּים *islands, coastlands* 67
אֵל *God* 25, 67
אֱלֹהֵי יִשְׁעִי *God my saviour, God of my salvation* 25
בֶּן־דָּוִיד *son of David* 140
דְּבַר־יהוה *word of the LORD* 146
חַיֵּי עוֹלָם *everlasting life* 36
חרשׁ *to keep silent* 67
חֶסֶד *steadfast love* 223
ישׁע *to deliver, save* 23, 24
כפר *to atone* 63
יְהוָה *Yahweh* 118, 146, 192, 193
לַפֹּשְׁעִים יַפְגִּיעַ *made intercession for the transgressors* 63

מַחְסֶה *refuge* 28
מִן־הָעוֹלָם וְעַד הָעֹלָם *from everlasting to everlasting* 190
סתר *to hide* 67
עֶבֶד יְהוָה *servant of the LORD* 192, 193
צַדִּיק *righteous* 39
פגע *to meet, interpose* 63
פלל *to intercede* 63
פשׁע *to sin* 63
קרא *to call* 118
רָשָׁע *wicked* 39
שֵׁם *name* 118
שׁפט *judge* 24

Greek Terms

ἀγαθός 160, 185, 210, 214, 216
ἀγαπάω 147, 208
ἀγάπη 34, 46-47, 69, 72, 79, 81, 82, 115
ἄγγελος 112, 168
ἁγιασμός 69, 72, 79, 81-83
ἅγιος 112, 115, 118, 214, 215, 216, 224, 225, 228
ἁγιωσύνη 136
ἀγνοέω 34, 40, 42, 49
ἄγνοια 42
ἀγών 38
ἀγωνίζομαι 38, 85, 93, 97
ἀδελφός 60, 85
ἄδηλος 29
ἀδηλότης 95
ἀδόκιμος 101, 185
ἀδύνατος 191
ἀθανασία 29, 38, 125, 126
- φάρμακον ἀθανασίας 126
ἀθάνατος 125
αἷμα 64, 231
αἰσχύνω 111, 112
αἰών 19, 34, 36, 37, 95, 121, 155, 166, 172, 190, 197, 199, 200, 203, 205, 212
- τὸ νῦν αἰών 19, 95, 197, 199, 200, 203, 205, 212
αἰώνιος 34, 36, 37, 38, 60, 115, 120, 121, 126, 135, 137, 148, 149, 151, 187, 188, 189, 190, 191, 193, 195, 196, 214, 215, 216, 261
- ζωὴ αἰώνιος 34, 36-38, 126, 137, 148, 187, 188, 193, 195-96, 214, 215, 216
- χρόνοι αἰώνιοι 115, 120, 121, 187, 189-90, 191, 261
ἀκούω 19, 56, 98, 166, 168, 169, 200
ἀκροβυστία 46
ἀλήθεια 51, 55-57, 67, 86, 113, 160, 161, 162, 183, 187, 193, 195, 200
- ἐπίγνωσις ἀληθείας 55-57, 113, 161, 162, 187, 193, 195
ἀληθινός 92, 127
ἄμαχος 214, 216

ἁμαρτάνω 217
ἁμαρτία 25, 40, 46, 62, 63, 208
ἁμαρτωλός 19, 34, 39-42, 48, 112
ἀνά 226
ἀναβίωσις 36
ἀναγεννάω 226
ἀνάγνωσις 99
ἀνακαινίζω 228
ἀνακαίνωσις 214, 215, 216, 224, 225, 227, 228
ἀνάλυσις 172
ἀνάστασις 29, 31, 66, 136, 140, 150
ἀνδρεία 207, 208
ἄνθρωπος 19, 22, 29, 51, 52, 54, 57, 58, 59, 60, 61, 62, 85, 86, 87, 88, 89, 91, 112, 127, 140, 171, 172, 197, 198, 199, 201, 202, 208, 212, 214, 215, 216, 217, 226
- πάντες ἄνθρωποι 19, 51, 52, 57, 85, 86, 87, 88, 89, 91, 197, 198, 201-02, 212, 214, 215, 216, 217
ἀνήρ 70
ἀνίστημι 29, 141, 161
ἀνόητος 214, 215, 216
ἀνομία 197, 205, 208, 209, 212, 213
ἄνομος 143
ἀνοχή 48
ἀντι- 62, 63, 208
ἀντίδοτος 126
ἀντίλυτρον 51, 58, 60, 62, 63-64, 208
ἀντίψυχον 64
ἀνυπότακτος 184
ἄνω 117
ἄνωθεν 226
ἄξιος 34, 87
ἀόρατος 34, 37
ἀπαίδευτος 161
ἀπαρνέομαι 153, 199
ἀπάρτισμα 126
ἅπας 34, 47
ἀπειθέω 218, 223, 227
ἀπειθής 214, 215, 216, 218, 223
ἀπεκδέχομαι 144
ἀπιστέω 135, 157, 260
ἀπιστία 34, 41, 42, 46, 49

ἄπιστος 158
ἁπλότης 170
ἀπόδεκτος 51
ἀποδοχή 34, 87
ἀποθνήσκω 61, 126
ἀποκαλύπτω 121
ἀποκρύπτω 121
ἀπόλαυσις 95
ἀπολογία 166, 167
ἀπολύτρωσις 60, 61
ἀπόστολος 21, 49, 51, 112, 115, 132, 133, 187, 193-96
ἀποστρέφω 161
ἀρετή ́ 96
ἀριθμός 36
ἀρνέομαι 113, 135, 151, 155-56, 157, 197, 203-05, 212, 260
ἀσεβ- 96
ἀσέβεια 197, 204, 212
ἀσεβής 39, 111
ἀστοχέω 160
αὐθεντέω 70
ἀψευδής 187, 190-91
ἀφθαρσία 38, 115, 125, 126, 141, 144
ἄφθαρτος 34, 37, 38
βασιλεία 110, 111, 117, 166, 172-73, 219
βασιλεύς 34, 37, 51, 53, 67
βασιλεύω 155
βέβηλος 161
βλασφημέω 42, 49, 214, 216
βλασφημία 48
βλάσφημος 34, 48
βοηθέω 23
βοηθός 28
γινώσκω 56, 167
γνήσιον τέκνον 187, 196
γνωρίζω 121
γράμματα, ἱερά 160-65
γυμνάζω 96
γυμνασία 96
γυνή 19, 70, 77, 184
διά 19, 34, 36, 60, 63, 69, 72, 79, 110, 115, 117, 118, 121, 126, 129, 133, 135, 142, 145, 146, 151, 160, 183, 214, 215, 216, 223, 224, 225, 228, 230, 231
- διὰ τοῦτο 142, 145, 151

διαβεβαιόομαι 214, 217
διάγω 51, 53, 214, 215, 216
διαθήκη 60, 231
διακονέω 208
διακονία 34, 45, 142
διάκονος 184
διαλλακτής 61
διαλογισμός 70
διαμένω 183
διασῴζω 23, 64
διαφθόρα 141
διδασκαλία 96, 98, 99, 145, 160, 161, 165, 191, 197, 198
διδάσκαλος 51, 115, 132, 133
διδάσκω 70, 202
διδαχή 191, 211
δίδωμι 24, 64, 65, 115, 116, 119, 121, 141, 197, 198, 208-09, 212
δίκαιος 39, 40
δικαιοσύνη 11, 30, 160, 207, 208, 214, 215, 216, 222, 223, 232
δικαιόω 11, 39, 147, 214, 215, 216, 223, 231, 232
δικαιῶς 197, 199, 207-08, 212
διωγμός 143
διώκτης 34, 38
διώκω 49
δόξα 112, 125, 135, 148, 149, 151, 166, 197, 206, 212
δοξάζω 147
δουλεύω 92, 205, 214, 215, 216
δοῦλος 187, 192, 193, 194, 261
δοῦλος θεοῦ 187, 192-93, 261
δυν- 113
δύναμαι 110, 113, 151, 160, 161, 162, 188
δύναμις 110, 113, 132, 136, 139, 142, 162, 199
δυνατός 113, 115, 131, 132, 135
ἐγείρω 137, 141, 188
ἐκαλέω 147
ἑδραίωμα 56, 86
ἔθνος 41, 64, 65, 66, 128, 166, 168, 169, 200
ἐκκλησία 49, 86, 90, 93-95, 258
ἐκχέω 214, 215, 216, 218, 224, 225, 228, 229, 230, 231, 232
ἐκλέγομαι 210

Indexes

ἐκλεκτός 36, 89, 110, 135, 142, 146-48, 151, 187, 193-94
ἐλεέω 34, 44-45, 46, 202, 227
ἔλεος 36, 41, 202, 214, 215, 216, 222, 223, 230
ἐλπίζω 85, 86, 89, 95, 144
ἐλπίς 95, 113, 187, 193, 195-96, 197, 206, 212, 214, 215, 216, 221, 255
ἐνδείκνυμι 34, 47-48, 214, 216
ἐνδυναμόω 34, 45-46, 113, 119, 166, 167
ἐνηρεμάζω 53
ἐνησυχάζω 53
ἐντυγχάνω 61
ἐν Χριστῷ see Χριστὸς Ἰησοῦς
ἐξαιρέω 23
ἐξαποστέλλω 194
ἐξιλάσκομαι 62, 63
ἐπαγγελία 91
ἐπαγγέλομαι 121, 187, 188-89, 191
ἐπαισχύνομαι 110, 111, 112, 115, 131, 132
ἐπακούω 33
ἐπανόρθωσις 54, 160, 165
ἐπέχω 99
ἐπιγείος 173
ἐπιγινώσκω 56, 200
ἐπίγνωσις 27, 51, 55, 56, 113, 161, 162, 187, 193, 195
ἐπιθυμία 197, 204, 205, 208, 212, 214, 215, 216
ἐπικαλέω 111
ἐπιλαμβάνομαι 38
ἐπιμένω 98, 99, 100
ἐπίσκοπος 184
ἐπιστήμων 96
ἐπιταγή 21, 192
ἐπιφαίνω 197, 198, 199-201, 202, 206, 214, 218, 219, 222, 244-45
ἐπιφάνεια 19, 38, 110, 115, 117, 121, 122, 129, 132, 197, 199, 205, 206, 210, 212, 215, 244-45, 259
ἐποστρέφω 92, 202
ἐπουράνιος 110, 117, 166, 172-73
ἔργον 11, 110, 115, 142, 160, 166, 171, 185, 197, 208, 209, 212, 214, 215, 216, 217, 221, 222, 223, 230, 261

- ἔργον ἀγαθόν 160, 185, 214, 216
- ἔργον πομηρόν 110, 166, 171-72, 261
- καλὰ ἔργα 185, 197, 208, 209-11, 212, 214, 217, 221, 230
εὐαγγελίζω 137
εὐαγγέλιον 31, 46, 66, 112, 115, 129-31, 132, 133, 135, 138, 142, 145, 151, 162, 183, 200
εὐαγγελιστής 142
εὐσεβ- 96
εὐσέβεια 36, 51, 53, 54-55, 70, 85, 86, 87, 89, 96, 103, 143, 144, 187, 193, 195, 196, 205, 208, 244, 245, 254, 256, 264
εὐσεβέω 54
εὐσεβής λογισμός 96
εὐσεβῶς 54, 55, 177, 197, 199, 204, 207-08, 212, 245
εὐφροσύνη 149
ἐξαιρέω 23
ζάω 38, 85, 86, 89, 90, 91, 92, 93, 94, 126, 177, 197, 198, 199, 203-08, 209, 212, 258
ζηλόω 197, 210
ζηλωτής 185, 208, 209-11, 212, 230
ζήτησις 161, 217
ζωὴ 19, 25, 29, 34, 36, 37, 38, 91, 96, 115, 125-26, 137, 148, 187, 188, 193, 195, 196, 214, 215, 216, 250
ζωὴ αἰώνιος 19, 34, 36-38, 125-26, 137, 148, 187, 188, 193, 195-96, 214, 215, 216
ζῳοποιέω 188
ἡδονή 205, 214, 215, 216
ἡμέρα 79, 94, 115, 118, 171, 172
ἡμέτερος 22, 64, 210, 221
ἤρεμος 51, 53-54
ἡσυχία, ἡσύχιος 51, 53-54, 70, 76, 256
θάνατος 60, 115, 123, 124, 143, 153
θέλω 51, 57, 91
θεομάχος 48
θεός 19, 21-28, 29, 30, 33, 38, 41, 42, 49, 51, 57, 58, 63, 85, 86, 89, 90-95, 101, 103-04, 113, 115, 116, 130, 131, 132, 135, 137, 140, 142, 145-46, 147, 148, 151, 158, 160, 162,

163, 167, 187, 188, 190-91, 192-93, 193-94, 197, 198, 200, 206, 208, 210, 212, 219, 214, 216, 230, 255, 258, 261
- θεὸς ζῶν 38, 85, 86, 89, 90-95, 258
- θεὸς σωτήρ 19, 21-28, 33, 51, 57, 85, 91, 103-04, 187, 191, 192, 197, 198, 206, 212, 214, 216, 255
Ἰησοῦς see Χριστὸς Ἰησοῦς
ἱλάσκομαι 25
ἱλαστήριον 61, 64
Ἰουδαῖος 40, 183
Ἰουδαϊκός 184
καθαρίζω 64, 197, 208, 209-11, 212
καθαρός 100
καί (epexegetical) 55, 125, 169, 195, 208, 227
καιρός 32, 51, 64, 65, 66-67, 80, 121, 187, 191, 192, 200, 203
- καιροὶ ἴδιοι 51, 64, 65, 66-68, 80, 121, 187, 191, 192, 200
κακοπαθεία/κακοπαθία 142, 143
κακοπαθέω 135, 142-43, 151
καλέω 49, 91, 115, 116, 117, 118, 147, 158
καλός 26, 38, 51, 96, 115, 130, 142, 185, 214, 215, 217, 221, 230
- καλὰ ἔργα see ἔργον
κατά 21, 42, 55, 60, 95, 96, 113, 115, 119, 132, 135, 136, 139, 142, 147, 151, 162, 187, 191, 192, 193, 194, 195, 196, 214, 215, 216, 222
- κατὰ δύναμιν θεοῦ 113, 132, 139, 142, 162
- κατ' ἔλεος 214, 215, 216, 222
- κατ' ἐπιταγην 21, 187, 192
- κατὰ τὸ εὐαγγέλιόν 135, 151
- κατ' εὐσέβειαν 55, 95, 187, 193
- κατὰ πίστιν 187, 193-94, 195, 196
- κατὰ πρόθεσιν 115, 147
- κατὰ σάρκα/κατὰ πνεῦμα 136
καταγγέλλω 128
καταισχύνω 111, 112, 113, 114
καταργέω 115, 116, 123, 124
καταφυγή 28
κενοφωνία
κήρυγμα 6, 93, 115, 145, 166, 168, 171, 175, 187, 191, 192, 200

κῆρυξ 51, 115, 132, 133
κηρύσσω 101
κληρονομέω 189, 195, 219
κληρονόμος 214, 215, 216, 223, 231, 232
κλῆσις 115, 117-18, 221
κλητός 147
κοινός 22, 31, 187, 194, 196
κοινωνία 153, 158
κοπιάω 85, 93, 97, 99
κοσμικός 197, 204, 205, 212
κόσμος 19, 27, 34, 35, 37, 43, 120, 121, 153, 202, 203, 205, 225, 226, 254, 263
κρίμα 202
κριτής 24
κύριος 25, 27, 29, 30, 31, 34, 45, 46, 66, 110, 111, 118, 132, 137, 145, 146, 148, 158, 166, 167, 168, 188, 193, 202, 209, 223, 230, 253
λαός 91, 189, 194, 197, 201, 208, 209, 210, 212
- λαὸς περιούσιος 189, 194, 197, 201, 208, 209-11, 212
λογομαχέω 161
λόγος 34, 38, 79, 83, 86, 87, 96, 99, 112, 115, 130, 131, 133, 136, 137, 145-46, 147, 148, 151, 158, 161, 187, 191-92, 194, 197, 200, 214, 215, 217, 263
- ὁ λόγος τοῦ θεοῦ 130, 131, 137, 145-46, 148, 151, 191
- πιστοὶ λόγοι see πιστός
λουτρόν 127, 214, 215, 216, 224, 225, 228, 229, 231
λούω 229
λύτρον 62, 63, 208
λυτρόω 197, 198, 208, 209-11, 212
λύτρωσις 60
μακάριος 96, 197, 206, 212
μακροθυμέω 230
μακροθυμία 34, 47-48, 143
μάλιστα 183, 184, 258
μανθάνω 83, 160, 221
μαρτύριον 51, 64-66, 67, 68, 111, 132, 145
μαρτυρέω 65
μάρτυς 64, 137

ματαιολόγος 184
μάταιος 217
μάχη 161, 217
μεγαλωσύνη 210
μέγας 86, 149, 197, 206, 212
μένω 8, 69, 72, 73, 77, 79, 80, 81-83, 143, 160, 263
μεσίτης 51, 58-63, 256
μετὰ πίστεως 34, 46-48
μετὰ σωφροσύνης 69, 72, 79, 81
μεταμορφόω 227
μετάνοια 161
μέχρι δεσμῶν 135, 143, 151
μέχρι θανάτου 143
μνημονεύω 135, 138, 139
μῦθος 161
μυστήριον 85, 86, 96
μωρός 161, 217
ναός 92
νεκρός 135, 137, 138, 139-40, 141, 150, 151, 188
νομικός 217
νόμος 39
νῦν 19, 95, 121, 197, 199, 200, 203, 205, 212, 227
οἶκος θεοῦ 86
ὁμολογέω 155
ὁμολογία 88
ὁμολογουμένως 86
ὄντως 38, 250
ὁράω 128, 137
ὀρθοτομέω 161
οὐράνιος 128
οὐρανός 173
πάθημα 143, 153
παιδεία 98, 160, 165, 202-03, 245
παιδεύω 49, 197, 199, 200, 202, 204, 209, 212
παλιγγενεσία/
  παλινγενεσία 37, 214, 215, 216, 224, 225-228, 232
παραγγελία 85
παραγγέλλω 21, 85
παραδίδωμι 63, 147, 208
παραθήκη 10, 115, 116, 130-31, 132, 145
παραιτέομαι 217
παρακαλέω 21, 51, 52, 197

παράκλησις 99
παρίστημι 166, 167, 168
πᾶς 19, 25, 33, 34, 51, 52, 53, 54, 57, 58, 60, 61, 63, 85, 86, 87, 88, 89, 91, 95, 100, 101, 110, 126, 135, 151, 166, 168, 197, 199, 202, 208, 209, 212, 214, 215, 216
- πάντες ἄνθρωποι see ἄνθρωπος
πάσχω 142, 143
πατήρ 112, 114, 183, 187
πείθω 28, 29, 89, 115
περιουσιασμός 210
πιστ- 49, 89
πιστεύω 28, 34, 36, 42-43, 46, 49, 52, 83, 112, 115, 131, 160, 187, 214, 217, 221, 232
πίστις 30, 34, 38, 42, 46-47, 49, 51, 56, 69, 72, 79, 81-83, 86, 90, 96, 115, 138, 160, 164-65, 187, 193-94, 195, 196, 208
πιστός 34, 45, 49, 79, 83, 85, 86, 87, 89-90, 94, 96, 97, 100, 135, 136, 151, 157-58, 191, 214, 215, 217, 263
- πιστοὶ λόγοι 34, 79, 83, 87, 133, 136, 263
πλανάω 161, 171, 214, 215, 216, 232
πληροφορέω 142, 166, 168
πνεῦμα 45, 113, 115, 136, 214, 215, 216, 224, 225, 228, 230
- πνεῦμα ἅγιον 115, 214, 215, 216, 224, 225, 228-231
πονηρός 110, 166, 171, 172, 203, 261
πρόγονος 144
προεπαγγέλλο-μαι 189
πρόθεσις 115, 119, 147
πρέπω 197
προγινώσκω 147
προκηρύσσω 137
προκοπή 96, 98
προκόπτω 160
προσδέχομαι 197, 199, 205-07, 212
προσέχω 94, 99, 100, 101
ῥύομαι 23, 25, 95, 110, 111, 114, 166, 167, 169, 170, 171
σάρξ 60, 80, 136, 202, 208
σεμνότης 51, 53, 54
σοφία 149
σοφίζω 110, 113, 160, 162, 163

σπέρμα 80
- ἐκ σπέρματος Δαυιδ 135, 137, 138, 139, 140-41, 151
στοιχεῖα τοῦ κοσμοῦ 153
στόμα λέοντος 153, 167, 169, 170
συμβασιλεύω 135, 152, 154-55
συμμορφίζω 153
συναποσθνήσκω 135, 152-53
συνείδησις 36
συνζάω 125, 135, 152, 153-54
συνκακοπαθέω 132, 142, 152, 162
σῶμα 61
σωματικός 96
σωτηρία 3, 23, 25, 36, 110, 113, 123, 135, 137, 148, 149, 151, 160, 163, 169, 171, 260
σωτήρ 3, 19, 21-28, 32, 33, 51, 53, 57, 85, 86, 88, 89, 90, 91, 95, 98, 100, 103, 110, 115, 117, 121, 122, 123, 137, 149, 171, 187, 188, 191, 192, 193, 197, 198, 201, 205, 206, 209, 212, 214, 215, 216, 219, 220, 224, 228, 231, 232, 234, 244, 246, 255, 261
σωτήριος 3, 197, 198, 201-02, 212, 217
σωτήριον 23, 25, 223
σωφρόνως 197, 199, 207-12
σωφροσύνη 69, 72, 79, 81, 82-83, 207, 208
σῴζω 3, 16, 19, 20, 21, 23, 24, 28, 29, 32, 34, 35-36, 44, 51, 52, 55, 57, 61, 69, 72, 73, 77, 79, 80, 83, 91, 99, 101, 110, 111, 114, 115, 116, 117, 123, 144, 166, 171, 214, 215, 216, 218, 220, 221, 222, 223, 227, 230, 231, 232
τεκνογονέω 80
τεκνογονία 19, 69, 72, 73, 80-81, 82
τέκνον 80, 187, 196
τυγχάνω 61, 110, 135, 142, 143, 150, 151
τύχη 22
ὕβρις 48, 82
ὑβριστής 34, 48, 82
ὑγιαίνω 115, 130, 145, 161, 197
- ὑγιαίνουσα διδασκαλία 145, 161, 197-98

- ὑγιαίνοντες λόγοι 115, 130
υἱός 91, 112, 158, 208, 226
- υἱὸς τοῦ ἀνθρώπου 112, 208, 226
ὑπέρ 51, 58, 61, 62, 63, 64, 147, 197, 208, 209, 212, 231
- ὑπὲρ ἡμῶν 61, 147, 197, 208, 209, 212
- ὑπὲρ πάντων 51, 58, 61, 63, 209
- ὑπὲρ πολλῶν 231
ὑπερασπιστής 25
ὑπερπλεονάζω 34, 46
ὑπερπερισσεύω 46
ὑπομένω 35, 83, 142, 143-44, 151, 154
ὑπομιμνήσκω 214, 216
ὑπομένω 35, 135, 142, 143-44, 151, 154
ὑπομονή 31, 32, 83, 143, 144
ὑποτύπωσις 34, 40, 45, 48, 130
φαίνω 122, 259
φανερόω 80, 115, 116, 117, 121, 132, 187, 191, 192, 200, 244
φθόνος 214, 215, 216
φθορά 37, 205
φιλανθρωπία 214, 215, 216, 218, 219, 220, 232
φρόνησις 207
φροντίζω 214, 217, 221
φυλάσσω 85, 115, 130, 132
φῶς 43, 127, 128, 137
φωτίζω 115, 116, 121, 122, 127-29, 132
φωτισμός 127
χάρις 11, 34, 42, 46, 56, 115, 116, 119, 187, 189, 197, 198, 199-201, 202, 212, 214, 215, 216, 223, 232
χοϊκός 173
χρηστότης 214, 215, 216, 218, 219, 220, 223, 227, 232
Χριστὸς Ἰησοῦς 19, 21, 28, 30, 31, 32, 33, 34, 36, 46-47, 47-48, 51, 58, 61, 65, 89, 115, 116, 117, 119, 122, 126, 135, 138, 139, 141, 142, 148-49, 151, 154, 155, 158, 160, 163, 164, 177, 187, 192, 193, 197, 198, 206, 212, 214, 216, 224, 228, 230, 231, 255, 256

- ἐν Χριστῷ Ἰησοῦ 34, 46-47, 89, 115, 119, 126, 135, 148-49, 151, 160, 164, 177, 256
χρόνος 42, 115, 120, 121, 187, 189-90, 191, 261

ψεύδομαι 51, 52, 67, 190, 191
ὠφελέω 54
ὠφέλιμος 54, 160, 214, 215, 217

General Index

Adam 61, 70, 71, 75, 76, 77
"All people" 25, 35, 52, 57, 85, 87, 88-89, 97, 102, 198, 201-02, 213, 217; see also πάντες ἄνθρωποι
Apostasy 61, 94, 155
Apostle(s), Apostolic, Apostleship 7, 8, 9, 10, 19, 21, 31, 32, 39, 40, 42, 65, 66, 74, 93, 101, 104, 128, 138, 150, 154, 155, 156, 162, 163, 164, 169, 171, 175, 177, 183, 185, 191, 193-96, 227, 235, 236, 237, 245, 261; see also ἀπόστολος
Apostolic Fathers 15, 27-28, 36, 254, 255; see also Biblical and Other Ancient Literature index
Asceticism 86, 257, 265
Assembly, see Church
Atonement 61, 62, 63, 64
Authorities, political/secular 51, 55, 66, 67, 144, 169, 174, 230
Authority
- of Gospel message 7, 236, 243
- of Paul 8, 21, 31, 32, 193, 196, 236, 242, 243, 252, 261
- of Timothy 19
- of Titus 188, 193, 196, 215, 216, 217, 236
- of church leaders 10, 230, 236, 266
- claimed by author of PE 9, 10, 148, 151
Author's strategy and purpose 9-10, 11, 20, 76-78, 96, 156, 158-59, 186, 214, 230, 252-53, 257
Authorship of PE 4-14, 109, 115-16, 252-54; see also Pauline/un-Pauline character of PE
Baptism 8, 10, 38, 126-27, 137, 152, 153, 154, 155, 204, 219, 222, 228, 229, 230, 249, 251
Believe, Believer, Belief 6, 7, 8, 15, 19, 29, 31, 32, 35, 36, 37, 38, 40, 41, 42-43, 44, 50, 53, 56, 73, 83, 85, 86, 87, 88, 89, 90, 93, 95, 96, 97, 100, 103, 104, 105, 106, 112, 126, 137, 146, 148, 153, 154, 155, 157, 163, 164, 165, 177, 185, 194, 201, 205, 207, 211, 220, 221, 222, 226, 227, 230, 232, 235, 237, 243, 244, 245, 246, 250, 252, 256, 258, 260, 261, 262, 265; see also πιστεύω, πίστις
Benefactor, Benefactrix 22, 24, 26, 88, 95, 103, 119, 123, 186, 220, 241, 250, 259
Blaspheme, Blasphemer 49, 137, 255, 256; see also βλασφημέω, -ία, -ος
Blessing, blessedness 25, 29, 117, 146, 148, 155, 156, 206, 221, 235
Chiasm, chiastic 131, 150, 215, 217, 220, 228, 229, 230, 231, 262
Christ, Jesus; see also Χριστὸς Ἰησοῦς
- "Jesus Christ"/"Christ Jesus" (word order) 138-39
- as saviour 3, 26, 27, 28, 32, 35, 39, 53, 122, 123, 126, 133, 176, 185, 188, 189, 193, 198, 199, 205, 206, 215, 216, 220, 229, 232, 233, 235, 241, 242, 244, 261
- salvation in/through 6, 7, 100, 105, 116, 117, 119-20, 125, 123, 129, 133, 139, 147, 149, 164, 165, 173, 175, 176, 177, 195, 199, 201, 203, 206, 209, 222, 228, 229, 241, 242, 243, 244, 249, 250, 253, 254, 261
- revelation through 7, 10, 86, 116, 117, 120-22, 133-34, 176, 177, 200, 219, 234, 244, 245, 262
- pretemporal involvement in salvation 117, 119-20, 129, 133, 176, 177, 241, 253
- historical appearing of, coming into the world, incarnation 6, 10, 35, 37, 43-44, 103, 117, 118, 120-22, 127, 128, 133, 199, 200, 209, 219, 222, 241, 244, 245, 246, 254, 263
- as human 59, 60, 62, 139, 140, 177, 209

Indexes 335

- Davidic descent of 135, 136, 137, 140-41, 158, 163, 178, 260
- death of 32, 64, 65, 143, 144, 149, 152, 153, 154, 158, 176, 199, 200, 209, 222, 253, 254
- self-giving of 26, 52, 60, 63-64, 66, 68, 102, 198, 200, 201, 208-11, 213, 230, 233, 234, 235, 236, 242, 253; see also *Hingabmotiv*
- sacrifice of 61, 62, 63-64, 68, 213, 231, 234, 257
- suffering of 142, 143, 153, 158, 170
- as mediator 19, 58-63, 64, 68, 241
- resurrection of 6, 7, 27, 30, 31, 32, 38, 92, 93, 123, 124, 128, 129, 134, 135, 136, 137, 138, 139-40, 141, 144, 146, 148, 149, 150, 151, 152, 153, 158, 163, 172, 173, 175, 177, 178, 188, 199, 222, 242, 245, 253, 254, 259, 260
- defeat of death 123-26, 129, 149, 241, 245, 259
- present activity of 8, 44-48, 104, 149, 154, 167, 168, 177, 200, 242
- future appearing of 5, 19, 31, 32, 38, 66, 102, 104, 122, 156, 168, 175, 199, 200, 204, 205-07, 218, 235, 242, 244, 245, 250
- as judge 156, 166, 167, 168, 172, 173, 175, 177, 242
- kingship, kingdom, reign 140, 149, 155, 158, 172, 174, 175, 176, 177, 242, 246, 253
- faith/belief in, 19, 29, 35, 36, 37, 38, 42-43, 44, 46-47, 50, 53, 56, 80, 81, 86, 100, 104, 105, 137, 160, 163, 164, 165, 177, 179, 204, 207, 234, 245, 246, 260
- faithfulness of 158, 159, 177, 260
- "Christ our hope" 28-33
- "in Christ" 6, 31, 37, 44, 46-47, 55, 104, 119-20, 125, 129, 139, 147, 148-49, 150, 151, 164, 165, 177, 222, 241, 256; see also Χριστὸς Ἰησοῦς - ἐν Χριστῷ Ἰησοῦ
- Christ and life 7, 31, 37, 38, 42, 50, 81, 82, 104, 125-29, 133, 139, 150, 152, 153, 154, 159, 172, 173, 175, 176, 177, 178, 195, 235, 242, 245, 250, 265
- witness of 64-66
- message about 30, 50, 67, 68, 83, 97, 163, 167, 175, 178, 179, 265
- and God: see God – and Christ
- "our great God and Saviour" 206-07
- and the Spirit 10, 228, 234, 235, 237, 242, 253
- fulfiment of promise to Israel 29, 30, 188
- worship of 173

Christ event 6, 7, 58-64, 65, 66, 86, 98, 102, 104, 122, 124, 129, 130, 132, 133, 163, 177, 212, 220, 222, 234, 237, 242, 244, 245, 265

Christian citizenship, *christliche Bürgerlichkeit* 5, 11, 54, 249-50, 265, 266

Christian community 8, 53, 84, 86, 90, 92, 94, 176, 184, 194, 199, 204, 208, 209, 210, 211, 234, 235, 237, 242, 243, 247, 265

Christian identity 8, 90, 147, 196, 207, 209, 210, 212-13, 247, 253, 265

Christian virtues, qualities, behaviour 6, 10, 38, 54, 69, 72, 96, 97, 131, 144, 163, 198, 207, 216, 217, 220, 230, 233, 234, 235, 237, 262, 263, 265

Christianity, early 12, 15, 26, 28, 29, 32, 33, 36, 38, 41, 44, 45, 48, 74, 76, 81, 91, 124, 141, 144, 158, 167-68, 190, 192, 193, 202, 209, 212, 220, 226, 255, 262, 264

Christianity, Greek/Hellenized 9, 41, 54, 211, 255

Christianity, Jewish 62, 136

Christology 8, 9, 10, 92, 96, 119, 120, 123, 124, 133, 148, 163, 164, 173, 200, 207, 212, 245, 251, 255, 259

christliche Bürgerlichkei /Good (Christian) citizenship 5, 11, 51, 249, 250, 255, 266

Church, assembly, Christian community 5, 6, 7, 8, 9, 19, 21, 25, 31, 33, 40, 43, 48, 49, 52, 55, 56, 69-

70, 71, 76, 77, 79, 81, 82, 83, 84, 86, 90, 92, 94, 95, 97, 100, 101, 104, 109, 130, 133, 142, 146, 155, 156, 165, 176, 191, 194, 195, 196, 198, 199, 202, 204, 207, 209, 210, 211, 212, 213, 215, 218, 219, 221, 222, 231, 234, 235, 236, 237, 242, 243, 247, 249, 251, 253, 258, 260, 262, 263, 264, 265, 266; see also ἐκκλησία

Church leaders, see Leaders, leadership

Circumcision 183-84

Coherence/incoherence
  of thought of PE 5, 6, 10, 11, 12-14, 52, 85, 115, 145, 248-29, 163, 266
  of PE as corpus 15-16, 248, 263

Commission, commissioning 19, 44, 45, 46, 49, 66, 93, 94, 99, 104, 116, 118, 133, 171, 172, 188, 242, 255

Conversion, convert 4, 44, 45, 48, 49, 50, 56, 65, 92, 118, 128, 152, 153, 154, 191, 195, 207, 228, 234, 235

Cosmology 10, 119, 120, 230, 251; see also κόσμος

Creation, Creator 25, 62, 70, 73, 74, 75, 76, 77, 80, 86, 88, 90, 92, 95, 97, 102, 103, 125, 189, 190, 226, 227, 246, 254, 257, 265

Crete 201, 237, 264

Daniel 170, 261

David 65, 68, 135, 136, 137, 140-41, 158, 163, 177, 178, 190, 192, 210, 241, 260

Day
- That Day 126, 130, 131, 156, 158, 172, 175, 176, 177
- Last Day(s) 37, 71, 86, 122, 144, 155, 171, 172, 250, 261
- Day of Christ 158, 236
- Day of Atonement 64
- Day of the Assembly 94

Death 7, 22, 23, 24, 29, 31, 32, 35, 37, 44, 60, 61, 64, 65, 66, 75, 109, 116, 122, 123-24, 125, 126, 129, 132, 138, 139-40, 141, 144, 146, 148, 149, 152-54, 159, 166, 169, 171, 172, 175, 176, 177, 178, 199, 200, 209, 222, 226, 242, 245, 253, 254, 259, 261, 165; see also θάνατος

Decalogue 39

Deceive, deceit 10, 55, 67, 70, 71, 74, 75, 77, 78, 86, 90, 144, 160, 161, 179, 190, 218, 236, 237; see also πλανάω; ψεύδομαι

Deutero-Pauline characteristics 66, 117, 120

Docetism 31

Doxology 26, 35, 37, 38, 167, 173

Earth, ends of/all of, etc. 25, 33, 45, 65, 68, 255

Ecclesiastic, see Church

Elders 99, 100

Elect 63, 117, 118, 135, 137, 145, 146-48, 158, 164, 177, 178, 179, 195, 196, 211, 237, 247, 253; see also ἐκλεκτός

Ephesus 69, 75, 100, 155, 264

Epiphany 5, 6, 10, 44, 66, 69, 122, 123, 127, 128, 129, 133, 195, 198, 200, 203, 205, 206, 207, 209, 217, 242, 244, 245, 246, 250, 259, 262; see also Christ - historical appearing of; future appearing of; ἐπιφάνεια; ἐπιφαίνω

Two-epiphany schema 245, 259

Eschatology 4, 6, 7, 11, 28, 29, 35, 37, 67, 68, 72, 73, 74, 75, 76, 88, 97, 122, 124, 125, 126, 129, 130, 131, 132, 133, 139, 140, 144, 149, 150, 153, 154, 156, 157, 159, 166, 167, 171, 172, 174, 175, 177, 178, 200, 205, 209, 221, 222, 226, 227, 232, 241, 242, 245, 246, 250, 253, 255, 257, 258, 259, 262, 265

Ethics 6, 8, 9, 10, 13, 14, 39, 41, 101, 153, 199, 200, 203, 205, 207, 212, 217, 219, 221, 230, 232, 236, 237, 241, 247, 262, 265

Eve 71-72, 74, 75, 77, 79, 80, 81, 102, 104, 257

Exclusivism 27, 40, 52, 63, 84, 91, 202, 209, 265

Faith 8, 11, 35, 38, 42-43, 44, 46-47, 48, 49, 56, 57, 73, 74, 78, 81, 82, 83,

84, 96, 89, 90, 96, 97, 100, 101, 102, 103, 104, 105, 109, 112, 113, 116, 117, 124, 138, 140, 144, 147, 148, 155, 156, 157, 158, 160, 162, 163, 164-65, 170, 177, 178, 179, 187, 188, 191, 193-95, 196, 201, 204, 207, 212, 221, 222, 230, 333, 234, 236, 237, 241, 243, 254, 257, 258, 260, 261, 263, 265; see also πιστεύω; πίστις

Faithful, faithfulness 19, 46, 49, 50, 86, 89-90, 102, 105, 106, 110, 123, 127, 139, 153, 154, 156, 157-58, 159, 166, 168-69, 170, 176, 177, 179, 194, 207, 242, 243, 244, 246, 247, 251, 252, 256, 258, 259, 260, 265, 266; see also πιστός

- "Faithful words/sayings" 3, 19, 34, 78, 79, 84, 135, 136, 178, 215, 257; see also πιστοὶ λόγοι

Forgive, forgiveness 30, 35, 40, 42, 62, 63, 64, 137, 158

Fragments Hypothesis 12, 13

Fulfilment of God's purpose/promises 26, 29, 30, 66, 37, 141, 146, 147, 149, 159, 169, 174, 188, 194, 196, 212, 234, 254, 265

Gentile(s) 29, 30, 31, 39, 40, 41, 42, 43, 48, 52, 65, 67, 68, 91, 92, 93, 94, 105, 126, 128, 137, 148, 174, 178, 179, 212, 230, 242, 243, 247, 256; see also Nations; ἔθνος, ἔθνη

Gideon 24, 45

Glory 29, 31, 114, 122, 125, 129, 139, 144, 147, 149, 150, 173, 176, 206, 207, 209, 235, 236, 244, 250, 253, 262; see also δόξα; δοξάζω

Gnosticism 58, 74, 75, 76, 77

God; see also θεός
- concept of 21, 25, 31, 33, 38, 41, 47, 48, 57, 58, 59, 62, 65, 68, 86, 90, 91-93, 96, 97, 98, 102, 103, 104, 112, 116, 126, 131, 132, 157-58, 167, 170, 190, 195, 199, 204, 206, 207, 215, 218, 219, 220, 223, 224, 226, 227, 232, 237, 243, 245, 246, 254, 258, 261, 265

- "Living God" 86, 87, 90-95, 96, 102, 103, 170, 258; see also θεὸς ζῶν
- as Father 31, 83, 167, 219, 220
- as Benefactor 24, 88, 95, 103, 119, 220, 241, 250, 259
- "God our saviour" 21-28, 32, 51, 57, 102, 103, 104, 229, 233, 234, 235, 237, 241, 244, 246; see also θεὸς σωτήρ
- saving purpose of 7, 9, 10, 19, 29, 30, 33, 35, 38, 42, 51, 52, 55, 57-58, 65, 66, 67, 68, 73, 78, 89, 99, 101, 102, 104, 105, 116, 117, 119-20, 121, 122, 123, 126, 128, 129, 132, 133, 137, 141, 145, 146, 147, 148, 149, 150, 151, 158, 169, 174, 175, 176, 177, 179, 188, 190, 191-92, 193, 194, 195, 196, 198, 203, 218, 222, 223, 230, 234, 235, 236, 242, 243, 245, 247, 256, 257, 259, 265
- saving activity of 3, 4, 5, 6, 19, 21-28, 32, 33, 37, 51, 57, 85, 86, 87, 88, 95, 96, 97, 98, 100, 102, 103-04, 110, 112, 113, 116, 117-18, 119-20, 123, 124, 126, 131, 132, 133, 134, 144, 147, 150, 157, 164, 165, 170, 172, 175, 176-77, 178, 187, 188-92, 198, 200, 201, 206, 207, 209, 210, 212, 213, 216, 217, 219, 220-31, 232, 233, 234, 235-36, 237, 241-42, 243, 246, 251, 253, 255, 258, 259, 261
- and Christ 3, 27, 28, 31, 32, 59, 60, 66, 93, 100, 103, 104, 112, 120, 121, 123, 124, 132, 133, 137, 141, 147, 157, 158, 165, 173, 177, 187, 188, 192, 193, 196, 201, 206-07, 213, 220, 233, 234, 235, 236, 241, 242, 244, 261
- and the world/all people 25, 33, 51, 65, 85, 87, 88, 90, 93, 95, 97, 102, 104, 105, 120, 169, 171, 179, 200, 201, 202, 207, 213, 250, 254, 255, 256

Godliness 29, 70, 82, 96, 97, 98, 102, 105, 113, 154, 156, 187, 195, 196, 236, 237, 246; see also εὐσέβεια

Gods (of the nations/Graeco-Roman) 22, 23, 91, 92, 210
Good (Christian) Citizenship see *christliche Bürgerlichkeit*
Good works/doing good 11, 37, 70, 82, 105, 126, 210, 211, 213, 215, 216, 217, 230, 232, 233, 237, 253, 263; see also ἔργον ἀγαθόν; καλὰ ἔργα
Gospel 4, 5, 7, 9, 30, 31, 34, 39, 41, 42, 45, 46, 49, 52, 53, 56, 57, 67, 97, 104, 105, 109, 110, 112, 113, 115, 116, 122, 123, 126, 127, 128, 129-31, 132, 133, 134, 135, 136-37, 138, 139, 140, 142, 143, 144, 145, 146, 149, 151, 158, 165, 169, 172, 175, 177, 178, 187, 189, 200, 202, 230, 237, 244, 245, 246, 247, 252, 254, 259, 264, 265, 266; see also εὐαγγελίζω; εὐαγγέλιον
Grace 6, 36, 37, 40, 41, 42, 46, 49, 50, 65, 88, 104, 113, 116, 117, 118, 119-22, 123, 126, 128, 129, 133, 137, 147, 164, 175, 176, 177, 179, 195, 196, 197, 198-208, 213, 215, 216, 217, 218, 219, 220, 223, 226, 230, 232, 234, 235, 236, 237, 241, 242, 244, 245, 246, 253, 256, 259, 262, 265, 266; see also χάρις
Graeco-Roman environment see Hellenistic environment
Haggada 71, 74, 84, 257
Halicarnassus inscription 22
Hapax 80, 94, 99, 118, 142, 165, 227
Hauptbriefe 5, 35, 37, 46, 47, 52, 61, 67, 109, 119, 128, 150, 191, 214, 252-54, 256; see also Biblical and Other Ancient Literature index
Heaven 26, 30, 36, 39, 54, 76, 126, 128, 140, 149, 154, 156, 171, 172-73, 174, 175, 176, 177, 178, 246, 247, 253, 259
Hell 23
Hellenistic environment 8, 9, 10, 15, 21, 22, 23, 26, 27, 33, 35, 36, 39, 41, 47, 48, 53, 54, 55, 63, 64, 68, 87, 88, 94, 98, 102, 110, 111, 112, 113, 122, 123, 125, 143, 152, 158, 161, 165, 169, 176, 190, 193, 198, 199, 202, 205, 207, 211, 212, 213, 220, 234, 243, 247, 255, 256, 259, 262, 264, 265; see also Salvation, Hellenistic ideas of; Philosophy, Hellenistic
Hendiadys 55, 119
Hingabmotiv 44, 68, 200, 208, 209, 257; see also Jesus Christ: self-giving of
Holiness, holy 49, 74, 78, 81, 82, 84, 105, 117, 118, 133, 175, 249; see also ἁγιασμός; ἅγιος; ἁγιωσύνη
Holy Spirit see Spirit
Hope 11, 22, 23, 26, 28-33, 38, 80, 86, 87, 90, 93, 95, 96, 97, 102, 103, 111, 113, 121, 124, 130, 137, 139, 141, 144, 154, 158, 172, 173, 177, 187, 188, 189, 190, 193, 195-96, 199, 205-07, 218, 221, 232, 235, 236, 237, 241, 250, 255, 261, 262; see also ἐλπίς; ἐλπίζω
Humanity of Christ – see Christ, Jesus – as human
Ignorance 41, 42, 43, 45, 68, 77, 105, 201, 218, 223, 256; see also ἀγνοέω; ἄγνοια
Immortality 29, 31, 37, 38, 104, 116, 122, 123, 125-29, 130, 132, 133, 144, 175, 176, 177, 226, 242, 244, 245, 246, 247; see also ἀθανασία; ἀφθαρσια; eternal life
Impietas 54-55, 256, 264
Inclusivist tendency of PE 89, 91, 92, 94, 105, 243, 258
Inheritance 30, 36, 38, 125, 126, 173, 188, 194, 219, 221, 223, 226, 231, 232, 235, 236, 250
Intercession 61, 62, 63, 257
Isis 22, 23
Israel 24, 25, 26, 29, 30, 33, 41, 42, 64. 67, 91, 92, 93, 94, 97, 102, 103, 118, 137, 138, 140, 141, 146, 154, 155, 167, 188, 189, 190, 194, 205, 207, 209, 210, 211, 218, 221, 223, 237, 241, 242, 255, 258, 260, 265
Jesus - see Christ, Jesus

Indexes

Johannine writings and traditions 26, 27, 37, 43, 56, 83, 84, 103, 127, 158, 263-64; see also Biblical and Other Ancient Literature index
Josephus 39; see also Biblical and Other Ancient Literature index
Joshua 94, 192, 193, 261
Judaism 8, 15, 23, 26, 27, 29, 30, 31, 32, 33, 39, 40, 42, 43, 48, 49, 58, 62, 67, 71, 74, 75, 91, 92, 102, 111, 112, 125, 126, 128, 136, 141, 147, 148, 155, 158, 161, 163, 165, 170, 176, 183, 189, 190, 193, 201, 205, 206, 207, 210, 211, 212, 213, 220, 234, 243, 247, 254, 255, 256, 258, 260, 261, 262, 264, 265; see also Salvation, Jewish ideas of; Ἰουδαῖος; Ἰουδαϊκός
- Alexandrian 8, 75, 185, 264
- Hellenistic 8, 15, 23-27, 33, 58, 67, 102, 110-11, 112, 125, 158, 161, 205, 208
- Intertestamental 29, 32, 64, 147, 174, 189, 261
Judaistic, Judaizing 32, 40, 49, 65, 201, 249; see also Ἰουδαϊκός
Judgment, God's 29, 30, 36, 37, 45, 48, 65, 112, 126, 156, 158, 159, 166, 168, 206
Justify, justification 7, 11, 39, 47, 119, 147, 164, 230, 231-32, 235, 236, 253; see also δικαιοσύνη; δικαιόω
Kairological framework 120, 133, 155, 243, 259
Kerygma 6, 93, 115, 171, 175; see also κήρυγμα
Kingdom of God/heaven 29, 30, 31, 35, 36, 76, 125, 126, 140, 144, 149, 154, 156, 166, 171, 172-73, 174, 175, 176, 177, 178, 179, 205, 206, 226, 232, 242, 249, 246, 247, 253; see also Heaven; βασιλεία
Law, Jewish 7, 30, 39, 40, 46, 53, 62, 66, 94, 143, 153, 162, 188, 208, 210, 223, 262; see also Nomism; νόμος
Law, Roman 55

Leaders, leadership 9, 55, 94, 155, 193, 202, 230, 243, 249, 250, 251, 258, 266
Life; see also ζωή
- future/eternal 6, 7, 11, 19, 22, 23, 29, 30, 31, 32, 33, 35, 36-38, 40, 42, 43, 46, 48, 50, 53, 73, 76, 87, 90-91, 92, 93, 95, 97, 98, 100, 102, 103, 104, 105, 106, 116, 121, 122, 123-24, 125-26, 127, 128, 129, 133, 137, 139-40, 144, 146, 149-50, 152-54, 154-55, 159, 161, 171, 172-73, 175, 176, 177, 178, 187, 188-91, 193, 194, 195-96, 200, 203, 218, 221, 223, 226, 227, 232, 233, 235, 236, 237, 241, 242, 244, 245, 246, 247, 250, 254, 255, 258, 261, 265; see also ζωὴ αἰώνιος
- present 6, 7, 10, 19, 22, 23, 28, 32, 50, 51, 53-55, 56, 57, 68, 70, 80, 82, 86, 97, 90-91, 95, 96, 97, 98, 99, 102, 103, 104, 118, 125, 126, 131, 135, 138, 152-54, 158, 164, 165, 166, 171, 176, 178, 179, 193, 195, 196, 198-208, 212, 217, 218, 219, 221, 226, 227, 233, 235, 236, 237, 241, 242, 243, 244, 245, 246, 249-50, 251, 253, 256, 266
Light, bring to 30, 83, 116, 122, 125-30, 133, 137, 175, 176, 177, 244, 245, 247
Liturgy 12, 34, 58, 115, 124, 127
Lucius 23
Luke-Acts 26; see also Biblical and Other Ancient Literature index
Luke and the PE 8, 21, 26, 27, 29, 100, 102, 137, 138, 141, 158, 168, 201, 207, 255, 259, 264
Maccabean martyrs and literature 15, 24, 29, 36, 38, 64, 96, 125, 143, 144, 158, 170, 206, 208, 260, 261, 262, 264
Marriage 74, 75, 76, 77, 90, 103, 190
Martyr, martyrdom 29, 38, 64, 125, 131, 143, 144, 152, 153, 155, 156, 158, 169, 176, 178, 242, 260, 264; see also μαρτύριον; μαρτυρέω; μάρτυς

Mary 26, 72, 76, 80
Mediator, mediation 19, 58, 59, 61, 62, 63, 64, 68, 104, 199, 241, 250, 251, 252, 254, 256, 257; see also μεσίτης
Mercy 36, 39, 41, 42, 43, 44-45, 47, 48, 49, 50, 64, 92, 104, 156, 172, 173, 175, 176, 177, 178, 220, 223, 224, 226, 227, 230, 232, 235, 241, 242, 253; see also ἐλεέω, ἔλεος
Messiah, messianic 23, 24, 27, 30, 35, 65, 72, 74, 80, 137, 139, 140, 141, 142, 143, 146, 158, 177, 178, 212, 241, 153, 157, 160
Ministry 19, 21, 32, 39, 40, 45, 46, 49, 50, 52, 60, 61, 63, 64, 95, 99-101, 102, 104, 105, 106, 110, 112, 113, 117, 118, 119, 127, 128, 132, 135, 139, 142-48, 150, 151, 153, 154, 158, 160, 161, 164, 165, 166, 168, 169, 172, 175, 176, 178, 192, 193, 194, 195, 196, 209, 229, 236, 241, 242, 243, 244, 246, 247, 251, 252, 259, 261, 262, 265, 266
Mission, missionary 6, 8, 33, 39, 44, 50, 52, 53, 54, 55, 67, 68, 91, 92-93, 95, 97, 102, 128, 133, 137, 138, 169, 171, 200, 202, 212, 213, 234, 242, 247, 250, 256, 257, 258, 259, 262, 263, 264, 265, 266
Moses 58, 61, 62, 65, 66, 94, 155, 176, 192, 193, 194, 204, 261
Mystery Religions 22, 23, 127, 165
Mysticism 22, 46, 47, 58, 127, 152, 168, 256
Nations, the 62, 67, 68, 91, 93, 95, 104, 105, 118, 144, 169, 170, 176, 188, 242, 257; see also Gentiles; ἔθνος, ἔθνη
Nomism 43, 65, 223
Old Testament 40, 41, 63, 64, 65, 68, 80, 92, 94, 95, 97, 103, 112, 113, 124, 131, 138, 146, 148, 160, 162, 163, 164, 165, 167, 170, 176, 177, 178, 188, 189, 190, 191, 192, 194, 196, 209, 212, 213, 221, 229, 230, 234, 237, 241, 244, 247, 258, 259, 260, 261, 262, 265; see also Biblical and Other Ancient Literature index
Opponents, opposition 10, 13, 19-20, 26, 27, 48, 49, 50, 52, 54, 55, 71, 72, 74, 75, 77, 81, 97, 113, 135, 137, 140, 146, 156, 160, 161, 162, 168, 169, 171, 172, 175, 176, 177, 178, 179, 201, 204, 215, 216, 217, 218, 220, 246, 247, 252, 257, 261, 262, 265, 266
Orthodoxy 10, 155
Paraenesis 14, 38, 49, 84, 86, 97, 98, 110, 130, 131-32, 135, 139, 142, 149, 151, 153, 154, 156, 158, 160, 166, 168, 195, 197, 209, 217, 219, 232, 233, 235, 246, 248, 251, 252, 253, 259, 260, 263, 265, 266
Parallelism, linguistic 25, 32, 38, 91, 111, 118, 157, 171, 211, 223, 228, 229
Patriarchs 31, 187
Paul
- as presented in PE 8, 19, 21, 32-33, 34-35, 36, 39-43, 44-48, 48-50, 52, 66-68, 82, 92-93, 95, 99, 102, 104-05, 110, 113, 116, 118, 125, 129, 130-31, 132, 133, 134, 135, 136-41, 139, 142-48, 150, 153, 154, 158, 160, 161, 166, 168-70, 171, 174, 175, 177-78, 179, 185, 188, 191, 192-96, 236, 237, 242-43, 244, 249, 251-52, 255-56, 261
- apostle 8, 9, 10, 21, 32, 33, 39, 40, 42, 66, 74, 93, 101, 104, 125, 128, 138, 150, 156, 163, 164, 169, 172, 175, 177, 191, 193-96, 227, 235, 267, 245, 261
- model of saved sinner 19, 35, 36, 40-50, 104, 255-56
- model of faithful minister 110, 116, 131, 132, 135, 142-48, 154, 158, 167-70, 172, 175, 178, 252
- in Luke-Acts 29-30, 91-92, 102, 128, 137, 141, 158, 168, 183, 201, 255, 259-60, 264
Pauline/un-Pauline character of PE 4-14, 41-42, 45, 46-47, 48, 57, 61, 73-74, 92-93, 94, 101, 109, 115, 117,

119-20, 121-22, 124, 126, 130, 133, 136-41, 146, 147-49, 152-54, 157-58, 164-65, 172-73, 185-86, 188-89, 197, 200, 205, 207-08, 214, 218-19, 221, 223, 227-28, 230, 252-54, 256, 258, 259, 260, 263, 264, 266
Pauline "fragments" 13
Pauline tradition 7, 8, 9, 10, 47, 67, 87, 94, 137, 140, 228, 244
"Paulology" 8, 251-52
People of God 24, 25, 33, 62, 64, 68, 91, 92, 94, 95, 117, 133, 146, 155, 193, 194, 196, 204, 209, 210, 211, 213, 221, 222, 223, 230, 234, 235, 236, 237, 243, 247, 258; see also λαός
Philo 39; see also Biblical and Other Ancient Literature index
Philosophy, Hellenistic 15, 22, 39, 53, 96, 98, 165, 207, 212, 234, 262
Philosophers as saviours 22
Phinehas 63
Piety 12, 36, 55, 96, 163, 165, 206, 260; see also *Pietas*; εὐσέβεια; εὐσεβέω; εὐσεβῶς
Pietas 54, 264; see also Piety; εὐσέβεια
Plato 58, 74
Power 22, 44, 45-46, 47, 65, 75, 92, 94, 110, 112, 113, 116, 124, 129, 131, 132, 139, 140, 146, 148, 153, 154, 156, 160, 162, 165, 166, 168, 170, 174, 175, 199, 205, 210, 226, 230, 242, 245, 249, 250, 251, 254, 258, 259, 260, 265; see also δύναμαι; δύναμις; δυνατός
Preaching 9, 45, 66, 67, 92, 93, 128, 129, 130, 133, 137, 138, 141, 143, 148, 158, 163, 167, 168, 169, 191, 192, 193, 194, 200, 201, 202, 230, 235, 237, 258, 259, 264, 265
Predestination 117, 146, 147, 148
Promise 26, 29, 30, 35, 37, 42, 61, 66, 78, 80, 84, 87, 90, 92, 97, 102, 105, 117, 121, 123, 125, 128, 129, 135, 137, 139, 141, 146, 147, 149, 153, 154, 157, 158, 172, 175, 176, 177, 187, 188-91, 193, 194, 195, 196, 200, 203, 211, 223, 229, 234, 235, 236, 237, 241, 242, 253, 257, 260, 261, 265; see also ἐπαγγελία; ἐπαγγέλομαι
Pseudepigraphy, pseudonymity 9, 10, 13, 109
Ransom 19, 59, 60, 62, 64, 104, 121, 254; see also ἀπολύτρωσις
Rebirth 22, 23, 224, 226, 227, 228, 236; see also παλιγγενεσία, ἀνακαίνωσις
Rechtfertigungslehre see Justification
Redeem, redemption 9, 22, 30, 60, 61, 149, 198, 205, 208-11, 213, 235, 242, 253; see also λύτρον; λυτρόω; λύτρωσις
Regeneration 224-31; see also παλιγγενεσία
Renewal 36, 67, 224-31, 233, 235, 236, 242; see also ἀνακαινίζω; ἀνακαίνωσις
Repentance 39, 42, 48, 49, 137, 161, 177, 179, 201
Rescue 22, 24, 31, 43, 92, 111, 149, 167-70, 171-73, 203, 205, 221, 235, 237, 246, 260, 261
Resurrection 6, 7, 27, 29, 30, 31, 32, 36, 37, 38, 92, 93, 95, 109, 123, 124, 125, 126, 128, 129, 134, 135, 136, 137, 138, 139-40, 141, 144, 146, 148, 149, 150, 151, 152, 153, 158, 163, 172, 173, 175, 177, 178, 188, 199, 206, 222, 225, 242, 245, 253, 254, 255, 259, 260; see also ἀνάστασις; ἐγείρω
Revelation of salvation; see also Light, bring to; Epiphany; ἐπιφάνεια; ἐπιφαίνω; φωτίζω; φωτισμός
- through Christ 9, 10, 116, 117, 120-22, 86, 129, 130, 132, 133, 176, 177, 200, 212, 219, 220, 234, 241, 244, 245
- through the Gospel and its messengers 9, 110, 116, 132, 175, 188, 190, 192, 194, 200, 203, 219, 234, 235, 236, 243, 244

- "once hidden/now revealed" schema 120-22, 189, 190
- Hellenistic revelation schema 9

Rhetoric 11, 48, 71, 85, 89, 91, 96, 218, 248, 250

Righteous, righteousness 29, 30, 36, 40, 46, 125, 165, 176, 177, 178, 205, 206, 207, 223, 224, 230, 232, 233; see also δίκαιος; δικαιοσύνη

Roman Empire, emperors 22, 26, 55, 169, 220, 264

Sacrament 7, 126-27, 204, 229, 230, 266

Sacrifice see Christ Jesus – Sacrifice of

Salvation *passim*, see entries under particular terms and subjects; see also σωτηρία; σωτήριος; σωτήριον; σῴζω; also summaries of:
- The Benefits of Salvation 103, 176, 235, 241
- God and Christ in relation to Salvation 103-04, 176-77, 235-36, 241-42
- Paul and Salvation 104-05, 177-78, 236, 242-43
- Those Who are Saved 105-06, 178-79, 236-38, 243

Salvation-historical schema 38, 66, 67, 68, 80, 84, 102, 104, 137, 146, 149, 150, 151, 158, 173, 177, 212, 254, 257, 265

Salvation, Early Christian ideas of 27-28, 31-32, 41, 75-76, 126-27, 140, 163, 254, 255, 264

Salvation, Hellenistic ideas of 21-23, 53, 58, 88, 95, 127, 143-44, 158, 186, 207, 213, 220, 226, 234, 243, 262, 265

Salvation, Jewish ideas of 23-26, 28-29, 32-33, 36, 47, 53-54, 58-59, 61-63, 63-64, 65, 74-75, 89-90, 91, 94, 95, 96, 102, 110-12, 114, 117-18, 124, 125, 131, 140-41, 146-47, 162, 170, 176, 191, 196, 199, 202, 205, 206, 207-08, 209-11, 212-13, 223, 225-26, 229, 230, 234, 241, 243, 256-57, 258, 260, 264, 265

Saviour 4, 5, 21-28, 31, 32, 33, 51, 52, 57, 67, 85, 87, 88, 95, 96, 97, 102, 103, 104, 105, 117, 118, 123, 126, 132, 133, 137, 141, 149, 164, 176, 177, 188, 192, 197, 199, 203, 206, 207, 209, 213, 216, 220, 229, 233, 234, 235, 236, 237, 241, 242, 244, 246, 255, 256, 258, 261, 265; see also Christ, Jesus – as saviour; God – "God our Saviour"; σωτήρ
- philosophers as saviours 22
- Emperor Augustus as saviour 22
- Isis as saviour 22-23
- saviour in Judaism 23-26
- saviour in NT 26-27
- saviour in Apostolic Fathers 27-28

Semitism 63, 118

Septuagint (LXX) 15, 23-25, 26, 28-29, 30, 32, 33, 36, 39, 42, 45, 47, 53, 58, 59, 63, 64, 65, 67-68, 79, 80, 89, 91, 92, 94, 95, 99, 111, 112, 118, 124, 125, 128, 144, 146, 149, 162, 167, 171, 190, 192, 202, 211, 223, 229, 231, 256, 261

Servant, serve, service 34, 46, 48, 49, 50, 63, 65, 97, 116, 117, 118, 139, 153, 154, 155, 156, 158, 165, 167, 168, 169, 170, 171, 172, 174, 175, 176, 177, 192-93, 194, 196, 243, 246, 247, 256, 259, 261, 265; see also δουλεύω; δοῦλος

Shame, ashamed, unashamed 110-12, 113-16, 131, 132, 143, 144, 156, 175, 178, 259; see also αἰσχύνω; ἐπαισχύνομαι; καταισχύνω

Shofar symbolism 45

Sin 3, 6, 7, 29, 30, 34, 35, 40, 41, 42, 46, 48, 61, 62, 63, 75, 78, 119, 137, 153, 158, 163, 203, 205, 209, 210, 211, 217, 223, 235, 236; see also ἁμαρτία

Sinner 8, 35, 36, 39-42, 44, 45, 47, 48, 49, 50, 53, 82, 104, 105, 118, 119, 243, 254, 255, 256; see also ἁμαρωλός

Indexes 343

Situation(s) of PE 4-11, 19-20, 48-50, 53-55, 57, 74-76, 109, 110, 135, 139-40, 155, 156, 167, 169, 176, 179, 183-86, 201, 218, 234, 243, 245-47, 263-64, 264-66

Spirit, spiritual 10, 37, 55, 71, 73, 75, 76, 77, 78, 86, 92, 94, 101, 113, 116, 127, 131, 163, 175, 221, 222, 224-31, 233, 234, 235, 236, 237, 242, 250, 251, 253; see also πνεῦμα

Structure of argumentation 6, 9-10, 12-14, 16, 21, 34-35, 52, 57, 58, 69-72, 76, 80, 85-87, 92, 96, 113, 116, 131-32, 135-36, 140, 141, 145, 147, 150-51, 160-61, 166, 187-88, 197-98, 198-99, 214, 215-17, 256, 263, 266

Substitution 61, 62, 63, 64

Suffering 37, 55, 61, 113, 115, 116, 131, 132, 133, 135, 137, 139, 140, 141, 142-48, 151, 153, 154, 158, 159, 169, 170, 174, 175, 176, 177, 178, 209, 242, 245, 247, 260, 264; see also κακοπαθεία; κακοπαθέω; πάσχω

Synoptic Gospels 35, 36, 37, 39, 66, 67, 83, 144, 147, 153, 154, 155, 156, 170, 173, 192, 231, 232, 257; see also Biblical and Other Ancient Literature index

Teaching, teachers; see also διδασκαλία; διδάσκαλος; διδάσκω; διδαχή
- teaching approved by PE (faithful/good/true/ health-giving etc) 19, 34, 56, 86, 97, 99, 102, 161, 175, 197, 202, 213, 216, 217, 237, 238, 243, 245, 247, 252, 262
- teaching disapproved by PE (false/opposing etc.) 19, 20, 32, 49, 52, 56, 71, 75, 76, 80, 84, 86, 90, 97, 98, 105, 113, 135, 156, 160, 161, 162, 179, 218, 237, 245, 256, 257, 265
- demonic teaching 71, 86, 90, 105
-command to teach/ teacher's task 86, 94, 97, 98, 99, 100, 127, 131, 135, 138, 143, 155, 156, 161, 175, 178, 193, 195, 197, 198, 215, 216, 217, 230, 236, 237, 243, 244, 245, 247, 251, 258, 262
- role of teaching in salvation 10, 20, 33, 98, 100, 101, 102, 179, 199, 202, 221, 238, 244, 250
  Paul's/Pauline teaching 7, 8, 56, 133, 135, 152, 193, 242, 250, 251, 252
- God as teacher 24, 202
- Christ's teaching 83, 138
- Moses' teaching 193, 261
- apostolic teaching 39, 40, 138, 196, 245
- women teaching 70, 76, 77
- primitive Christian teaching 211

Time; see also καιρός; χρόνος
- Mediterranean concept of 189-90, 261
- God's control of 65, 66-68, 102, 104, 105, 120-22, 176, 188-90, 191, 192, 201, 242, 257, 259
- before time, pretemporal 117, 119-21, 129, 133, 175, 176, 177, 179, 188-90, 194, 236, 241, 242, 243, 253, 259, 261
- present time, soteriological significance of 66-68, 175, 196, 203, 217-19, 242, 246, 257
- "End Time" 29, 35, 36, 37, 125, 144, 174, 177, 242; see also Day – "That Day", Last Day(s), Day of Christ
- Then/now contrasts 120-121, 205, 217-19, 227

Timothy 19, 21, 33, 35, 38, 49, 52, 86, 90, 95, 97, 98, 99-100, 102, 105, 109, 110, 113, 116, 117, 119, 120, 130, 131-33, 134, 135, 139, 142, 160, 161, 162, 164, 165, 166, 168, 175, 178, 179, 243, 245, 247, 260

Titus 188, 192-96, 197, 201, 236, 237, 243, 261

Traditional material 3, 6, 7, 8, 9, 10, 12, 13, 14, 15, 16, 34, 43, 44, 47, 51, 62, 65, 66, 67, 71, 75, 83, 87, 94, 103, 111, 112, 115, 119, 122, 129, 133, 136, 137, 138, 139, 140, 144,

151, 154, 157, 158, 187, 210, 212, 215, 220, 227, 228, 244, 247, 255, 256, 257, 261, 263, 264
Transformation 39, 50, 128, 200, 203, 204, 213, 217, 219, 220, 221, 227, 234, 235, 237, 241, 263, 265
Truth 41, 42, 46, 51, 53, 55-57, 58, 66, 86, 90, 96, 99, 100, 102, 103, 104, 105, 109, 138, 156, 160, 161, 162, 175, 177, 179, 190, 195, 196, 226, 230, 237, 244 ; see also ἀλήθεια
- come to knowledge of truth 51, 53, 55-57, 58, 66, 90, 96, 100, 102, 103, 104, 105, 161, 162, 177, 179, 195, 196, 237, 244; see also ἐπίγνωσις ἀληθείας
Unbelief 41, 42, 45, 105, 137, 158, 211; see also ἀπιστέω; ἀπιστία; ἄπιστος
Virtues 10, 46, 73, 74, 82, 96, 143, 163, 199, 207-08, 217, 250, 251, 256, 262
Washing 224-25, 228-30; see also καθαρίζω; καθαρός; λουτρόν
Witness 55, 64-68, 92, 104, 110, 113-14, 131, 132, 134, 137, 156, 166, 168, 169, 170, 171, 174, 177, 178, 179, 197, 198, 201, 210, 242, 246, 247, 253, 257, 259, 260, 263; see also μαρτύριον; μαρτυρέω; μάρτυς
Woman, women 4, 27, 69-84, 113, 243, 257; see also γυνή
Works - see Good works
World; see also κόσμος
- attitudes towards the world 5, 6, 7, 11, 14, 53, 72, 204, 205, 246, 249, 250, 255, 256
- worldliness 199, 204, 205; see also κοσμικός
- pagan/Gentile world 23, 26, 42, 51, 54, 58, 92, 169, 174, 176, 189, 190, 218; see also Gentile
- God's saving extending to the world 78, 118, 169, 171, 202, 215, 250
- salvation experienced in present world 10, 35, 95, 199, 204, 213, 220
- Christ's coming into the world 35, 36, 43-44, 47, 50, 103, 104, 118, 133, 245
- cosmos 120, 225, 254
Worship, worshipper 8, 24, 25, 52, 53, 55, 61, 70, 91, 170, 192, 194, 222, 258, 263
Yahweh 24, 47, 65, 118, 167, 168, 223; see also יְהוָה

Paternoster Biblical Monographs

(All titles uniform with this volume)
Dates in bold are of projected publication

Joseph Abraham
Eve: Accused or Acquitted?
A Reconsideration of Feminist Readings of the Creation Narrative Texts in Genesis 1–3
Two contrary views dominate contemporary feminist biblical scholarship. One finds in the Bible an unequivocal equality between the sexes from the very creation of humanity, whilst the other sees the biblical text as irredeemably patriarchal and androcentric. Dr Abraham enters into dialogue with both camps as well as introducing his own method of approach. An invaluable tool for any one who is interested in this contemporary debate.
2002 / 0-85364-971-5 / xxiv + 272pp

Octavian D. Baban
Mimesis and Luke's on the Road Encounters in Luke-Acts
Luke's Theology of the Way and its Literary Representation
The book argues on theological and literary (mimetic) grounds that Luke's on-the-road encounters, especially those belonging to the post-Easter period, are part of his complex theology of the Way. Jesus' teaching and that of the apostles is presented by Luke as a challenging answer to the Hellenistic reader's thirst for adventure, good literature, and existential paradigms.
2005 */ 1-84227-253-5 / approx. 374pp*

Paul Barker
The Triumph of Grace in Deuteronomy
This book is a textual and theological analysis of the interaction between the sin and faithlessness of Israel and the grace of Yahweh in response, looking especially at Deuteronomy chapters 1–3, 8–10 and 29–30. The author argues that the grace of Yahweh is determinative for the ongoing relationship between Yahweh and Israel and that Deuteronomy anticipates and fully expects Israel to be faithless.
2004 / 1-84227-226-8 / xxii + 270pp

Jonathan F. Bayes
The Weakness of the Law
God's Law and the Christian in New Testament Perspective
A study of the four New Testament books which refer to the law as weak (Acts, Romans, Galatians, Hebrews) leads to a defence of the third use in the Reformed debate about the law in the life of the believer.
2000 / 0-85364-957-X / xii + 244pp

Mark Bonnington
The Antioch Episode of Galatians 2:11-14 in Historical and Cultural Context

The Galatians 2 'incident' in Antioch over table-fellowship suggests significant disagreement between the leading apostles. This book analyses the background to the disagreement by locating the incident within the dynamics of social interaction between Jews and Gentiles. It proposes a new way of understanding the relationship between the individuals and issues involved.

2005 / 1-84227-050-8 / approx. 350pp

David Bostock
A Portrayal of Trust
The Theme of Faith in the Hezekiah Narratives

This study provides detailed and sensitive readings of the Hezekiah narratives (2 Kings 18–20 and Isaiah 36–39) from a theological perspective. It concentrates on the theme of faith, using narrative criticism as its methodology. Attention is paid especially to setting, plot, point of view and characterization within the narratives. A largely positive portrayal of Hezekiah emerges that underlines the importance and relevance of scripture.

2005 / 1-84227-314-0 / approx. 300pp

Mark Bredin
Jesus, Revolutionary of Peace
A Non-violent Christology in the Book of Revelation

This book aims to demonstrate that the figure of Jesus in the Book of Revelation can best be understood as an active non-violent revolutionary.

2003 / 1-84227-153-9 / xviii + 262pp

Robinson Butarbutar
Paul and Conflict Resolution
An Exegetical Study of Paul's Apostolic Paradigm in 1 Corinthians 9

The author sees the apostolic paradigm in 1 Corinthians 9 as part of Paul's unified arguments in 1 Corinthians 8–10 in which he seeks to mediate in the dispute over the issue of food offered to idols. The book also sees its relevance for dispute-resolution today, taking the conflict within the author's church as an example.

2006 / 1-84227-315-9 / approx. 280pp

Daniel J-S Chae
Paul as Apostle to the Gentiles
His Apostolic Self-awareness and its Influence on the Soteriological Argument in Romans

Opposing 'the post-Holocaust interpretation of Romans', Daniel Chae competently demonstrates that Paul argues for the equality of Jew and Gentile in Romans. Chae's fresh exegetical interpretation is academically outstanding and spiritually encouraging.

1997 / 0-85364-829-8 / xiv + 378pp

Luke L. Cheung
The Genre, Composition and Hermeneutics of the Epistle of James

The present work examines the employment of the wisdom genre with a certain compositional structure and the interpretation of the law through the Jesus tradition of the double love command by the author of the Epistle of James to serve his purpose in promoting perfection and warning against doubleness among the eschatologically renewed people of God in the Diaspora.

2003 / 1-84227-062-1 / xvi + 372pp

Youngmo Cho
Spirit and Kingdom in the Writings of Luke and Paul

The relationship between Spirit and Kingdom is a relatively unexplored area in Lukan and Pauline studies. This book offers a fresh perspective of two biblical writers on the subject. It explores the difference between Luke's and Paul's understanding of the Spirit by examining the specific question of the relationship of the concept of the Spirit to the concept of the Kingdom of God in each writer.

2005 / 1-84227-316-7 / approx. 270pp

Andrew C. Clark
Parallel Lives
The Relation of Paul to the Apostles in the Lucan Perspective

This study of the Peter-Paul parallels in Acts argues that their purpose was to emphasize the themes of continuity in salvation history and the unity of the Jewish and Gentile missions. New light is shed on Luke's literary techniques, partly through a comparison with Plutarch.

2001 / 1-84227-035-4 / xviii + 386pp

Andrew D. Clarke
Secular and Christian Leadership in Corinth
A Socio-Historical and Exegetical Study of 1 Corinthians 1–6

This volume is an investigation into the leadership structures and dynamics of first-century Roman Corinth. These are compared with the practice of leadership in the Corinthian Christian community which are reflected in 1 Corinthians 1–6, and contrasted with Paul's own principles of Christian leadership.

2005 / 1-84227-229-2 / 200pp

Stephen Finamore
God, Order and Chaos
René Girard and the Apocalypse

Readers are often disturbed by the images of destruction in the book of Revelation and unsure why they are unleashed after the exaltation of Jesus. This book examines past approaches to these texts and uses René Girard's theories to revive some old ideas and propose some new ones.

2005 / 1-84227-197-0 / approx. 344pp

David G. Firth
Surrendering Retribution in the Psalms
Responses to Violence in the Individual Complaints

In *Surrendering Retribution in the Psalms*, David Firth examines the ways in which the book of Psalms inculcates a model response to violence through the repetition of standard patterns of prayer. Rather than seeking justification for retributive violence, Psalms encourages not only a surrender of the right of retribution to Yahweh, but also sets limits on the retribution that can be sought in imprecations. Arising initially from the author's experience in South Africa, the possibilities of this model to a particular context of violence is then briefly explored.

2005 / 1-84227-337-X / xviii + 154pp

Scott J. Hafemann
Suffering and Ministry in the Spirit
Paul's Defence of His Ministry in II Corinthians 2:14–3:3

Shedding new light on the way Paul defended his apostleship, the author offers a careful, detailed study of 2 Corinthians 2:14–3:3 linked with other key passages throughout 1 and 2 Corinthians. Demonstrating the unity and coherence of Paul's argument in this passage, the author shows that Paul's suffering served as the vehicle for revealing God's power and glory through the Spirit.

2000 / 0-85364-967-7 / xiv + 262pp

Scott J. Hafemann
Paul, Moses and the History of Israel
The Letter/Spirit Contrast and the Argument from Scripture in 2 Corinthians 3
An exegetical study of the call of Moses, the second giving of the Law (Exodus 32–34), the new covenant, and the prophetic understanding of the history of Israel in 2 Corinthians 3. Hafemann's work demonstrates Paul's contextual use of the Old Testament and the essential unity between the Law and the Gospel within the context of the distinctive ministries of Moses and Paul.
2005 / 1-84227-317-5 / xii + 498pp

Douglas S. McComiskey
Lukan Theology in the Light of the Gospel's Literary Structure
Luke's Gospel was purposefully written with theology embedded in its patterned literary structure. A critical analysis of this cyclical structure provides new windows into Luke's interpretation of the individual pericopes comprising the Gospel and illuminates several of his theological interests.
2004 / 1-84227-148-2 / xviii + 388pp

Stephen Motyer
Your Father the Devil?
A New Approach to John and 'The Jews'
Who are 'the Jews' in John's Gospel? Defending John against the charge of antisemitism, Motyer argues that, far from demonising the Jews, the Gospel seeks to present Jesus as 'Good News for Jews' in a late first century setting.
1997 / 0-85364-832-8 / xiv + 260pp

Esther Ng
Reconstructing Christian Origins?
The Feminist Theology of Elizabeth Schüssler Fiorenza: An Evaluation
In a detailed evaluation, the author challenges Elizabeth Schüssler Fiorenza's reconstruction of early Christian origins and her underlying presuppositions. The author also presents her own views on women's roles both then and now.
2002 / 1-84227-055-9 / xxiv + 468pp

July 2005

Robin Parry
Old Testament Story and Christian Ethics
The Rape of Dinah as a Case Study

What is the role of story in ethics and, more particularly, what is the role of Old Testament story in Christian ethics? This book, drawing on the work of contemporary philosophers, argues that narrative is crucial in the ethical shaping of people and, drawing on the work of contemporary Old Testament scholars, that story plays a key role in Old Testament ethics. Parry then argues that when situated in canonical context Old Testament stories can be reappropriated by Christian readers in their own ethical formation. The shocking story of the rape of Dinah and the massacre of the Shechemites provides a fascinating case study for exploring the parameters within which Christian ethical appropriations of Old Testament stories can live.

2004 / 1-84227-210-1 / xx + 350pp

Ian Paul
Power to See the World Anew
The Value of Paul Ricoeur's Hermeneutic of Metaphor in Interpreting the Symbolism of Revelation 12 and 13

This book is a study of the hermeneutics of metaphor of Paul Ricoeur, one of the most important writers on hermeneutics and metaphor of the last century. It sets out the key points of his theory, important criticisms of his work, and how his approach, modified in the light of these criticisms, offers a methodological framework for reading apocalyptic texts.

2006 / 1-84227-056-7 / approx. 350pp

Robert L. Plummer
Paul's Understanding of the Church's Mission
Did the Apostle Paul Expect the Early Christian Communities to Evangelize?

This book engages in a careful study of Paul's letters to determine if the apostle expected the communities to which he wrote to engage in missionary activity. It helpfully summarizes the discussion on this debated issue, judiciously handling contested texts, and provides a way forward in addressing this critical question. While admitting that Paul rarely explicitly commands the communities he founded to evangelize, Plummer amasses significant incidental data to provide a convincing case that Paul did indeed expect his churches to engage in mission activity. Throughout the study, Plummer progressively builds a theological basis for the church's mission that is both distinctively Pauline and compelling.

2006 / 1-84227-333-7 / approx. 324pp

David Powys
'Hell': A Hard Look at a Hard Question
The Fate of the Unrighteous in New Testament Thought

This comprehensive treatment seeks to unlock the original meaning of terms and phrases long thought to support the traditional doctrine of hell. It concludes that there is an alternative—one which is more biblical, and which can positively revive the rationale for Christian mission.

1997 / 0-85364-831-X / xxii + 478pp

Sorin Sabou
Between Horror and Hope
Paul's Metaphorical Language of Death in Romans 6.1-11

This book argues that Paul's metaphorical language of death in Romans 6.1-11 conveys two aspects: horror and hope. The 'horror' aspect is conveyed by the 'crucifixion' language, and the 'hope' aspect by 'burial' language. The life of the Christian believer is understood, as relationship with sin is concerned ('death to sin'), between these two realities: horror and hope.

2005 / 1-84227-322-1 / approx. 224pp

Rosalind Selby
The Comical Doctrine
The Epistemology of New Testament Hermeneutics

This book argues that the gospel breaks through postmodernity's critique of truth and the referential possibilities of textuality with its gift of grace. With a rigorous, philosophical challenge to modernist and postmodernist assumptions, Selby offers an alternative epistemology to all who would still read with faith *and* with academic credibility.

2005 / 1-84227-212-8 / approx. 350pp

Kiwoong Son
Zion Symbolism in Hebrews
Hebrews 12.18-24 as a Hermeneutical Key to the Epistle

This book challenges the general tendency of understanding the Epistle to the Hebrews against a Hellenistic background and suggests that the Epistle should be understood in the light of the Jewish apocalyptic tradition. The author especially argues for the importance of the theological symbolism of Sinai and Zion (Heb. 12:18-24) as it provides the Epistle's theological background as well as the rhetorical basis of the superiority motif of Jesus throughout the Epistle.

2005 / 1-84227-368-X / approx. 280pp

Kevin Walton
Thou Traveller Unknown
The Presence and Absence of God in the Jacob Narrative

The author offers a fresh reading of the story of Jacob in the book of Genesis through the paradox of divine presence and absence. The work also seeks to make a contribution to Pentateuchal studies by bringing together a close reading of the final text with historical critical insights, doing justice to the text's historical depth, final form and canonical status.

2003 / 1-84227-059-1 / xvi + 238pp

George M. Wieland
The Significance of Salvation
A Study of Salvation Language in the Pastoral Epistles

The language and ideas of salvation pervade the three Pastoral Epistles. This study offers a close examination of their soteriological statements. In all three letters the idea of salvation is found to play a vital paraenetic role, but each also exhibits distinctive soteriological emphases. The results challenge common assumptions about the Pastoral Epistles as a corpus.

2005 / 1-84227-257-8 / approx. 324pp

Alistair Wilson
When Will These Things Happen?
A Study of Jesus as Judge in Matthew 21–25

This study seeks to allow Matthew's carefully constructed presentation of Jesus to be given full weight in the modern evaluation of Jesus' eschatology. Careful analysis of the text of Matthew 21–25 reveals Jesus to be standing firmly in the Jewish prophetic and wisdom traditions as he proclaims and enacts imminent judgement on the Jewish authorities then boldly claims the central role in the final and universal judgement.

2004 / 1-84227-146-6 / xxii + 272pp

Lindsay Wilson
Joseph Wise and Otherwise
The Intersection of Covenant and Wisdom in Genesis 37–50

This book offers a careful literary reading of Genesis 37–50 that argues that the Joseph story contains both strong covenant themes and many wisdom-like elements. The connections between the two helps to explore how covenant and wisdom might intersect in an integrated biblical theology.

2004 / 1-84227-140-7 / xvi + 340pp

Stephen I. Wright
The Voice of Jesus
Studies in the Interpretation of Six Gospel Parables
This literary study considers how the 'voice' of Jesus has been heard in different periods of parable interpretation, and how the categories of figure and trope may help us towards a sensitive reading of the parables today.
2000 / 0-85364-975-8 / xiv + 280pp

Paternoster
9 Holdom Avenue,
Bletchley,
Milton Keynes MK1 1QR,
United Kingdom
Web: www.authenticmedia.co.uk/paternoster

Paternoster Theological Monographs
(All titles uniform with this volume)
Dates in bold are of projected publication

Emil Bartos
Deification in Eastern Orthodox Theology
An Evaluation and Critique of the Theology of Dumitru Staniloae

Bartos studies a fundamental yet neglected aspect of Orthodox theology: deification. By examining the doctrines of anthropology, christology, soteriology and ecclesiology as they relate to deification, he provides an important contribution to contemporary dialogue between Eastern and Western theologians.

1999 / 0-85364-956-1 / xii + 370pp

Graham Buxton
The Trinity, Creation and Pastoral Ministry
Imaging the Perichoretic God

In this book the author proposes a three-way conversation between theology, science and pastoral ministry. His approach draws on a Trinitarian understanding of God as a relational being of love, whose life 'spills over' into all created reality, human and non-human. By locating human meaning and purpose within God's 'creation-community' this book offers the possibility of a transforming engagement between those in pastoral ministry and the scientific community.

***2005** / 1-84227-369-8 / approx. 380 pp*

Iain D. Campbell
Fixing the Indemnity
The Life and Work of George Adam Smith

When Old Testament scholar George Adam Smith (1856–1942) delivered the Lyman Beecher lectures at Yale University in 1899, he confidently declared that 'modern criticism has won its war against traditional theories. It only remains to fix the amount of the indemnity.' In this biography, Iain D. Campbell assesses Smith's critical approach to the Old Testament and evaluates its consequences, showing that Smith's life and work still raises questions about the relationship between biblical scholarship and evangelical faith.

2004 / 1-84227-228-4 / xx + 256pp

Tim Chester
Mission and the Coming of God
Eschatology, the Trinity and Mission in the Theology of Jürgen Moltmann
This book explores the theology and missiology of the influential contemporary theologian, Jürgen Moltmann. It highlights the important contribution Moltmann has made while offering a critique of his thought from an evangelical perspective. In so doing, it touches on pertinent issues for evangelical missiology. The conclusion takes Calvin as a starting point, proposing 'an eschatology of the cross' which offers a critique of the over-realised eschatologies in liberation theology and certain forms of evangelicalism.
2006 / 1-84227-320-5 / approx. 224pp

Sylvia Wilkey Collinson
Making Disciples
The Significance of Jesus' Educational Strategy for Today's Church
This study examines the biblical practice of discipling, formulates a definition, and makes comparisons with modern models of education. A recommendation is made for greater attention to its practice today.
2004 / 1-84227-116-4 / xiv + 278pp

Darrell Cosden
A Theology of Work
Work and the New Creation
Through dialogue with Moltmann, Pope John Paul II and others, this book develops a genitive 'theology of work', presenting a theological definition of work and a model for a theological ethics of work that shows work's nature, value and meaning now and eschatologically. Work is shown to be a transformative activity consisting of three dynamically inter-related dimensions: the instrumental, relational and ontological.
2005 / 1-84227-332-9 / xvi + 208pp

Stephen M. Dunning
The Crisis and the Quest
A Kierkegaardian Reading of Charles Williams
Employing Kierkegaardian categories and analysis, this study investigates both the central crisis in Charles Williams's authorship between hermetism and Christianity (Kierkegaard's Religions A and B), and the quest to resolve this crisis, a quest that ultimately presses the bounds of orthodoxy.
2000 / 0-85364-985-5 / xxiv + 254pp

Keith Ferdinando
The Triumph of Christ in African Perspective
A Study of Demonology and Redemption in the African Context
The book explores the implications of the gospel for traditional African fears of occult aggression. It analyses such traditional approaches to suffering and biblical responses to fears of demonic evil, concluding with an evaluation of African beliefs from the perspective of the gospel.
1999 / 0-85364-830-1 / xviii + 450pp

Andrew Goddard
Living the Word, Resisting the World
The Life and Thought of Jacques Ellul
This work offers a definitive study of both the life and thought of the French Reformed thinker Jacques Ellul (1912-1994). It will prove an indispensable resource for those interested in this influential theologian and sociologist and for Christian ethics and political thought generally.
2002 / 1-84227-053-2 / xxiv + 378pp

David Hilborn
The Words of our Lips
Language-Use in Free Church Worship
Studies of liturgical language have tended to focus on the written canons of Roman Catholic and Anglican communities. By contrast, David Hilborn analyses the more extemporary approach of English Nonconformity. Drawing on recent developments in linguistic pragmatics, he explores similarities and differences between 'fixed' and 'free' worship, and argues for the interdependence of each.
2006 / 0-85364-977-4 / approx. 350pp

Roger Hitching
The Church and Deaf People
A Study of Identity, Communication and Relationships with Special Reference to the Ecclesiology of Jürgen Moltmann
In *The Church and Deaf People* Roger Hitching sensitively examines the history and present experience of deaf people and finds similarities between aspects of sign language and Moltmann's theological method that 'open up' new ways of understanding theological concepts.
2003 / 1-84227-222-5 / xxii + 236pp

John G. Kelly
One God, One People
The Differentiated Unity of the People of God in the Theology of Jürgen Moltmann

The author expounds and critiques Moltmann's doctrine of God and highlights the systematic connections between it and Moltmann's influential discussion of Israel. He then proposes a fresh approach to Jewish–Christian relations building on Moltmann's work using insights from Habermas and Rawls.

2005 / 0-85346-969-3 / approx. 350pp

Mark F.W. Lovatt
Confronting the Will-to-Power
A Reconsideration of the Theology of Reinhold Niebuhr

Confronting the Will-to-Power is an analysis of the theology of Reinhold Niebuhr, arguing that his work is an attempt to identify, and provide a practical theological answer to, the existence and nature of human evil.

2001 / 1-84227-054-0 / xviii + 216pp

Neil B. MacDonald
Karl Barth and the Strange New World within the Bible
Barth, Wittgenstein, and the Metadilemmas of the Enlightenment

Barth's discovery of the strange new world within the Bible is examined in the context of Kant, Hume, Overbeck, and, most importantly, Wittgenstein. MacDonald covers some fundamental issues in theology today: epistemology, the final form of the text and biblical truth-claims.

2000 / 0-85364-970-7 / xxvi + 374pp

Keith A. Mascord
Alvin Plantinga and Christian Apologetics

This book draws together the contributions of the philosopher Alvin Plantinga to the major contemporary challenges to Christian belief, highlighting in particular his ground-breaking work in epistemology and the problem of evil. Plantinga's theory that both theistic and Christian belief is warrantedly basic is explored and critiqued, and an assessment offered as to the significance of his work for apologetic theory and practice.

2005 / 1-84227-256-X / approx. 304pp

Gillian McCulloch
The Deconstruction of Dualism in Theology
With Reference to Ecofeminist Theology and New Age Spirituality
This book challenges eco-theological anti-dualism in Christian theology, arguing that dualism has a twofold function in Christian religious discourse. Firstly, it enables us to express the discontinuities and divisions that are part of the process of reality. Secondly, dualistic language allows us to express the mysteries of divine transcendence/immanence and the survival of the soul without collapsing into monism and materialism, both of which are problematic for Christian epistemology.

2002 / 1-84227-044-3 / xii + 282pp

Leslie McCurdy
Attributes and Atonement
The Holy Love of God in the Theology of P.T. Forsyth
Attributes and Atonement is an intriguing full-length study of P.T. Forsyth's doctrine of the cross as it relates particularly to God's holy love. It includes an unparalleled bibliography of both primary and secondary material relating to Forsyth.

1999 / 0-85364-833-6 / xiv + 328pp

Nozomu Miyahira
Towards a Theology of the Concord of God
A Japanese Perspective on the Trinity
This book introduces a new Japanese theology and a unique Trinitarian formula based on the Japanese intellectual climate: three betweennesses and one concord. It also presents a new interpretation of the Trinity, a co-subordinationism, which is in line with orthodox Trinitarianism; each single person of the Trinity is eternally and equally subordinate (or serviceable) to the other persons, so that they retain the mutual dynamic equality.

2000 / 0-85364-863-8 / xiv + 256pp

Eddy José Muskus
The Origins and Early Development of Liberation Theology in Latin America
With Particular Reference to Gustavo Gutiérrez
This work challenges the fundamental premise of Liberation Theology, 'opting for the poor', and its claim that Christ is found in them. It also argues that Liberation Theology emerged as a direct result of the failure of the Roman Catholic Church in Latin America.

2002 / 0-85364-974-X / xiv + 296pp

Jim Purves
The Triune God and the Charismatic Movement
A Critical Appraisal from a Scottish Perspective

All emotion and no theology? Or a fundamental challenge to reappraise and realign our trinitarian theology in the light of Christian experience? This study of charismatic renewal as it found expression within Scotland at the end of the twentieth century evaluates the use of Patristic, Reformed and contemporary models of the Trinity in explaining the workings of the Holy Spirit.

2004 / 1-84227-321-3 / xxiv + 246pp

Anna Robbins
Methods in the Madness
Diversity in Twentieth-Century Christian Social Ethics

The author compares the ethical methods of Walter Rauschenbusch, Reinhold Niebuhr and others. She argues that unless Christians are clear about the ways that theology and philosophy are expressed practically they may lose the ability to discuss social ethics across contexts, let alone reach effective agreements.

2004 / 1-84227-211-X / xx + 294pp

Ed Rybarczyk
Beyond Salvation
Eastern Orthodoxy and Classical Pentecostalism on Becoming Like Christ

At first glance eastern Orthodoxy and classical Pentecostalism seem quite distinct. This ground-breaking study shows they share much in common, especially as it concerns the experiential elements of following Christ. Both traditions assert that authentic Christianity transcends the wooden categories of modernism.

2004 / 1-84227-144-X / xii + 356pp

Signe Sandsmark
Is World View Neutral Education Possible and Desirable?
A Christian Response to Liberal Arguments
(Published jointly with The Stapleford Centre)

This book discusses reasons for belief in world view neutrality, and argues that 'neutral' education will have a hidden, but strong world view influence. It discusses the place for Christian education in the common school.

2000 / 0-85364-973-1 / xiv + 182pp

Hazel Sherman
Reading Zechariah
The Allegorical Tradition of Biblical Interpretation through the Commentary of Didymus the Blind and Theodore of Mopsuestia
A close reading of the commentary on Zechariah by Didymus the Blind alongside that of Theodore of Mopsuestia suggests that popular categorising of Antiochene and Alexandrian biblical exegesis as 'historical' or 'allegorical' is inadequate and misleading.
2005 / 1-84227-213-6 / approx. 280pp

Andrew Sloane
On Being a Christian in the Academy
Nicholas Wolterstorff and the Practice of Christian Scholarship
An exposition and critical appraisal of Nicholas Wolterstorff's epistemology in the light of the philosophy of science, and an application of his thought to the practice of Christian scholarship.
2003 / 1-84227-058-3 / xvi + 274pp

Damon W.K. So
Jesus' Revelation of His Father
A Narrative-Conceptual Study of the Trinity with Special Reference to Karl Barth
This book explores the trinitarian dynamics in the context of Jesus' revelation of his Father in his earthly ministry with references to key passages in Matthew's Gospel. It develops from the exegeses of these passages a non-linear concept of revelation which links Jesus' communion with his Father to his revelatory words and actions through a nuanced understanding of the Holy Spirit, with references to K. Barth, G.W.H. Lampe, J.D.G. Dunn and E. Irving.
2005 / 1-84227-323-X / approx. 380pp

Daniel Strange
The Possibility of Salvation Among the Unevangelised
An Analysis of Inclusivism in Recent Evangelical Theology
For evangelical theologians the 'fate of the unevangelised' impinges upon fundamental tenets of evangelical identity. The position known as 'inclusivism', defined by the belief that the unevangelised can be ontologically saved by Christ whilst being epistemologically unaware of him, has been defended most vigorously by the Canadian evangelical Clark H. Pinnock. Through a detailed analysis and critique of Pinnock's work, this book examines a cluster of issues surrounding the unevangelised and its implications for christology, soteriology and the doctrine of revelation.
2002 / 1-84227-047-8 / xviii + 362pp

Scott Swain
God According to the Gospel
Biblical Narrative and the Identity of God in the Theology of Robert W. Jenson
Robert W. Jenson is one of the leading voices in contemporary Trinitarian theology. His boldest contribution in this area concerns his use of biblical narrative both to ground and explicate the Christian doctrine of God. *God According to the Gospel* critically examines Jenson's proposal and suggests an alternative way of reading the biblical portrayal of the triune God.
2006 / 1-84227-258-6 / approx. 180pp

Justyn Terry
The Justifying Judgement of God
A Reassessment of the Place of Judgement in the Saving Work of Christ
The argument of this book is that judgement, understood as the whole process of bringing justice, is the primary metaphor of atonement, with others, such as victory, redemption and sacrifice, subordinate to it. Judgement also provides the proper context for understanding penal substitution and the call to repentance, baptism, eucharist and holiness.
2005 / 1-84227-370-1 / approx. 274 pp

Graham Tomlin
The Power of the Cross
Theology and the Death of Christ in Paul, Luther and Pascal
This book explores the theology of the cross in St Paul, Luther and Pascal. It offers new perspectives on the theology of each, and some implications for the nature of power, apologetics, theology and church life in a postmodern context.
1999 / 0-85364-984-7 / xiv + 344pp

Adonis Vidu
Postliberal Theological Method
A Critical Study
The postliberal theology of Hans Frei, George Lindbeck, Ronald Thiemann, John Milbank and others is one of the more influential contemporary options. This book focuses on several aspects pertaining to its theological method, specifically its understanding of background, hermeneutics, epistemic justification, ontology, the nature of doctrine and, finally, Christological method.
2005 / 1-84227-395-7 / approx. 324pp

Graham J. Watts
Revelation and the Spirit
A Comparative Study of the Relationship between the Doctrine of Revelation and Pneumatology in the Theology of Eberhard Jüngel and of Wolfhart Pannenberg

The relationship between revelation and pneumatology is relatively unexplored. This approach offers a fresh angle on two important twentieth century theologians and raises pneumatological questions which are theologically crucial and relevant to mission in a postmodern culture.

2005 / 1-84227-104-0 / xxii + 232pp

Nigel G. Wright
Disavowing Constantine
Mission, Church and the Social Order in the Theologies of John Howard Yoder and Jürgen Moltmann

This book is a timely restatement of a radical theology of church and state in the Anabaptist and Baptist tradition. Dr Wright constructs his argument in dialogue and debate with Yoder and Moltmann, major contributors to a free church perspective.

2000 / 0-85364-978-2 / xvi + 252pp

Paternoster
9 Holdom Avenue,
Bletchley,
Milton Keynes MK1 1QR,
United Kingdom
Web: www.authenticmedia.co.uk/paternoster